LEARN, TEACH...

SUCCEED...

With **REA's PRAXIS II® Elementary Education:**
Content Knowledge (0014/5014) with TestWare®
you'll be in a class all your own.

WE'D LIKE TO HEAR FROM YOU!
Visit **www.rea.com** to send us your comments
or email us at **info@rea.com**

2nd Edition

PRAXIS II® ELEMENTARY EDUCATION
Content Knowledge (0014/5014)

TestWare® Edition

Shannon Grey, Ed.D.
Associate Professor
Princeton University, Princeton, N.J.

Anita Price Davis, Ed.D.
Professor Emerita
Converse College, Spartanburg, S.C.

Research & Education Association
Visit our Educator Support Center: www.rea.com/teacher
Updates to the test and this book: www.rea.com/PRAXIS/eled14.htm

The competencies presented in this book were created and implemented by Educational Testing Service. For individual state requirements, consult your state education agency. For further information visit the PRAXIS website at www.ets.org.

PRAXIS II® and The PRAXIS Series™ are trademarks of Educational Testing Service (ETS). Windows® is a registered trademark of Microsoft Corporation. All other trademarks cited in this publication are the property of their respective owners.

Research & Education Association
61 Ethel Road West
Piscataway, New Jersey 08854
E-mail: info@rea.com

Praxis II Elementary Education: Content Knowledge (0014/5014) with TestWare®, 2ⁿᵈ Edition

Library of Congress Control Number 2011923795

ISBN-13: 978-0-7386-0914-0
ISBN-10: 0-7386-0914-5

REA® and TestWare® are registered trademarks of Research & Education Association, Inc.

About Research & Education Association

Founded in 1959, Research & Education Association is dedicated to publishing the finest and most effective educational materials—including software, study guides, and test preps—for students in middle school, high school, college, graduate school, and beyond.

REA's Test Preparation series includes books and software for all academic levels in almost all disciplines. Research & Education Association publishes test preps for students who have not yet entered high school, as well as for high school students preparing to enter college. Students from countries around the world seeking to attend college in the United States will find the assistance they need in REA's publications. For college students seeking advanced degrees, REA publishes test preps for many major graduate school admission examinations in a wide variety of disciplines, including engineering, law, and medicine. Students at every level, in every field, with every ambition can find what they are looking for among REA's publications.

REA's practice tests are always based upon the most recently administered exams and include every type of question that you can expect on the actual exams.

REA's publications and educational materials are highly regarded and continually receive an unprecedented amount of praise from professionals, instructors, librarians, parents, and students. Our authors are as diverse as the fields represented in the books we publish. They are well-known in their respective disciplines and serve on the faculties of prestigious high schools, colleges, and universities throughout the United States and Canada.

Today, REA's wide-ranging catalog is a leading resource for teachers, students, and professionals.

We invite you to visit us at *www.rea.com* to find out how "REA is making the world smarter."

Acknowledgments

We would like to thank Larry Kling, Vice President, Editorial, for his editorial direction; Pam Weston, Publisher, for setting the quality standards for production integrity and managing the publication to completion; John Cording, Vice President, Technology, for coordinating the design, development, and testing of REA's TestWare®; Alice Leonard, Senior Editor, and Kathleen Casey, Senior Editor, for project management and preflight editorial review; Diane Goldschmidt, Senior Editor, for post-production quality assurance; Heena Patel, Technology Project Manager, for software testing efforts; Christine Saul, Senior Graphic Artist, for cover design; and Maureen Mulligan, Graphic Artist, for typesetting revisions.

We also gratefully acknowledge Marianne L'Abbate for copyediting, Kathy Caratozzolo for typesetting, Ellen Gong for proofreading, and Terry Casey for indexing the manuscript.

About the Authors

Dr. Shannon Grey has had a successful career in education for over sixteen years. Dr. Grey graduated with honors with a B.S. in Early Childhood Development from New York University. She received her Master of Education degree from Rutgers, The State University of New Jersey's Graduate School of Education with a specialization in Elementary Language Arts. Dr. Grey earned her Ed.D. from Rutgers in the area of Sociological and Philosophical Foundations of Education, sppecializing in Curriculum Theory and Development.

Dr. Grey taught elementary school for thirteen years in highly acclaimed public schools. During her time as a teacher she served as a mentor for novice educators, staff developer, and chairperson for several school-based and district-wide committees. Dr. Grey was also the co-creator of a summer institute aimed at instructing students in the areas of language arts and mathematics. As a faculty lecturer, she has taught classes in teacher education at Rutgers University. Currently Dr. Grey teaches and supervises student teachers for Princeton University's Program in Teacher Preparation.

Dr. Anita Price Davis is The Charles Dana Professor Emerita of Education and was the Director of Elementary Education at Converse College, Spartanburg, South Carolina. Dr. Davis earned her B.S. and M.A. from Appalachian State University and her doctorate from Duke University. She also received a postdoctoral fellowship to Ohio State University for two additional years of study.

Dr. Davis had worked more than 36 years at Converse College, where she served as the faculty advisor for Kappa Delta Epsilon, a national education honor organization. She also worked 5 years as a public school teacher. Dr. Davis has received wide recognition for her work, including a letter of appreciation from the U.S. Department of the Interior, inclusion in *Contemporary Authors*, and a citation of appreciation from the Michigan Council of the Social Studies. She has authored/coauthored 23 funded grants for Converse College. She has served as a mentor and was a two-time President of the Spartanburg County Council of the International Reading Association. The state of South Carolina twice named her an outstanding educator, and she was twice a nominee for the CASE U.S. Professor of the Year.

Dr. Davis has authored, co-authored, and edited more than 80 books. She has written two college textbooks titled *Reading Instruction Essentials* and *Children's Literature Essentials*. Dr. Davis has published several history books and is also the author of more than 80 papers, book reviews, journal articles, and encyclopedia entries.

CONTENTS

Introduction

ABOUT THIS BOOK AND TESTWARE®

If you're looking to secure certification as an elementary teacher, you'll find that many states require the Praxis II: Elementary Education: Content Knowledge (0014/5014) test. Think of this book as your toolkit to pass the test.

Deciding to pursue a teaching career already speaks volumes about you. You would not have gotten to this point without being highly motivated and able to synthesize considerable amounts of information.

But, of course, it's a different matter when you have to show what you know on a test. That's where we come in. We're here to help take the mystery and anxiety out of the process. We're here to equip you not only with the nuts and bolts, but, ultimately, the confidence to succeed alongside your peers across the United States.

We've put a lot of thinking into this, and the result is a book that pulls together all the critical information you need to know to pass the Praxis Elementary Education 0014/5014 Test.

Let us help you fill in the blanks—literally and figuratively!—while providing you with the touchstones that will allow you to do your very best come test day and beyond.

In this guide, REA offers our customarily in-depth, up-to-date, objective coverage, with test-specific modules devoted to targeted review and realistic practice exams complete with the kind of detail that makes a difference when you're coming down the homestretch in your preparation. Practice tests 1 and 2 for the PRAXIS 0014/5014 are included in two formats: in printed form in this book and on the enclosed TestWare® on CD-ROM. We strongly recommend that you begin your preparation with the TestWare® tests. The software provides timed conditions and instantaneous, accurate scoring, which makes it easier to pinpoint your strengths and weaknesses. We also include a quick-view answer key and competency-categorized chart to enable you to track your progress.

ABOUT THE PRAXIS SERIES

Praxis is Educational Testing Service's (ETS) shorthand for Professional Assessments for Beginning Teachers. The Praxis Series is a group of teacher licensing tests that ETS developed in concert with states across the nation. There are three categories of tests in the series: Praxis I, Praxis II and Praxis III. Praxis I includes the paper-based Pre-Professional Skills Tests (PPST) and the Praxis I Computer-Based Tests (CBT). Both versions cover essentially the same subject matter. These exams measure reading, mathematics, and writing skills and are often a requirement for admission to a teacher education program. Praxis II embraces Subject Assessment/Specialty Area Tests, including the Praxis II Elementary Education series, of which the Praxis II 0014/5014 exam is a part. The Praxis II examinations cover the subject matter that students typically study in teacher education courses–such content as human growth and development, school curriculum, methods of teaching, and other professional development courses. In most teacher-training programs, students take these tests after having completed their classroom training, the course work, and practicum. Praxis III is different from the multiple-choice and essay tests typically used for assessment purposes. With this assessment, ETS-trained observers evaluate an instructor's performance in the classroom, using nationally validated criteria. The observers may videotape the lesson, and other teaching experts may critique the resulting tapes.

The Praxis II 0014/5014 covers the content areas of reading and language arts, mathematics, science, and social studies. This study guide addresses each of these broader content areas and the subareas of social studies such as geography, anthropology, economics, United States history and world history.

Who Takes the Test?

Most people who take the Praxis II 0014/5014 are seeking initial licensure. You should check with your state's education agency to determine which Praxis examination(s) you should take; the ETS Praxis website (*www.ets.org/praxis/*) and registration bulletin may also help you determine the test(s) you need to take for certification. You should also consult your education program for its own test requirements. Remember that colleges and universities often require Praxis examinations for entry into programs, for graduation, and for the completion of a teacher certification program. These requirements may differ from the baseline requirements the state has for teacher certification. You will need to meet both sets of requirements.

When Should I Take the Test?

The Praxis II 0014/5014 is a test for those who have completed or almost completed their teacher education programs. Each state establishes its own requirements for certification; some states specify the passing of other tests. Some states may require the test for initial certification; other states may require the test for beginning teachers during their first months on the job. Generally, each college and university establishes its own requirements for program admission and for graduation. Some colleges and universities require certain tests for graduation and/or for completion of a teacher education program. Check with your college and the state teacher certification agency for details.

When and Where Can I Take the Test?

ETS offers the Praxis 0014/5014 seven times a year at a number of locations across the nation. The usual testing day is Saturday, but examinees may request an administration on an alternate day if a conflict—such as a religious obligation—exists.

How Do I Get More Information on the ETS Praxis Exams?

To receive information on upcoming administrations of the Praxis II 0014/5014 test or any other test consult the ETS registration bulletin or website. Contact ETS at:

ETS-The Praxis Series
P.O. Box 6051
Princeton, NJ 08541-6051
Phone: (609) 771-7395; (800) 772-9476

Website: *www.ets.org/praxis*
E-mail: http://www.ets.org/praxis/contact/email_praxis and use the online form

Special accommodations are available for candidates who are visually impaired, hearing impaired, physically disabled, or specific learning disabled. For questions concerning disability services, contact:

ETS Disability Services: (609) 771-7780; (866) 387-8602
TTY only: (609) 771-7714

Provisions are also available for examinees whose primary language is not English. The ETS registration bulletin and website include directions for those requesting such accommodations.

You can also consult ETS with regard to available test sites; reporting test scores; requesting changes in tests, centers, and dates of test; purchasing additional score reports; retaking tests; and other basic facts.

Is there a registration fee?

To take a Praxis examination, you must pay a registration fee, which is payable by check, money order, or with American Express, Discover, MasterCard, or Visa credit cards. In certain cases, ETS offers fee waivers. The registration bulletin and Web site give qualifications for receiving this benefit and describe the application process. Cash is not accepted for payment.

Can I retake the Test?

Some states, institutions, and associations limit the number of times you can retest. Contact your state or licensing authority to confirm their retest policies.

HOW TO USE THIS BOOK AND TESTWARE®

What do I study first?

To begin your studies, read over REA's subject reviews and follow the Study Schedule found on page 12. Take Practice Test 1 on the CD-ROM to determine your areas of weakness, and then restudy the material focusing on your specific problem areas. Studying the reviews thoroughly will reinforce the basic skills you need to do well on the exam. Make sure to follow up your diagnostic work by taking the practice exams in this book so that you will be familiar with the format and procedures involved with taking the actual test.

When should I start studying?

It is never too early to start studying; the earlier you begin, the more time you will have to sharpen your skills. Do not procrastinate! Cramming is not an effective way to study because it does not allow you the time needed to learn the test material.

FORMAT OF THE TEST

The Praxis II 0014/5014 is a two-hour exam composed of 120 multiple-choice questions.

Content Categories	Approximate Number of Questions	Approximate Percentage of Examination
I. Reading/Language Arts	30	25%
II. Mathematics	30	25%
III. Social Studies	30	25%
IV. Science	30	25%

About Computer-Based Testing

The test numbered 5014 is offered only on computer at flexible times and locations throughout the year. Minimal computer and typing skills are required to complete the computer-based tests. You need to be comfortable with a Windows environment, using a mouse (including clicking, double-clicking, dragging, and scrolling), and typing at a rate that will allow you to complete the assignment in the allotted time (approximately 30 words per minute). In computer-based testing, examinees complete the tests by selecting answers on-screen to multiple-choice questions.

Multiple-Choice Question Formats

The multiple-choice questions assess a beginning teacher's knowledge of certain job-related skills and knowledge. Four choices are available on each multiple-choice question;

the options bear the letters A through D. The exam uses four types of multiple-choice questions:

1. The Roman Numeral Multiple-Choice Question

2. The "Which of the Following?" Multiple-Choice Question

3. The "Complete the Statement" Multiple-Choice Question

4. The Multiple-Choice Question with Qualifiers

The following sections describe each type of question and suggested strategies.

Roman Numeral Multiple-Choice Questions

Perhaps the most difficult of the types of multiple-choice questions is the Roman numeral question because it allows for more than one correct answer. **Strategy:** Assess each answer before looking at the Roman numeral choices. Consider the following Roman numeral multiple-choice question designed to test science content:

The drop in temperature that occurs when sugar is added to coffee is the result of

    I.   sugar passing from a solid to a liquid state.
    II.   sugar absorbing calories from the water
    III. heat becoming latent when it was sensible

    (A) I only
    (B) I and II only
    (C) I, II and III
    (D) I and III only

In reviewing the questions, you should note that you may choose two or three answers by selecting (B), (C), or (D), while it is possible to choose only one answer by choosing answer (A).

The correct answer is (C) because it includes three correct statements. The sugar does pass from a solid to a liquid state (I), the sugar does absorb calories from the water (II), and the heat does become latent when it is sensible (III). Since I, II, and III are all causes of the drop of temperature when sugar is added to coffee, *all three* must be included when choosing an answer.

"Which of the Following?" Multiple-Choice Questions

In a "Which of the Following?" question, one of the answers is correct among the various choices.

Strategy: Form a sentence by replacing the first part of the question with each of the answer choices in turn, and then determine which of the resulting sentences is correct. Consider the following example:

Which of the following geological processes displaces solids as a result of gravity ?

    (A) Weathering
    (B) Soil erosion
    (C) Glacial activity
    (D) Volcanic activity

Using the suggested technique, one would read:

    (A) Weathering is the geological process that displaces solids as a result of gravity.
    (B) Soil erosion is the geological process that displaces solids as a result of gravity.
    (C) Glacial activity is the geological process that displaces solids as a result of gravity.
    (D) Volcanic activity is the geological process that displaces solids as a result of gravity.

The correct answer is (B). *Volcanic* activity is the only process by which material is from inside the Earth is brought to the surface, and it is not by force of gravity. The other processes (A) and (C) are the means of wearing down of the Earth's surface.

Not all "Which of the Following?" multiple-choice questions are as straightforward and simple as the previous example. Consider the following multiple-choice question.

An experiment is planned to test the effect of microwave radiation on the success of seed germination. One hundred corn seeds will be divided into four sets of 25 each. Seeds in Group 1 will be microwaved for 1 minute, seeds in Group 2 for 2 minutes, and seeds in Group 3 for 10 minutes. Seeds in Group 4 will not be placed in the microwave. Each group of seeds will be soaked overnight and placed between the folds of water-saturated newspaper. During the measurement of seed and root length, students note that many of the roots are not growing straight. Efforts to straighten the roots manually for measurement are only minimally successful as the roots are fragile and susceptible to breakage.

Which of the following approaches is consistent with the stated hypothesis?

(A) At the end of the experiment, straighten the roots and measure them.
(B) Use a string as a flexible measuring instrument for curved roots.
(C) Record the mass instead of length as an indicator of growth.
(D) Record only the number of seeds that have sprouted, regardless of length.

The answer to the question is (D). The hypothesis is to evaluate seed germination as a function of microwave irradiation. Recording the overall growth or length of the seed root, while interesting, is not the stated hypothesis. Choice (C) would be a good approach if the hypothesis were to relate seed growth to some variable, as it would more accurately reflect the growth of thicker or multiple roots in a way that root length might not measure.

Strategy: Underline key information as you read the question. For instance, as you read the previous question, you might underline or highlight the sentence: "An experiment is planned to test the effect of microwave radiation on the success of seed germination." This sentence will remind you of the stated hypothesis of the experiment and will prevent your having to read the entire question again. The highlighting will thus save you time; saving time is helpful when you must answer 110 questions in two hours.

Complete the Statement Multiple-Choice Questions

The "Complete the Statement" multiple-choice question consists of an incomplete statement for which you must select the answer choice that will complete the statement correctly. Here is an example:

A circular region rotated 360° around its diameter as an axis generates a

    (A) cube.
    (B) cylinder.
    (C) cone.
    (D) sphere.

The correct answer is (D), a sphere, which results when a circle is rotated 360°.

Multiple-Choice Questions with Qualifiers

Some of the multiple-choice questions may contain qualifiers—words like *not, least,* and *except.* These added words make the test questions more difficult because rather than having to choose the best answer, as is usually the case, you now must actually select the opposite. **Strategy:** Circle the qualifier. It is easy to forget to select the negative; circling the qualifier in the question stem is a flag. This will serve as a reminder as you are reading the question and especially if you must re-read or check the answer at a later time. Now consider this question with a qualifier:

Which of the following is NOT characteristic of Italian Renaissance humanism?

    (A) Its foundation is in the study of the classics.
    (B) Intellectual life was its focus.
    (C) It was noticeable in the artistic accomplishments of the period.
    (D) It was based on learning and understanding about what it means to be human.

You are looking for the *exception* in this question, so you want to compare each answer choice to the question to find which answer is *not* representative of Italian Renaissance humanism. Humanism is NOT learning and understanding, nor is it the study of being human, so (D) is the correct answer. Humanism was an intellectual movement based on the study of the classics. And, artistic accomplishments of the period did reflect the characteristics of the Renaissance.

You should spend approximately one minute on each multiple-choice question on each of the practice tests—and on the real exams, of course. The reviews in this book will help you sharpen the basic skills needed to approach the exam and offer you strategies for attacking the questions. By using the reviews in conjunction with the practice tests, you will better prepare yourself for the actual tests.

You have learned through your course work and your practical experience in schools most of what you need to know to answer the questions on the test. In your education classes, you gained the expertise to make important decisions about situations you will face as a teacher; in your content courses, you should have acquired the knowledge you will need to teach specific content. The reviews in this book will help you fit the information you have acquired into its specific testable category. Reviewing your class notes and textbooks along with systematic use of this book will give you an excellent springboard for passing the Praxis II 0014/5014.

SCORING THE TEST

The number of raw points awarded on the Praxis II 0014/5014 is based on the number of correct answers given. Most Praxis examinations vary by edition, which means that each test has several variations that contain different questions. The different questions are intended to measure the same general types of knowledge or skills. However, there is no way to guarantee that the questions on all editions of the test will have the same degree of difficulty. To avoid penalizing test takers who answer more difficult questions, the initial scores are adjusted for difficulty by using a statistical process known as equating. To avoid confusion between the *adjusted* and *unadjusted scores*, ETS reports the *adjusted scores* on a score scale that makes them clearly different from the *unadjusted scores*. *Unadjusted scores* or "raw scores" are simply the number of questions answered correctly. *Adjusted scores*, which are equated to the scale ETS uses for reporting the scores are called "scaled scores." For each edition of a Praxis test, a "raw-to-scale conversion table" is used to translate raw to scaled scores. The easier the questions are on a test edition, the more questions must be answered correctly to earn a given scaled score.

The college or university in which you are enrolled may set passing scores for the completion of your teacher education program and for graduation. Be sure to check the requirements in the catalogues or bulletins. You will also want to talk with your advisor. The passing scores for the Praxis II tests vary from state to state. To find out which of the Praxis II tests your state requires and what your state's set passing score is, contact your state's education department directly.

To gage how you are doing using our practice tests, if you score a 75% or above you can be assured that you passed the practice test.

Score Reporting

When Will I Receive My Examinee Score Report and in What Form Will It Be?

ETS mails test-score reports six weeks after the test date. There is an exception for computer-based tests and for the Praxis I examinations. Score reports will list your current score and the highest score you have earned on each test you have taken over the last 10 years.

Along with your score report, ETS will provide you with a booklet that offers details on your scores. For each test date, you may request that ETS send a copy of your scores to as many as three score recipients, provided that each institution or agency is eligible to receive the scores.

STUDYING FOR THE PRAXIS II 0014/5014

It is critical to your success that you study effectively. Throughout this guide you will find *Praxis Pointers* that will give you tips for successful test taking. The following are a few tips to help get you going:

- Choose a time and place for studying that works best for you. Some people set aside a certain number of hours every morning to study; others may choose to study at night before retiring. Only you know what is most effective for you.

- Use your time wisely and be consistent. Work out a study routine and stick to it; don't let your personal schedule interfere. Remember, seven weeks of studying is a modest investment to put you on your chosen path.

- Don't cram the night before the test. You may have heard many amazing tales about effective cramming, but don't kid yourself: most of them are false, and the rest are about exceptional people who, by definition, aren't like most of us.

- When you take the practice tests, try to make your testing conditions as much like the actual test as possible. Turn off your television, radio, and telephone. Sit down at a quiet table free from distraction.

- As you complete the practice test, score your test and thoroughly review the explanations to the questions you answered incorrectly.

- Take notes on material you will want to go over again or research further.

- Keep track of your scores. By doing so, you will be able to gauge your progress and discover your strengths and weaknesses. You should carefully study the material relevant to your areas of difficulty. This will build your test-taking skills and your confidence!

Study Schedule

The following study schedule allows for thorough preparation to pass the Praxis II 0014/5014. This is a suggested seven-week course of study. However, you can condense this schedule if you are in a time crunch or expand it if you have more time. You may decide to use your weekends for study and preparation and go about your other business during the week. You may even want to record information and listen to your mp3 player or tape as you travel in your car. However you decide to study, be sure to adhere to the structured schedule you devise.

WEEK	ACTIVITY
1	After reading the first chapter to understand the format and content of this exam, take the first practice test on CD-ROM. Our computerized tests are drawn from the tests we present in our book and provide a scored report which includes a progress chart indicating the percentage right in each category. This will pinpoint your strengths and weaknesses. The instantaneous, accurate scoring allows you to customize your review process. Make sure you simulate real exam conditions when you take the test.
2	Review the explanations for the questions you missed, and review the appropriate chapter sections. Useful study techniques include highlighting key terms and information, taking notes as you review each section, and putting new terms and information on note cards to help retain the information.
3 and 4	Reread all your note cards, refresh your understanding of the exam's subareas and related skills, review your college textbooks, and read over notes you took in your college classes. This is also the time to consider any other supplementary materials suggested by your counselor or your state education agency.

WEEK	ACTIVITY
5	Begin to condense your notes and findings. A structured list of important facts and concepts, based on your note cards, college textbook, course notes, and this book's review chapters will help you thoroughly review for the test. Review the answers and explanations for any questions you missed on the practice test.
6	Have someone quiz you using the note cards you created. Take the second practice test on CD-ROM, adhering to the time limits and simulated test-day conditions.
7	Review your areas of weakness using all your study materials. This is a good time to take the practice tests printed in this book, if time allows.

THE DAY OF THE TEST

Before the Test

- Dress comfortably in layers. You do not want to be distracted by being too hot or too cold while you are taking the test.

- Check your registration ticket to verify your arrival time.

- Plan to arrive at the test center early. This will allow you to collect your thoughts and relax before the test; your early arrival will also spare you the anguish that comes with being late.

- Make sure to bring your admission ticket with you and two forms of identification, one of which must contain a recent photograph, your name, and your signature (e.g., a driver's license). You will not gain entry to the test center without proper identification.

- Bring several sharpened No. 2 pencils with erasers for the multiple-choice section; pens if you are taking another test that might have essay or constructed-response questions. You will not want to waste time searching for a replacement pencil or pen if you break a pencil point or run out of ink when you are trying to complete your test. The proctor will not provide pencils or pens at the test center.

- Wear a watch to the test center so you can apportion your testing time wisely. You may not, however, wear one that makes noise or that will otherwise disturb the other test takers.

- Leave all dictionaries, textbooks, notebooks, briefcases, and packages at home. You may not take these items into the test center.

- You may bring a four-function or scientific calculator for use on the test.

- Do not eat or drink too much before the test. The proctor will not allow you to make up time you miss if you have to take a bathroom break. You will not be allowed to take materials with you, and you must secure permission before leaving the room.

During the Test

- Pace yourself. ETS administers the Praxis II 0014/5014 in one two-hour sitting with no breaks.

- Follow all of the rules and instructions that the test proctor gives you. Proctors will enforce these procedures to maintain test security. If you do not abide by the regulations, the proctor may dismiss you from the test and notify ETS to cancel your score.

- Listen closely as the test instructor provides the directions for completing the test. Follow the directions carefully.

- Be sure to mark only one answer per multiple-choice question, erase all unwanted answers and marks completely, and fill in the answers darkly and neatly. There is no penalty for guessing at an answer, do not leave any answer ovals blank. Remember: a blank oval is just scored as wrong, but a guessed answer has a chance of being right!

Take the test! Do your best! Afterward, make notes about the multiple-choice questions you remember. You may not share this information with others, but you may find that the information proves useful on other exams that you take. Relax! Wait for that passing score to arrive.

Reading and Language Arts

2

This chapter provides a review of the Reading and Language Arts portion of the Praxis II Elementary Education Content Knowledge exam. It is designed to assess objectives related to concepts of print and phonological awareness, word identification strategies, vocabulary knowledge and skills across the curriculum as well as reading fluency and comprehension across the curriculum. It comprises 25% of the whole exam.

FOUNDATIONS OF READING

This first objective deals with concepts related to emerging literacy and will account for 50% of the Reading and Language Arts portion of the exam. Remember, the more you know about the skills tested, the better you will perform on the test. You will be assessed on how well you understand the

- foundations of literacy and reading development (e.g., language acquisition, support of second-language learners, concept of print)

- role of phonological awareness (e.g., rhyming, segmenting) and phonics (e.g., decoding, letter-sound correspondence, syllabication) in literacy development

- role of fluency (e.g., rate, accuracy) in literacy development

- role of vocabulary (e.g., affixes, root words, context clues) in literacy development

- role of comprehension (e.g., role of prior knowledge, literal and critical comprehension, metacognition) in literacy development

- the basic elements of fiction and nonfiction texts for children

- basic elements of poetry (e.g., mood, rhythm) and drama (e.g., puppetry, story theater) for children

- uses of figurative language (e.g., metaphor, simile, alliteration)

- use of resource materials (e.g., types of resources, graphic organizers) in reading and language arts

The Foundations of Literacy and Reading Development

This category includes the stages of reading and writing development, concepts of print, phonological and phonemic awareness and effective strategies teaching phonological and phonemic awareness.

Language learning is a very complex process involving a system for creating meaning through socially shared conventions. Children come to school with a basic mastery of their native oral language. In school, they learn how to apply that knowledge of oral language as they learn more formal concepts of written language.

Language is organized using four systems that together make oral and written communication possible. The four systems are: the phonological or sound system, the syntactic or structural system, the semantic or meaning system and pragmatic or social and cultural use system of language. No one system is more important than the others but the phonological system is a critical part of early literacy.

Reading and Writing Development

Children's reading and writing develop gradually and naturally as they interact within a language-rich environment. Children's understanding of the relationship between speech and print is a vital first step in learning to read. Without learning the relationship between speech and print, the beginner will never make sense of reading or achieve independence in it.

Children's writing develops through stages from scribbling to conventional writing. The stages are 1) **emergent writing**, 2) **beginning writing** and 3) **fluent writing**. The **emergent writing** stage begins with the first marks they make on a page and they move from scribbles to the use of single letters to represent an idea. They begin making a distinction between drawing and writing, showing an interest in writing.

As children begin to learn about letter–sound relationships they move into the beginning writing stage. In the beginning writing stage children begin to write using sentences, they begin to use multiple letters to represent words through invented or temporary spelling. Their early attempts at writing sentences may lack spaces between words. They move from capitalizing random words and the use of punctuation only at the end of sentences to more conventional use of capitalization and punctuation within sentences. In the fluent writing stage, children's writing appears more conventional. They use the writing process to write including one or more paragraphs and apply knowledge of spelling patterns and rules of mechanics and usage as well as more advanced vocabulary to write text in various genres (Tompkins, 2007).

Similarly, reading develops through a series of developmental stages. As in writing development, children move through three stages: 1) **emergent reading**, 2) **beginning reading** and 3) **fluent reading**. They begin by "pretend reading" with no real connection to what is on the page to picture reading whereby they make up a story in their own words based on the illustrations in the story. They may also retell a story from memory. They are demonstrating awareness that print is used for communication in this stage as they "read" print in the environment.

As children begin to develop the basic concepts of print they move into the beginning reading stage. They begin making one-to-one correspondence between spoken words with the printed text and are able to recognize a few words as sight words and begin decoding words. As children are exposed to more formal reading instruction they begin to build on this knowledge of basic sight words and predictable text patterns to navigate text. They use word identification tactics such as picture, semantic and syntactic clues when they encounter a word not known by sight. With further instruction these word identification skills are applied strategically as they read more complex texts in the final, fluent reading stage. Knowledge of these developmental stages is critical for making instructional decisions as we facilitate children's writing and reading development.

Knowledge of Print

Concepts of print refer to the knowledge of how print looks and how it works. Emergent readers recognize that print is organized in predictable ways. The words are read from left-to-right and top-to-bottom. The letters are grouped together to form words, and the words are grouped to form sentences that represent ideas.

Concepts of print can be divided into two categories: print awareness and technical aspects of print. Children who demonstrate print awareness understand that the words carry the message and that the function of print is dependent on the context. They understand that what can be said orally can be written then later read. Print awareness is the basis for all future literacy learning.

Technical aspects of print address directionality, organization of books, and terminology related to books. Students should understand that we read from left to right, swing back, and continue from the top of the page to the bottom. We turn the pages from left to right, and the book has a "beginning," "middle," and "end." Students should be able to identify the cover of the book and the title page, and they should hold the book right side up. They should be able to find the first and last page of the book, and they should identify the top and bottom of the page. Students should distinguish between letters and words, and they should be able to point to the punctuation at the end of sentences.

As children interact in a language-rich environment they begin to learn that print carries meaning and that reading and writing are used for many different purposes. These purposes are demonstrated as children learn to read and write through natural experiences involving oral and written language. Teachers can involve children in many authentic learning activities including language-experience activities that allow children to share and discuss experiences as the teacher models written language. Language experiences that revolve around speaking and listening, visual expression, singing, movement and rhythmic activities build on children's natural language abilities. This connection between oral and written language is a vital first step in learning to read and write.

Dramatic play centers also allow children to use language naturally as they role-play a variety of roles. Shared reading experiences such as the reading aloud of big books allow children to participate in real reading, exposing them to the basic concepts of print. Centers that allow children to reread favorite stories give students practice in authentic "reading" as they retell stories from illustrations or memory. Other activities such as drawing and writing in journals, writing messages to other classmates, and recording information on charts allow students to use language for a variety of purposes as they communicate naturally.

Phonological and Phonemic Awareness

Phonological awareness is based on the phonological or sound system of language. Phonological awareness is defined as a student's awareness of the phonological structure of a spoken word. The focus of phonological awareness includes identifying and manipulating larger parts of spoken language, such as words, syllables, onsets and rimes as well as the individual phonemes that make up the word. Phonological awareness relates only to speech sounds, not to written symbols that represent sounds. Phonological awareness instruction includes activities at the syllable level such as onsets and rimes and phoneme manipulation.

Phonemic awareness is a subcategory of phonological awareness. It is the ability to notice, think about, and work with the individual sounds in spoken language. An example of how beginning readers show they are phonemically aware is by combining or blending the separate sounds of a word to say the word ("/d/ /o/ /g/ - *dog*."). Phonemic awareness tasks used for assessment and instructional purposes include: rhyming, phoneme identification, phoneme blending, phoneme substitution, phoneme addition, phoneme deletion, and phoneme segmentation. Phonemic awareness is not phonics. Phonemic awareness is an auditory skill that enables students to identify and orally manipulate the sounds of language.

Other parts of phonological awareness are auditory syllabication and parts of syllables called onsets and rimes. An onset is the initial consonant sound of a syllable (the onset of *bat* is *b-*; of *swim* is *sw-*). The rime is the part of a syllable that contains the vowel and all that follows it (the rime of *bat* is *-at*; of *swim* is *-im*). Onset and rime substitution tasks are often referred to as "word family" activities.

The ability to segment and blend phonemes is critical for the development of decoding skills, reading fluency, and spelling. Understanding the relationship between speech and print is a vital first step in learning to read and spell.

Teaching Phonological and Phonemic Awareness

Children develop phonemic awareness by singing songs, chanting rhymes, and listening to parents and teachers read books read aloud. Teachers also teach lessons to help students understand that their speech is composed of sounds. Big books are valuable tools for interactive reading, which assists children in developing phonemic awareness.

Phonemic and phonological awareness can be that directly through a variety of strategies. For example:

1. Teach the child to isolate sounds in a word. To follow a pattern from the simplest to the most difficult, begin with initial and final sounds first, then add medial phonemes. For example: "What is the first sound in *bat*?" (The first sound is /b/), "What is the last sound in *bat*?" (The last sound is /t/), "What sound do you hear in the middle of *bat*?" (The medial sound is /a/)

2. Teach blending by guiding children to identify the word created when the following sounds are blended: /c/, /a/, /t/.

3. Teach word segmentation by saying a word then guiding children to identify the sounds that they hear. For example, "What sounds do you hear in the word *dog*?" (The sounds are /d/ /o/ /g/)

4. Teach minimal pairs, which are sets of words that differ in only one phoneme like *pail* and *bail*, to guide students to notice the difference. Teachers should pronounce both words and ask students if the words are the same or different. Begin with words with the same initial consonant sounds like *cat* and *mat*, then later expand to include more complex pairs like b*i*t, b*ee*t.

5. Guide children to blend onsets and rimes. For example: "What word can you make when you blend the sounds *b* and *oat*, or *c* and *oat*?"

6. Guide children to identify a word like *tape* and then remove the onset and ask the child: "What word is left when we remove the first sound?"

Phonics

Phonics builds on phonemic awareness. Using the rules of phonics we teach children to associate symbols—a specific written letter or letter combinations—to represent each speech sound. There are several components, including consonants, consonant blends, consonant digraphs, vowels, vowel digraphs, vowel diphthongs, and *r*-controlled vowels.

Consonants are all sounds represented by letters of the alphabet except *a, e, i, o, u*. There are twenty-one single consonant letters in our language.

Consonant digraphs are two or more consonants combined to produce a new sound. Examples include *ch, sh, th* as in the words *ch*air, *sh*oe or *th*e. The digraphs, in this case consonant digraphs, are two-letter combinations that represent a single speech sound.

Consonant blends are two or more consonants appearing together in words whose individual sounds are blended together. Examples include *bl, cr, sk, str* such as in the words *bl*ue, *cr*ack, *sk*ate or *str*ong. These are called blends because the consonants are sounded—neither the *b*–or *l* in *blue* loses its identity—but they are blended.

Vowels are all sounds represented by *a, e, i, o, u*, and sometimes *y* or *w*. Vowels have either the long or short sound. The long vowel sound is a speech sound similar to the letter name of the vowel as in the word *be*. Short vowels are also sounds represented by vowel letter as in the word *bat*.

Vowel diphthongs are sounds that consist of a blend of two separate vowel sounds. Examples are *oi, oy, au, aw, ou, ow* such as in the words *oi*l, b*oy*, t*au*ght, s*aw*, pr*ou*d and h*ow*. Vowel digraphs are two vowels that are adjacent to one another and only form one sound. The first vowel is usually a long sound and the 2nd is usually silent. Examples include *oa, ee, ea, ai, ay* as in the words b*oa*t, b*ee*t, *ea*t, r*ai*n and s*ay*.

Some consonants affect vowels. For example, the letter *a* has a different sound when followed by an *l* such as in the word *shallow*. The most important example of consonant influenced vowels are r-controlled vowels such as in the words *fir, far, for*, etc.

Structural analysis is closely related to phonics. It involves the use of known word parts to identify unknown words. This includes the use of affixes, inflectional endings such as -s, -ed, -ing, -ly, contractions and compound words.

Affixes and **root words** are a common word-identification strategy. Affixes may be either **prefixes** that come before the root word, or **suffixes** that are at the end of a word. By pulling the word apart one can identify parts of the words that may help with identifying the word as a whole. Common prefixes include *un-* (not), *re-* (do again), *pre-* (before). Common suffixes include *-ist* (one who does), *-ment* (quality or act), *-able* (capable of). Added to root words prefixes and suffixes carry meaning. **Inflectional endings** such as *-s, -ed, -ing, -ly*, are suffixes that change the tense or degree of a word but not its meaning.

Contractions and compound words are also taught as part of structural analysis. **Contractions** are formed when two or more words are shortened into one word. An apostrophe is used to indicate one or more missing letters. The word meaning does not change but the word is spelled differently. For example, the words *do not* are combined into the contraction *don't* or the words *we will* are combined into the contraction *we'll* (Fox, 2010).

Compound words are two or more root words that are combined into a new word. For example, *butter* and *fly* are combined to form the new word *butterfly*. This is an important word identification strategy because it uses known words to attack or figure out unknown or unrecognized words.

Spelling patterns and syllabication are useful as techniques for decoding unfamiliar words. The following are common vowel patterns and spelling patterns:

Long vowel sounds:

- CV—consonant, vowel such as in the word *me*

- Cve— consonant, vowel, silent *e* as in the word *bike*

- CVVC—consonant, vowel, vowel, consonant as in the word *meet*

Short vowel sounds:

- VC—vowel, consonant such as in the word *at*

- CVC—consonant, vowel, consonant, as in the word *pot*.

R-controlled sounds:

- Vr—vowel followed by *r* as in the word *art*

- CVr—consonant, vowel followed by *r* as in the word *car*

Digraph/dipthong variations:

- VV—vowel digraph as in *look* or vowel diphthong as in *soil*

There are the three primary syllabication patterns that signal how to break down a word into syllabic units. They are:

VCCV: When there are two consonants between two vowels the word is usually divided between the consonants. There is one exception to this rule: Do not split consonant digraphs *–sh, -th, -ng* (as in *fa-ther, sing-er*)

VCV #1: When one consonant is between two vowels the word is usually divided before the consonant. For example *apart* would be divided into *a-part*

VCV #2: If using the VCV pattern #1 doesn't result in familiar word, divide the word after the consonant. For example: *salad* (if divided after the vowel would be sā lad) (Vacca, et al, 2009, pp. 210–211)

Teaching Word Identification

Teaching decoding and word identification strategies is a process that varies based on the developmental needs of students. The stages of spelling development provide a guide for the teaching of phonics and structural analysis. All instruction should be done in the context of authentic, hands-on opportunities for manipulating word concepts and applying critical thinking skills (Bear, Invernizzi, Templeton & Johnston, 2007).

Table 2.1 Activities to Develop Word Study Skills

Skill	Activity	Explanation
Vocabulary Development	Concept sorts	Use picture-sorting cards
Phoneme Awareness	Phoneme isolation	The first sound of the word mat is /m/
	Phoneme identity	Matching words with the same beginning sounds or the same ending sounds
	Phoneme categorization	Identifying a word that begins with a different sound than the others in a group of words: bat, ball, cow.
	Rhyming games	Blend sounds to identify a word: m//a//t/ says mat
	Segmenting activities	Identify individual sounds in a word

Skill	Activity	Explanation
Phonemic & Phonological Awareness	Clapping syllables in spoken words	Identify onset and rimes
	Alphabet games	Letter recognition

At the beginning writing and reading stage, instruction shifts to a focus on sound-symbol relationships. In the early grades students learn beginning and ending consonants, digraphs, blends and word families. They progress to reading one-syllable words, some vowel patterns including long vowels and *r*-controlled vowels. Instruction focuses on manipulating words through word sorts using word tiles or flip books.

As students progress to the fluent stage of reading and writing development, they are ready for lessons in structural analysis—including prefixes, suffixes and root words—as well as long vowel patterns in multisyllabic words and words with inflected endings. As students mature in the upper elementary grades and above they begin learning alternative consonant and vowel sounds as well as learning Greek and Latin prefixes, suffixes, and roots.

Fluency is the ability to read text with **accuracy**, **appropriate rate**, and good **expression** or prosody. Fluent readers read smoothly, maintaining a natural rhythm that resembles speaking. The fluent reader is focused on the meaning of the text rather than on decoding unfamiliar words, resulting in improved comprehension.

Accuracy in word identification is vital. Readers need to be able to accurately identify words, both through effective decoding skills and immediate word recognition, in order to focus attention on making meaning. Skill in accuracy directly impacts reading rate.

Reading rate refers to the speed with which the student reads a given text. Since students with faster reading rates read more than those with slower reading rates in the same amount of time, therefore they read less and are often unmotivated to read.

Another element that indicates that a student is reading fluently is expression, or prosody. Prosodic features affect expression and include stress, intonation, and phrasing. Prosodic reading reflects understanding of the meaning through appropriate phrasing and intonation, and reflects understanding of text features such as punctuation and headings.

Relationship between Fluency and Comprehension

There is a direct correlation between reading fluency and comprehension. Poor readers are characterized by slowly plodding through a passage as they struggle to decode many unknown words. By the time they finish reading the passage, it is a struggle to remember what was read. Comprehension is compromised for students who read with insufficient fluency because they are more focused on decoding than on the meaning of the text. Students for whom reading is a struggle have fewer experiences with text and get less meaningful practice which, in turn, limits the development of comprehension skills and slows vocabulary growth.

Teachers help readers to chunk ideas into phrases in a sentence in order to read more fluently. This is done through activities such as read-aloud or choral reading.

Factors that Influence Fluency and Comprehension

Factors that influence fluency and comprehension include prior knowledge, context, vocabulary knowledge, and attention to graphic cues. A sound comprehensive language arts program addresses all of these factors through assessment and instruction. Attention to these elements is necessary for students' literacy growth.

Prior Knowledge

Comprehension demands prior knowledge because written language contains semantic interruptions where knowledge is taken for granted. Subsequently, understanding is based on making sound inferences, asking questions, or using research and reference tools.

Disruptions in comprehension impact fluency. For example, the student reads, "Larry kept jumping in front of Moe to reach the jar on the shelf until Moe told him to knock it off." In this sentence Larry is continually jumping in front of Moe. Moe tells Larry to "knock it off" or stop the action. The intent of the text is compromised if the student's background knowledge lacks an understanding of the idiom "knock it off."

Three ways to increase background knowledge include: questioning to build on what students already know about a topic, providing more in-depth information about the topic, to add to prior knowledge, and providing real or vicarious experiences, to scaffold knowledge about the topic. Teachers have a wealth of resources to aid this process efficiently through technology.

Context

Language arts instruction spans genres and content areas. Comprehension strategies for literature differ from strategies for mathematics. Story structure for folk tales does not match story structure of other genres. For many students the transference of skills from story reading to non-fiction text is difficult, therefore students should have guided experience using strategies for understanding different kinds of text.

Levels of Comprehension

Comprehension skills include the ability to identify supporting details and facts, the main idea or essential message, the author's purpose, fact and opinion, point of view, inference and conclusion. To help students develop these skills teachers can consistently emphasize meaning in the classroom and should focus on three levels of comprehension: 1) literal, 2) interpretive and 3) evaluative.

Literal Level of Comprehension

The most basic, or lowest, level of comprehension is **literal**. This level of comprehension involves *reading the lines*, or reading and understanding exactly what is on the page. Students may give back facts or details directly from the passages as they read. For example, a teacher works with students as they make their own play dough and use the recipe to practice authentic reading (Davis, 2004). The teacher might question the students on the literal level as they mix their ingredients. For example:

Factual Question: How much salt do you add to the mixture?

Sequence Question: What is the first step in making the play dough?

Contrast Question: Do you add more or less salt than you did flour?

All of the information needed to answers the questions is literally stated in the text (in this case, a recipe).

Interpretive Level of Comprehension

The second level of comprehension is the **interpretive** level, which requires students to *read between the lines*. At this level of comprehension, the student must explain figurative language, define terms and answer interpretive and inferential questions. Inferential questions require the students to infer, or figure out, the answers. Asking students to identify the author's purpose, the main idea or essential message, the point of view and the conclusion are examples of inferential questions. Inferential questions may require students to draw conclusion, generalize, derive meaning from the language, speculate anticipate, predict and summarize. All such questions are from the interpretive level.

The following are examples of interpretive questions the teacher could ask at the cooking center while the students are making play dough:

> **Contrast Question**: How is the dry measuring cup different from the liquid measuring cup? Why are they different?

> **Deriving Meaning Question:** What does the word *blend* mean?

> **Purpose Question**: What is the purpose of making play dough? Why would you want to make play dough instead of buying it ready-made as the product Play-Doh?

> **Cause and Effect Question:** Why do the directions say to store the play dough in a covered, airtight container?

Evaluative Level of Comprehension

The **evaluative** level of comprehension requires a higher level of understanding. The students must judge the passage they have read. The evaluative level is the highest level of understanding; it requires students to ***read beyond the lines***. Having students determine whether a passage is true or false, deciding whether a statement is a fact or opinion, detecting propaganda or judging the qualifications of the author for writing the passage are examples of using the critical level of comprehension. The following are some examples of questions the teacher could ask students as they make play dough to encourage understanding at the evaluative level:

> **Checking Author's Reputation:** The recipe for the play dough comes from a book of chemistry experiments. A chemist wrote the book. Do you think that a chemist would be a good person to write about play dough? Why or why not?

Responding Emotionally: Do you prefer to use the play dough we made in class or the play dough that the local stores carry?

Judging: Do you think the recipe for play dough that is on the recipe card will work? Why or why not?

Strategies for Promoting the Literal, Inferential and Evaluative Comprehension

Questioning: Questioning is vital strategy. When readers ask questions, even before they read, they clarify understanding and forge ahead to make meaning. Asking questions is at the heart of thoughtful reading. Vacca, et al. (2009) also recommend the following questioning strategies for extending students' understanding of the texts they read.

Reciprocal Questioning (ReQuest)

This strategy encourages students to think as they read in any situation that requires reading. Modeling appropriate questions—those that go beyond the literal level of comprehension—is vital.

Question-Answer Relationships (QARs)

This is a very important strategy that helps readers determine the most likely source of information needed to answer comprehension questions. As they point out, some questions can be thought of as textually explicit because they promote recall or recognition of *information actually stated in the text* as in literal-level questions. Other questions can be thought of as textually implicit because they provoke thinking, requiring students to provide information that is **not** actually stated in the text as in interpretive and evaluative levels of comprehension.

Strategies that Facilitate Comprehension Before, During and After Reading

Different strategies are important at different points of the reading process.

For example, **before reading** strategies include:

Activate prior knowledge: Readers attend better when they relate to the text. Readers naturally bring their prior knowledge and experience to reading but they comprehend better when they think about the connections they make between the text, their lives and the larger world.

Predicting: Making predictions based on the cover, the title and the first page or so is an effective strategy to keep students focused on the text. Predictions focus attention as children read to verify or reject earlier predictions, both as they read and after they read. They can do this through a picture walk with a story or by pre-viewing content using title, table of contents and glossary for important vocabulary with informational texts. Both help students anticipate content and possible events in the story.

During reading, students use strategies to monitor comprehension and maximize understanding. For example:

Mapping text structures: Students identify the text structures, whether narrative or expository. Story maps are effective for stories. For expository texts students can use the K-W-L strategy in order to record what they are learning.

Visualizing: Active readers create visual images based on the words they read in the text. These created "pictures" enhance their understanding.

Drawing inferences: Inferring is done when readers take what they know, garner clues from the text and think ahead to make a judgment, discern a theme or speculate about what is to come.

Determining important ideas: Effective readers grasp essential ideas and important information when reading. Readers must differentiate between less important ideas and key ideas that are central to the meaning of the text. This involves main ideas and important supporting details.

Repairing understanding: If confusing disrupts meaning, readers need to stop and clarify their understanding. Readers may use a variety of strategies to "fix up" comprehension. This may involve rereading parts of the texts in order to better understand the author's meaning.

Using the parts of a book: Students should use all parts of the book, including charts, diagrams, indexes, and the table of contents, to improve their understanding of the content in the text.

Reflect: Stop and reflect on literal, interpretive, or evaluative questions.

After reading, students reflect, relook and extend their knowledge of the text. For example, readers:

Synthesize information: Synthesizing involves combining new information with existing knowledge to form an original idea or interpretation. Reviewing, sorting and sifting important information can lead to new insights that change the way readers think.

Reflecting: Reflection is an important comprehension strategy. It requires the reader to think about or reflect on what they have just read. It can be done through rethinking the content, through written activities such as in a journal writing activities or through visually representing.

The more students know about the organization of texts the better able they are to make meaning of them. Knowing the underlying structure of texts helps readers to set a purpose for reading, allowing them to anticipate possible events or content in the text they are reading, thereby enhancing comprehension.

Vocabulary Knowledge

A major determinant of reading comprehension is vocabulary knowledge. If the student sounds out a word and fails to recognize its meaning, the ability to understand the text is lost. In order for the reader to understand what is written, the words must reside in their meaning vocabulary. According to the National Reading Panel (2000), vocabulary instruction is a major component of a comprehensive reading program.

Vocabulary knowledge is grounded in the semantic, or meaning, system of language. This includes development in both oral and written vocabularies. The more words children can recognize immediately the more likely they are to comprehend more quickly and easily. Also, the more deeply a concept is developed, the more fluent a child can make meaning through varied language use.

When choosing words it is important to select those that students will read or hear most often and that are useful to them. This includes sight words such as *the, of* or *is*, since they are not easily decoded through word identification strategies such as phonics. Another important consideration is selecting words that tend to be confusing and key words in content area learning. All are important sources for vocabulary instruction. Overall, the following are types of words that are taught as part of vocabulary instruction.

Antonyms are words that are opposite in meaning. For example, *day* is the opposite of *night* or *wet* is the opposite of *dry*. There are also different shades of meaning. For example, *hot* is the opposite of *cold* but there are a continuum of words that express varying degrees of meaning. For example, *cold, frigid, chilly* or *cool* are all opposite of *hot* but some are more extreme than others. Antonyms provide variety in expressing meaning.

Synonyms are words that have the same or nearly the same meaning. As with antonyms there are varying shades of meaning. For example, synonyms for *hot* are *scorching sizzling* or *sultry*. All have similar meanings but provide variety in written text.

Multiple-meaning words are, as the phrase suggests, words that have more than one meaning. As students progress through the elementary grades they begin to enrich their vocabularies as they learn the various meaning of words. For example, there are multiple meanings for the word *bat*. It could mean 1) what you use to hit a baseball, 2) a nocturnal flying creature or 3) to swing at something (as in my cat bats at the ball of yarn). Similarly, there are as many as 12 different meanings for the word *bank*. Knowledge of the multiple meanings of words provide enhanced comprehension in reading and listening and provide variety for writing and speaking.

Homonyms are another category of words that are important for vocabulary development. Homonyms are words that have similar sounds or spellings. Words can be either homophones, homographs or homographic homophones.

Homophones are words that sound the same but are spelled differently. Each conveys a separate meaning. For example, *two, to* and *too* are all pronounced the same but have different meanings. Other common homophones are *their, there* and *they're; our and hour; bare,* and *bear*.

Homographs are words that are spelled the same but are pronounced differently. Again, each conveys a different meaning. For example, *tear*, meaning to rip something (as in "don't tear it") or droplets from the eye (as in "dry your tears").

Though these two words are spelled the same, the pronunciation varies. Therefore, context becomes vital to determining the meaning of the word.

Homographic homophones are words that are spelled the same and pronounced the same but have different meanings. For example, *ball* could be a spherical object that is thrown, a dance (as in "Cinderella went to the ball"), or a good time (as in "we had a ball"). Again, because they are spelled the same and pronounced the same, context becomes vital to determining meaning.

Idioms are words that have a figurative rather than literal meaning. For example, don't "let the cat out of the bag" or don't "spill the beans" both mean don't tell the secret. Other examples of idioms include "an arm and a leg," meaning something is very expensive, "up for grabs" meaning something is available and whoever is first or best will get it or "hold your horses," meaning you need to slow down or be patient.

Vocabulary Instruction

Vocabulary knowledge deals with both concept development and word knowledge as labels for concepts. Vocabulary should be taught in the context of their own reading, writing, speaking and listening activities. When planning vocabulary instruction it is important to consider the levels of word knowledge. Beck, McKeown and Kucan (2002) identify a continuum of word knowledge from no knowledge, to incidental knowledge or partial knowledge, to full knowledge.

Vocabulary should be taught indirectly though activities such as read-aloud, conversations, discussions, and independent reading. Direct instruction involves students in learning words that they do not commonly come into contact with in their everyday, incidental experiences. These include words in the content areas such as science, social studies and mathematics as well as words students come into contact with in their basal or other reading materials. Word study involves students in meaningful study of word meanings that moves beyond the superficial "word and definition." Students are given the chance to act upon their knowledge as they participate in activities such as word posters, word maps, dramatizations, word sorts, word chains or semantic feature analysis (Tompkins, 2009).

Classifying or categorizing words helps students to study words in relation to other words. This involves them in more critical thinking skills as they work through the relationships between words, leading to deeper, richer vocabulary knowledge. This is especially true in vocabulary that is specific to the content areas across the curriculum.

Attention to Graphic Cues

Graphic cues include spacing, text size or font, bolding, highlighting and underlining of text, and punctuation. The cues are used primarily to show emphasis or importance. Graphic cues can be introduced to students at a young age through shared reading. Shared writing using technology is also effective for using graphic cues to aid comprehension.

Context Clues

Context clues are those clues taken from words, phrases, sentences surrounding the unknown word used as recognition aids. These include picture clues that use accompanying pictures as clues for unknown words, semantic clues that are clues derived from meanings of surrounding words and syntactic clues that are clues derived from grammar knowledge (i.e., certain words appear in certain positions in sentences).

Illustrations in books can often help children determine the meaning of unfamiliar words. This is a good first step for teaching about context clues. This is not a good strategy in the upper grades, though, since the texts will have fewer and fewer illustrations. Semantic clues require a child to think about the meanings of words and what is already known about the topic being read. For example, when reading a story about bats, good teachers begin by activating background knowledge about bats. This helps to develop an expectation that the selection may contain words such as *swoop, wings, mammal*, or *nocturnal* that are associated with bats. This prereading discussion helps children gain a sense of what vocabulary might be reasonable in a sentence. Finally, syntactic clues relate to word order based on grammar rules. For example, in the sentence, "Bats can _____ at night," the order of the words in the sentence gives clues that the missing word must be a verb. Based on their knowledge of verbs students can determine that the missing word would indicate an action.

Dictionaries and thesauri can be useful for a range of information related to vocabulary.

Dictionaries include important information such as definitions, pronunciation guides, grammatical information, possible synonyms, etc. They usually have an introduction that gives information on how to use the dictionary including an explanation of the marks, abbreviations and symbols used. Dictionaries are arranged in alphabetical order and include guide words, the first and last words on a page, to aide in locating a word.

Thesauri are used to find synonyms and antonyms and, like dictionaries, are arranged in alphabetical order. They are useful for finding a variety of words in order to express meaning more effectively in order to avoid repeating the same words monotonously.

Literary Text Structures

As pointed out earlier, comprehension strategies differ according to the literary type. Strategies for comprehending stories or poetry are different than those for comprehending informational text. Therefore, it is important that students learn the characteristics of a variety of literary structures.

Stories have a specific structure including a clear beginning, middle and end. In the beginning of stories, characters are introduced, a setting is established and a story problem or initiating event is identified. In the middle, the character attempts to solve the story problem. The story continues with multiple attempts at resolving the problem. This continues to a climax and the story ends with a resolution of the story problem. Story grammar is the knowledge about the basic parts of stories and how they tie together to form a well-constructed story. Important elements of stories are characters (those involved in the story), setting (where the story takes place), plot (sequence of events from the story problem introduction to the solution of the problem) and point of view (narrator of the story). Knowledge of these elements helps students anticipate story events and read for confirmation or rejection of the predicted events.

Poetry uses vivid and colorful words arranged in lines, stanzas or other shapes depending on the type of poetry. Poems uses poetic devices such as comparison (using similes or metaphors), alliteration (repetition of initial consonant sound), onomatopoeia (words that mimic sounds) or rhyme (repetition of ending sounds) to elicit a specific response or emotion. There are a variety of types, each with its own structure.

Informational texts convey information through the use of **expository text structures**. These include:

Description: Describe a topic by listing characteristics, features, and examples. Details are used to support the main idea.

Sequence: Organizes topic or events in numerical or the order in which they occurred.

Comparison: Discusses topic by explaining how two or more things are alike or different.

Cause and Effect: Discusses topic by explaining the relationship between two or more events. The focus is on the triggering event/s (cause/s) and the resulting effect/s.

Problem and Solution: A problem is explained and one or more solutions are offered.

Informational books may also make use of a table of contents or glossary and other graphic organizers. Sometimes the pattern is clearly identified through titles, topic sentences or cue words (Tompkins, 2004).

Strategies for Developing Students' Literary Response Skills

Response and reflection are the hallmarks of literary comprehension. Reading response is an important part of the reading process. Here students continue to make text-to-self and text-to-world connections. Strategies such as journal writing, literature discussions, or visually representing help students examine the author's meaning.

Some strategies that extend knowledge enhance comprehension include:

Semantic Feature Analysis: Helps students think about similarities and differences between and among related concepts in the text.

Story Mapping Activities: Mapping activities require visually representing the story. Younger students use pictures, older ones use diagrams, maps, arrows, labels, etc.

Sketch-to-Stretch: This is a nonverbal response activity. Individual students draw a picture of a favorite or memorable event or scene from the story. The student shows the illustration to a small group, inviting classmates to provide their own interpretation of the drawing (Tompkins, 2009).

Compare-and-Contrast Chart: An important aspect of comprehension is the ability to make thoughtful comparisons across texts, between events within stories, and across other aspects of stories that students read. Activity begins with a grid, either a large one on chart paper or individual sheets of paper. Along one axis of the chart are listed the items to be compared. On the other axis, students brainstorm key characteristics that distinguish at least one item from another.

K-W-L charts: Provide an opportunity to reflect on and record what was learned from the text.

Response Journals: Journals are an effective way to extend comprehension in all types of literary text. Journals are a place for capturing reactions and thoughts related to the books students have read or take notes on important information.

Comprehension of informational texts involves reading to obtain information in the text. In order to maximize comprehension of informational texts it is important to understand how text is organized. Children need to identify key components of the organizational format and identify the type of information offered. Teachers guide children to notice and study the structure of text including the table of contents, titles, subtitles and headings.

Helping students focus on the main idea or the essential message in texts and the supporting details that make the main idea stronger. These may be stated explicitly or implied through factual information in the text.

Chats, tables, graphs, pictures and print and nonprint media are examples of materials writers use to present information. A graphic can expand a concept, serve as an illustration, support points, summarize data, organize facts, compare information or furnish additional information.

Strategies for promoting comprehension include:

Previewing and Skimming: This begins with previewing through questions about elements such as the table of contents, titles of chapters, headings and subheadings, highlighted text, index or glossary. Skimming is done by looking through the content quickly to get an overall sense of what the content is about.

Graphic Organizers: These highlight the key concepts and the children's prior knowledge. K-W-L is a good example of this strategy. In the K-W-L students complete what they *K*now and what they *W*ant to know before reading. Then later, after the reading, *L*earned is recorded as they discover the information. Other examples include webs or clusters.

Anticipation Guides: These include written statements for students to think about and discuss before they read. Statements are designed to activate prior knowledge and arouse curiosity about the issues addressed in the text.

Children's Literature

Children's literature is a vital part of the language arts curriculum. High-quality children's literature provides excellent models of good texts, enhancing both reading comprehension and children's own writing.

Genre refers to the category of literature. There are a variety of classifications, but the most common include fiction, nonfiction and poetry. Fiction includes traditional literature, modern fantasy, contemporary realistic fiction, historical fiction. Nonfiction includes informational books or biographies and autobiographies. There is also a variety of poetry types. Most genres can be further divided into a variety of subcategories. There is also a variety of formats across genre. These include picture books, in which the illustrations and the text work together to communicate the story, chapter books and multimedia versions.

Traditional literature includes tales that have been handed down from one generation to the next through oral stories. There are four types of traditional tales: folktales, fables, myths, and legends.

Folktales usually tell the adventures of animal or human characters. They contain common narrative motifs such as supernatural adversaries (ogres, witches, giants, etc.); supernatural helpers, magic and marvels, tasks and quests, and common themes such as reward of good and punishment of evil. Example: *Cinderella*

Fables are brief tales in which animal characters that talk and act like humans teach a moral lesson. Example: *The Tortoise and the Hare*

Myths explain something in life or in nature such as thunder and lightning and/or illustrated human emotions and experiences such as love or death. The main characters may be animals, deities, or humans. Example: *How the Elephant Got its Trunk*

Legends are based on some fact but are exaggerated. For example, the hero tales such as *John Henry* or *Johnny Appleseed*

Modern fantasy includes story with unrealistic or unworldly elements but that are written by an identifiable original author. Examples include *The Emperor's New Clothes* by Hans Christian Anderson, *Arthur's Loose Tooth* by L. Hoban, or C.S. Lewis's *Narnia* series.

Contemporary realistic fiction includes stories that are consistent with the lives of real people in our contemporary world. The word *realistic* doesn't mean that the story is true, however; it means the story could have happened. Examples include *Dear Mr. Henshaw* by Beverly Cleary, *Amber Brown* books by Paula Danziger, or *Jacob Have I Loved* by Betsy Paterson.

Historical fiction tells realistic stories of history. Like contemporary realistic fiction, events reflect what has happened or could have happened. Realistic doesn't mean that the story is true however; it means the story could have happened. Examples: *Sarah Plain and Tall*, by Patricia MacLachlan, *Roll of Thunder, Hear My Cry* by Mildred Taylor, or *Number the Stars* by Lois Lowry.

Informational books are available on almost any subject. These include ideas, facts or principles related to the physical, biological or social world. Reference books include dictionaries, thesauri or encyclopedias.

Biographies and autobiographies are factual stories about people. In biographies authors tell about another's life. Autobiographies are stories about the author's life.

Poetry can be a difficult genre to define for children; there is no single accepted definition of poetry (Norton, 2007). There are multiple forms of poetry:

Narrative: poem tells a story

Lyric: statement of mood or feeling (e.g., song lyrics)

Limericks: five-line poems in which the first, second and fifth lines rhyme and have three pronounced beats each, and the third and fourth lines rhyme and have two beats each

Concrete: poem written in the shape of its meaning, forming a picture

Haiku: three unrhymed lines: the first and last lines have five syllables each, the second line has seven syllables

LANGUAGE IN WRITING

Language in writing will comprise approximately 33% of the Reading and Language Arts exam. This objective focuses on concepts related to writing in the elementary curriculum. This includes the developmental stages of children's writing and the key strategies and skills within each of the stages of the writing process. The specific topics you are expected to know are:

- the components of written language (e.g., elements of grammar, usage, syntax)

- the types (e.g., narrative, persuasive, journaling) and traits (e.g., tone, purpose, audience) of writing

- the stages of the writing process (e.g., draft, edit, publish)

- the stages of writing development (e.g., picture, scribble, letter for words)

- sentence types (e.g., declarative, imperative) and sentence structure (e.g., simple, compound, complex)

- structures (e.g., description, definition, examples) and organization (e.g., descriptive, comparison/contrast, persuasion) of writing

Developmental stages of writing are evident in children's writing. Young children's writing begins as they make marks on paper. This begins with the earliest attempts of expression as children use pictures to convey meaning. These pictures become the story; children will "read" these as they communicate their meaning. As children begin to notice writing in their environment they make early attempts at "writing" through scribbling. These start out as random scribbles but eventually progress to a left-to-right, top-to-bottom orientation on the page. These scribbles later evolve into a child's first attempts at forming letters and numbers. Letters are pulled from those which are most important to the child, such as letters in his or her name. The letters will appear in random order or string together shapes, scribbles and familiar letter-like forms. As children become more phonemically aware and start in early phonics instruction, they begin to form their own spellings for words. One letter may represent the whole word and the words may be strung together without spaces in sentences. As children mature, their writing becomes more conventional.

The stages of spelling development most commonly agreed upon are identified by Bear, Invernizzi, Templeton, and Johnston (2007). These include the following stages: **emergent**, **letter-name**, **within-word**, **syllables**, and affixes and derivational relations. The earliest stage, 1) emergent spelling, is characterized by random marks, representational drawing, mock letter-like writing and random letters and numbers. In stage 2, the letter-name spelling stage, children begin to represent the sounds in words with letters. In this stage, children use their knowledge of the names of letters of the alphabet to spell their words. This is characteristic of writers in the early grades of elementary school, and corresponds to early phonics instruction in short vowels, consonant sounds and consonant blends and digraphs. At stage 3, the within-word spelling phase, children's knowledge of the alphabetic principle is further developed. In this stage, children learn the long-vowel spelling patterns, diphthongs and r-controlled vowels. Stage 4 is the syllable and affixes spelling stage. At this stage students are learning to spell more complex words. Lessons in structural analysis support the spellers in this stage as they learn inflectional endings, syllabication, contractions, homophones and possessives. Finally, in the derivational-relations spelling stage, older children begin to learn concepts as consonant alternations, vowel alternations, as well as Greek and Latin roots of words and word origins.

Genres of Writing

There is a variety of writing modes and formats that all serve different purposes. One must determine the purpose and audience of writing in order to select the best form to use. The most common writing modes are 1) **narrative**, that which tells a story, 2) **expository**, which informs, 3) **descriptive**, which describes or paints a picture with words, and 4) persuasive, which is used to convince the reader of a position or point of view.

There are a variety of writing forms that may be used within each of the modes. For example, narrative writing may take the form of fictional stories or nonfictional stories such as biographies; persuasive writing may take the form of advertisements, letters to the editor or persuasive essays. Based on these, the most common writing genres taught in the K-5 curriculum are: 1) stories, 2) personal writing, such as response journals and letters, 3) informational writing, 4) poetry and 5) persuasive writing.

Stories have a specific structure used to tell a story and entertain the reader. Whether fictional or nonfictional, stories have a clear beginning, middle and end. They are told through a plot that involves characters in conflicts; this is termed the *story problem*. Important elements are characters (those involved in the story), setting (where the story takes place), plot (sequence of events from story problem introduction to solution of the problem) and point of view (narrator of the story). Stories are told through both actions of characters and dialogue. All of these elements must be considered when composing stories.

Personal writing includes journal writing, which is used to record personal experiences, respond to literature or record and analyze information and letter writing. The most common types of journals are reading-response journals and learning logs, but may also include journals—personal, dialogue, or simulated. All are effective for learning across the curriculum. Letter-writing is used to develop and maintain relationships or to convey information. There is a variety of letter writing forms taught. These vary from the less formal, such as friendly letters and email, to the more formal, such as business letters and persuasive letters to the editor of a newspaper or magazine. Each has a specific structure (e.g., greeting, body, closing) varying from very informal (email) to more formal business letters and letters to editors.

Informational writing is valuable for both learning and sharing information across the curriculum as students study social studies, science and other curricular areas. As with other genres, informational writing has a specific structure. The most common organizational patterns are:

Description: Writers describe a topic by listing characteristics, features, and examples

Sequence: Writers list items or events in numerical or chronological order

Comparison: Writers explain how two or more things are alike or different

Cause and Effect: Writers describe one or more causes and the resulting effect or effects in this pattern

Problem and Solution: Writers present a problem and offer one or more solutions in this expository structure

Graphic organizers are also important as we teach students to use charts, tables, graphs, webs, etc., to convey meaning.

Poetry is used to entertain, create visual and oral images or to explore feelings. It includes a variety of poetic formulas. These include formula poems that provide a framework for writing (e.g., "I wish. . ." poems, "If I were. . ." poems, acrostic poems, etc.), free-form poems that allow the writer to put the poem together without concern about rhyme or other patterns (e.g., concrete/word picture poems, found poems, etc.), syllable/word-count poems such as haiku, cinquain or diamante poems, as well as the more traditional rhymed verse poems such as limericks and clerihews (Tompkins, 2008).

Persuasive writing is used to share opinions and support them by presenting facts in a clear, logical and convincing way, present an alternate viewpoint or persuade someone to do something. The structure of persuasive writing includes stating a position or opinion, developing the position or opinion by supporting facts or reasons and drawing conclusions to persuade the reader to accept their position or viewpoint. This can be done in the form of advertisements, posters, letters or essays.

Writing Process

The stages of the writing process are 1) prewriting, 2) drafting, 3) revision, 4) editing, and 5) publishing. The process is a focus on what writers do as they create a written piece.

Prewriting includes everything a writer does before writing. This includes considering the purpose for writing, deciding on what form or genre would be most appropriate for the specific writing purpose, the audience for whom the writing is being done, the topic, as well as generating and organizing ideas for writing. Children should be encouraged to select topics that are of interest to them and to consider the purpose of the writing before selecting the appropriate genre or form to write. Prewriting activities should help children to activate background knowledge as they explore ideas for writing. Appropriate activities include drawing, talking, reading, webbing ideas, dramatizing, etc.

Drafting is the second stage of writing. In this stage writers get their ideas down on paper in the form of a first draft. The emphasis here is on ideas and content rather than mechanics so it should be clearly labeled as a rough draft. This is where a writer gets the initial ideas down. Developing those ideas can then come in the revision stage.

Revision allows writers to look again at the ideas as well as seek feedback from others. The focus here is still on the ideas and content. Revision strategies are used during the revision stage of the writing process to improve the written product. Revision involves looking to see how you presented your ideas. One important strategy involves getting distance from the work. That distance is important for viewing the piece with a more objective eye. After rethinking what has been written it is important to get feedback from others in conferences or writer's workshops.

Changes are made based on the feedback given. This involves adding, deleting, consolidating, clarifying, and rearranging words and sentences to clarify meaning and expand ideas. Though the various genres have different structures, they all should be clear, concise and effectively organized. The six-trait model is an effective framework for relooking at the written products. Spandel (2008) identifies the following traits:

1. Ideas: The main message or story line of the piece. It involves focusing or narrowing the topic, developing the main idea, using details that build understanding or hold the reader's attention.

2. Organization: The design and structure of the written piece. This includes an original title, an opening that attracts interest, transitions that connect the main ideas in the piece, clear ideas that are easy to follow and an effective ending.

3. Voice: A sense of the writer behind the words. It is the writer's personal imprint on the page. It shows concern for the reader and enthusiasm about the topic.

4. Word choice: Words should paint a picture in the reader's mind. This includes the use of strong verbs, specific nouns, descriptive adjectives, figurative language such as similes or metaphors and avoidance of overused words, slang or clichés.

5. Sentence fluency: The flow or rhythm of the language. Writers use a variety of well-structured sentences that lend to the flow of the piece of writing. This includes a variety of sentence structures and beginnings.

These traits provide a framework for revision as students rethink their writing. The writer may find the need to return to the prewriting stage to do more research or to the drafting stage to do more writing. Once the content is complete and organized the writer moves on to polishing the final form.

Editing allows students put the writing in its final form. This is where the mechanical elements are addressed. Misspelled words, errors in grammar, capitalization and punctuation are addressed here. Students need to get distance from their written product before editing. They then proofread their writing (or the writing of another) in order to locate errors. This is the time to teach lessons on mechanics. Once the errors are corrected, they are ready to move to the final stage, publishing.

Publishing is the final stage of the writing process. The ultimate goal of publishing is to share the written product with the audience. This stage allows a celebration of the completed product. It can take the form of sharing from the author's chair or publishing a book for the classroom library.

Research skills and technology provide vital support for writing. There is a huge variety of resources that provide useful information as students develop their written products. It is important that we teach students both to locate and apply information effectively.

Students can use a number of resources to aid writing. These include dictionaries, thesauri, encyclopedias, electronic information such as the internet of CD-ROM, almanacs, atlases, magazines and newspapers. It is important that students choose the resources appropriately. For example, a dictionary provides useful information about word meanings and spelling, encyclopedias provide information on a variety of topics about events or historical figures and a newspaper is useful for current news and events. Guiding students to the appropriate resource is vital.

Other skills related to the effective use of references are also important. This includes such concepts as locating information in reference texts by using organizational features such as the preface, appendix, index, glossary, table of contents, citations, end notes or bibliographic references. Students need to be knowledgeable about using features such as guide words, alphabetical and numerical order in order to obtain and organize information and thoughts.

While research skills are useful in many genres, they are especially critical skills in writing informational research reports. Technology provides a wide variety of research options through the internet. Resources such as online databases, encyclopedias and other internet references are plentiful. Programs such as *Kid Pix*, *Kidspiration*, *VoiceThread* (to name only a very few) allow tools for gathering, organizing and presenting multimedia and written projects.

Other tools such as digital cameras, smart boards, electronic notebooks for note taking are also useful. Graphic organizers, such as data charts, allow students to record information and document sources. Elementary grade students learn basic keyboarding skills and become familiar with computer terminology such as software, memory, disk drive, hard drive, passwords, entry and pull-down menus, word searches, bookmarking, thesaurus and spell check as useful tools for researching, drafting, revising, editing, and publishing research reports.

Grammar

Grammar is part of the syntactic system of language. Grammar involves principles of word and sentence formation that are the structure of language (Tompkins, 2009). Usage deals with socially acceptable correctness in applying those rules or principles of grammar. Usage is part of the pragmatic system of language. Grammar, usage and mechanics are taught as a part of the language arts curriculum.

In traditional grammar there are eight parts of speech. They are: 1) noun, 2) pronoun, 3) adjective, 4) verb, 5) adverb, 6) preposition, 7) conjunction and 8) interjection.

A **noun** is used to name a person, place or thing. There are two types of nouns, **common nouns** and **proper nouns**. Examples of common nouns include *boy, house,* or *dog.* Common nouns are not capitalized. Proper nouns name a specific person, place or thing as in *Brian, White House* or *Drew.* Proper nouns are capitalized.

Nouns may be **singular**, **plural**, or **possessive**. When a noun refers to one thing it is considered singular, as in *boy, dog* or *book.* For example, *The boy is gone.* When a noun refers to more than one it is said to be plural, as in *boys, dogs* or *books.* For example, *The boys are outside.* The plural is made by adding *–s.* There are exceptions when a plural noun ends in *x, z, s, ch* or *sh, y, o, f* or *fe.* There are also irregular plural forms such as *man/men, foot/feet,* etc.

A possessive noun shows possession. It shows who or what has something. Possessive nouns are formed by adding apostrophes which are explained in a later section. For example, *The dog is Brian's.* Most singular possessives are formed by adding an *apostrophe -s ('s)* such as in the sentence *The car is Candace's.* To form a possessive of a plural noun one adds just an apostrophe (') if the noun ends in *-s,* such as in the sentence *The Kents' house.* An *apostrophe -s ('s)* for plural nouns not ending with *–s* such as in the sentence *The men's team won the game.*

A **pronoun** is used to take the place of a noun. For example, instead of saying *Jordan likes to play,* you could say *He likes to play.* Other examples of pronouns are *she, it, we,* or *they.* Singular pronouns take the place of singular pronouns; plural pronouns take the place of plural pronouns. **Possessive pronouns** take the place of nouns and show possession. For example, *The dog is his.* Other possessive pronouns include *her, their* or *our.* **Personal pronouns** represent specific people. For example *I, we, he,* or *she.*

An **adjective** describes, defines, or limits a noun or pronoun. For example, *blue, sticky,* or *big.* An **adverb** is used to modify a verb, adjective or other another adverb. It tells how, when, where, why, how often or how much. For example: *very, later, inside, well, really* or *badly*.

In general, we use adjectives as subject complements with linking verbs and adverbs with action verbs. For example: The sentence *Please be careful* uses an adjective (*careful*) whereas the sentence *Please walk carefully* uses the related adverb (*carefully*).

A **preposition** is a word that shows a relationship between the noun or pronoun and other words in a sentence. For example: *on, under,* or *above.* A **conjunction** is a word that connects a word and other words or phrases. For example: *and, or,* and *but.* **Interjections** are expressive words such as *wow, ah,* or *oh.* They are used to show strong emotion.

A **verb** is used to show action, as in *jump, run* or *hop,* or to show a state of being, as in *is, will* or *seem.* Students learn about present, past and past participle tenses of verbs. The use of regular verbs, such as *look* and *receive,* poses few problems since the past and past participle forms end in –*ed.*

The present, past and past participle forms of irregular verbs can cause problems however. Examples include *catch/caught, ring/rang/rung or swim/swam/swum.* These verbs are taught individually since there is no standard rule for irregular verb forms.

Sentence Structure and Types

Sentences can be classified by structure or by types. The structure of sentences includes **simple, compound, complex** or **compound-complex,** depending on the number and types of clauses used. Sentences can also be classified by the type. These include **declarative, interrogative, imperative** or **exclamatory** sentences.

A sentence is made up of one or more words and expresses a complete thought. Simple sentences are made up of a **subject** and a **predicate.** The subject is a noun or pronoun and the predicate is the verb and anything that completes or modifies the verb. Sentences may also include phrases or clauses. Phrases do not express a complete thought and do not contain a subject and a predicate. Clauses contain a subject and a predicate and may include a complete thought. Independent clauses contain a subject, a predicate and can stand alone as a complete thought. Dependent clauses contain a subject and a predicate but are not a complete thought.

The **four structures of sentences** are: **simple, compound, complex,** and **compound-complex.** A simple sentence is contains one independent clause. A compound sentence has two or more independent clauses. A complex sentence has one independent clause and one or more dependent clauses. Finally a compound-complex sentence two or more independent clauses and one or more dependent clauses.

There are also **four types of sentences**: **declarative**, **interrogative**, **imperative**, and **exclamatory**. Declarative sentences make statements. They begin with a capital letter and end with a period. An example would be, *I am going to the store.* Interrogative sentences ask a question and end with a question mark. An example would be *Are you going to the store?* Imperative sentences make commands and end either with a period or an exclamation point. For example, *Go to the store.* Exclamatory sentences show strong emotion or surprise. For example, *Wow, you went to the store!*

Mechanics

Mechanics in writing usually refers to rules of capitalization and punctuation. The rules of capitalization and punctuation are taught throughout the K–5 curriculum.

Capitalization

The most common rules of capitalization include: 1) the first word in a sentence, 2) proper nouns or 3) the word *I* when used alone or in a contraction.

All sentences begin with a capital letter. This is true of all types of complete sentences.

Proper nouns are always capitalized. This includes names of persons, geographical places, organizations and the months of the year.

> *Derek Lowe* is a pitcher for the *Atlanta Braves,* who play in the *National League.* Their first game is in *March.*

The word I is also capitalized if it used alone or as a contraction.

> Anna and *I* live in Georgia or
>
> Give me a minute and *I'll* go.

Punctuation

The most common components of punctuation include 1) ending marks such as periods, question marks, and exclamation points, 2) commas, 3) quotation marks, and 4) apostrophes.

End marks

The type of ending punctuation varies depending on the type or purpose of the sentence. The end marks are period (.), question mark (?) and exclamation point (!). As we saw earlier, different types of sentences end with different types end marks.

Commas

The following are the most common rules for commas taught in the K–5 curriculum:

In dates: In sentences with the month, day and year, a comma is placed between the day and the year.

> *It is January 5, 2010.* If only the month and year appear in the sentence, no comma is needed. For example: *It is January 2010 already!*

In a series: When more than one adjective describes a noun, use a comma to separate and emphasize each adjective.

> *the wet, smelly dog* or *the white, fluffy rabbit.*

In a letter greeting and closing:

> In the greeting: *Dear Matthew,*
>
> In the closing: *Your friend,*

Between city and state:

> *We live in Statesboro, Georgia.*

Before conjunctions forming compound sentences:

The children were sleeping, so I read my book.

After interjections at the beginning of sentences:

Oh, that was a great story.

Quotation marks

Quotation marks (" ") are used to set off quoted words, phrases and sentences.

"If everyone treated others as they want to be treated," said Ms. Smith, "the world would be a better place."

Commas and periods at the end of quotations are always placed inside the quotation marks, even if they are not part of the quote.

Apostrophes

Apostrophes are used to make a noun possessive.

For example: The coat is Abby's.

Apostrophes are also used in contractions.

Cannot = can't

Do not = don't.

COMMUNICATION SKILLS (SPEAKING, LISTENING, AND VIEWING)

This category, which will embrace approximately 17% of the exam questions, focuses on concepts related to speaking, listening and viewing. It requires the examinee to understand:

- different aspects of speaking (e.g., purpose, audience, tone)

- different aspects of listening (e.g., following directions, responding to questions appropriately, focusing on the speaker)

- different aspects of viewing (e.g., interpreting images, evaluating media techniques, understanding the message)

- the role that speaking, listening, and viewing play in language acquisition for second-language learners

Listening, talking and viewing are involved in all learning areas of the curriculum. Concepts related to oral and visual language are taught explicitly and incidentally through instruction in the other parts of language arts. They are also taught and reinforced in activities such as classroom routines (following directions, conversations and discussions).

Language uses a complex system for creating meaning through socially shared conventions. During the first months of life, babies are active listeners. Long before they can respond orally they communicate nonverbally by waving their arms, smiling or wiggling. They are also capable of communicating their needs and wants through non-verbal communication, including body language and crying. Through listening they develop the receptive language needed to begin communicating orally.

Oral communication then becomes the foundation for literacy. Proficiency in oral language can lead to success in written language. Therefore, speaking, listening and viewing are important parts of the elementary curriculum.

Learning opportunities in oral language should include a range of activities. These include informal conversations, projects involving cooperative learning, drama and role-play, storytelling and read-aloud, as well as oral language to both present information (oral reports, etc.) and gain information (listening to instruction, viewing videos, etc.).

While children have acquired basic oral language by the time they come to school, it is important to reinforce the basic concepts of verbal interactions. This includes things such as:

1. Asking and answering relevant questions

2. Displaying appropriate turn-taking behaviors

3. Speaking in appropriate volume and speed

4. Staying on topic

5. Actively soliciting the comments or opinions of others

6. Offering one's own opinion forcefully without being domineering

7. Providing reasons in support of opinions expressed

8. Clarifying, illustrating or expanding on a response when asked to do so

9. Employing a group decision-making technique such as brainstorming or a problem-solving sequence (e.g., recognizes problem, defines problem, identifies possible solutions, selects optimal solution, implements solutions, evaluates solution)

Both verbal and nonverbal cues are also important when communicating. Speakers use a variety of cues that help focus attention on important information. For example:

1. Emphasizes important information with words such as *you need to know. . .*, *let me emphasize. . .*, or *let me repeat. . .* to provide emphasis for important information.

2. Provides organizational cues such as *first we will. . .*, *next. . .*, *lastly. . .*, *or in review. . .*

3. Provides emphasis on information by repeating phrases, stressing key words, speak more slowly or more loudly, etc.

Nonverbal communication ranges from facial expression to body language. Gestures, signs, and use of space are also important in nonverbal communication. Multicultural differences in body language, facial expression, use of space, and especially gestures, are enormous and can be open to misinterpretation. Helping children become aware of these differences can increase listening comprehension.

Listening Strategies

Listening strategies vary depending on purpose. Strategies for aesthetic listening differ from those used for efferent or critical listening.

Students listen aesthetically to stories or poems read aloud or view plays or videotapes of stories. Strategies for aesthetic listening include:

- activating prior knowledge

- making predictions that help them anticipate upcoming story events, listening to confirm or reject predictions

- visualizing the story elements such as the characters or setting

- summarizing or retelling a story to reinforce the story elements

- reflecting on what was heard by writing about the story in a journal or discussing the story. This helps students make connections between the story and their lives, or other stories they have heard.

Students listen for efferent purposes as they listen to informational books read aloud, videos or informational presentations. The focus is on listening to take away information so the comprehension strategies are similar to those used for reading content area texts.

Efferent listening strategies such as organizing, summarizing, note-taking and monitoring are important. Teaching students to listen for the verbal and nonverbal cues discussed above are vital. Students should also be taught to using visual aids such as pictures or graphic organizers such as charts, diagrams, or boxes as important sources of information.

Critical-listening skills are also important. We are exposed to much persuasion through commercials, politics, etc. Critical thinking is important in other areas of the curriculum as students learn about science, social studies and other areas of the curriculum as well. Teaching critical listening should involve lessons in propaganda and deceptive language.

Viewing and Visually Representing

Children learn through viewing from a very early age. According to Cox (2008), the United States is the most mass-mediated country in the world. Media is also an important component of effective communication. As with critical listening, critical viewing is important.

Multimedia presentations provide visual methods for enhancing the communication of factual information through the use of graphics, sound clips, and video clips in order to deliver a message. Cox (pp. 427-428) presents a range of steps important in producing effective media. These include:

- Envisioning—discovering ideas and visions

- Arranging—brainstorming and recording ideas using graphic organizers such as webs, drawings and note taking

- Storyboarding—breaking up the ideas into meaningful chunks of images and action

- Producing—use of storyboard to guide production

- Editing—through the camera or camcorder

- Presenting—publicizing the created piece

According to Cox, "participation in viewing and visually representing activities such as media, the visual arts, and drama performance provides great opportunities for developing language and literacy, communicating in social contexts, learning across the curriculum, and experiencing personal growth and development" (page 440).

REFERENCES

Bear, D., Invernizzi, M., Templeton, S. & Johnston, F. (2007). *Words their way: Word study for phonics, vocabulary and spelling instruction.* (4th ed.). Upper Saddle River, NJ: Pearson.

Beck, I., McKeown, M., & Kucan, L. (2002). *Bringing words to life: Robust vocabulary instruction.* New York: Guilford Press.

Cox, C. (2008). *Teaching language arts: A student-centered classroom.* (6th ed.). Boston: Allyn & Bacon.

Davis, A. (2004). *Reading instruction essentials.* (3rd ed.). Boston: American Press.

Fox, B. (2010). *Phonics and structural analysis for the teacher of reading: Programmed for self-instruction.* (10th ed.). Boston: Allyn & Bacon.

Norton, D. & Norton, S. (2007). *Through the eyes of a child: An introduction to children's literature.* (7th ed.). Upper Saddle River, NJ: Pearson.

Report of the National Reading Panel. Teaching Children to Read: An Evidence-Based Assessment of the Scientific Research Literature on Reading and Its Implications for Reading Instruction. National Institute of Child Health and Human Development. (April 2000).

Spandel, V. (2008). *Creating young writers: Using the six traits to enrich writing process in primary classrooms.* (2nd ed.). Boston: Allyn & Bacon.

Tompkins, G. (2004). *Literacy for the 21st century: Teaching reading and writing in grades 4 through 8.* Upper Saddle River, NJ: Pearson.

Tompkins, G. (2007). *Literacy for the 21st century: Teaching reading and writing in pre-kindergarten through grade 4.* (2nd ed.). Upper Saddle River, NJ: Pearson.

Tompkins, G. (2008). *Teaching writing: Balancing process and product.* (5th ed.). Upper Saddle River, NJ: Pearson.

Tompkins, G. (2009). *Language arts: Patterns of practice.* (7th ed.). Upper Saddle River, NJ: Pearson.

Vacca, J., Vacca, R, Gove, M., Burkey, L., Lenhart, L., & McKeon, C. (2009). *Reading and learning to read.* (7th ed.). Boston: Allyn & Bacon.

Mathematics

SCOPE AND SEQUENCE OF SKILLS

The main topics (scope) in elementary mathematics and the sequence (order) in which the school introduces the topics is essentially the same in all states. The table below details these main topics and their introduction order.

**Table 3.1 Mathematics Curriculum:
Number Concepts Strand for Pre-K–Grade 6**

Grade Level	Numbers and Operations
Pre-K	1. Able to explore concrete models and materials, begins to arrange sets of concrete objects in one-to-one correspondence, count by ones to 10 or higher, by fives or higher, and combine, separate, and name "how many" concrete objects. 2. Begins to recognize and describe the concept of zero (meaning there are none), to identify first and last in a series, to compare the numbers of concrete objects using language (e.g., "same" or "equal," "one more," "more than," or "less than").
Kindergarten	1. Uses whole number concepts to describe how many objects are in a set (through 20) using verbal and symbolic descriptions, uses sets of concrete objects to represent quantities given in verbal or written form (through 20), uses one-to-one correspondence and language such as more than, same number as, or two less than to describe relative sizes of sets of concrete objects, and names the ordinal positions in a sequence such as first, second, third, etc. 2. Begins to demonstrate part of and whole with real objects. 3. Sorts to explore numbers, uses patterns, and able to model and create addition and subtraction problems in real situations with concrete objects.

Grade Level	Numbers and Operations
First	1. Is able to create sets of tens and ones using concrete objects to describe, compare, and order whole numbers, read and write numbers to 99 to describe sets of concrete objects, compare and order whole numbers up to 99 (less than, greater than, or equal to) using sets of concrete objects and pictorial models. 2. Separates a whole into two, three, or four equal parts and uses appropriate language to describe the parts such as three out of four equal parts. 3. Models and creates addition and subtraction problem situations with concrete objects and writes corresponding number sentences. 4. Identifies individual coins by name and value and describes relationships among them.
Second	1. Uses concrete models of hundreds, tens, and ones to represent a given whole number (up to 999) in various ways. Begins to use place value to read, write, and describe the value of whole numbers to 999, uses models to compare and order whole numbers to 999, and records the comparisons using numbers and symbols ($<$, $=$, $>$). 2. Uses concrete models to represent and name fractional parts of a whole object (with denominators of 12 or less). 3. Models addition and subtraction of two-digit numbers with objects, pictures, words, and numbers, solve problems with and without regrouping, and is able to recall and apply basic addition and subtraction facts (to 18). 4. Determines the value of a collection of coins up to one dollar and describes how the cent symbol, dollar symbol, and the decimal point are used to name the value of a collection of coins.
Third	1. Uses place value to read and write (in symbols and words), and describes the value of whole numbers and compares and orders whole numbers through 9,999. 2. Uses fraction names and symbols to describe fractional parts of whole objects or sets of objects and compares fractional parts of whole objects or sets of objects in a problem situation using concrete models 3. Selects addition or subtraction and uses the operation to solve problems involving whole numbers through 999. Uses problem-solving strategies, is able to use rounding and compatible numbers to estimate solutions to addition and subtraction problems. 4. Applies multiplication facts through 12 by using concrete models and objects (up to two digits times one digit), uses models to solve division problems, and uses number sentences to record the solutions. Identifies patterns in related multiplication and division sentences (fact families).

Grade Level	Numbers and Operations
Fourth	1. Uses place value to read, write, compare, and order: whole numbers through 999,999,999 and decimals involving tenths and hundredths, including money, using concrete objects and pictorial models. 2. Uses concrete objects and pictorial models to generate equivalent fractions. 3. Uses multiplication to solve problems (no more than two digits, times two digits) and uses division to solve problems (no more than one-digit divisors and three-digit dividends). 4. Uses strategies, including rounding and compatible numbers to estimate solutions to addition, subtraction, multiplication, and division problems.
Fifth	1. Uses place value to read, write, compare, and order whole numbers through 999,999,999,999 and decimals through the thousandths place. 2. Identifies common factors of a set of whole numbers, uses multiplication to solve problems involving whole numbers (no more than three digits times two digits) and uses division to solve problems involving whole numbers (no more than two-digit divisors and three-digit dividends), including solutions with a remainder.
Sixth	1. Compares and orders non-negative rational numbers, generates equivalent forms of rational numbers including whole numbers, fractions, and decimals, uses integers to represent real-life situations. 2. Is able to write prime factorizations using exponents, identifies factors of a positive integer, common factors, and the greatest common factor of a set of positive integers.

MATHEMATICAL PROCESSES

Examinees are expected to understand mathematical processes (e.g., representation, problem solving, making connections). In 2000, the National Council of Teachers of Mathematics (NCTM) published the Principles and Standards for School Mathematics. The national organization's goals include the development and improvement of mathematics education. In the NCTM publication, the council identified six principles and ten standards that children in K-12 ought to master. The document guides states and district curricula development and specifies the mathematics content knowledge students should develop.

Principles of Mathematics

The NCTM (2000) identified six principles that should guide mathematics instruction. These include: equity, curriculum, teaching, learning, assessment, and technology. These are defined as follows:

- **Equity**—Excellence in mathematics education requires equity: high expectations and strong support for all students.

- **Curriculum**—A curriculum must be coherent, focused on important mathematics, and well-articulated concepts across the grades.

- **Teaching**—Effective mathematics teaching requires understanding of what students know and need to learn and then challenging and supporting students to learn it well.

- **Learning**—Students must learn mathematics with understanding, actively building new knowledge from experience and previous knowledge.

- **Assessment**—Assessment should support the learning of important mathematics concepts, and furnish useful information to both teachers and students.

- **Technology**—Technology is essential in teaching and learning mathematics; it influences the teaching of mathematics and enhances students' learning.

Standards for Mathematics

The Content Standards describe the five strands of content that students should learn; and the Process Standards highlight ways of acquiring and applying content knowledge.

Content Standards

1. *Numbers and Operations.* This standard deals with understanding numbers, developing meanings of operations, and computing fluently.

2. *Algebra.* Algebraic symbols and procedures for working with them are a towering mathematical accomplishment in the history of mathematics, and are critical in mathematical work. Algebra is best learned as a set of concepts and techniques tied to the representation of quantitative relations and as a style of mathematical thinking for formalizing patterns, functions, and generalizations.

3. *Geometry.* Geometry has long been regarded as the place in high school where students learn to prove geometric theorems. The Geometry standard

takes a broader view of the power of geometry by calling on students to analyze characteristics of geometric shapes and make mathematical arguments about the geometric relationship, as well as to use visualization, spatial reasoning, and geometric modeling to solve problems.

4. *Measurement.* The study of measurement is crucial in the school mathematics curriculum because of its practicality and pervasiveness in so many aspects of life. The Measurement standard includes understanding the attributes, units, systems, and processes of measurement as well as applying the techniques, tools, and formulas to determine measurements.

5. *Data Analysis and Probability.* Students must formulate questions and collect, organize, and display relevant data to answer key questions. Additionally, it emphasizes learning appropriate statistical methods to analyze data, making inferences and predictions based on data, and understanding and using the basic concepts of probability.

Process Standards

1. *Problem Solving.* Students require frequent opportunities to formulate, grapple with, and solve complex problems that involve a significant amount of effort. Students are able to acquire ways of thinking, habits of persistence and curiosity, and confidence in unfamiliar situations that serve them well outside the mathematics classroom.

2. *Ways of Reasoning and Proof.* Mathematical reasoning and proof offer powerful ways of developing and expressing insights. Students are able to identify patterns, structure, or regularities in both real-world and mathematical situations. They make and investigate mathematical conjectures; and develop and evaluate mathematical arguments and proofs, which are ways reasoning and providing justification.

3. *Communication.* Mathematical communication is a way of sharing ideas and clarifying understanding. Through communication, ideas become objects of reflection, refinement, discussion, and amendment.

4. *Connections.* Mathematics is an integrated field of study. When students connect mathematical ideas, their understanding is deeper and more lasting, and they come to view mathematics as a coherent whole.

5. *Representations.* Mathematical ideas can be represented in a variety of ways: pictures, concrete materials, tables, graphs, number and letter symbols, spreadsheet displays, and so on.

PROBLEM-SOLVING STRATEGIES

The instruction of problem-solving strategies involves engaging students to use their existing knowledge to assist them in acquiring new knowledge. This process can be difficult if students do not have appropriate problem-solving skills. At the start of the problem-solving process, teachers can provide the students with some basic background information and perhaps show the students how to reduce a complex problem into simpler parts. Teachers may need to guide the students in helping to isolate the pertinent information of what is given, what is assumed, and what needs to be proven. Characteristics of the actual problem, such as the number of possible solutions, may indicate that one particular strategy is the best choice for solving the problem.

Once a strategy has been used successfully to solving the problem, teachers should direct the students to determine whether the solution makes sense within the context of the problem. As an example, if the problem requires finding the length of a side of a triangle, then any negative number solution would have to be discarded. Similarly, if a problem involves rational solutions, then an answer of $\sqrt{2}$ could not be acceptable.

Reasonableness and Estimation

Throughout the problem solving process, students should ask whether the results of the steps that are used actually make sense. In particular, students must be able to recognize if a quantity is either exceptionally large or exceptionally small. As an example, if an investment of $1000 is split by placing it into two separate accounts, it would be impossible for one account to contain $1500. By asking students to estimate the answer to either part of a problem or the entire problem, students will become better mathematical thinkers. For example, if $100 is to be given to three people A, B, and C in the ratio of 1 : 2 : 7 respectively, the student must recognize that C will receive more money than either A or B. The ability to estimate an answer is an excellent assessment of the students' comprehension and readiness for more advanced problems.

Constructing a Table

When a problem provides a data set that can be organized by specific characteristics or groups, constructing tables of values will assist students to recognize patterns inherent in the data. For example, suppose the student has collected the following data for two variables, x and y.

Figure 3.2

x	1	2	3	4	5	6	7
y	0	3	8	15	24	35	48

At first glance, it may appear that there is no relationship between the values of x and y. However, if a student does some "experimenting" by squaring the x values, the corresponding squared values will be 1, 4, 9, 16, 25, 36, and 49. Hopefully, the student recognizes that each y valuc is 1 less than the square of its corresponding x value. Thus, the relationship can be expressed as $y = x^2 - 1$. The construction of a table has the advantage of organizing the information into a form that can facilitate finding a solution.

Guess-and-Check

Although it may seem unusual, guessing is a valid problem-solving strategy that should be used when there are a relatively small number of possible solutions or when the list of potential solutions can be tested easily. As an example, suppose that it is known that the solution to the equation $3^x + 5x^2 - x^3 = 693$ is a positive integer less than 10. Since this would be a difficult equation to solve by algebraic techniques, a suggestion would be to simply guess, using an integer from 1 to 9. The student can readily see that the value of 1 could not possibly be a solution. Suppose the student decides to use the value of 5. Then, $3^5 + 5(5)^2 - 5^3 = 243 + 125 - 125 = 243$, which is too low. At this point, the student might believe that the number 7 is the correct solution. This leads to $3^7 + 5(7)^2 + 7^3 = 2187 + 245 - 343 = 2089$, which is too large. The only choice left is to select 6. Then $3^6 + 5(6)^2 - 6^3 = 729 + 180 - 216 = 693$, which is the correct answer.

Working Backwards

This is a strategy that works best when the solution is already known, and thus we need to provide the steps that lead to the solution. As an example, suppose that the student is asked to factor completely the polynomial $x^4 + 2x^3 + 2x^2 + x - 6$. The student decides to graph $y = x^4 + 2x^3 + 2x^2 + x - 6$, and finds that the points $(1, 0)$ and $(22, 0)$ lie on the graph. Hopefully, the student recognizes that this means that both $(x - 1)$ and $(x + 2)$ must be factors of $x^4 + 2x^3 + 2x^2 + x - 6$. In order to determine the other factor(s), the student should divide the product of $(x - 1)$ and $(x + 2)$ into $x^4 + 2x^3 + 2x^2 + x - 6$. Now $(x - 1)(x + 2) = x^2 + x - 2$, and by long division, $(x^4 + 2x^3 + 2x^2 + x - 6) \div (x^2 + x + 2) = x^2 + x + 3$. It becomes fairly easy to check that $x^2 + x + 3$ cannot be factored, so the complete factoring is $(x - 1)(x + 2)(x^2 + x + 3)$.

Using a Diagram

The use of a diagram can never be overemphasized. Consider the following mixture problem, which is typically found in a second-year algebra textbook.

A solution of 10 quarts of alcohol and water contains 20% alcohol. How many quarts of a solution of alcohol and water that contains 30% alcohol should be added in order that the resulting mixture contains 28% alcohol?

This would be challenging to solve without a diagram for even an experienced mathematics teacher. But Figure 3.3 shows an appropriate diagram that can certainly clarify the direction of the solution to this problem.

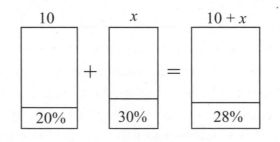

Figure 3.3

NUMBER SENSE AND NUMERATION

This portion of the test will account for 40% of your score in the Mathematics category. You will be tested on your ability to understand:

- prenumeration concepts (e.g., informal counting, meaning of number, patterns)

- basic number systems (e.g., whole numbers, integers, fractions, decimals)

- basic four operations (e.g., addition, subtraction, multiplication, and division) and their properties (e.g., commutativity, order of operations)

- basic concepts of number theory (e.g., factors, multiples, prime and composite)

- how to solve problems (e.g., modeling, estimation, algorithms) and recognize the reasonableness of results

- how to make, describe, and explore numerical patterns and engage in mathematical investigations

Sets and Number Concepts

The basic mathematical concept is that of **set**. A set is a collection of things, real or imagined, related or unrelated. Students may manipulate the objects within the set in various ways.

Classifying Objects in a Set

Classification allows the students to sort materials according to some specific criteria. A child who is not yet able to count, for example, might sort objects by whether the objects are soft or hard, by whether a magnet will attract them, or by other attributes.

Ordering objects in a set. Students may **order** the objects or arrange them in size from smallest to largest or from largest to smallest.

Patterning objects in a set. Students may try arranging the objects in a set to duplicate **a pattern that they observe**. The students may, for instance, try to replicate a color pattern with beads: red, yellow, red, yellow, and so on. Later, they may try to replicate a number pattern using magnetic numbers; the pattern may be 2, 4, 6, etc. They may even match the correct number of pennies to the magnetic number for another type of patterning. Making a pattern of geometric shapes would be another example, for instance, square, circle, triangle, square, circle, triangle, etc.

Comparing objects in a set. Students may **compare** objects in a set to objects in another set as a help in preparing for number skills. Is there a chair for each toy bear? Does each child in the set of children in the classroom have a carton of milk? Does each carton of milk have a straw for the child to use? Later, the students will compare each object in a set with a counting number; this will give the total number of objects in the set.

Students may try pairing objects with the numbers that they have memorized through rote; this is **oral counting**. After classifying objects, a student may try counting the objects in the groups. For example, if the teacher asks, "How many objects were soft?" the answer is a number that tells how many, and the student will have to count to find the answer.

Number

Number is a concept or idea that indicates how many. Children may memorize the counting numbers from 1 to 10 and be able to count by rote before they start school. Many times, however, there is little understanding in the beginning of what a number is. After the students have some idea of the value of the numbers, they may arrange the numbers from largest to smallest or smallest to largest. Students may try counting by pairing the objects with a number on the number line; this will give a visual comparison. The set {1, 2, 3, 4, . . . } can represent counting numbers. Study the following number line. Notice that the counting numbers start with 1 and that 0 is not in the set of counting numbers.

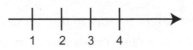

Whole numbers are the counting numbers plus 0: {0, 1, 2, 3, . . . }. Study the following number line. Notice that 0 is part of the set of whole numbers.

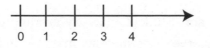

A **number** is a concept; a **numeral** is a symbol used to represent a number. The students must be able to read and to write the numerals. This skill is an important part of a student's early mathematical development. An important part of mathematical learning and of language arts learning is being able to read and to represent the numbers in words: *one*, *two*, *three*, and so on. Students may also try another way of counting: **skip counting**.

They may start with 1 and count only the odd numbers: 3, 5, 7, 9, and so on. **Odd numbers** are those that cannot be evenly divided by 2. Students may also try skip counting with another beginning point; for instance, they may start with 2 and count only the even numbers: 2, 4, 6, 8, 10, and so on. **Even numbers** are those that one can evenly divide by 2.

Base-10 Numeration System and Place Value

Our numeration system uses the Hindu-Arabic numerals (0, 1, 2, 3, 4, 5, 6, 7, 8, 9) to represent numbers. Our numeration system follows a **base-10 place-value** scheme. As we move to the left in any number, each place value is 10 times the place value to the right. Similarly, as we move to the right, each place value is one-tenth the place value to the left. For example, in the number 543, the value of the place that the 5 is in (100s) is 10 times the value of the place that the 4 occupies (10s). The place value of the 3 is one-tenth the place value of the 4.

Expanded notation can show the value of each number in its place. Using the same number 543, the values are $(5 \times [10 \times 10]) + (4 \times [10 \times 1]) + (3 \times 1)$. **Exponential notation** can show the value of each number. Using the same number 543, the exponential values are $(5 \times 10^2) + (4 \times 10^1) + (3 \times 10^0)$.

The Four Basic Operations

Operations indicate what one is to do with numbers. There are four main operations: addition, subtraction, multiplication, and division. Multiplication is repeated addition. Division is repeated subtraction.

Addition is an operation that, when performed on numbers of disjoint sets (sets with different members), results in a **sum**. One can show addition on a number line by counting forward. Addition is also a **binary operation**, meaning it combines only two numbers at a time to produce a third, unique number. Adding two whole numbers always results in a whole number. The **algorithm** of addition is the form in which we write and solve an addition example. Familiar short forms are

2 (addend) + 3 (addend) = 5 (sum) and

$$\begin{array}{r} 2\ (\text{addend}) \\ +\ 3\ (\text{addend}) \\ \hline 5\ (\text{sum}) \end{array}$$

The operation of **subtraction** is the **inverse** of addition: what addition does, subtraction undoes. Like addition, subtraction is a binary operation; that is, we work on only two numbers at a time. The result is a third, unique number called the **difference**. Given two whole numbers, subtracting the smaller number from the larger one results in a whole number. However, subtraction of whole numbers does not result in a whole number if the larger whole number is subtracted from the smaller one. The algorithm of subtraction is the form in which we write and solve a subtraction example. Familiar short forms are

$$5 - 3 = 2 \text{ and}$$

$$\begin{array}{r} 5 \ \text{(minuend)} \\ -\ 3 \ \text{(subtrahend)} \\ \hline 2 \ \text{(difference)} \end{array}$$

Addition problems with a missing addend are solved with the operation of subtraction, for example, ___ (addend) + 3 (addend) = 5 (sum).

Multiplication, like addition and subtraction, is a binary operation. The result of the operation of multiplication is the **product**. The product of multiplying two whole numbers is always a whole number.

The operation of **division** has the same inverse relation to multiplication as subtraction has to addition: what multiplication does, division undoes. For example, multiplying 4 by 9 results in a product of 36; dividing 36 by 9 "gives back" a **quotient** of 4. Teaching division should parallel teaching multiplication.

> **PRAXIS Pointer**
>
> **Work quickly and steadily. You have two hours to complete the test. Avoid focusing on any one problem too long. Taking the practice tests in this book will help you learn to budget your precious time.**

Number Concepts and Algorithms

One of the key challenges in mathematics education is the teaching of technical vocabulary and concepts. Teachers as well as students need to have an understanding of the key terms used in mathematics to communicate effectively in the classroom. An **algorithm** is an established and well-defined step-by-step problem solving method used to achieve a desired mathematical result. A summary of key mathematical terms and concepts follows.

Integers

An integer is a whole number that includes all positive and negative numbers, including zero. This may be represented on a number line that extends in both directions from 0. You might have –45, –450,000, 0, 234, or 78,306. Integers do not include decimals or fractions. The set of integers: {..., –6, –5, –4, –3, –2, –1, 0, 1, 2, 3, 4, 5, 6...}

You can represent many real-life situations with integers.

Natural Numbers

A natural number is a positive integer or a non-negative integer. There is a small difference because non-negative integers also include "0." A list of positive integers would only include whole numbers, but not zero. Natural numbers include 1, 2, 3, 4, 5 ... ∞ (Note: ∞ is the symbol for infinity). They are all whole numbers. Natural numbers do not include negative numbers, fractions, or decimals.

Rational Numbers

A number that can be expressed as a ratio or quotient of two non-zero integers is known as a rational number. Rational numbers can be expressed as common fractions or decimals, such as $\frac{3}{5}$ or 0.6. Finite decimals, repeating decimals, mixed numbers, and whole numbers are all rational numbers. Non-repeating decimals cannot be expressed in this way, and are said to be irrational.

Irrational Numbers

An irrational number is a number that cannot be represented as an exact ratio of two integers. The decimal form of the number never terminates and never repeats. Examples: The square root of 2 ($\sqrt{2}$) or Pi (π).

Real Numbers

A real number describes any number that is positive, negative, or zero and is used to measure continuous quantities. A real number also includes numbers, which have decimal representations, even those with infinite decimal sequences (e.g., Pi (π)).

Exponential Notation

Exponential notation is a symbolic way of showing how many times a number or variable is used as a factor. In the notation 5^3, the exponent 3 shows that 5 is a factor used three times; that is calculated in the following way: $5^3 = 5 \times 5 \times 5 = 125$.

Scientific Notation

Scientific notation is a form of writing a number as the product of a power of 10 and a decimal number greater than or equal to 1 and less than 10.

$$2,400,000 = 2.4 \times 10^6, \ 240.2 = 2.402 \times 10^2, \ 0.0024 = 2.4 \times 10^{-3}$$

Absolute Value

The absolute value is the number's distance from zero on the number line. This action ignores the + or – sign of a number. $|x|$ is the graphic used to describe the action of absolute value. Example: $|-5| = 5$ or $|5| = 5$.

Expanded Form

The expanded form of an algebraic expression is the equivalent expression without parentheses, for example the expanded form of $(a + b)^2$ is $a^2 + 2ab + b^2$. A way to write numbers that shows the place value of each digit, for example: $263 = 200 + 60 + 3$ or 263 which is equal to 2 hundreds, 6 tens, and 3 ones.

Expanded Notation

Expanded notation is showing place value by multiplying each digit in a number by the appropriate power of 10.

$$523 = 5 \times 100 + 2 \times 10 + 3 \times 1 \text{ or } 5 \times 10^2 + 2 \times 10^1 + 3 \times 10^0$$

Estimating

Estimating is generally done by rounding the numbers to the nearest decimal place required for accuracy. For example, a sum 23 + 35 can be solved easily by rounding 23 to **20** and 35 to **40** to obtain the estimation 20 + 40 = 60.

Place Values

Place values are the basic foundation for understanding mathematic computation. A simple number like 1984 can be explained based on the positions of the numbers in the value scale. See the example in table 3.2.

Table 3.2 Place Value

Thousand	Hundred	Ten	One
1000	900	80	4
1	9	8	4

Number Theory

Teacher candidates have to have a solid command of basic number theory. Some of the elements required are covered in the Praxis II Elementary Education: Content Knowledge (0014/5014) curricula are discussed next:

Prime Factorization

You can use exponents to write the prime factorization of a number. Every composite number can be written as a product of prime numbers. This is called the prime factorization of the number. When a factor is repeated in a prime factorization, express the repeated factor using an exponent. A factor tree can also help you find the prime factorization of a composite number. It does not matter which factor pair you start with, as long as you continue factoring until you have only prime numbers. What is the prime factorization of 48 using exponents?

$$48 = 3 \times 16$$
$$48 = 3 \times 2 \times 8$$
$$48 = 3 \times 2 \times 2 \times 4$$
$$48 = 3 \times 2 \times 2 \times 2 \times 2$$

The prime factorization of 48 is 3×2^4.

The exponent 4 shows how many times the base number 2 is used as a factor. The factor 3 is used only once. It has an exponent of 1. Exponents of 1 do not need to be written because they are implied. Prime factorizations are usually written in order from least to greatest base number. The prime factorization of 48 can also be written $2^4 \times 3$.

Greatest Common Divisor (GCD)

The greatest common divisor (GCD) of two or more non-zero integers is the largest positive integer that divides into the numbers without producing a remainder. This is useful for simplifying fractions into their lowest terms, for example: GCD (42, 56) = 14.

$$\frac{42}{56} = \frac{3 \times 14}{4 \times 14} = \frac{3}{4}$$

Although 42 and 56 are divisible by larger numbers (21 and 28, respectively), the largest number, which is a factor of both 42 and 56, is 14.

Common Multiple

A common multiple is a whole number that is a multiple of two or more given numbers, for example: The common multiples of 2, 3, and 4 are 12, 24, 36, 48 . . .

Composite Number

A number greater than zero which is divisible by at least one other number besides **one (1) and itself** resulting in an integer (i.e., it has at least 3 factors). For example: 9 is a composite number because it has three factors: 1, 3, and 9.

MODELING THE OPERATIONS

There are four ways to model the operations:

1. Concrete method. With the concrete method, the teacher allows the students to use real objects. The students can represent a set and take away objects from it (subtraction), or they can combine two sets with no common objects (addition).

2. Semiconcrete method. With the semiconcrete method, the students work with visual representations (pictures) instead of actual objects.

3. Semiabstract method. With the semiabstract method, the students work with one symbol (tally marks, x's, y's, etc.) to represent objects; instead of actual objects, pictures, or abstract (numerical) representations, the students use one symbol. The semiabstract method can be used to represent, for instance, a multiplication problem. If there are three rabbits and if each rabbit eats four carrots each day, how many carrots will the rabbits eat in one day?

Rabbit 1	////
Rabbit 2	////
Rabbit 3	////

4. Abstract method. With the abstract method, the student matches the elements of a given group with abstract numbers. To represent three rabbits eating four carrots daily using the abstract method, the student would set up the problem as 3×4.

Regrouping in Addition and Subtraction

Regrouping in addition, a process that teachers and students once called *carrying*, is evident in addition problems, such as $16 + 7$ and $26 + 6$. To begin working with students on this process, the teacher would ideally drop back to the concrete level. For example, to work on the problem $16 + 7$, the teacher would have the students make one bundle of 10 straws and lay 6 straws to the side; when the students see 7 straws added to the 6 straws, they realize that they need to make another bundle of 10 straws. When they make that second bundle, they have the answer: two groups of 10 and 3 extra straws, or 23.

Regrouping in subtraction, a process that teachers and students once called *borrowing*, is evident in problems such as $23 - 7$. The students can readily see that they cannot subtract the big number 7 from the small number 3; to accomplish this process, the students again can use concrete objects to begin the process. With two bundles of 10 straws and one group of 3 straws on the table, the students should count out 7 straws; when the students see that they cannot subtract 7 from 3, they can unbundle one packet of 10 straws and place the 10 straws with the 3 straws. The students can pull 7 straws from the 13; 6 straws will be left along with one bundle of 10—the answer: 16.

Modeling Multiplication

As noted earlier, pairs of operations that "undo" each other are **inverse**. Multiplication and division are inverse, that is, they "undo" one another.

An **array** can model a multiplication problem. The first number in a multiplication problem is the vertical number in an array; the second number is the horizontal number. The following is the array for $2 \times 3 = 6$.

x	x	x
x	x	x

Multiplication Properties and Algorithms

The **multiples** of any counting number are the results of multiplying that counting number by all the counting numbers. For example, the multiples of 7 are 7, 14, 21, 28, and so on. Every whole number has an infinite number of multiples.

Terms related to multiplication and key properties of the multiplication operation include the following:

Multiplicative identity property of 1. Any number multiplied by 1 remains the same, for instance, $34 \times 1 = 34$. The number 1 is called the **multiplicative identity**.

Property of reciprocals. The product of any number (except 0) multiplied by its reciprocal is 1. The **reciprocal** of a number is 1 divided by that number. Remember that dividing by 0 has no meaning; avoid dividing by 0 when computing or solving equations and inequalities.

Commutative property for addition and multiplication. The order of adding addends or multiplying factors does not determine the sum or product. For example, 6×9 gives the same product as 9×6. Division and subtraction are not commutative.

Associative property for addition and multiplication. Associating, or grouping, three or more addends or factors in a different way does not change the sum or product. For example, $(3 + 7) + 5$ results in the same sum as $3 + (7 + 5)$. Division and subtraction are not associative.

Distributive property of multiplication over addition. A number multiplied by the sum of two other numbers can be handed out, or distributed, to both numbers, multiplied by each of them separately, and the products added together. For example, multiplying 6 by 47 gives the same result as multiplying 6 by 40, multiplying 6 by 7, and then adding the products. That is, $6 \times 47 = (6 \times 40) + (6 \times 7)$. The definition of the distributive property of multiplication over addition can be stated simply: the product of a number and a sum can be expressed as a sum of two products. The simple notation form of the distributive property is

$$a(b + c) = (a\ 3\ b) + (a\ 3\ c).$$

Another major concept in multiplication is **regrouping**, or carrying. The term *regrouping* indicates the renaming of a number from one place value to another. The short algorithm we are most familiar with does not show the steps that illustrate the regrouping. Students must be able to use the multiplication facts, multiply by 0, and apply regrouping to solve problems such as 268×26.

Factors, Primes, Composites, and Multiples

Factors are any of the numbers or symbols in mathematics that, when multiplied together, form a product. For example, the counting number factors of 12 are 1, 2, 3, 4, 6, and 12. A number with only two counting number factors—1 and the number itself—is a **prime number**. The first few primes are 2, 3, 5, 7, 11, 13, and 17. Most other counting numbers are **composite numbers** because they are *composed* of several counting number factors. The number 1 is neither prime nor composite; it has only one counting number factor: 1.

As noted earlier, the **multiples** of any counting number are the results of multiplying that whole number by all the counting numbers. For example, the multiples of 7 are 7, 14, 21, 28, and so on. Every whole number has an infinite number of multiples.

Modeling Division

Division, the inverse of multiplication, can be represented in two ways: measurement and partition. With **measurement division**, the students know how many in each group (set) but do not know how many sets. Here is an example: A homeowner has a group of 400 pennies. He plans to give each trick-or-treater five pennies. How many trick-or-treaters can receive a treat before the homeowner has to turn out the porch light? In this case, the students know the number of pennies (measurement) each child will receive; they need to find the number of children.

In **partitive division**, students know the number of groups (sets), but they do not know the number of objects in each set. Here is an example: There is a plate of eight cookies on the table. There are four children at the table. How many cookies does each child get if they divide the cookies evenly? The question asks the students to determine how many are in each group.

No properties of division—commutative, associative, and so on—hold true at all times. Division is the most difficult of the algorithms for students to use. Division begins at the left, rather than at the right. Also, to solve a division problem, students must not only divide but subtract and multiply as well. Students must use estimation with the trial quotients; sometimes it takes several trials before the trial is successful.

ALGEBRAIC CONCEPTS

This portion of the test will account for 25% of your score in the Mathematics category. You will be tested on your ability to understand:

- basic algebraic methods and representations

- the associative, commutative, and distributive properties

- additive and multiplicative inverses

- the special properties of zero and one

- equalities and inequalities

- the appropriate application of formulas

An understanding of patterns is essential to mastering the skills associated with algebra. According to Suggate et al. (1998), "Algebra is a very powerful way of expressing patterns concisely. It is concerned with generalities and finding equivalences among expressions" (p. 100). Therefore, the primary concepts addressed by this objective include patterns, expressions, and algebraic functions. Algebraic skills are closely tied to problem solving, as many word problems require us to recognize and extend patterns or create algebraic expressions to find a solution.

1. Patterns

In algebra, a pattern is a sequence governed by a rule that can be expressed in words or symbols. An understanding of patterns involves recognizing the basic characteristics of patterns, identifying correct extensions of patterns, recognizing relationships among patterns, and demonstrating knowledge of applications of algebra in representing relationships and patterns in everyday life. The following example illustrates the concept of pattern characteristics and extensions:

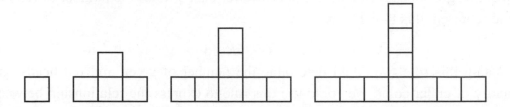

Look at the four models above. If the pattern continues, how many squares would be needed to build the 6th model?

Explanation of Example:

The example asks us to extend the pattern based on the information we are given. The first step in extending the pattern is to recognize the relationships between the four models by counting and recording the number of squares in each one. The creation of a simple table is a useful aid in recording what is known and what must be determined:

Model	1	2	3	4	5	6
Squares	1	4	7	10	?	?

By looking at the table, we can see that the number of squares increases by three each time a new model is constructed. Following this rule, we can determine that the 5th model would contain 13 squares, while the 6th model would contain 16 squares. Since this problem requires us to extend the pattern only twice beyond what is illustrated, we could solve it without the use of the table. However, creating a table is a reliable way of recording patterns and ensuring accuracy as the pattern is extended, particularly as the number of extensions increases.

2. Algebraic Expressions

Understanding algebraic expressions requires knowledge of the concepts of variable, function, and equation. These concepts are essential to the expression of algebraic relationships, the application of algebraic methods to solve equations and inequalities, and the use of algebraic functions to plot points, describe graphs, and determine slope.

At the elementary level, algebraic expressions typically contain numbers, operational symbols and variables. The expression is part of the number sentence, or equation, which includes the equal sign. In elementary mathematics, functions are algebraic equations that express rules or patterns to determine the relationship between values. For example, if the number of green beads of a necklace is 3 fewer than 5 times the number of red beads, we could represent this function as:

$$G = 5R - 3$$

Using this rule, we could determine the number of green and red beads, given the quantity of either color. We could use this rule to express the relationship between x and y in order to plot points using the coordinate system and create a graphic representation of the function. The example that follows illustrates the use of algebraic functions to plot points and determine slope.

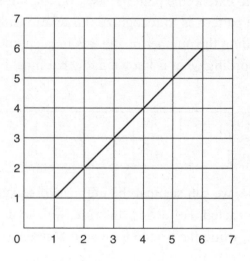

Which function is illustrated in the graph above?

   a. $y = 2x + 3$

   b. $y = x - 1$

   c. $y = \dfrac{x}{2}$

   d. $y = x$

In the example above, we are asked to determine the function represented by the graph that is pictured in the figure. To determine the relationship between the x and y variables, we can plot some points along the line. Focusing on the first quadrant alone, we could plot the following ordered pairs: (1, 1), (2, 2), (3, 3), and so on. This tells us that the value of x is equal to the value of y. Therefore, the function is $y = x$.

Numbers and their Properties

Numbers have basic properties that can help simplify mathematics problem solving and reasoning skills. Some of these are:

Commutative Property

The order of the **addends** or **factors** do not change the result.

$$a + b = b + a \quad \text{and} \quad a \times b = b \times a$$

Addition: $6 + 8 = 14$ is the same as $8 + 6 = 14$
Multiplication: $5 \times 8 = 40$ is the same as $8 \times 5 = 40$

Associative Property of Multiplication and Addition

The order of the addends or product will not change the sum or the product.

$$(a + b) + c = a + (b + c) \text{ and } (a \times b) \times c = a \times (b \times c)$$

Addition: $(2 + 3) + 5 = 10, 2 + (3 + 5) = 10$
Multiplication: $(2 \times 3) \times 5 = 30, 2 \times (3 \times 5) = 30$

Property of Zero

The sum of a number and zero is the number itself, and the product of a number and zero is zero.

Addition: $8 + 0 = 8$
Multiplication: $8 \times 0 = 0$

Distributive Property

You can add and then multiply or multiply then add.

$$a(b + c) = (a \times b) + (a \times c)$$

$$8(5 + 2) = (8 \times 5) + (8 \times 2) = 56$$

Linear and Nonlinear Functional Relationships

Many functions can be represented by pairs of numbers. When the graph of those pairs results in points lying on a straight line, a function is said to be linear. When not on a line, the function is nonlinear.

A real-valued function for a real variable is a rule that assigns to each real number x in a specified set of numbers, called the domain of f, a single real number $f(x)$. The variable x is called the independent variable. If $y = f(x)$ we call y the dependent variable. A function can be specified in the following ways: 1) numerically by the means of a table, 2) algebraically by means of a formula, or 3) graphically by means of a graph. A **numerical specified function** is listed in Table 3.3:

Table 3.3 Numerical Specified Function

x	0	1	2	3
$f(x)$	3.01	−1.03	2.22	0.01

Then, $f(0)$ is the value of the function when $x = 0$. From the table, we may have the following values: $f(0) = 3.01$ and $f(1) = -1.03$

An algebraically specified function: Suppose you had function f specified by $f(x) = 3x^2 - 4x + 1$. Then:

$f(x) = 3x^2 - 4x + 1$ (Substitute 2 for x) $f(2) = 3(2)^2—4(2) + 1$

The answer: $f(2) = 12 - 8 + 1$, this would $= 5$

$f(-1) = 3(-1)^2 - 4(-1) + 1$ (Substitute -1 for x) $= 3 + 4 + 1$, this would $= 8$

A **linear function** is one whose graph is a straight line (that is why it is called "linear"). A linear function is one of the most fundamental and important relationship concepts as a foundation for advanced mathematics. A linear function is one which always satisfies the following: $f(x + y) = f(x) + f(y)$ and $f(\alpha x) = \alpha f(x)$. In this definition, x and y are input variables and α is a constant.

For example: Consider the function $f(x) = 2x$. Assuming there are two input values $(x = a + b)$, the function now becomes $f(x) = f(a + b) = 2(a + b) = 2a + 2b$. We see that if we substitute $(x = a$ and then $x = b)$ we obtain $f(a) = 2a$ and $f(b) = 2b$ where we see that $f(a + b) = f(a) + f(b)$ and satisfies the first rule. Checking the second constraint we have $f(\alpha x) = 2\alpha x$ which is equivalent to $\alpha f(x) = \alpha 2x$ due to the associative/commutative properties of multiplication.

A non-linear function is one that does not satisfy the constraints stated previously. For example, the function $f(x) = x^2$ is non-linear because $f(a + b) = (a + b)^2 = a^2 + 2ab + b^2$ is not equal to $f(a) + f(b) = a^2 + b^2$.

We will revisit the concept of linear and non-linear functions in the proceeding sections.

Algebraic Pattern

An algebraic pattern is a set of numbers and/or variables in a specific order that form a pattern. An example would be a chart showing the distance in feet if Max travels on his bicycle a different number of seconds. Given the chart below, what is one way to find the number of feet Max travels on his bicycle in 1 second?

# of seconds	6	8	9
# of feet	90	120	135

First, students need to be able to understand the algebraic pattern presented in the chart and how the numbers are listed. Students should divide the number of feet by the number of seconds to find the correct answer. However, in this problem the answer 15 does not answer the test question. Students need to be able to tell which operation they used to derive the answer to the question.

Special Properties of 0 and 1

The **natural numbers** are equivalent to the set of counting numbers. The number 0 has special mathematical significance with respect to the operation of addition. The number 0 added to any natural number yields a sum that is the same as the other natural number; 0 is, therefore, the **additive identity**, or the **identity element of addition**.

Because multiplication is repeated addition, 0 holds a special property with both multiplication and addition. The **multiplication property of 0** states that when a factor is multiplied by 0, then the product is 0. The **identity element of multiplication** is 1; the identity element of multiplication means that any factor multiplied by 1 gives that factor. Zero is not an identity element for subtraction or for division. Subtraction does not have an identity element. Even though $4 - 0 = 4$, it is not true that $0 - 4 = 4$. Division by 0 is not possible, so 0 is not an identity element for division.

Formulas: Variables, Equations and Inequalities

Equations

An equation is a mathematical sentence stating that two expressions are equal. Many mathematical expressions include letters called variables. Variables are classified as either free or bound. For a given combination of values for the free variables, an expression may be evaluated, although for some combinations of values of the free variables, the value of the expression may be undefined. Thus an expression represents a function whose inputs are the values assigned the free variables and whose output is the resulting value of the expression.

For example, the expression $\frac{x}{y}$ evaluated for $x = 10$, $y = 5$, will give 2; but is undefined for $y = 0$.

The evaluation of an expression is dependent on the definition of the mathematical operators and on the system of values that is its context. See Formal Semantics and Interpretation (logic) for the study of this question in logic.

Two expressions are said to be equivalent if, for each combination of values for the free variables, they have the same output, i.e., they represent the same function. Example:

The expression $\sum_{n=1}^{3}(2nx)$ has free variable x, bound variable n, constants 1, 2, and 3, two occurrences of an implicit multiplication operator, and a summation operator. The expression is equivalent with the simpler expression $12x$. The value for $x = 3$ is 36.

The '+' and '−' (addition and subtraction) symbols have their usual meanings. Division can be expressed with the ÷, /, or with horizontal dash, i.e., $x / 2$ or $\frac{x}{2}$. Also, for multiplication one can use the symbols × or a "•" (dot), or else simply omit it (multiplication is implicit); so: $x2$ or $2x$ or $\times 2$ or $x • 2$ are all acceptable (please notice in the first example above how the "times" symbol resembles an "x" and also how the "." symbol resembles a decimal point, so to avoid confusion it's best to use one of the latter two forms).

An **expression** must be well-formed. That is, the operators must have the correct number of inputs, in the correct places. The expression 2 + 3 is well formed; the expression * 2 + is not, at least, not in the usual notation of arithmetic.

Algebraic Inequality

An algebraic inequality is a statement that is written using one or more variables and constants that shows a greater than or less than relationship. Example: $2x + 8 > 24$.

Solving an algebraic inequality means finding all of its solutions. A "solution" of an inequality is a number which when substituted for the variable (for example: x) makes the inequality a true statement. An algebraic inequality is defined as a statement that is written using one or more variables and constants that shows a greater than or less than relationship. As in the case of solving equations, there are certain manipulations of the inequality, which do not change the solution. Consider the algebraic inequality in the following example: $2x + 8 > 24$.

Here is a list of possible manipulations:

1. Adding/subtracting the same number on both sides: $2x + 8 > 24$ has the same solution as the inequality $2x > 16$. (The second inequality was obtained from the first one by subtracting 8 on both sides.)

2. Switching sides and changing the orientation of the inequality sign: $2x + 8 > 24$ has the same solution as $24 < 2x + 8$. (We merely switched sides and turned the ">" into a "<".)

Last, the operation which is at the source of all the trouble with inequalities:

3a. Multiplying/dividing by the same POSITIVE number on both sides.

3b. Multiplying/dividing by the same NEGATIVE number on both sides AND changing the orientation of the inequality sign.

This does not seem too difficult. The inequality $2x < 6$ has the same solution as the inequality $x < 3$. (We divided by +2 on both sides.) The inequality $-2x > 4$ has the same solutions as the inequality $x < -2$. (We divided by (-2) on both sides and switched ">" to "<".)

The inequality $x^2 > x$ does not have the same solutions as the inequality $x > 1$. (We were planning on dividing both sides by x, but this is not possible, because we do not know whether x will be positive or negative.) In fact, it is easy to check that $x = -2$, that solves the first inequality, but does not solve the second inequality.

Consider the inequality: $2x + 8 > 24$

The basic strategy for inequalities and equations is the same: isolate x on one side. Following this strategy, let's move $+8$ to the right side. We accomplish this by subtracting 8 on both sides (Rule 1) to obtain $(2x + 8) - 8 > 24 - 8$, after simplifying we obtain $2x > 16$. Once we divide by $+2$ on both sides (Rule 3a), we have succeeded in isolating x on the left: $2x/2 > 16/2$, or simplified, $x > 8$. All real numbers greater than 8 solve the inequality. We say that the "set of solutions'" of the inequality consists of all real numbers greater than 8.

An algebraic inequality is an algebraic statement about the relative size of one or more variables and/or constants. Inequalities are used to determine the relationship between these values. Example: Taking x as a variable and saying, "*x is less than 5*," may be written as $x < 5$.

INFORMAL GEOMETRY AND MEASUREMENT

Geometry and measurement are significant strands of mathematics. In the elementary classroom, children's experience in geometry should provide for the development of the concepts of direction, shape, size, symmetry, congruence, and similarity in using two-dimensional and three-dimensional shapes. Experiences for children should begin with exploring, playing, and building with shapes using familiar objects and a wide variety of concrete materials. Children must use these experiences to develop appropriate vocabulary and build on their understanding. Middle school students use formal generalizations to understand geometric relationships. The Geometry portion of the Praxis Elementary Education Content Knowledge exam will count towards 20% of your mathematics score and test how well you understand

- properties of figures and relationships in two- and three-dimensional objects

- transformations (e.g., slides, flips, and turns), geometric models, and nets

- nonstandard, customary, and metric units of measurement (e.g., length, time, temperature)

Concepts and skills in the measurement strand of mathematics deal with making comparisons between what is being measured and the standard for measurement. Children need first-hand experiences with measuring activities that require them to practice the skill. Additionally, children should be aware that measurement is never exact, but is actually an estimation. However, it is important that children learn to practice making estimates. Measuring gives children practical applications to apply their computation skills. It also provides a way to link geometric concepts to number concepts.

The van Hiele Theory

Although the van Hiele theory (van Hiele, 1986) has been recognized for its role in describing the levels of thinking associated with the learning of geometry, it has also been developed as a general theory of mathematics education. In 1988, Fuys, Gedds, and Tischler interpreted much of that work. The van Hiele theory is a stage theory, set out in levels. The theory does not stop at the description of "levels of thinking," but provides a foundation for understanding the movement between these levels, and the role of the teacher in assisting with this progression. The theory goes beyond the concerns of Piaget, who did not address the question of how students may be encouraged to progress from level to level. The van Hiele theory, in addition to describing levels of thinking, offers an important addition. This is the notion of *stages of learning* as means by which the learner may be assisted to use higher level thinking skills.

Principles and Properties of Geometry

A fundamental concept of geometry is the notion of a *point*. A point is a specific location, taking up no space, having no area, and frequently represented by a dot. A point is considered to have no dimensions. In other words, it has neither length nor breadth nor depth.

Through any two points there is exactly one straight line; straight lines are one-dimensional. Planes (think of flat surfaces without edges) are two-dimensional, meaning they have infinite length and breadth but no depth. From these foundational ideas you can move to some other important geometric terms and ideas.

- A segment is any portion of a line between two points on that line. It has a definite start and a definite end. The notation for a segment extending from point A to point B is $\overline{AB}$.

- A ray is like a line segment, except it extends forever in one direction. The notation for a ray originating at point X (an *endpoint*) through point Y is $\overrightarrow{XY}$.

Formulas for Lengths, Perimeters, Area, and Volume

Finding the Perimeter

The *perimeter* of a two-dimensional (flat) shape or object is the distance around the object (think of a fence, for example). Perimeter is measured in linear units (e.g., inches, feet, and meters). See the chart for the formulas used to find perimeter:

Perimeter of a Square	$P = 4s$
Perimeter of a Rectangle	$P = 2l + 2w$ or $P = 2(l + w)$

The **perimeter of a square** is found by multiplying four times the measure of a side of the square. This relationship is commonly given by the formula $P = 4s$, where s is the measure of a side of the square. For example, if a square has $s = 5$ feet, then the perimeter of the square is given by $P = 4(5 \text{ feet}) = 20$ feet.

The **perimeter of a rectangle** is found by adding twice the length of the rectangle to twice the width of the rectangle. This relationship is commonly given by the formula:

$P = 2l + 2w$, where l is the measure of the length and w is the measure of the width. For example, if a rectangle has $l = 10$ m and $w = 5$ m, then the perimeter of the rectangle is given by $P = 2(10 \text{ m}) + 2(5 \text{ m}) = 30$ m.

The **perimeter of a triangle** is found by adding the measures of the three sides of the triangle. This relationship can be represented by $P = s_1 + s_2 + s_3$, where s_1, s_2, and s_3 are the measures of the sides of the triangle. For example, if a triangle has three sides measuring 3 inches, 4 inches, and 5 inches, then the perimeter of the triangle is given by $P = 3 \text{ inches} + 4 \text{ inches} + 5 \text{ inches} = 12$ inches.

Finding the Area

The **area of a rectangle** is found by multiplying the measure of the length of the rectangle by the measure of the width of the rectangle. This relationship is commonly given by $A = l \times w$, where l is the measure of the length and w is the measure of the width. For example, if a rectangle has $l = 10$ m and $w = 5$ m, then the area of the rectangle is given by $A = 10$ m $\times 5$ m $= 50$ m^2.

The **area of a square** is found by *squaring the measure* of the side of the square. This relationship is commonly given by $A = s^2$, where s is the measure of a side. For example, if a square has $s = 5$ ft, then the area of the square is given by $A = (5 \text{ ft})^2 = 25$ ft^2.

Volume

Volume refers to how much space is inside of three-dimensional, closed containers. It is useful to think of volume as how many cubic units could fit into a solid. If the container is a rectangular solid, multiplying width, length, and height together computes the volume.

If all six faces (surfaces) of a rectangular solid are squares, then the object is a cube.

Cube

A **cube** is a three-dimensional solid figure. This figure has 6 faces, 12 edges, and 8 vertices. The number of faces, edges and faces can be identified visually, or through the application of the following formula:

Formula for the figure: $F + V = E + 2$

- **Vertex**: A vertex is the union of two segments or point of intersection of two sides of a polygon.

- **Faces:** Each of the plain regions of a geometric body is a face.

- **Edge:** An edge is a line segment where two faces of a three-dimensional figure meet.

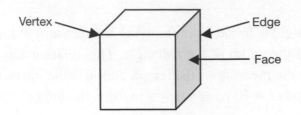

Using Triangles to Explore Geometric Relationships

Sufficient evidence for congruence between two triangles can be shown through the following comparisons:

- **SAS** (Side-Angle-Side): If two pairs of sides of two triangles are equal in length, and the included angles are equal in measurement, then the triangles are congruent.

- **SSS** (Side-Side-Side): If three pairs of sides of two triangles are equal in length, then the triangles are congruent.

- **ASA** (Angle-Side-Angle): If two pairs of angles of two triangles are equal in measurement, and the included sides are equal in length, then the triangles are congruent.

- **AAS** (Angle-Angle-Side): If two pairs of angles of two triangles are equal in measurement and a pair of ***corresponding*** sides equal in length, then the triangles are congruent.

Points, Lines, Angles, Lengths, and Distances

Points

Points are most often considered within the framework of Euclidean geometry, where they are one of the fundamental objects. Euclid originally defined the point vaguely, as "that which has no part." In two-dimensional Euclidean space, a point is represented by an ordered pair, *(x, y)*, of numbers, where the first number conventionally represents the horizontal and is often denoted by *x,* and the second number conventionally represents the vertical and is often denoted by *y*. This idea is easily generalized to three-dimensional Euclidean space, where a point is represented by an ordered triplet, *(x, y, z)*, with the additional third number representing depth and often denoted by *z*.

Many constructs within Euclidean geometry consist of an infinite collection of points that conform to certain axioms. This is usually represented by a set of points. As an example, a line is an infinite set of points of the form $L = \{(a_1, a_2, \ldots , a_n) \lfloor a_1 c_1 + a_2 c_2 + \ldots a_n c_n = d\}$, where c_1 through c_n and d are constants and n is the dimension of the space. Similar constructions exist that define the plane, line segment, and other related concepts.

In addition to defining points and constructs related to points, Euclid also postulated a key idea about points. He claimed that any two points can be connected by a straight line, this is easily confirmed under modern expansions of Euclidean geometry, and had grave consequences at the time of its introduction, allowing the construction of almost all the geometric concepts of the time. However, Euclid's axiomatization of points was neither complete nor definitive, as he occasionally assumed facts that didn't follow directly from his axioms, such as the ordering of points on the line or the existence of specific points, but in spite of this, modern expansions of the system have since removed these assumptions.

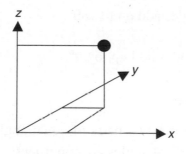

Angles

When two rays (or lines) share an endpoint, an *angle* is formed. Typically, a *degree* is the unit of measure of the angle created. If a circle is divided into 360 even slices, each slice has an angle measure of 1 degree.

- If an angle has exactly 90 degrees it is called a ***right*** **angle**.

- Angles of less than 90 degrees are ***acute* angles**.

- Angles greater than 90 degrees but less than 180 degrees are ***obtuse* angles**.

- If two angles have the same size (regardless of how long their rays might be drawn), they are *congruent*. Congruence is shown this way: $\angle m \cong \angle n$ (read "angle m is congruent to angle n").

Angle Measure

Angles are often measured in degrees. A circle has a measure of 360°, a half-circle 180°, a quarter-circle 90°, and so forth. If the measures of two angles are the same, then the angles are said to be congruent as stated earlier. Three types of angles are commonly identified—right, acute, and obtuse.

- Right angles measure 90°.

- Acute angles measure less than 90°.

- Obtuse angles measures more than 90° but less than 180°.

In addition to the traditional type of angles, combinations of two angles are classified as complementary and supplementary.

- Supplementary angles add up to 180°.

- Complementary angles add up to 90°.

Vertical (Opposite) Angles

If two lines intersect, they form two pairs of equal angles. The measures of vertical angles are equivalent; that is, vertical angles are congruent.

Parallel and Perpendicular Lines

Parallel lines

Parallel and *perpendicular* are important concepts in geometry. Consider the two parallel lines that follow, and the third line (a *transversal*), which crosses them. Note that among the many individual angles created, there are only two angle measures: (30° noted in the figure) and 150° (180° − 30°).

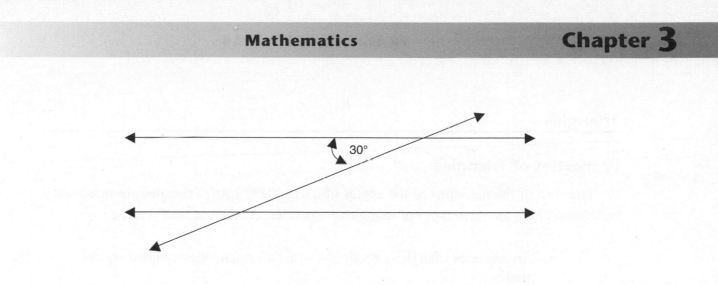

Perpendicular lines

Perpendicular simply means "at right angles". A line meeting another at a right angle, or 90° is said to be perpendicular to it. In the figure below, the line AB is perpendicular to the line DF.

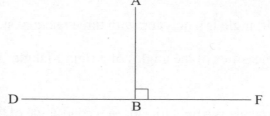

Two- and Three-Dimensional Figures

Circle

To find the circumference of a circle, you would use the following formula:

C = $2\pi r$ or C = πd (pi is the ratio of a circle's circumference to its diameter).

The value of π is the same for all circles: approximately 3.14159. The approximation 3.14 is adequate for most calculations. In the formula the *d represents the diameter and the r stands for the radius* of the circle.

Diameter and Radius

The *diameter* of a circle is a straight line segment that goes from an outside point on the circle to the other side, passing through the center. The *radius* of a circle is half of its diameter (from the center to an edge). A *chord* is any segment that goes from one point on a circle to any other point. (All diameters are chords, but not all chords are diameters.)

Triangles

Properties of Triangles

The sum of the measures of the angles of a triangle is 180°. Triangles are three-sided polygons. There are three types of triangles—isosceles, equilateral, and scalene.

- An **isosceles** triangle is a polygon with two equal sides and two equal angles.

- All equilateral triangles are isosceles triangle, but not vice versa.

- If the measures of all sides of the triangle are equal, then the triangle is called an **equilateral** triangle (this means all angles will be equal).

- A **scalene** triangle is a polygon with three unequal sides.

Problem: Find the measures of the angles of a right triangle if one of the angles measures 30°.

Solution: Since the triangle is a right triangle, a second angle of the triangle measures 90°. We know the sum of the measures of a triangle is 180°, so that $90° + 30° + x° = 180°$. Solving for $x°$, we get $x° = 60°$. The measures of the angles of the triangle are 90°, 60° and 30°.

Formulas for Basic Polygons

Area of a square	$A = s^2$
Area of a rectangle	$A = lw$ or $A = bh$
Area of a triangle	$A = \frac{1}{2} bh$ or $A = bh/2$
Area of a trapezoid	$A = \frac{1}{2}(b_1 + b_2)h$ or $A = \frac{(b_1 + b_2)h}{2}$
Area of a circle	$A = \pi r^2$
s = side, l = length, w = width, b = base, h = height, π = pi	

Polygons

A polygon is a many-sided plane figure bounded by a finite number of straight lines or a closed figure on a circle bounded by arcs. These figures are described based on the number of sides. Some of the most common are the following:

- Three-sided polygons are *triangles*.

- Four-sided polygons are *quadrilaterals*.

- Five-sided polygons are *pentagons*.

- Six-sided polygons are *hexagons*.

- Eight-sided polygons are *octagons*.

If two polygons (or any figures) have exactly the same size and shape, they are *congruent*. If they are the same shape, but different sizes, they are *similar*.

The following are formulas for finding the areas of basic polygons (formally defined as closed, coplanar geometric figures with three or more straight sides). Abbreviations used are as follows: A stands for area, l stands for length, w stands for width, h stands for height, and b stands for length of the base.

Triangle (a three-sided polygon): $A = \dfrac{b \times h}{2}$

(Note that, as shown in the figure that follows, the height of a triangle is not necessarily the same as the length of any of its sides.)

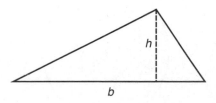

Rectangle (a four-sided polygon with four right angles): $A = l \times w$

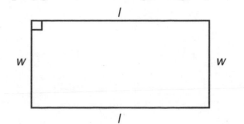

Parallelogram (a four-sided polygon with two pairs of parallel sides): $A = b \times h$ (Note that, as with triangles, and as shown in the figure below, the height of a parallelogram is not necessarily the same as the length of its sides.)

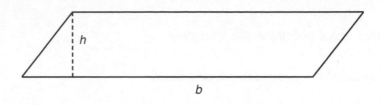

A **rhomboid** is a parallelogram that is neither a rhombus nor a rectangle. The formula for the area of a rhomboid is the same as that for all parallelograms: If b is the length of its base and h is the length of its height, then A=bh . In *The Elements*, Euclid defined a rhomboid this way: "Of quadrilateral figures....a rhomboid (is) that which has its opposite sides and angles equal to each other but is neither equilateral nor right-angled."

Circle The area of a circle can be found by squaring the length of its radius, then multiplying that product by π. The formula is given as $A = \pi r^2$ (Pi is the ratio of a circle's circumference to its diameter).

The value of π is the same for all circles; approximately 3.14159. (The approximation 3.14 is adequate for most calculations.) The approximate area of the circle shown below can be found by squaring 6 (giving 36), then multiplying 36 by 3.14, giving an area of about 113 square units.

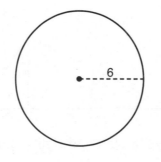

Here are several commonly used **volume formulas**:

The volume of a rectangular solid is equal to the product of its length, width, and height; $A = l \times w \times h$. (A rectangular solid can be thought of as a box, wherein all intersecting edges form right angles.)

A prism is a polyhedron—a three-dimensional solid consisting of a collection of polygons—with two congruent, parallel faces (called bases) and whose lateral (side) faces are parallelograms. The volume of a prism can be found by multiplying the area of the prism's base by its height. The volume of the triangular prism shown below is 60 cubic units. (The area of the triangular base is 10 square units, and the height is 6 units.)

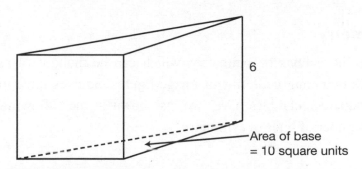

6

Area of base
= 10 square units

A cylinder is like a prism in that it has parallel faces, but its rounded "side" is smooth. The formula for finding the volume of a cylinder is the same as the formula for finding the volume of a prism: the area of the cylinder's base is multiplied by the height. The volume of the cylinder in the following figure is approximately 628 cubic units ($5 \times 5 \times \pi \times 8$).

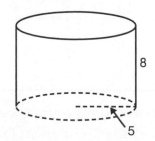

8

5

A property of all triangles is that the sum of the measures of the three angles is 180°. If, therefore, the measures of two angles are known, the third can be deduced using addition, then subtraction. Right triangles (those with a right angle) have several special properties. A chief property is described by the Pythagorean theorem, which states that in any right triangle with legs (shorter sides) a and b, and hypotenuse (the longest side) c, the sum of the squares of the sides will be equal to the square of the hypotenuse ($a^2 + b^2 = c^2$). Note that in the following right triangle, $3^2 + 4^2 = 5^2$.

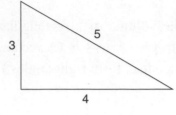

Symmetry

Symmetry—The correspondence in size, form, and arrangement of parts on opposite sides of a plane, line, or point. For example, a figure that has line symmetry has two halves that coincide if folded along its line of symmetry.

Lines of Symmetry

Polygons may have lines of symmetry, which can be thought of as imaginary fold lines that produce two congruent, mirror-image figures. Squares have four lines of symmetry, and non-square rectangles have two, as shown in the following figures. Circles have an infinite number of lines of symmetry.

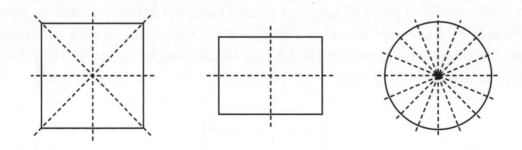

Tessellations

The arrangement of polygons that forms a grid is called a tessellation; however, other shapes may also tessellate. A tessellation is a pattern formed by the repetition of a single unit or shape that, when repeated, fills the plane with no gaps and no overlaps. Familiar examples of tessellations are the patterns formed by paving stones or bricks, and cross-sections of beehives. (See Math Forum at: *http://mathforum.org/geometry/rugs/symmetry/grids.html*).

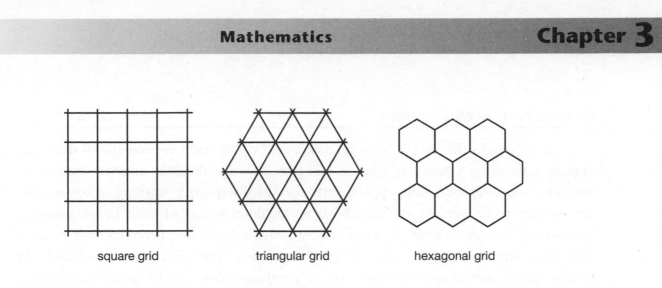

square grid   triangular grid   hexagonal grid

Grids

Grids are usually bascd on regular polygons: squares, equilateral triangles, and hexagons. Or they can be based on rectangles, parallelograms, and rhomboids.

Translations, Rotations, and Reflections

Translation (also called a slide)—In geometry a translation simply means moving. Every translation has a direction and distance. This is known as a transformation that moves a geometric figure by sliding. Each of the points of the geometric figure moves the same distance in the same direction. This may be shown on a graph by moving the figure without rotating or reflecting it.

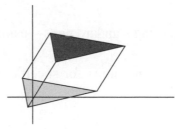

Rotation (also called a turn)—In geometry this is known as a transformation that means a rotation or to turn the shape around. Each rotation has a center and an angle for movement around a given number of degrees.

Reflection (also called a flip)—This is known as a transformation that means to reflect an object or to make the figure/object appear to be backwards or flipped. It produces the mirror image of a geometric figure.

Concepts of Measurement

Concepts and skills in the Measurement strand of the math curriculum all deal with making comparisons between what is being measured and some suitable standard of measure. Measurement offers opportunities for interdisciplinary learning in social studies, geography, science, art and music. Key to the development of skills in measurement is allowing for various types of measurement activities. Children need firsthand practice with measuring and making estimates in measurement. The principles of measurement involve an understanding of the attributes of length, capacity, weight, area, volume, time, temperature, and angles. Being able to measure connects mathematics to the environment and gives children practical applications for computation skills. The ability to use measurement tools—rulers, thermometers, measuring cups, and scales—to estimate is necessary skills for children to develop. According to Burns (2000), concepts in measurement include four stages in learning when developing classroom activities. Instruction should progress using the four stages of measurement.

Concepts in Measurement Include Four Stages in Learning

1. Comparing objects by matching—ordering items based on size

2. Comparing a variety of objects for measuring—using body parts, blocks, cubes, etc.

3. Comparing objects using standard units—using standard and metric systems

4. Comparing using suitable units for specific measurements—choosing standard units

Time

There are two kinds of clocks: analog and digital. The digital represents the time using Arabic numbers separating the hours from the minutes with a colon (12:45), which makes it relatively easy to read. However, the analog clock uses two hands to represent the hours and minutes based on 60 minutes for an hour and 60 seconds for a minute. Students must have a mathematical understanding of each of the numbers on a face when using analog clocks.

> **Time**
>
> 1 year = 365 days
>
> 1 year = 12 months
>
> 1 year = 52 weeks
>
> 1 week = 7 days
>
> 1 day = 24 hours
>
> 1 hour = 60 minutes
>
> 1 minute = 60 seconds

Temperature

Temperature is measured using a thermometer, which may be filled with mercury (a liquid metallic element that expands with heat). The **Fahrenheit** scale is used in the U.S., whereas the **Celsius** scale is used in countries throughout the world. The Celsius scale is specifically useful in scientific experimentation. Water boils at 212°F or 100°C, and freezes at 32°F or 0°C.

Money

Teaching the concept of money involves the understanding of base ten. Children learn how to relate each denomination to pennies and understand the relationship between the other coins. Use real currency to introduce this concept. Children begin by observing the various coins and their attributes. They learn to associate the value for each of the coins and make equivalences. Suggest that students begin by counting out a bag of coins and then trade out the various coins for larger denominations, for example 5 pennies for one nickel, etc.

Conversions Within and Between Measurement Systems

Units of Measurement

Students in kindergarten through grade 6 should become familiar with and apply knowledge of measurement using both U.S. Customary (standard) and metric systems. Table 3.4 provides a comparison of these two units of measurement.

Customary Units

- Linear measurement: Customary units of length include inches, feet, yards, and miles.

- Measurement of mass: Customary units of weight include ounces, pounds, and tons.

- Volume measurement: Customary units of capacity include teaspoons, tablespoons, cups, pints, quarts, and gallons.

Metric Units

- Linear measurement: Metric units of length include millimeters, centimeters, meters, and kilometers. The centimeter is the basic metric unit of length, at least for short distances. There are about 2.5 centimeters to 1 inch. The kilometer is a metric unit of length used for longer distances. It takes more than 1.5 kilometers to make a mile.

- Measurement of mass: Metric units of weight include grams and kilograms. The gram is the basic metric unit of mass (which for many purposes is the same as *weight*). A large paper clip weighs about 1 gram. It takes about 28 grams to make 1 ounce.

- Volume measurement: Metric units of capacity include milliliters and liters. The liter is the basic metric unit of volume. A liter is slightly larger than a quart, so it takes fewer than four liters to make a gallon.

Table 3.4 The Customary and Metric Systems

Customary System	Metric System
Linear 12 inches (in.) = 1 foot (ft.) 3 feet (ft.) = 1 yard (yd.) 1,760 yards (yds.) = 1 mile (mi.) 5,280 feet (ft.) = 1 mile (mi.)	**Linear** 10 millimeters (mm) = 1 centimeter (cm) 100 centimeters (cm) = 1 meter (m) 1000 meters (m) = 1 kilometer (km)
Capacity and Volume 1 gallon (gal.) = 4 quarts (qt.) 1 gallon (gal.) = 128 fluid ounces 1 quart (qt.) = 2 pints (pt.) 1 pint (pt.) = 2 cups (C.) 1 pint (pt.) = 16 fluid ounces (oz.) 1 cup (C.) = 8 fluid ounces (oz.)	**Capacity and Volume** 1 liter (L) = 1000 milliliters (ml) 1 liter (L) = 1.0556 quarts (qt.)
Mass and Weight 1 ton = 2000 pounds (lbs.) 1 pound (lb.) = 16 ounces (oz.)	**Mass and Weight** 1 kilogram (kg) = 1000 grams (g) 1 gram (g) = 1000 milligrams (mg)

DATA ORGANIZATION AND INTERPRETATION

Specifically, this category tests your ability to organize and interpret data in a variety of formats, such as tables, frequency distributions, line graphs, and circle graphs. Identifying the best format for displaying different types of data is also important. This category is worth 15% of your Mathematics score. You will be expected to understand:

- visual displays of quantitative information (e.g., bar graphs, pie charts, line graphs)

- simple probability and intuitive concepts of chance (e.g., flipping a coin, spinning a spinner, rolling a number cube)

- fundamental counting techniques (e.g., permutations, combinations, tree diagrams)

- basic descriptive statistics (e.g., mean, median, and mode)

When presented with data in any type of graph, we should be able to identify trends and patterns in the data and describe it using standard measures such as mean, median, mode, and range. Finally, we should also be able to draw valid conclusions based on the data presented and demonstrate knowledge of how data analysis applies to everyday life. Let's look at example of a question involving data analysis skills:

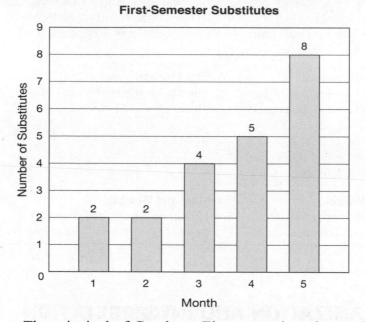

The principal of Goodyear Elementary is trying to determine how much he needs to budget for substitute teacher pay for the upcoming school year. The graph above shows the number of substitutes needed for each of the first five months of the school year, beginning in August. Which of the following statements regarding teacher substitutes is consistent with the data depicted above?

    a.   Fewer than five substitutes were needed during the first three months of the school year.

    b.   More than half of the substitutes required between August and December were needed for the last two months of the semester.

    c.   The mean number of substitutes for the five-month period above is 2.

    d.   Four substitutes were needed in the 5th month of the semester.

The example above requires us to use the graph to draw some conclusions about the data presented. We are asked to determine which of the statements is consistent with the data presented. Let's look at each how each statement compares to the data:

a. Upon first glance, this statement might be deceiving, because we might look at the number of substitutes needed for the third month and see that it is four, which is less than five. However, this statement indicates that fewer than five substitutes were needed for the first three months combined, which is not true. Examining the first three months, we see that 2 substitutes were needed in August, 2 were needed in September, and 4 in October. A total of 8 substitutes were needed in the first three months.

b. Looking at November and December, we see that a total of 13 substitutes were needed. When we add up the total from each month, we find that 21 substitutes were needed over the five-month period. Thirteen is more than half of 21, so this statement is true.

c. To determine if this statement applies to our data, we must understand that the mean is the numerical average. In order to find the average, we add the numbers together and divide by the total number of items. When we divide 21 by 5, we get 4.2. Therefore, the average is not approximately 2, as the statement indicates.

d. This statement tests our ability to distinguish the x-axis from the y-axis. If we confused the two, we might notice the 5 and the 4 together in the fourth data set, and assume the statement is true. However, if we are familiar with the x-axis and its titles, we know that we must move horizontally to the 5th position on the x-axis before moving up the y-axis to determine the number of substitutes needed in the 5th month, which equals 8.

Statistics

Statistics is the science or study of data. Statistical methods are used to describe, analyze, evaluate, and interpret information. The information is then used for predicting, drawing inferences, and making decisions. Data analysis involves both probability and statistics. Probability gives a way to measure uncertainty and is essential for understanding statistical methods. It explains data sets to give a type of generalized statistic, to make a prediction, or to infer something beyond the specific data collected. Probability is used to create experimental and theoretical models of situations involving probabilities.

There is some general agreement with regard to six underlying facts about the learning and teaching of data analysis. These include the following:

Research on Teaching Data Analysis

1. Problem-solving approach to teaching is consistent with how learners develop data analysis knowledge. (Lajoie, Jacobs, & Lavigne, 1995)

2. Concept knowledge must be developed first before developing procedural knowledge. This can then be further developed using problem solving, for example understanding the concept of sample before gathering data to analysis a problem/situation. (Horvath & Lehrer, 1998)

3. Concepts and procedures are interdependent. (Konold & Higgins, 2003)

4. Statistical representations can become more sophisticated using technology and as students have more experiences with data. (Friel, S.N., Curcio, F.R., & Bright, G. W. (2001))

5. Data organization can be improved by using technology tools. (Konold, 2002; Lehrer & Romberg, 1996)

6. Teachers must sequence instruction based on developmental age-appropriate situations and so students may examine certain types of situations before other types. For example, students should study situations in which all outcomes are equally likely before studying situations in which all outcomes are **not equally likely.** (Horvath & Lehrer, 1998)

Probability

Learning probability and statistics provides real applications of arithmetic. When basic computation skills are used in context, students have the opportunity to see the advantages and limitations of their calculations. Most arithmetic is done with a degree of uncertainty, for example estimating costs, making calculations of needed building materials, approximating estimated time of arrival (ETA) on trips, and estimating time for baking or cooking food.

A set of data can be describe by its range, mean, median, and/or mode.

The **range** of a set of data is the difference between the greatest and the least numbers in the data set. Subtract to find the difference.

The **mean** of a set of data is the average of the data values. To find the mean, add all the data values and then divide this sum by the number of values in the set.

The **median** of a set of data is the middle value of all the numbers. To find the middle value, list the numbers in order from the least to greatest or from greatest to least. Cross out one value on each end of the list until you reach the middle. If there are two values in the middle, find the number halfway between the two values by adding them together and dividing their sum by 2.

The **mode** is the value (or values) that appear in a set of data more frequently than any other value. If all the values in a set of data appear once, the set does not have a mode. A set of data may have more than one mode.

Studying probability and statistics should involve real problems and/or simulations. A theoretical or abstract approach is not appropriate for students in elementary mathematics. The approach should be based on experiments that draw on children's experience and interests. Children's intuition needs to be challenged. Once they understand or can say what "should happen" in a situation, then they may be able to conduct experiments to test their predictions. Basic to probability and statistics are the following steps:

1. Data Collections

2. Sampling

3. Organizing and Representing Data

4. Interpreting Data

5. Assigning Probabilities

6. Making Inferences

Probability is a way of describing how likely it is a particular outcome will occur. A random event occurs when a selection is made without looking. A fraction can be used to describe the results of a probability experiment in this way: 1) the numerator of the fraction is the number of favorable outcomes for the experiment. 2) The denominator of the fraction is the number of all the possible outcomes for the experiment.

Gabrielle is randomly choosing a marble from a bag containing three marbles—1 red marble, 1 blue marble, and 1 green marble. What is the probability that she will choose a green marble on a single pull?

- There is 1 green marble in the bag.

- There is 1 favorable outcome.

- There are 1 + 1 + 1 = 3 marbles in the bag.

- There are 3 possible outcomes.

$$\text{Probability of choosing a green marble} = \frac{\text{Number of favorable outcomes}}{\text{Total number of possible outcomes}} = \frac{1}{3}$$

The probability that Gabrielle will choose a green marble on a single pull is $\frac{1}{3}$, or 1 out of 3.

Students need to demonstrate an understanding of probability and statistics and be able to do the following: 1) use experimental and theoretical probability to make predictions; and 2) use statistical representations to analyze data. A **sample space** is the set of all possible outcomes of an experiment. For example, if you flip a coin, it will land either heads or tails. Students learn to list all the possible outcomes: heads or tails. Sample spaces may also be listed on a chart or tree diagram.

Determining Odds For and Against a Given Situation

Odds are related to but different from probability. The odds that any given event *will* occur can be expressed as the ratio of the probability that the event *will* occur to the probability that the event will *not* occur.

If there are four marbles—three red and one blue—in a jar, the probability of drawing the blue is 1/4. There is one chance of a blue marble, and there are four total chances (marbles). Odds describe the number of chances for (or against) versus the number of chances against (or for). Because there is one chance of picking blue and three chances of picking red, the odds are three to one *against* picking the blue. For odds in favor, just reverse the numbers: the odds are one to three *in favor* of picking the blue. To repeat, if you express odds as *against*, you put the number of chances against first, versus the number of chances for. If you express odds as *in favor of*, you put the number of chances for first.

Note that the odds in the marbles example do not mean that the probability is 1/3 for or against. To convert odds to probability, one must add the chances. For example, if the odds against a horse winning are four to one, this means that, out of five (4 + 1) chances, the horse has one chance in favor of winning; the probability of the horse winning is 1/5 or 20 percent (*www.mathforum.org/library/drmath/view/56495.html*).

Fundamental Counting Principles

As noted earlier, probability is calculated as follows:

$$\text{Probability of a particular event occurring} = \frac{\text{Number of ways the event can occur}}{\text{Total number of possible events}}$$

Human sex type is determined by the genetic material in the sperm and egg. The genetic sex code for human females is XX. The genetic sex code for human males is XY. Eggs carry only X genes. Sperm carry both X and Y genes; the Y gene is the absence of the X gene. The following chart illustrates the probability of a fertilized human egg being male or female:

		Female	
		X	X
Male			
	X	*XX*	*XX*
	Y	*XY*	*XY*

The chart shows that the probability of a female (XX) is 2 out of 4, and the probability of a male (XY) is 2 out of 4. Therefore, there is a 50 percent chance of a boy and a 50 percent chance of a girl.

Permutations—All possible arrangements of a given number of items in which the order of the items makes a difference, for example the different ways that a set of four books can be placed on a shelf.

Jones, Langral, Thornton, and Mogill (1999) have developed a four-stage framework that attempts to explain the learning process for probability. Learners begin at the subjective level, at which they are easily swayed by personal experiences when making probabilistic statements. At the second level, transitional learners begin to recognize the importance of organizing information. The third level involves students becoming informal quantitative thinkers. Finally, students work at the purely numerical level in which they understand the nuances of numerical argument and use sophisticated procedures to determine numerical facts.

Students should learn to read graphs, making quick visual summaries as well as further interpretations and comparisons of data through finding means, medians, and modes. Students use tables, line graphs, bar graphs, circle graphs, line plots, and pictographs to organize and display data. This is a helpful strategy used in problem solving. A **line plot** represents a set of data by showing how often a piece of data appears in that set. It consists of a number line that indicates the values of the data set. An X is placed above the corresponding number each time that value appears in the data set; for example, the weights of 10 twelve-year-old girls were measured and recorded. A line plot is used to record the data from a chart. Then, students may make comparisons of the range of height, find the tallest or shortest girl, and interpret the data found.

In real-world problems, students may sample a part of a population. Students need to learn the difference between random and nonrandom samples and the importance this difference makes in statistical studies, for example to determine the percentage of people who are left-handed. Students would not poll famous athletes as a random sampling.

For students to fully understand data analysis, all frameworks and researchers agree that students should generate their own data. They should work with simulations that model real situations. They should use dice, spinners, two-color counters, and coins. As students begin to understand how to gather their own data, they need to be consciously aware of any graphical representations they might choose to use, recognizing the difference between discrete and continuous situations. Finally, technology is a highly useful tool in data analysis and in making sense of the data.

REFERENCES

Burns, M. 2000. *About teaching mathematics: A K-8 resource.* Sausalito, CA: Math Solutions Publications.

Carpenter, T.M., E. Fennema, M. L. Franke, L. Levi, and S. B. Empson. 1999.

Children's mathematics: Cognitively guided instruction. Portsmouth, NH: Heinemann.

Fredericks, A. D., B. Blake-Kline, and J. V. Kristo. 1997. *Teaching the integrated language arts: Process and practice.* New York: Longman.

Friel, S.N., F. R. Curcio, and G. W. Bright. 2001. Making sense of graphs: Critical factors influencing comprehension and instructional implication. *Journal of Research in Mathematics Education,* 32(2), 124–158.

Flavell, J.H. 1985. *Cognitive development.* 2nd ed. Upper Saddle River, NJ: Prentice Hall.

Fuson, K. 1988. *Children's counting and concepts of numbers.* New York: Springer.

Fuson, K. C., and J. W. Hall. 1983. The acquisition of early number word meanings: A conceptual analysis and review. In *The development of mathematical thinking,* ed. H. P. Ginsburg, pp. 49–107. Orlando, FL: Academic Press.

Fuys, D., D. Gedds, and R. Tischler. 1988. The van Hiele model of thinking in geometry among adolescent. *Journal of Research in Mathematics Education Monograph #3.* Reston, VA: NCTM.

Horvath, J.K. & R. Lehrer. 1998. A model-based perspective on the development of children's understanding of chance and uncertainty. In *Reflections on statistics: Learning teaching, and assessment in grades K-12,* ed. S.P. Lajoie, pp. 121–148. Mahwah, NJ: Lawrence Erlbaum Associates.

Jones, G.A., C. W. Langrall, C. A. Thorton, and A. T. Mogill. 1999. Student's probabilistic thinking in instruction. *Journal for Research in Mathematics Education,* 30(5), 487–519.

Kamii, C. 2000. *Young children reinvent arithmetic: Implications of Piaget's theory.* New York: Teacher College Press.

Konold, C. 2002. Teaching concepts rather than conventions. *New England Journal of Mathematics Education, 34(2),* 69–81.

Konold, C. and T. Higgins. 2003. Reasoning about data. In *A research companion to principles and standards for school mathematics,* eds. J. Kilpatrick, W.G. Martin, and D.E. Schifter, Reston, VA: NCTM.

Lejoie, S.P., V. R. Jacobs, and N. C. Lavigne. 1995. Empowering children in the use of statistics. *Journal of Mathematics Behavior, 14(4),* 401–425.

Lehrer, R. and T. Romberg. 1996. Exploring children's data modeling. *Cognition and Instruction, 14(1),* 69–108.

National Council of Teachers of Mathematics 2007. *Professional standards for teaching mathematics.*

National Council of Teachers of Mathematics 2000. *Principles and standards for school mathematics.* Reston, VA: NCTM.

Pepper, C. and R. P. Hunting. 1998. Preschooler's counting and sharing. Journal for *Research in Mathematics Education, 29(2),* 14–183.

Piaget, J. and B. Inhelder. 1969. *The psychology of the child.* New York: Basic Books.

Santrock, J.W. 2003. *Children,* 7th ed. Boston, MA: McGraw-Hill.

Sperry Smith, S. 2008. *Early childhood mathematics,* 4th ed. Boston, MA: Allyn and Bacon.

U. S. Department of Labor 2008–09. Bureau of Labor Statistics, U.S. Department of Labor Occupational Outlook Handbook, 2008–09 edition, Bulletin 2700. Superintendent of Documents, U.S. Government Printing Office, Washington, DC: Author. *http://www.bls.gov/OCO/* (accessed August 1, 2009)

van Hiele, P.M. 1986. *Structure and Insight.* Orlando, FL: Academic Press.

Vygotsky, L. S. 1986. *Thought and language* (new rev.ed.) Cambridge, MA: MIT Press

Social Studies I

Geography, Anthropology, Sociology, World History and Economics

The National Council for the Social Studies defines social studies as "the integrated study of the social sciences and humanities to promote civic competence." Within the school program, social studies provides coordinated, systematic study drawing upon such disciplines as anthropology, archaeology, economics, geography, history, law, philosophy, political science, psychology, religion, and sociology, as well as appropriate content from the humanities, mathematics, and natural sciences. In essence, social studies promotes knowledge of and involvement in civic affairs. And because civic issues—such as health care, crime, and foreign policy—are multidisciplinary in nature, understanding these issues and developing resolutions to them require multidisciplinary education. These characteristics are the key defining aspects of social studies.

In 2010, NCSS published *National Curriculum Standards for Social Studies: A Framework for Teaching, Learning, and Assessment.* The revised standards, like the earlier social studies standards published in 1994, are stuctured around the ten themes of social studies. However, the revised standards offer a sharper focus on Purposes; Questions for Exploration; Knowledge (what learners need to understand); Processes (what learners will be capable of doing); and Products (how learners demonstrate understanding). NCSS standards ensure that an integrated social science, behavioral science, and humanities approach for achieving academic and civic competence is available to guide social studies decision makers in K-12 schools.

The NCSS framework consists of ten themes incorporating fields of study that correspond with one or more relevant disciplines. The organization believes that effective social studies programs include experiences that provide for the study of:

- Culture

- Time, Continuity, and Change

- People, Places, and Environment

- Individual Development and Identity

- Individuals, Groups, and Institutions

- Power, Authority, and Governance

- Production, Distribution, and Consumption

- Science, Technology, and Society

- Global Connections

- Civic Ideals and Practices

Social studies is taught in kindergarten through grade 12 in schools across the nation. As a field of study, social studies may be more difficult to define than a single discipline such as history or geography, precisely because it is multidisciplinary and interdisciplinary and because it is sometimes taught in one class (perhaps called "social studies") and sometimes in separate discipline-based classes within a department of social studies. Two main characteristics, however, distinguish social studies as a field of study: it is designed to promote civic competence; and it is integrative, incorporating many fields of endeavor.

The topic of Social Studies will have a approximately 30 questions and account for 25% of your overall score for the Elementrary Education: Content Knowledge 0014/5014 exam.

GEOGRAPHY, ANTHROPOLOGY, AND SOCIOLOGY

The categories of geography, anthropology, and sociology will account for 30% of your social studies score. You will be tested on these factors:

- Your knowledge of world and regional geography (e.g., spatial terms, places, and regions)

- Your understanding of the interaction of physical and human systems (e.g., how humans change the environment, how the environment changes humans, importance of natural and human resources)

- Your knowledge of the uses of geography (e.g., apply geography to interpret past, to interpret present, to plan for future)

- Your knowledge of how people of different cultural backgrounds interact with their environment, self, family, neighborhoods, and communities

Five Themes of Geography

The five themes of geography are place; location; human-environmental interaction; movement and connections; and regions, patterns, and processes. An understanding of these themes includes the ability to use them to analyze regions, states, countries, and the world to gain a perspective about interrelationships among those areas. When a teacher uses the five themes, students should gain the ability to compare regions:

1. In this world of fast-breaking news from throughout the globe, students must be able to recognize the **place** names of continents, countries, and even cities. In addition to geography, the theme of place encompasses the fields of political science.

2. An understanding of the theme of **location** requires knowledge of both absolute and relative location. **Absolute location** is determined by longitude and latitude. **Relative location** deals with the interactions that occur between and among places. Relative location involves the interconnectedness among people because of land, water, and technology. For example, the Silver River brought commerce and steamboats to the Silver Springs area of Florida; the 99.8 percent pure artesian spring waters in one of the largest artesian spring formations in the world offered respite and beauty to settlers and tourists alike. Hullam Jones invented the glass-bottom boat there in 1878 and enabled visitors to view the underwater world of fish, turtles, crustaceans, and fossils more than 10,000 years old. The location of Silver Springs has contributed to the area's economic development and vitality. In addition to geography, the theme of location encompasses the fields of technology, history, and economics.

3. An understanding of the theme of **human-environmental interaction** involves consideration of how people rely on the environment, how people alter it, and how the environment may limit what people are able to do. For example, Silver Springs, a nature park in Florida, is at the headwaters of the Silver River. In the 1850s, barges carried cotton, lumber, and nonperishables up the Silver River to the area's growing population. The development of a stagecoach line and the arrival of conventional steamboats in Silver Springs in 1860 aided in the development of Silver Springs and the nearby areas as a destination. In addition to geography, the theme of human-environmental interaction encompasses the field of ecology.

4. An understanding of the theme of **movement and connections** requires identifying how people are connected through different forms of transportation and communication networks and how those networks have changed over time. This would include identifying channels for the movement of people, goods, and information. For example, the automobile industry had a profound impact on the number of visitors to Silver Springs, Florida, and on the movement patterns of ideas, fashion, and people. In addition to geography, the theme of movement and connections encompasses the fields of communications, history, anthropology, economics, and sociology.

5. An understanding of the theme of **regions, patterns, and processes** involves identifying climatic, economic, political, and cultural patterns within regions. To comprehend why these patterns were created, students need to understand how climatic systems, communication networks, international trade, political systems, and population changes contributed to a region's development. With an understanding of a particular region, students can study its uniqueness and relationship to other regions. In addition to geography, the theme of regions, patterns, and processes encompasses the fields of economics, sociology, and politics.

The study of global issues and events includes comprehending the interconnectedness of peoples throughout the world (sociology and political science). For example, knowing the relationship between world oil consumption and oil production helps students understand the impact that increased demand for oil in China would have on the price of a barrel of oil, which in turn could affect the purchasing decisions of consumers of new vehicles in the United States.

Using Geologic Maps

Any study of maps should begin with a study of the globe—a model of the earth with a map on its surface. The globe is more accurate than a flat map. Constantly using the globe helps bring understanding of the earth's shape and structure.

Some of the points on the globe that students should be able to locate include the equator, Antarctic Circle, Arctic Circle, prime meridian, international date line, North Pole, South Pole, meridians, parallels, the Great Circle Route, and time zones. The use of maps requires students to identify four main types of map projections: conic, cylindrical, interrupted, and plane. Additional graphics that students use in geography include charts, graphs, and picture maps.

Interpreting Geologic Maps

Geologic maps provide much information about the earth and present a perfect opportunity to integrate social studies and science. By reading a **topographical map**, a student can find out about **altitudes** (heights above and below sea level) and landforms. **Symbols** on the map may represent rivers, lakes, rapids, and forests. **Map scales** allow the student to determine distances. The **legends** of a map furnish additional information, including the locations of mineral deposits and quarries, dams and boat ramps, fire and ranger stations, and more. Often a map displays a **compass rose**, which gives the cardinal directions: north, south, east, and west.

Parallels and meridians grid the earth. **Meridians** run from pole to pole, and 360 of them surround the earth in one-degree increments. Every hour a given location on the earth's surface rotates through 15 degrees of longitude. Meridians help measure longitude, the distance east and west of the prime meridian, which has a measurement of 0° east-west. **Parallels** are the lines that run in an east-west direction; parallels help measure **latitude**, the distance north and south of the equator. Geologic maps often contain all this information. A geologic map usually differs from a political map, which shows political boundaries, counties, cities, towns, churches, schools, and other representations of government and people.

How Tools and Technology Affect the Environment

The period from the emergence of the first-known hominids, or humans, around 2.5 million years ago until approximately 10,000 B.C.E. has been designated as the Paleolithic period, or the Old Stone Age. During that period, human beings lived in very small groups of perhaps 10 to 20 nomadic people who were constantly moving from place to place. Human beings had the ability to make tools and weapons from stone and the bones of the animals they killed. Hunting large game such as mammoths, which the hunters sometimes drove off cliffs in large numbers, was crucial to the survival of early humans. The meat, fur, and bones of the hunted animals were essential to the survival of prehistoric people, who supplemented their diets by foraging for food.

Early human beings found shelter in caves and other natural formations and took the time to paint and draw on the walls of their shelters. Created during the prehistoric period, cave paintings in France and northern Spain depict scenes of animals, such as lions, owls, and oxen. Around 500,000 years ago, humans developed the means of creating fire and used it to provide light and warmth in shelters and to cook meat and other foods. They also developed improved techniques of producing tools and weapons. Tools and technology can improve the lives of people; needless to say, tools and technology can also harm the lives of people. Likewise, people can use tools and technology both to improve their environment and to harm or even destroy their immediate areas or even the world. For example, as Alfred Nobel learned after he developed dynamite, escalating the power of weapons has never successfully prevented war. As weapons become more powerful, the danger from the technology increases.

Reasons for the Movement of People in the World, Nation, or State

The people living in a particular area determine the characteristics of that area. The physical, cultural, economic, and political characteristics are important to most area residents and may affect their original decision to settle there.

If the characteristics of an area become unacceptable to residents, the residents may consider moving to a different location. With the ease of transportation today, most people can move more easily than they could a generation ago. The move may be to another region of their state, the nation, or the world.

Economic reasons for moving include the finances of the individual considering relocation and the economic level required to live comfortably in the area. Some residents may move to a more expensive area, but others may decide to go to a less expensive area. Many change their places of residence, therefore, to get ahead economically or to raise their standard of living.

Some people decide to relocate for **cultural reasons**. These people might consider their neighbors too similar to them and decide to move to an area with more diversity. On the other hand, some people would rather live with others who are similar to them.

Physical reasons can also affect a person's decision to relocate. An understanding of the theme of human-environmental interaction involves considering how people rely on the environment, how they alter it, and how the environment can limit what people are able to do. Sometimes people move to a place where they can satisfy their physical wants or needs. In some cases, people can modify their environment or bring the needed goods to their area without having to relocate. For example, an adaptation of the environment that aided the Illinois shipping industry was the development of the lock and dam system on the Mississippi River.

An understanding of the theme of location, movement, and connections involves identifying how people are connected through different forms of transportation and communication networks and how those networks have changed over time. This would include identifying the channels of movement for people, goods, and information. For example, the textile industry in North Carolina in the 1930s had a profound impact on the movement patterns of ideas and people; many of those without work came to the textile regions seeking jobs. When the textile mills began closing in the 1990s, many people began to leave the area in search of other employment.

Political reasons also compel the movement of people. Many people equate the political system with government. There is a distinction, however. Government carries out the decisions of the political system. The organizations and processes that contribute to the decision-making process make up the political system. Individuals may move to another region or area if they are unhappy with the government and/or political systems in their area and are unable to bring about change. On the other hand, an attractive system of government may bring people to an area.

Comparing and Contrasting Major Regions of the World

There are many ways of dividing the world into regions. Perhaps the simplest is to consider the equator as a dividing line between the Northern Hemisphere and the Southern Hemisphere. Another way of dividing the world into regions is to draw a line from pole to pole. Such a line may separate the globe into the Eastern Hemisphere and Western Hemisphere. Another way geographers might divide the world into regions is by land-masses, or continents, specifically Africa, Asia, Australia, Europe, North America, and South America; some geographers also include Antarctica as a separate continent. Other geographers prefer to group the regions according to political characteristics. Still others prefer to designate regions by latitudes: low, middle, and high.

Two important higher-order thinking skills that teachers should encourage among their students are comparing and contrasting. The use of regions is an ideal place to work with these skills of comparing and contrasting two (or more) things (or concepts). The process of finding similarities between or among the things or concepts that appear dissimilar on the surface requires deeper thought. W. J. J. Gordon describes a process of synectics, which forces students to make an analogy between two concepts, one familiar and the other new. At first, the concepts might seem completely different, but through a series of steps, the students discover underlying similarities. By comparing something new with something familiar, students have a "hook" that will help them remember and understand the new information (Huitt 1998; Gordon 1961).

For example, a biology teacher might ask students to draw an analogy between a cell (new concept) and a city government (familiar concept). Although they seem impossibly different, both concepts involve systems for transportation, systems for disposing of unwanted materials, and parts that govern those systems. After discussion of this analogy, students trying to remember the functions of a cell would find help by relating the functions of the cell to the systems of city government.

Anthropology

Anthropology is the study of human behavior in all places and at all times. It combines humanistic, scientific, biological, historical, psychological, and social views of human behavior. Anthropology is divided into two broad subfields:

Physical Anthropology is the study of the biological, physiological, anatomical, and genetic characteristics of both ancient and modern human populations. Physical anthropologists study the evolutionary development of the human species by a comparative analysis of both fossil and living primates. They study the mechanics of evolutionary change through an analysis of genetic variation in human populations.

Cultural Anthropology is the study of learned behavior in human societies. Most cultural anthropologists specialize in one or two geographic areas. They may also specialize in selected aspects of culture (e.g., politics, medicine, religion) in the context of the larger social whole. Cultural anthropology is further subdivided as follows:

Archaeology is the study of the cultures of prehistoric peoples. It also includes the study of modern societies, but from the evidence of their material remains rather than from direct interviews with or observations of the people under study.

Ethnography is the systematic description of a human society, usually based on first-hand fieldwork. All generalizations about human behavior are based on the descriptive evidence of ethnography.

Ethnology is the interpretive explanation of human behavior, based on ethnography.

Social Anthropology is the study of human groups, with a particular emphasis on social structure (social relations, family dynamics, social control mechanisms, economic exchange).

Linguistics is the study of how language works as a medium of communication among humans. Language is the vehicle through which all culture is learned and transmitted.

Defining Characteristics of Anthropology

Holism is the belief that the experiences of a human group are unified and patterned. No one aspect of human behavior can be understood in isolation from all the rest.

Culture is the organized sum of everything a people produces, does, and thinks about—all of which they learn as members of a particular social group. A people's culture develops over time as they adapt to their environment.

Comparative Method is the belief that generalizations about human behavior can only be made on the basis of data collected from the widest possible range of cultures, both contemporary and historical.

Relativism is the belief that we cannot make value judgments about a culture based on standards appropriate to another culture. When such judgments are made on the basis of one's own culturally derived values, it is said that we are making **ethnocentric** judgments.

Fieldwork is the study of cultures in their natural settings, the communities in which people live, work, and interact on a regular basis.

Anthropologists attempt to live for an extended period of time among the people they study. They are both **participants** in and **observers** of the culture of the group.

Sociology

Interpretative sociology studies the processes whereby human beings attach meaning to their lives. Derived from the work of Mead and Blumer, symbolic interaction is focused on the process of social interaction and on the meanings that are constructed and reconstructed in that process. Human beings are viewed as shaping their actions based upon both the real and anticipated responses of others. Thus, defined by an ongoing process of negotiation, social life is considered far from stable.

Actors are thought to be continually engaged in the process of interpreting, defining, and evaluating their own and others' actions, a process that defies explanation in law-like terms or in terms of sociological theories proceeding deductively. Thus, out of the **symbolic interactionist** school of thought, the social construction of reality—the familiar notion that human beings shape their world and are shaped by social interaction—was conceived (Berger & Luckman, 1967).

Focused on the details of everyday life, the dramaturgical approach of Erving Goffman conceives social interaction as a series of episodes or human dramas in which we are more or less aware of playing roles and, thereby, engaging in impression management. We are actors seeking 1) to manipulate our audience, or control the reaction of other people in our immediate presence by presenting a certain image of ourselves; 2) to protect or hide our true selves, or who we really are offstage through "onstage," "frontstage," and "backstage" behavior; and 3) to amplify the rules of conduct that circumscribe our daily encounters.

WORLD HISTORY

Your knowledge of the history of the world requires that you

- know the major contributions of classical civilizations (e.g., Egypt, Greece, Rome)

- understand twentieth-century developments and transformations in World History

- understand the role of cross-cultural comparisons in World History instruction

- can make cross-cultural comparisons

This part of the test will count for 10% of your overall social studies score, which, is 25% of your total Social Studies score.

Prehistory and Early Civilization

Major Leaders and Events

The earth is estimated to be approximately 6 billion years old. The earliest known humans, called **hominids**, lived in Africa 3 to 4 million years ago. Of the several species of hominids that developed, all modern humans descended from just one group, the **Homo sapiens sapiens**. *Homo sapiens sapiens* is a subspecies of *Homo sapiens* (along with Neanderthals, who became extinct) and appeared in Africa between 200,000 and 150,000 years ago.

Historians divide prehistory into three periods. The period when people first appeared (around 2.5 million years ago until approximately 10,000 B.C.E.) is the **Paleolithic period**, or **Old Stone Age**. These nomads lived in groups of 10 to 20 and **made tools and weapons** from stone and from the bones of the animals they killed. Large animals were crucial to their survival; they sometimes drove the animals off cliffs. The early people foraged for food and took shelter in caves and other natural formations. About 500,000 years ago humans began to use fire for light, cooking, and warmth. They improved their methods of making tools and weapons, and learned how to create fire.

The **Mesolithic period**, or **Middle Stone Age**, from 10,000 to 7000 B.C.E., marks the beginning of a major transformation known as the Neolithic Revolution. Previously, historians and archeologists thought this change occurred later. Thus, they called it the Neolithic Revolution because they thought it took place entirely within the Neolithic period, or New Stone Age. Beginning in the Mesolithic period, humans domesticated plants and began to shift away from a reliance on hunting large game and foraging. Human beings had previously relied on gathering food where they found it and had moved almost constantly in search of game and wild berries and other vegetation. During the Mesolithic period, humans were able to **plant and harvest** some crops and began to stay in one place for longer periods. Early humans also improved their tool-making techniques and developed various kinds of tools and weapons.

During the **Neolithic period**, or **New Stone Age**, this revolution was complete, and humans engaged in systematic agriculture and began domesticating animals. Although humans continued to hunt animals to supplement their diet with **meat** and to use the skins and bones to make clothing and weapons, major changes in society occurred. Human beings became settled and lived in farming villages or towns, the population increased, and people began to live in much larger communities. A more settled way of life led to a **more structured social system**; a higher level of organization within societies; the development of **crafts**, such as the production of **pottery**; and a rise in **trade** or exchange of goods among groups.

Between 4000 and 3000 B.C.E., **writing** developed, and the towns and villages settled during the Neolithic period developed a more complex pattern of existence. The establishment of written records marks the **end of the prehistoric period**. The beginning of history coincides with the emergence of the earliest societies that exhibit characteristics enabling them to be considered civilizations. The first civilizations emerged in Mesopotamia and Egypt.

Ancient and Medieval Times

Appearance of Civilization and Related Cultural and Technological Developments

Between 6000 and 3000 B.C.E., humans invented the **plow**, developed the **wheel**, harnessed the **wind**, discovered how to smelt **copper ores**, and began to develop accurate **solar calendars**. Small villages gradually grew into populous cities. The **invention of writing** in 3500 B.C.E. in Mesopotamia marks the beginning of civilization and divides prehistoric from historic times.

Mesopotamia

Sumer (4000–2000 B.C.E.) included the city of Ur. The Sumerians constructed **dikes and reservoirs** and established a loose confederation of **city-states**. They probably invented writing (called **cuneiform** because of its wedge-shaped letters). After 538 B.C.E., the peoples of Mesopotamia, whose natural boundaries were insufficient to thwart invaders, were absorbed into other empires and dynasties.

Egypt. During the end of the Middle Archaic Period (6000–3000 B.C.E.), in about 3200 B.C.E., Menes, or Narmer, probably unified Upper and Lower Egypt. The capital moved to Memphis during the Third Dynasty (ca. 2650 B.C.E.). The **pyramids** were built during the Fourth Dynasty (ca. 2613–2494 B.C.E.). After 1085 B.C.E., in the Post-Empire period, Egypt came under the successive control of the Assyrians; the Persians; Alexander the Great; and finally, in 30 B.C.E., the Roman Empire. The Egyptians developed papyrus and made many medical advances.

Palestine and the Hebrews. Phoenicians settled along the present-day Lebanon coast (Sidon, Tyre, Beirut, Byblos) and established colonies at Carthage and in Spain. They spread **Mesopotamian culture** through their trade networks. The Hebrews probably moved to Egypt in about 1700 B.C.E. and suffered enslavement in about 1500 B.C.E. The Hebrews fled Egypt under Moses and, around 1200 B.C.E., returned to Palestine. King David (reigned ca. 1012–972 B.C.E.) defeated the Philistines and established Jerusalem as a capital. The poor and less attractive state of Judah continued until 586 B.C.E., when the Chaldeans transported the Jews ("the people of Judah" or, in some translations, "the people of God") to Chaldea as advisors and slaves (Babylonian captivity). The Persians conquered Babylon in 539 B.C.E. and allowed the Jews to return to Palestine.

Greece. In the period from about 800–500 B.C.E., the Greeks organized around the **polis**, or city-state. Oligarchs controlled most of the polis until near the end of the sixth century, when individuals holding absolute power (tyrants) replaced them. By the end of the sixth century, **democratic governments** in turn replaced many tyrants.

The Classical Age. The fifth century B.C.E. was the high point of Greek civilization. It opened with the Persian Wars (560–479 B.C.E.), after which Athens organized the Delian League. **Pericles** (ca. 495–429 B.C.E.) used money from the league to rebuild Athens, including construction of the Parthenon and other buildings on the Acropolis hill. Athens's dominance spurred war with Sparta. At the same time, a revolution in philosophy occurred in classical Athens. The **Sophists** emphasized the individual and the attainment of excellence through rhetoric, grammar, music, and mathematics. **Socrates** (ca. 470–399 B.C.E.) criticized the Sophists' emphasis on rhetoric and emphasized a process of questioning, or dialogue, with his students. Like Socrates, **Plato** (ca. 428–348 B.C.E.) emphasized ethics. Aristotle (ca. 384–322 B.C.E.) was Plato's pupil. He criticized Plato and argued that ideas or forms did not exist outside things. He contended that, in treating any object, it was necessary to examine four factors: its matter, its form, its cause of origin, and its end or purpose.

Rome. The traditional founding date for Rome is 753 B.C.E. Between 800 and 500 B.C.E., Greek tribes colonized southern Italy, bringing their alphabet and religious practices to Roman tribes. In the sixth and seventh centuries B.C.E., the Etruscans expanded southward and conquered Rome. In the early Republic, power was in the hands of the patricians (wealthy landowners). During the 70s and 60s, **Pompey** (106–48 B.C.E.) and **Julius Caesar** (100–44 B.C.E.) emerged as Rome's most powerful men.

In 60 B.C.E., Caesar convinced Pompey and Crassus (ca. 115–53 B.C.E.) to form the First Triumvirate. When Crassus died, Caesar and Pompey fought for leadership. In 47 B.C.E., the Senate proclaimed Caesar dictator and later named him consul for life. **Brutus** and **Cassius** believed that Caesar had destroyed the Republic. They formed a conspiracy, and on March 15, 44 B.C.E. (the Ides of March), Brutus and Cassius assassinated Caesar in the Roman forum. Caesar's 18-year-old nephew and adopted son, Octavian, succeeded him.

The Roman Empire. After some power struggles, Octavian (reigned 27 B.C.E.–14 C.E.) was eventually named as Caesar's heir. Octavian kept up the appearances of administering a republic while he gained absolute control of Rome. When he offered to relinquish his power in 27 B.C.E., the Senate gave him a vote of confidence and a new title, Augustus. He introduced many reforms, including new coinage, new tax collection, fire and police protection, and land for settlers in the provinces. By the first century C.E., Christianity had spread throughout the Empire. Around 312 C.E., Emperor Constantine converted to Christianity and ordered toleration in the Edict of Milan (ca. 313 C.E.). In 391 C.E., Emperor Theodosius I (reigned 371–395 C.E.) proclaimed Christianity the empire's official religion.

The Byzantine Empire. Emperor Theodosius II (reigned 408–450 C.E.) divided his empire between his two sons, one ruling the East and the other ruling the West. After the Vandals sacked Rome in 455 C.E., Constantinople was the undisputed leading city of the Byzantine Empire. In 1453 C.E., Constantinople fell to the Ottoman Turks.

Islamic Civilization in the Middle Ages. Mohammed was born about 570 C.E. In 630 C.E., he marched into Mecca. The Shari'ah (code of law and theology) outlines five pillars of faith for Muslims to observe. The beliefs that there is one God and that Mohammed is his prophet form the first pillar. Second, the faithful must pray five times a day. Third, they must perform charitable acts. Fourth, they must fast from sunrise to sunset during the holy month of Ramadan. Finally, they must make a *haj*, or pilgrimage, to Mecca. The Koran, which consists of 114 *suras* (verses), contains Mohammed's teachings.

The Umayyad caliphs, with their base in Damascus, governed from 661–750 C.E. They called themselves **Shiites** and believed they were Mohammed's true successors.

(Most Muslims were **Sunnis**, from the word *sunna*, meaning "oral traditions about the prophet.")

The Abbāsid caliphs ruled from 750–1258 C.E. They moved the capital to Baghdad and treated Arab and non-Arab Muslims as equals. Genghis (or Chingis) Khan (reigned 1206–1227 C.E.) and his army invaded the Abbāsids. In 1258 C.E., they seized Baghdad and murdered the last caliph.

Feudalism in Japan. Feudalism in Japan began with the arrival of mounted nomadic warriors from throughout Asia during the Kofun Era (300–710 C.E.). Some members of the nomadic groups formed an elite class and became part of the court aristocracy in the capital city of Kyoto, in western Japan. During the Heian Era (794–1185 C.E.), a hereditary military aristocracy arose in the Japanese provinces; by the late Heian Era, many of these formerly nomadic warriors had established themselves as independent landowners, or as managers of landed estates, or *shoen* owned by Kyoto aristocrats. These aristocrats depended on the warriors to defend their *shoen,* and in response to this need, the warriors organized into small groups called *bushidan*.

After victory in the Taira-Minamoto War (1180–1185 C.E.), Minamoto no Yorimoto forced the emperor to award him the title of **shogun**, which is short for "barbarian-subduing generalissimo." Yorimoto used this power to found the Kamakura shogunate, a feudal military dictatorship that survived for 148 years.

By the fourteenth century C.E., the great military governors (*shugo*) had augmented their power enough to become a threat to the Kamakura, and in 1333 C.E., they led a rebellion that overthrew the shogunate. The Tokugawa shogunate was the final and most unified of the three shogunates. Under the Tokugawa, the *daimyo* were direct vassals of the shoguns and were under strict control. The warriors gradually became scholars and bureaucrats under the *bushido*, or code of chivalry, and the principles of neo-Confucianism. Under the Meji Restoration of 1868, the emperor again received power and the samurai class lost its special privileges.

Chinese and Indian Empires. In the third century B.C.E., the Indian kingdoms fell under the Mauryan Empire. Ashoka, the grandson of the founder of this empire, opened a new era in the cultural history of India by promulgating the Buddhist religion.

Buddha had disregarded the Vedic gods and the institutions of caste and had preached a relatively simple ethical religion that advocated two levels of aspiration—a monastic life that renounced the world and a high, but not too difficult, morality for the layperson.

Although the two religions of Hinduism and Buddhism flourished together for centuries in a tolerant rivalry, Buddhism had almost disappeared from India by the thirteenth century C.E.

Chinese civilization originated in the Yellow River Valley, and only gradually extending to the southern regions. Three dynasties ruled early China: the Xia or Hsia, the Shang (ca. 1500 to 1122 B.C.E.), and the Zhou (ca. 1122 to 211 B.C.E.). After the Zhou Dynasty fell, China welcomed the teachings of **Confucius**; warfare between states and philosophical speculation created circumstances ripe for such teachings. Confucius made the good order of society depend on an ethical ruler, who would receive advice from scholar-moralists like Confucius himself. In contrast to the Confucians, the Chinese Taoists professed a kind of anarchism; the best kind of government was none at all. Wise people did not concern themselves with political affairs but with mystical contemplation that identified them with the forces of nature.

African Kingdoms and Cultures. The **Bantu** peoples lived across large sections of Africa. Bantu societies lived in tiny chiefdoms, starting in the third millennium B.C.E., and each group developed its own version of the original Bantu language.

The **Nok** people lived in the area now known as Nigeria. Artifacts indicate that they were peaceful farmers who built small communities consisting of houses of wattle and daub (poles and sticks). The **Ghanaians** lived about 500 miles from what is now Ghana. Their kingdom fell to a Berber group in the late eleventh century C.E., and Mali emerged as the next great kingdom in the thirteenth century. The Malians lived in a huge kingdom that lay mostly on the savanna bordering the Sahara Desert. Timbuktu, built in the thirteenth century C.E., was a thriving city of culture where traders visited **stone houses**, **shops**, **libraries, and mosques**. The Songhai lived near the Niger River and gained their independence from the Mali in the early 1400s. The major growth of the empire came after 1464 C.E., under the leadership of Sunni 'Ali, who devoted his reign to warfare and expansion of the empire.

Civilizations of the Americas. The great civilizations of early America were agricultural, and the foremost civilization was the Mayan in Yucatan, Guatemala, and eastern Honduras. Farther north, in present-day Mexico, a series of advanced cultures derived much of their substance from the Maya. Peoples, such as the Zapotecs, Totonacs, Olmecs, and Toltecs, evolved into a high level of civilization. By 500 B.C.E., agricultural peoples had begun to use a **ceremonial calendar** and had built **stone pyramids** on which they held religious observances.

The Aztecs then took over Mexican culture, and a major feature of their culture was human sacrifice in repeated propitiation of their chief god. Aztec government was centralized, with an elective king and a large army. Andean civilization was characterized by the evolution of **beautifully made pottery**, **intricate fabrics**, **and flat-topped mounds**, or *huacas*.

In the interior of South America, the Inca, who called themselves "Children of the Sun," controlled an area stretching from Ecuador to central Chile. As sun worshippers, they believed that they were the sun god's vice regents on earth and were more powerful than any other humans. They believed that every person's place in society was fixed and immutable and that the state and the army were supreme. They were at the apex of their power just before the Spanish conquest.

In the present-day southwestern United States and northern Mexico, two varieties of ancient culture are still identifiable. The Anasazi developed **adobe architecture**, worked the land extensively, had a highly developed system of **irrigation**, and made cloth and baskets. The Hohokam built separate stone and timber houses around a central plaza.

Europe in Antiquity. The Frankish Kingdom was the most important medieval Germanic state. Under Clovis I (reigned 481–511 C.E.), the Franks finished conquering France and the Gauls in 486 C.E. Clovis converted to Christianity and founded the Merovingian dynasty.

Charles the Great, or **Charlemagne** (reigned 768–814 C.E.), founded the Carolingian dynasty. In 800 C.E., Pope Leo III named Charlemagne emperor of the Holy Roman Empire. In the Treaty of Aix-la-Chapelle (812 C.E.), the Byzantine emperor recognized Charles's authority in the West. The purpose of the Holy Roman Empire was to reestablish the Roman Empire in the West. Charles's son, Louis the Pious (reigned 814–840 C.E.), succeeded him. On Louis's death, his three sons vied for control of the Empire. The three eventually signed the Treaty of Verdun in 843 C.E. This gave Charles the Western Kingdom (France), Louis the Eastern Kingdom (Germany), and Lothair the Middle Kingdom, a narrow strip of land running from the North Sea to the Mediterranean.

In this period, **manorialism** developed as an economic system in which large estates, granted by the king to nobles, strove for self-sufficiency. The lord and his serfs (also called villeins) divided the ownership. The church was the only institution to survive the Germanic invasions intact. The power of the popes grew in this period. **Gregory I** (reigned 590–604 C.E.) was the first member of a monastic order to rise to the papacy. He advanced the ideas of penance and purgatory. He centralized church administration and was the first pope to rule as the secular head of Rome. Monasteries preserved the few remnants that survived the decline of antiquity.

The year 1050 marked the beginning of the High Middle Ages. Europe was poised to emerge from five centuries of decline. Between 1000 and 1350, the population of Europe grew from 38 million to 75 million. New technologies, such as **heavy plows**, and a slight temperature rise produced a longer growing season and contributed to agricultural productivity.

The Holy Roman Empire. Charlemagne's grandson, Louis the German, became Holy Roman Emperor under the Treaty of Verdun. Otto became Holy Roman Emperor in 962. His descendants governed the empire until 1024, when the Franconian dynasty assumed power, reigning until 1125. Under the leadership of **William the Conqueror** (reigned 1066–1087), the Normans conquered England in 1066. William stripped the Anglo-Saxon nobility of its privileges and instituted feudalism. He ordered a survey of all property of the realm; the Domesday Book (1086) records the findings.

William introduced feudalism to England. **Feudalism** was the decentralized political system of personal ties and obligations that bound vassals to their lords. Serfs were peasants who were bound to the land. They worked on the *demesne*, or lord's property, three or four days a week in return for the right to work their own land. In 1215, the English barons forced King John I to sign the **Magna Carta Libertatum**, acknowledging their "ancient" privileges. The Magna Carta established the principle of a limited English monarchy.

From 710 to 711, the Moors conquered Spain, which had been ruled by the Visigoths. Under the Moors, Spain enjoyed a stable, prosperous government. The caliphate of Córdoba became a center of scientific and intellectual activity. The Reconquista (1085–1340) wrested control from the Moors. The fall of Córdoba in 1234 completed the Reconquista, except for the small state of Granada.

Most of eastern Europe and Russia was never under Rome's control; Germanic invasions separated the areas from Western influence. In Russia, Vladimir I converted to Orthodox Christianity in 988. He established the basis of Kievian Russia. After 1054, Russia broke into competing principalities. The **Mongols (Tartars)** invaded in 1221. They completed their conquest in 1245 and cut Russia's contact with the West for almost a century.

The **Crusades** attempted to liberate the Holy Land from infidels. Seven major crusades occurred between 1096 and 1300. Urban II called Christians to the First Crusade (1096–1099) with the promise of a plenary indulgence (exemption from punishment in purgatory). Younger sons who would not inherit their fathers' lands were also attracted. The Crusades helped to renew interest in the ancient world. The Crusaders massacred thousands of Jews and Muslims, however, and relations between Europe and the Byzantine Empire collapsed.

Scholasticism. Scholasticism was an effort to reconcile reason and faith and to instruct Christians on how to make sense of the pagan tradition. The most influential proponent of this effort was Thomas Aquinas (ca. 1225–1274), who believed that there were two orders of truth. The lower level, reason, could demonstrate propositions such as the existence of God, but the higher level necessitated that some of God's mysteries, such as the nature of the Trinity, be accepted on faith. Aquinas viewed the universe as a great chain of being, with humans midway on the chain, between the material and the spiritual.

Late Middle Ages and the Renaissance

The Black Death

Conditions in Europe encouraged the quick spread of disease. Refuse, excrement, and dead animals filled the streets of the cities, which lacked any form of urban sanitation. Living conditions were overcrowded, with families often sleeping in one room or one bed; poor nutrition was rampant; and there was often little personal cleanliness. Merchants helped bring the plague to Asia; carried by fleas on rats, the disease arrived in Europe in 1347. By 1350, the disease had killed 25 percent to 40 percent of the European population.

Literature, Art, and Scholarship. Humanists, as both orators and poets, often imitated the classical works that inspired them. The literature of the period was more secular and wide ranging than that of the Middle Ages. **Dante Alighieri** (1265–1321) was a Florentine writer whose *Divine Comedy*, describing a journey through hell, purgatory, and heaven, shows that reason can take people only so far and that attaining heaven requires God's grace and revelation. Francesco Petrarch (1304–1374) encouraged the study of ancient Rome, collected and preserved works of ancient writers, and produced a large body of work in the classical literary style.

Giovanni Boccaccio (1313–1375) wrote *The Decameron*, a collection of short stories that the Italian author meant to amuse, not edify, the reader. Artists also broke with the medieval past in both technique and content. Renaissance art sometimes used religious topics but often dealt with secular themes or portraits of individuals. Oil paints, chiaroscuro, and linear perspectives produced works of energy in three dimensions. **Leonardo** da Vinci (1452–1519) produced numerous works, including *The Last Supper* and *Mona Lisa*. Raphael Santi (1483–1520), a master of Renaissance grace and style, theory, and technique, brought all his skills to his painting *The School of Athens*. **Michelangelo** Buonarroti (1475–1564) produced masterpieces in architecture, sculpture (*David*), and painting (the Sistine Chapel ceiling). His work was a bridge to a new, non-Renaissance style: mannerism.

Renaissance scholars were more practical and secular than medieval ones. **Manuscript collections** enabled scholars to study the primary sources and to reject traditions established since classical times. Also, scholars participated in the lives of their cities as active politicians. Leonardo Bruni (1370–1444), a civic humanist, served as chancellor of Florence, where he used his rhetorical skills to rouse the citizens against external enemies. Niccolo **Machiavelli** (1469–1527) wrote *The Prince*, which analyzes politics from the standpoint of expedience rising above morality in the name of maintaining political power.

The Reformation. The Reformation destroyed western Europe's religious unity and introduced new ideas about the relationships among God, the individual, and society. Politics greatly influenced the course of the Reformation and led, in most areas, to the subjection of the church to the political rulers.

Martin Luther (1483–1546), to his personal distress, could not reconcile the sinfulness of humans with the justice of God. During his studies of the Bible, Luther came to believe that personal efforts—good works such as a Christian life and attention to the sacraments of the church—could not "earn" the sinner salvation but that belief and faith were the only way to obtain grace. By 1515, Luther believed that "justification by faith alone" was the road to salvation.

On October 31, 1517, Luther nailed 95 theses, or statements, about **indulgences** (the cancellation of a sin in return for money) to the door of the Wittenberg church and challenged the practice of selling them. At this time he was seeking to reform the church, not divide it. In 1519, Luther presented various criticisms of the church and declared that only the Bible, not religious traditions or papal statements, could determine correct religious practices and beliefs. In 1521, Pope Leo X excommunicated Luther for his beliefs.

In 1536, **John Calvin** (1509–1564), a Frenchman, arrived in Geneva, a Swiss city-state that had adopted an anti-Catholic position. In 1540, Geneva became the center of the Reformation. Calvin's *Institutes of the Christian Religion* (1536), a strictly logical analysis of Christianity, had a universal appeal. Calvin emphasized the doctrine of **predestination**, which indicated that God knew who would obtain salvation before those people were born. Calvin believed that church and state should unite. Calvinism triumphed as the majority religion in Scotland under the leadership of John Knox (ca. 1514–1572), and in the United Provinces of the Netherlands. Puritans in England and New England also accepted Calvinism.

The Thirty Years' War. Between 1618 and 1648, the European powers fought a series of wars. The reasons for the wars varied; religious, dynastic, commercial, and territorial rivalries all played a part. The battles were fought over most of Europe and ended with the Treaty of Westphalia in 1648. The Thirty Years' War changed the boundaries of most European countries.

Revolution and the New World Order

The Scientific Revolution

For the first time in human history, a secular worldview emerged: the Age of Enlightenment. The philosophical starting point for the Enlightenment was the belief in the autonomy of man's intellect apart from God's. The most basic assumption was faith in reason rather than faith in revelation. René Descartes (1596–1650) sought a basis for logic and believed he found it in man's ability to think. "I think; therefore, I am" was his most famous statement.

Benedict de Spinoza (1632–1677) developed a rational pantheism in which he equated God and nature. He denied all free will and ended up with an impersonal, mechanical universe. Gottfried Wilhelm Leibniz (1646–1716) worked on symbolic logic and calculus and invented a calculating machine. He, too, had a mechanistic view of the world and life and thought of God as a hypothetical abstraction rather than a persona.

John Locke (1632–1704) pioneered the empiricist approach to knowledge; he stressed the importance of the environment in human development. Locke classified knowledge as either (1) according to reason, (2) contrary to reason, or (3) above reason. Locke thought reason and revelation were complementary and derived from God.

The Enlightenment's Effect on Society

The Enlightenment affected more than science and religion. New political and economic theories originated as well. John Locke and **Jean-Jacques Rousseau** (1712–1778) believed that people were capable of governing themselves, either through a political (Locke) or social (Rousseau) contract forming the basis of society.

Most philosophers opposed democracy, preferring a limited monarchy that shared power with the nobility. The assault on mercantilist economic theory was begun by the physiocrats in France; the physiocrats proposed a laissez-faire (minimal governmental interference) attitude toward land use. The culmination of their beliefs was the theory of economic capitalism, which was associated with Adam Smith (1723–1790) and his notions of free trade, free enterprise, and the law of supply and demand.

The French Revolution

The increased criticism directed toward governmental inefficiency and corruption and toward the privileged classes demonstrated the rising expectations of "enlightened" society in France. The remainder of the population (called the Third Estate) consisted of the middle class, urban workers, and the mass of peasants, who bore the entire burden of taxation and the imposition of feudal obligations.

The most notorious event of the French Revolution was the so-called Reign of Terror (1793–1794), the government's campaign against its internal enemies and counterrevolutionaries. **Louis XVI** faced charges of treason, was declared guilty, and suffered execution on January 21, 1793. Later the same year, the queen, **Marie Antoinette**, met the same fate. The middle class controlled the Directory (1795–1799). Members of the Directory believed that, through peace, they would gain more wealth and establish a society in which money and property would become the only requirements for prestige and power. Rising inflation and mass public dissatisfaction led to the downfall of the Directory.

The Era of Napoleon

On December 25, 1799, a new government and constitution concentrated supreme power in the hands of **Napoleon**. Napoleon's domestic reforms and policies affected every aspect of society.

French-ruled peoples viewed Napoleon as a tyrant who repressed and exploited them for France's glory and advantage. Enlightened reformers believed Napoleon had betrayed the ideals of the Revolution. The downfall of Napoleon resulted from his inability to conquer England, economic distress caused by the Continental System (boycott of British goods), the Peninsular War with Spain, the German War of Liberation, and his invasion of Russia. The actual defeat of Napoleon occurred at the **Battle of Waterloo** in 1815.

The Industrial Revolution

The term *Industrial Revolution* describes a period of transition, when machines began to significantly displace human and animal power in methods of producing and distributing goods so that an agricultural and commercial society became an industrial one.

Roots of the Industrial Revolution are evident in these ways:

- the Commercial Revolution (1500–1700) that spurred the great economic growth of Europe and brought about the Age of Discovery and Exploration, which in turn helped to solidify the economic doctrines of mercantilism;

- the effect of the Scientific Revolution, which produced the first wave of mechanical inventions and technological advances;

- the increase in population in Europe from 140 million people in 1750 to 266 million people by the mid-nineteenth century (more producers, more consumers); and

- the nineteenth-century political and social revolutions that began the rise to power of the middle class and that provided leadership for the economic revolution.

A transportation revolution ensued to distribute the productivity of machinery and to deliver raw materials to the eager factories. This led to the growth of canal systems; the construction of hard-surfaced **"macadam" roads**; the commercial use of the **steamboat**, which **Robert Fulton** (1765–1815) demonstrated; and the **railway locomotive**, which **George Stephenson** (1781–1848) made commercially successful. The Industrial Revolution created a unique new category of people who depended on their jobs for income and who needed job security. Until 1850, workers as a whole did not share in the general wealth produced by the Industrial Revolution. Conditions improved as the century neared an end. Union action, general prosperity, and a developing social conscience all combined to improve the working conditions, wages, and hours of skilled labor first and unskilled labor later.

Socialism

The Utopian Socialists were the earliest writers to propose an equitable solution to improve the distribution of society's wealth. The name of this group comes from *Utopia*, **Saint Thomas More's** (1478–1535) book on a fictional ideal society. While they endorsed the productive capacity of industrialism, the Utopian Socialists denounced its mismanagement. Human society was ideally a community rather than a mixture of competing, selfish individuals. All the goods a person needed could be produced in one community.

Scientific socialism, or **Marxism**, was the creation of **Karl Marx** (1818–1883), a German scholar who, with the help of **Friedrich Engels** (1820–1895), intended to replace utopian hopes and dreams with a militant blueprint for socialist working-class success. The principal works of this revolutionary school of socialism were *The Communist Manifesto* and *Das Kapital*. Marxism has four key propositions:

1. An economic interpretation of history that asserts that economic factors (mainly centered on who controls the means of production and distribution) determines all human history.

2. The belief that there has always been a class struggle between the rich and the poor (or the exploiters and the exploited).

3. The theory of surplus value, which holds that the true value of a product is labor; because workers receive a small portion of their just labor price, the difference is surplus value "stolen" from workers by capitalists.

4. The belief that socialism is inevitable because capitalism contains the seeds of its own destruction (overproduction, unemployment, etc.): The rich grow richer and the poor grow poorer until the gap between each class (proletariat and bourgeoisie) becomes so great that the working classes rise up in revolution and overthrow the elite bourgeoisie to install a "dictatorship of the proletariat." The creation of a classless society guided by the principle, "From each according to his abilities, to each according to his needs" is the result of dismantling capitalism.

Causes and Consequences of Exploration, Settlement, and Growth

Beginnings of European Exploration

Europeans were largely unaware of the existence of the American continent, even though a Norse seaman, **Leif Eriksson**, had sailed within sight of the continent in the eleventh century. Few other explorers ventured nearly as far as America. Before the fifteenth century, Europeans had little desire to explore and were not ready to face the many challenges of a long sea voyage. Just as developments led to changes and conflict in North America and produced an increasing number of distinct cultures and systems, developments in Europe were about to make possible the great voyages that led to contact between Europe and the Americas. In the fifteenth and sixteenth centuries, technological devices such as the **compass** and **astrolabe** freed explorers from some of the constraints that had limited early voyages. Three primary factors—God, gold, and glory—led to increased interest in exploration and eventually to a desire to settle in the newly discovered lands.

Although Europeans, such as Italians, participated in overland trade with the East and sailed through the Mediterranean and beyond, it was the Arabs who played the largest part in such trade and who benefited the most economically. **Prince Henry the Navigator**, ruler of Portugal, sponsored voyages aimed at adding territory and gaining control of trading routes to increase the power and wealth of Portugal. Prince Henry also wanted to spread Christianity and prevent the further expansion of Islam in Africa. Prince Henry the Navigator brought a number of Italian merchant traders to his court at Cape St. Vincent, and subsequently they sailed in Portuguese ships down the western coast of Africa. These initial voyages were extremely difficult because the voyagers lacked navigational instruments and any kind of maps or charts. Europeans had charted the entire Mediterranean Sea, including harbors and the coastline, but they had no knowledge or maps of the African coast.

The first task of the explorers was to create accurate charts of the African shoreline. The crews on these initial voyages did not encounter horrible monsters or boiling water, which rumors had said existed in the ocean beyond Cape Bojador, the farthest point Europeans had previously reached. They did discover, however, that strong southward winds made it easy to sail out of the Mediterranean but difficult to return. Most people believed that Africa and China were joined by a southern continent, eliminating any possibility of an eastern maritime route to the Indian Ocean. Prince Henry, however, sent ships along the coast of Africa because he believed it was possible to sail east through the Atlantic and reach the Indian Ocean.

Technical Innovations Aiding Exploration

One of the reasons that the explorers sailing from Portugal traveled along the coast was to avoid losing sight of land. By the thirteenth century, explorers were using the compass, borrowed from China, to determine direction; it was more difficult to determine the relative position from the North and South Poles and from landmasses or anything else. In the Northern Hemisphere, a navigator could determine the relative north-south position, or latitude, by calculating the height of the **Pole Star** from the horizon. South of the equator, one cannot see the Pole Star; until around 1460, captains had no way to determine their position if they sailed too far south. Although longitude (relative east-west position) remained unknown until the eighteenth century, the introduction of the astrolabe allowed sailors to calculate their latitude south of the equator.

Along with navigational aids, improvements in shipbuilding and in weaponry also facilitated exploration. Unlike the Mediterranean, it was not possible to use ships propelled only by oarsmen in the Atlantic because the waves were high and the currents and winds were strong. Europeans had initially used very broad sails on ships that went out into the Atlantic; the ships were heavy and often became stranded by the absence of the favorable tailwinds upon which the ships and sailors depended. The Portuguese borrowed techniques from Arab and European shipbuilding and developed the Caravela Redondo. This ship proved to be more worthy of long voyages because it combined square rigging for speed with lateen sails that were more responsive and easier to handle. Other European states adopted the ship and also the practice of mounting artillery and other weapons on exploration vessels.

Main Elements of European Exploration

As the Portuguese began to trade and explore along the coast of Africa, they brought back slaves, ivory, gold, and knowledge of the African coast. It looked as though the Portuguese might find a route to the Indian Ocean, and it was clear that the voyages sponsored by Prince Henry were benefiting Portugal in many ways.

Other European states wanted to increase their territory and wealth and to establish trade routes to the East. Although the desire for control of trade routes and wealth was a primary motive in launching voyages of exploration, it was not the only incentive. Europe in the fifteenth and sixteenth centuries, despite the increase in dissenting views, was still extremely religious. The Catholic Church continued to exert a tremendous influence, and some Christians were motivated to go on voyages of discovery to conduct missionary activities and spread the word of God. In addition, after the beginning of the Reformation, many Lutherans, Calvinists, and other groups who had left the Catholic Church emigrated from Europe in the hope of settling where they would be free from religious persecution or violent conflicts.

Other individuals sponsored or participated in voyages in the hope of gaining wealth or increased opportunities. For example, younger sons of families in Europe were able to secure prominent positions in the church, but they were often not able to find lucrative opportunities at home because the eldest son usually inherited lands and wealth. The voyages of exploration were a means of securing fame and fortune and of obtaining opportunities that would not be available otherwise.

Although the motivation of fame and fortune was often secondary to God and glory, many individuals were attracted to exploration by the possibility of adventure and by their desire to explore uncharted territory. These three factors—gold, God, and glory—operated on both individual and state levels; kings and heads of states were as interested as the seamen were in spreading their faith and increasing the wealth and prestige of their states.

Portugal was the first European state to establish sugar plantations on an island off the west coast of Africa and to import slaves from Africa to labor there. This marked the beginning of the slave trade. The level of trading was initially far less extensive and intense than during the later period of the slave trade, when Spain and England became involved. In an attempt to maintain control of the slave trade and of the eastern routes to India, the Portuguese appealed to the pope; he ruled in their favor and forbade the Spanish and others to sail south and east in an attempt to reach India or Asia.

When **Ferdinand and Isabella** married and united Spain's two largest provinces (Castile and Aragon), they not only began the process of uniting all of Spain but also agreed to sponsor **Christopher Columbus** in his voyage of exploration. Only the heads of states had the necessary resources and could afford the risk involved in sponsoring a major voyage across the oceans of the world, but most monarchs were unwilling to take such a risk. Columbus was an Italian explorer looking for a sponsor and had approached Ferdinand and Isabella after being turned down by the English government. He convinced the Spanish monarchs that a western route to the Indian Ocean existed and that it would be possible to make the voyage.

However, Columbus had miscalculated the distance of the voyage from Europe to Asia. His estimate of the circumference of the earth was much less than it should have been for an accurate calculation, and no Europeans were aware of the existence of the American continents. One of the reasons that Ferdinand and Isabella were willing to support Columbus was that the previous agreements prevented all states but Portugal from sailing east to reach India. Therefore, the only chance for Spain to launch an expedition to India and to participate in trade and exploration was in the discovery of a western route to India.

European Contact with the Americas

In 1492, Columbus sailed from Spain with 90 men on three ships, the *Niña*, the *Pinta*, and the *Santa María*. After a 10-week voyage, they landed in the Bahamas. On his second trip, Columbus reached Cuba; and then in 1498, during his third trip, he reached the mainland and sailed along the northern coast of South America. Columbus originally thought he had reached India; he referred to the people he encountered in the Bahamas and on his second landing in Cuba as Indians.

There is considerable debate over whether Columbus realized, either during his third voyage or just before his death, that he had landed not in India but on an entirely unknown continent between Europe and Asia. Another question is whether Columbus, who died in obscurity despite his fame for having discovered America, should receive credit for this discovery; earlier explorers had reached the American continent.

However, because Columbus's voyages prompted extensive exploration and settlement of the Americas, it is accurate to state that he was responsible for the discovery of the New World by Europeans. Another result of Columbus's voyages was the increased focus of Spain on exploration and conquest. Nevertheless, the New World took its name from the Florentine merchant **Amerigo Vespucci**—not Columbus. Vespucci took part in several voyages to the New World and wrote a series of descriptions that not only gave Europeans an image of this "New World" but also spread the idea that the discovered lands were not part of Asia or India. Vespucci, then, popularized the image of the Americas and the idea that the Americas were continents separate from those previously known.

A Portuguese navigator, **Vasco da Gama**, crossed the Isthmus of Panama and came to another ocean, which separates the American continents from China. The Spanish sponsored another Portuguese sailor, **Ferdinand Magellan**, who discovered at the southern end of South America a strait that provided access to the ocean west of the Americas. Magellan named this ocean the Pacific because it was much calmer than the strait through which he had sailed to reach it. Later, he reached the Philippines and met his death in a conflict with the natives. Magellan's voyage, nevertheless, was the final stage of the process whereby Europeans completed the first known circumnavigation of the globe. Although initially the Spanish were eager to find a route around the Americas that would enable them to sail on toward their original goal, the treasures of the Far East, they began to consider the Americas as a possible source of untapped wealth.

The Spanish claimed all the New World except Brazil, which papal decree gave to the Portuguese. The first Spanish settlements were on the islands of the Caribbean Sea. It was not until 1518 that Spain appointed **Hernando Cortez** as a government official in Cuba; Cortez led a small military expedition against the Aztecs in Mexico. Cortez and his men failed in their first attack on the Aztec capital city, Tenochtitlán, but were ultimately successful.

A combination of factors allowed the small force of approximately 600 Spanish soldiers to overcome the extensive Aztec Empire. The Spanish were armed with rifles and bows, which provided an advantage over Aztec fighters armed only with spears. However, weapons and armor were not the main reason that the Spanish were able to overcome the military forces of the natives.

The Aztec ruler, Montezuma, allowed a delegation, which included Cortez, into the capital city because the description of the Spanish soldiers in their armor and with feathers in their helmets was similar to the description in Aztec legend of messengers who would be sent by the chief Aztec god, Quetzalco'atl. The members of Cortez's expedition exposed the natives to smallpox and other diseases that devastated the native population. Finally, the Spanish expedition was able to form alliances with other native tribes that the Aztecs had conquered; these tribes were willing to cooperate to defeat the Aztecs and thus break up their empire.

Twenty years after Cortez defeated the Aztecs, another conquistador, **Francisco Pizarro**, defeated the Incas in Peru. Pizarro's expedition enabled the Spanish to begin to explore and settle South America. Spain funded the conquistadors, or conquerors, who were the first Europeans to explore some areas of the Americas. However, the sole purpose of the conquistadors' explorations was defeating the natives to gain access to gold, silver, and other wealth. Spain established mines in the territory it claimed and produced a tremendous amount of gold and silver. In the 300 years after the Spanish conquest of the Americas in the sixteenth century, those mines produced 10 times more gold and silver than the total produced by all the mines in the rest of the world.

Spain had come to view the New World as more than an obstacle to voyages toward India; over time, Spain began to think that it might be possible to exploit this territory for more than just mining. The conquistadors made it possible for the Spanish to settle the New World, but they were not responsible for forming settlements or for overseeing Spanish colonies there. Instead, Spain sent officials and administrators from Spain to oversee settlements after their initial formation.

Spanish settlers came to the New World for various reasons: Some went in search of land to settle or buy, others went looking for opportunities that were not available to them in Europe, and priests and missionaries went to spread Christianity to the natives. By the end of the sixteenth century, Spain had established firm control over not only the several islands in the Caribbean, Mexico, and southern North America but also in the territory currently within the modern states of Chile, Argentina, and Peru.

Spanish Settlements in the New World

The first permanent settlement established by the Spanish was the predominantly military fort of St. Augustine, located in present-day Florida. In 1598, Don Juan de Oñate led a group of 500 settlers north from Mexico and established a colony in what is now New Mexico.

Oñate granted *encomiendas* to the most prominent Spaniards who had accompanied him. Under the *encomienda* system, which the Spanish in Mexico and parts of North America established, these distinguished individuals had the right to exact tribute and/or labor from the native population, which continued to live on the land in exchange for the services the native peoples provided. Spanish colonists founded Santa Fe in 1609, and by 1680 about 2,000 Spaniards were living in New Mexico. Most of the colonists raised sheep and cattle on large ranches and lived among approximately 30,000 Pueblo Indians. The Spanish crushed a major revolt that threatened to destroy Santa Fe in 1680. Attempts to prevent the natives—both those who had converted to Catholicism and those who had not—from performing religious rituals that predated the Spaniards' arrival provoked the revolt. The natives drove the Spanish from Santa Fe, but they returned in 1696, crushed the Pueblos, and seized the land.

Although the Spanish ultimately quelled the revolt, they began to change their policies toward the natives, who still greatly outnumbered the Spanish settlers. The Spanish continued to try to Christianize and "civilize" the native population, but they also began to allow the Pueblos to own land. In addition, the Spanish unofficially tolerated native religious rituals, although Catholicism officially condemned all such practices. By 1700, the Spanish population in New Mexico had increased and reached about 4,000 and the native population had decreased to about 13,000; intermarriage between natives and Spaniards increased. Nevertheless, disease, war, and migration resulted in the steady decline in the Pueblo population. New Mexico had become a prosperous and stable region, but it was still relatively weak and, as the only major Spanish settlement in northern Mexico, was isolated.

Effects of Contact between Europe and the Americas

One cannot underestimate the impact of the Europeans on the New World, both before and after the arrival of the English and French. The most immediate effect was the spread of disease, which decimated the native population. In some areas of Mexico, for example, 95 percent of the native population died as a result of contact with Europeans and the subsequent outbreaks of diseases like smallpox. In South America, the native population was devastated not only by disease but also by deliberate policies instituted to control and in some cases eliminate native peoples.

Although Europeans passed most diseases to the natives, the natives passed syphilis to the Europeans, who carried it back to Europe. The European and American continents exchanged plants and animals. Europeans brought animals to the New World, and they took plants, such as potatoes, corn, and squash, back to Europe, where introduction of these crops led to an explosion of the European population. The decimation of the native population and the establishment of large plantations led to a shortage of workers, and Europeans began to transport slaves from Africa to the New World to fill the shortage.

Chronological Relationships Among Historical Events

Students of history understand that there is a complex relationship between sequential events. An example of a complex relationship is that of the migration of African-Americans from the South in search of better paying jobs, during each of the world wars and the subsequent race riots that took place in some urban areas after the wars. While some would argue that the riots were largely due to overcrowding (seemingly an isolated cause), others might argue that, while overcrowding was a factor, it was the fact that African-Americans, having left the socially oppressive and segregated South, were unwilling to retreat from their gains.

Historical understanding includes the use of reasoning, resulting in a thorough exploration of cause-effect relationships to reach defensible historical interpretations through inquiry. This is true with all levels of history, such as discussed above in the previous sections. Another example, this time in world history, would be the relationship between the Industrial Revolution and the emergence of a new category of people who depended on their jobs for income and who thus needed job security. From the practices employed during industrialization came new theories of the relationship between work and the worker (e.g., Marxism, socialism and capitalism). Without those practices and the subsequent historical analysis, comparing pre-industrialization work to that of industrialization, the important concepts which help us think about the socio-political systems most likely would not have emerged.

Strategies and Resources for Historical Inquiry

The ability to understand and apply skills and procedures related to the study of history involves knowledge of the use of systematic inquiry. Inquiry is essential for use in not only examining a single discipline, such as history, but also integrated social studies.

Being able to engage in inquiry involves the ability to acquire information from a wide variety of resources, and organize that information, which leads to the interpretation of information. Inquiry involves the ability to design and conduct investigations, which in turn leads to the identification and analysis of social studies issues.

Also, this understanding includes knowledge about and the use of the various resources used in systematic social science inquiry. Those resources include primary (e.g., letters, diaries, speeches, photos, and autobiographies) and secondary sources (e.g., encyclopedias, almanacs, atlases, government documents, artifacts, and oral histories).

However, there are instances where secondary source materials can function as primary sources. One example is Lytton Strachey's famous history of nineteenth century England, *Eminent Victorians*, published in 1918. *Eminent Victorians* is a secondary source, a history of English society and culture in the 1800s based on Strachey's research and analysis of primary sources. And yet, to a present-day scholar *Eminent Victorians* itself as a primary source for use in analyzing the mores and attitudes of Lytton Strachey and the early twentieth-century English society of which he was a part.

Twentieth-Century Developments and Transformations: Causes and Effects

World War I

CAUSES

- There are many different interpretations about what caused the war, but the Treaty of Versailles, after the war, blamed it all on Germany.

- Direct cause of WWI: the **assassination of Archduke Franz Ferdinand** at Sarajevo on **28 June 1914**

- Intense nationalism—specifically Serbian nationalism

  1. Germany: **Weltpolitik**—desire for world power status

  2. France: Revenge over Alsace and Lorraine

  3. British—fighting own imperialist issues and emergent nationalism in its colonies

- Alliance system and the rivalry between powers

    1. Before 1914, Europe's main powers were divided into two armed camps by a series of alliances. These were the **Triple Alliance** of Germany, Austria-Hungary, and Italy (1882) and the **Triple Entente** of Britain, Russia, and France (1907)

    2. Although these alliances were defensive in nature, they meant that any conflict between two countries involved all of the other countries.

- The main rivalries between the powers were:

    1. Germany and France over Alsace. This division made an alliance between both countries impossible.

    2. Russia and Austria over the Balkans.

    3. Britain and Germany over their navies and economic power.

- Crises before 1914 that exposed rivalries and rifts:

    1. First Moroccan Crisis—1905 Kaiser Wilhelm II visited Morocco and denounced French influence there. This prompted outcry by both France and England, who were sensitive to other countries getting involved in their colonies. Brought an Anglo-French entente.

    2. Second Moroccan Crisis—Germans sent a gunboat to Morocco to protect German citizens there and said that France had ignored terms of Algeciras Conference. Germans agreed to leave Morocco in return for rights to the Congo.

    3. Annexation of Bosnia-Herzegovinia by Austria; angered Serbia and almost caused war to break out between supporters of each side.

- **Militarism:** The arms race was running amok, with military spending and sizes of armies doubling between 1870 and 1914.

Country	1910–1914 Increase in Defense Expenditures
France	10%
Britain	13%
Russia	39%
Germany	73%

Economic rivalry

- International competition among European powers for colonies and economic markets.

Imperialism

- Germans trying to distract their population from problems and fears about Russians, set their sights on more colonies and territory in Europe.

- Growth of German power in Central Europe challenged Great Powers (France, Great Britain, and Russia).

- Naval rivalry between Great Britain and Germany due to colonial rivalry.

- Breakdown of the European treaty system and the "Balance of Power."

- The Eastern Question—both Austria and Russia wanted control of the Balkan as the Ottoman Empire was losing its grip on the area. Russia encouraged Slav nationalism there, and Austria feared nationalism would spill over to their territory the Balkans.

- Domestic political factors—hopes among elites that a war would erase issue of socialism and would lose its favor among those groups clamoring for it.

EFFECTS

<u>Political</u>

- Socialist ideas experienced a boom in Europe, spreading from Germany and the Austrian Empire to Britain (1923) and France (1924).

- Republic became the most popular type of government to gain influence after the war in Europe. Before the war, Europe contained 19 monarchies and 3 republics, yet only a few years afterward, they had 13 monarchies, 14 republics, and 2 regencies.

PRAXIS *Pointer*

Take the practice tests under the same conditions you will take the actual test.

- 1919 Treaty of Versailles had deleterious effects on the post-war environment as it caused hostilities and resentment that later paved the way for World War II.

- Germany was singled out for harsh treatment:

  1. forced to sign a humiliating treaty accepting blame for causing the war and ordered to pay compensation for it;

  2. size of the German state was reduced, while Italy and France was enlarged;

  3. Weimar government not liked by most of the citizens and maintained little power in controlling the German state;

  4. many German soldiers refused to give up fighting, even though Germany's military was ordered to be drastically reduced. Given such orders, numerous German ex-soldiers joined the Freikorps, an establishment of mercenaries available for street-fighting. The open hostility and simmering feelings of revenge exhibited by Germany foreshadowed the start of World War II.

- Colonies who supported Europe during the war, like India and protectorates, like Egypt, thought they would be rewarded for their support. When Britain shot down one of Wilson's 14 Points that advocated the right of **self-determination** for all countries, the colonies rebelled. World War I also showed the vulnerabilities of the colonizer and massive nationalist movements started in many of the colonized states.

- The boundaries of the Middle East were redrawn, introduction of new states and leaders, sparked long-term crises and problems that continue today.

- Women acquired the right to vote throughout most of the countries in Europe (exceptions were France and Switzerland).

- Status of working classes increased.

- United States's position in the world was elevated.

- Break-up of the Ottoman Empire

- Rise of the Turkish Republic

- Increased involvement of government in society

- Increased propaganda

Economic

- Technology changed tremendously after the war, in part because of developments in mass production made during the war, like automobiles, airplanes, radios, and even certain chemicals.

- Tremendous war debt caused European governments to print more and more money, only to spur on uncontrollable inflation.

- Members of the middle class who had been living reasonably comfortably on investments began to experience a rocky financial period.

- German mark devalued tremendously. For instance, in 1923, in just three months, the mark's value jumped from 4.6 million marks to the dollar to 4.2 *trillion* marks to the dollar.

- War debt shifted world's financial center from England to the United States.

- Property damages were quite heavy in Europe, particularly France.

- War strained resources of each country to the maximum.

Creation of New States After World War I

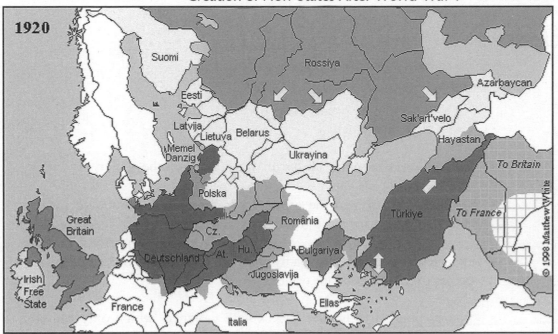

Source: http://users.erols.com/mwhite28.post-ww1.htm. © Matthew White 1998

- Many social customs faded out, and society became more open (at least for a time).

- There was also a rapid development of new technology.

- There was a disruption of world trade.

Social

- Growing distrust with political and government officials over some of the horrors of the war and the reluctance that government officials had toward pursuing peace during the war.

- Tremendous sense of loss and anger in some parts of Western Europe where one in four young men died in battle. The war killed 10 to 13 million people.

Russian Revolution of 1917

CAUSES

Economic

- Tsar's mismanagement

- Tremendous economic strains of World War I on the society

- So many men joined the army (15 million) that there were insufficient numbers to run the factories and farms, which led to widespread shortages of basic food, and working conditions in the factories deteriorated so badly that workers rioted and engaged in strikes to try to get better wages.

- Tsar responded to worker strikes with violence, which only caused more strikes, including strikes by transportation workers that further paralyzed the country.

- Prices soared as availability of goods plummeted.

- Famine threats to big cities

Political

- Dire economic situation was faced by the urban workers. Most worked eleven-hour days, and health and safety conditions were dismal.

- Upper classes and educated classes resented Tsar Nicholas's autocracy.

- Perception of government decadence and ineptness affected each level of society who saw the Romanov regime as corrupt.

- Irritation when Tsar Nicholas decided to take direct command of the army during World War I, leaving his German wife at the helm of the government (and she was under the sway of **Rasputin**).

- Army's morale was terrible. By October 1916, Russia had lost between 1.6 and 1.8 million soldiers, with an addition two million prisoners of war and one million who had gone missing. Mutinies occurred as soldiers lacked food, shoes, and weapons.

- Tsar Nicholas was blamed for the poor condition of the army as well as his handling of the War.

- Unwillingness of Tsar Nicholas to grant political reforms, his failure to let the Duma be effective, and his active attempt to diminish its power, caused all political opposition to become revolutionary.

- Rise of radical socialist political parties dedicated to overthrowing both Tsarism and (eventually) capitalism: Liberals—Kadets and Octoberists; Socialist Populists (the SRs); Marxists (Bolsheviks and Mensheviks).

Social

- Continuance of popular opposition to the Tsar and his policies due to discontent of peasants, worker, and minorities

- Centuries of oppression towards the lower classes, about 85% of whom were peasants who had been emancipated in 1861 by Tsar **Alexander II of Russia**, and had been given land to work on by the government, but the land was insufficient and peasants frequently rioted over their conditions and feelings of being "second-class subjects"

- Need for workers in the factories and lack of land for peasants resulted in many moving to the cities, which quickly became overrun and living conditions worsened.

- Vast discontent among Russian citizens

- Growing student and intelligentsia political radicalism, inspired by the West, who wanted quick change

- Failure of middle class to provide a base for liberal reforms to be enacted

Effects

- End of autocratic rule

- Establishment of a socialist/communist government

- Withdrawal of Russia from World War I

- Industrial growth and organization of economy on five-year plans

- Complete transformation of Russian society, government, and economy

- Formation of the Soviet Union

- Emergence of Russia as a world power

- Spread of communism throughout the world

- Criticism of imperialism, which lent a hand to nationalist movements in colonized countries

- Tremendous focus on education in the Soviet Union had an enormous impact on the population, which started the twentieth century as mainly illiterate but grew into one of the world's most well-rounded educational systems

- Division of world into communist and capitalist camps—Cold War

World War II

CAUSES

Economic

- Great Depression created environment for the emergence of the Nazi Party

Political

- Treaty of Versailles:

    1. Germans unhappy with elements of the treaty that they considered to be humiliating and burdensome:

    2. War Guilt Clause: they had to accept blame for starting the war.

    3. Reparations: Germany had to pay tremendous costs for the war.

    4. Disarmament: Germany only allowed to have a small army and six naval ships; no tanks, air force, or submarines allowed, and the Rhineland was to be demilitarized.

- Territorial Losses: Land taken away from Germany and given to other countries; no merger with Austria allowed.

- Hitler's Actions—He built up the military, ordered troops into the Rhineland, made alliances with Mussolini and Japan, and marched into Austria. He responded to world concern about his expansionist moves, and he replied that he had no more interest in expansion; however, it was clear that he did when he demanded the Sudetenland and invaded first Czechoslovakia and then Poland.

- Failure of Appeasement: In order to make up for the harshness of the Treaty of Versailles, Neville Chamberlain thought that if they gave into Hitler's demands, he would be appeased. Hitler's response was to invade Czechoslovakia. Chamberlain acquiesced and said Britain would only step in if Hitler invaded Poland. Hitler invaded Poland.

- Failure of the League of Nations: Weak and ineffective and unable to stop war from happening because: not all countries had joined the League (chief among them, the United States, Germany, and Russia); the League had no power; the League had no army; the League was unable to act quickly because it only met four times a year and all decisions had to be agreed upon by all nations.

<u>Social</u>

- Emergence of fascism, which glorified the military, denounced international organization and cooperation, and considered war an accepted means for achieving national goals

EFFECT

- Massive human dislocations

- Extensive casualties

- Nuremberg war trials in which former Nazi leaders were tried for crimes against humanity carried out in the systematic murder of millions of Jews and others in the Holocaust

PRAXIS Pointer

When you feel anxious, close your eyes and take a couple of long, deep breaths. Then hold it and exhale slowly. Imagine a peaceful place to visit.

- Space Race begins

- Early computer technology came out of World War II

- Emergence of third-world nationalist movements

- De-colonization of European empires

- Colonized countries, bolstered by weaknesses of England and France, galvanized to fight for independence

<u>Political</u>

- United States and USSR emerged as the two superpowers of the twentieth century.

- The bi-polarization of Europe and the beginning of the Cold War

- Division of Germany

  - Germany divided into four zones of occupation, each controlled by one of the victorious powers.

- Creation of the UN

- Japanese war trials

- Japan temporarily placed under United States rule; in ruins from extensive bombing and U.S. nuclear attack; military leaders tried and convicted of war crimes; emperor retains crown.

- England and France take a back seat to the United States and the USSR.

- Russian army built up to fight against Germans and by the end of the war, they occupied most of Eastern Europe.

Economic

- Creation of the International Monetary Fund (IMF) and General Agreement on Tariffs and Trade (GATT)

- England had been devastated by bombing and had to rely on aid from the United States.

- U.S. economy booms and actually have labor shortages, rather than any unemployment.

Social

- New technology developed during the war to fight diseases would sharply lower mortality rate and increase population growth.

- Technological developments during war had a significant impact— for instance, the English developed radar, which paved the way for television; progress in computers and electronics were important.

- Development of atomic bomb changed the nature of future wars.

- Women involved in workforce and this sparked changes.

Globalization

Globalization has many definitions and many perspectives. The one thing to remember is that it is not a new concept—globalization has been happening for thousands of years. Basically, behind the definition of globalization is the notion that no one nation stands by itself, for the world really is one in which we see the interaction and integration of people, governments, and businesses with people of other nations through trade and investment. It challenges the idea that a state's influence stops at its borders, which really are just man-made designations of where a country should stop.

Today we see more examples of globalization than we may have seen previously, simply in its scope and diversity. In the past few decades, the flow of information and technology between and among peoples has spurred increases in cross-border trade, as goods and services are distributed more quickly than ever before. As a result, the world seems more connected in its day-to-day operations than previously. Such interaction has its effects on all aspects of life—environmental, cultural, political, economic, and social.

There are two principal drivers of globalization today: economic policies and technology. In terms of economic policies dictating the extent and direction of global interaction, we have seen that the adoption of free-market economic systems throughout the world has resulted in new international opportunities for trade and investment. Knocking down trade and political barriers has resulted in expansion of foreign markets and a re-honing of domestic ones. It is this constant integration with the world beyond one's borders that has made both countries and businesses realize that they need to have a carefully crafted international business and financial structure in place in order to meet needs. The other driver in globalization is technology, which has dramatically transformed the economic life of individuals, companies, and nations. These new tools make it easier to communicate worldwide, conduct international financial transactions with a flick of a switch, and collaborate with partners all over the world.

Globalization, however, is not without its detractors. Opponents of globalization have argued that the hold that multinational corporations now have over societies worldwide has been at the expense of local enterprise, development, culture, and the common people. Resistance to globalization has pushed such movements as "buy local," "sustainability efforts," and calls for increased attention to regulation of these megalith countries. Environmentalists express concern about the destruction of resources, like the rainforest, to meet the temporary needs of these corporations.

Below are some big issues that are happening today. The best way to become familiar with the latest on any of these issues is to pick up some copies of reputable, thoughtful newspapers and/or magazines and read about current thought and developments on any of the following topics. By no means is this an exhaustive list.

Political

- Clash of Civilizations: Inter-religious conflict, especially the tensions between Islam and Christianity

- Terrorism and the Rule of Law

- How can nations fit into an increasingly global world that emphasizes internationalism?

- Role of the United Nations and NGOs

- Palestinian-Israeli Conflict

- Change in the world's power structure—emergence of China and India

- Widening of the gap between political views on the right and left and disappearance of true "left" with the fall of the Soviet Union

- "War on Terror"

- Uprisings in the Middle East (Egypt, Libya, Yemen and Saudi Arabia)

- Controversies about genocide—who defines it, where is it happening, when should other countries intervene?

- Peace-keeping missions

Social

- Women, children, and family issues

- Sex trade

- Role of the media

- "Bread and Circuses" idea and the use of entertainment to turn people away from focusing on current problems

- Health crises and ethical questions of who should receive health care and who pays

Economic

- Current global economic crises and their causes and consequences

- Successes and stresses of global economic development

- Global poverty and hunger

- Reform of World Bank and the International Monetary Fund, focusing particularly on international coordination of macroeconomic policy

- Global economic imbalances and their affects on the U.S. dollar

- Monetary integration in Europe and elsewhere

- Trade reform

- Development gap and ways of closing it

- Intellectual property rights in an increasingly technological and global world

Geographic

- Impact of environmental disasters like oil spills, eathquakes, and tsunamis. (e.g., Japan, Haiti)

- Impact of global climate change

- Mass migrations and demographic challenge

- Global environmental crisis (e.g., Cherynobyl and Three Mile Island nuclear disasters, Gulf Oil crisis, Japanese nuclear crisis)

- Genetic engineering of food and the future

- Creation of sustainable societies

ECONOMICS

The teacher understands the concepts and processes of government and the responsibilities of citizenship; knows how people organize economic systems to produce, distribute, and consume goods and services; and applies social science skills to information, ideas, and issues related to government and economics.

- Knows key terms and basic concepts of economics (e.g., supply and demand, scarcity and choice, money and resources)

- Understands how economics effects population, resources, and technology

- Understands the government's role in economics and impact of economics on government

How Resources Affect Economic Choices

A basic understanding relating to economics is that wants are unlimited while resources are limited. When resources are limited, the limitation affects prices (the amount of money needed to buy goods, services, or resources). Therefore, individuals and institutions must make choices when purchasing. These seemingly local decisions may affect other people and even other nations.

A true sense of global interdependence results from an understanding of the relationship between local decisions and global issues. For example, individual or community actions regarding waste disposal or recycling can affect the availability of resources worldwide. A country's fuel standards can affect air pollution, oil supplies, and gas prices. The government can provide the legal structure and help needed to maintain competition, redistribute income, reallocate resources, and promote stability. There are two main types of resources: economic resources and human resources.

Basic Principles of Economy

Economics is a social science that analyzes the principles that regulate the production, distribution, and consumption of resources in society. It emphasizes how these principles operate within the economic choices of individuals, households, businesses, and governments. Economics can be divided into two main areas: macroeconomics and microeconomics. *Macroeconomics* is the study of the economy at the world, regional, state, and local levels. Some of the topics include reasons and ways to control inflation, causes of unemployment, and economic growth in general. *Microeconomics* deals with specific issues related to the decision-making process at the household, firm, or industry levels.

Theory of Supply and Demand

This theory of supply and demand states that prices vary based on balance between the availability of a product or service at a certain price (supply) and the desire of potential purchasers to pay that price (demand). This balance of supply and demand can occur naturally or be created artificially. An example of an artificially created balance is the intentional destruction of a surplus of a given product on the world market to maintain the price level. Another way is to control the production and availability of the product to create a scarcity of a product. For instance, the Organization of Petroleum Exporting Countries (OPEC) often reduces its production of oil to cause an increase in price.

Goods and Services

The use of machines increases the availability of goods and services to the population. This kind of production can decrease the cost of producing the goods and consequently its price. For example, as a result of the division of labor and the use of assembly lines developed by Eli Whitney in 1799, production costs of manufactured goods decreased and productivity increased. Mass production that came as a result of the Industrial Revolution made contemporary families and children more likely to become consumers rather than producers. However, before the Industrial Revolution, especially in colonial America, children were used to produce goods and contribute to the group.

Free Enterprise

Free enterprise is an economic and political doctrine of the capitalist system. The concept is based on the premise that the economy can regulate itself in a freely competitive market through the relationship of supply and demand, and with minimum governmental intervention. One of the main benefits of the system of free enterprise is the competition among businesses that results in a greater choice and better prices for consumers. The system of free enterprise has led to globalization. *Globalization* can be defined as a continuous increase of cross-border financial, economic, and social activities. It implies some level of economic interdependence among individuals, financial entities, and nations. As a result of globalization, trade barriers have been eliminated and tariffs imposed on imported products have been largely discontinued. In a global market, it is difficult to determine the origins of products. For example, Toyota from Japan and Ford from the United States joined forces to build cars using parts and labor from Mexico.

The concept of *economic interdependence* describes a positive, close connection between producers and consumers of goods and services within a nation or across nations. This economic interdependence has guided nations to establish large markets of free trade zones like the European Union (EU) trade agreement and the North American Free Trade Agreement (NAFTA) for Canada, Mexico, and the United States. The members of the European Union went a step further; in 2002 they adopted a common currency for the Union—the euro. As a result of this alliance, the euro is today one of the strongest currencies in the world.

Money and Banking

Under the presidency of Woodrow Wilson, the Federal Reserve System was established. The main purpose of this institution is to keep the banking industry strong to ensure a supply of currency. The Federal Reserve is run by the Federal Reserve Board of Governors, a seven-member body appointed to a four-year term, with the option of being reappointed to a maximum of fourteen-year terms. Alan Greenspan served as chairman of the Federal Reserve Board from 1987 to 2006. He finished an unexpired term and then served for a full fourteen-year term for a total of eighteen and a half years. The current chair is Ben S. Bernanke. His term as chairman will expire in January 2014. The main function of the Federal Reserve Bank is to promote fiscal stability and economic growth in the nation and to regulate inflation and deflation. The Board of Governors controls the flow of money and sets the interest rate that banks use to lend money. They increase the interest rate to control inflation and lower the interest rate when business slows down.

Inflation and Deflation

Inflation reduces the purchasing power of money, which technically affects the value of the currency. Countries generally devalue their currency to keep up with inflation. Deflation is the opposite of inflation: the purchasing power of money increases, thereby lowering the prices of goods and services. In a period of deflation, consumers benefit but industry suffers. The Federal Reserve controls the flow of money and keeps a healthy balance between inflation and deflation.

American Federal Income Tax System

In 1913, the Sixteenth Amendment of the U.S. Constitution allowed the imposition of direct taxation of citizens. This direct taxation is known as the federal income tax.

Interdependence of State, National, and World Economies

Taking Texas as an example, let's looks at how interdependency works. The economy of Texas is based primarily on telecommunications, software, financial services, business products and services, semiconductors, biotechnology, and oil and coal. Agriculture and ranching are still viable economic activities, but they are no longer carrying the economy. A large percentage of these products are exported to members of NAFTA—Mexico and Canada—and to the world markets. According to the Texas Economic Update, if Texas were a nation, it would rank as the eighth-largest economy in the world (Strayhorn 2004).

The Texas economy relies heavily on exports of goods and services. From 2002 through 2005, Texas was ranked as the number one state in terms of export revenues (BIDC 2006). Without its exports, the Texas economy could not sustain its growth. Because of the interdependence of state and global economies, political turmoil and economic problems in the world can have a direct impact on the Texas economy. For example, because part of the economy of Texas is based on petroleum, the decisions of OPEC have a direct impact on the state's economy.

Economic resources. The land (natural), labor (human), capital, and entrepreneurial ability used in the production of goods and services; productive agents; factors of production.

Human resources. The physical and mental talents and efforts of people; these resources are necessary to help produce goods and services.

The result of combining resources may be entrepreneurship. As a human resource that also takes advantage of economic resources to create a product, **entrepreneurship** is characterized by nonroutine decisions, innovation, and the willingness to take risks.

Characteristics of Different Economic Institutions

Two important higher-order thinking skills that teachers should encourage in their students are comparing and contrasting. The study of various economic institutions is an ideal place to work with these two skills. The following are the main economic institutions of the United States: banks, credit unions, the Federal Reserve System, and the stock market.

Banks. Banks serve anyone in the general public. Small groups of investors who expect a certain return on their investments own the banks. Only the investors have voting privileges; customers do not have voting rights, cannot be elected board members, and do not participate in governing the institution. The Federal Deposit Insurance Corporation insures the banks. Typically, banks do not share information, ideas, or resources.

Credit unions. Credit unions are owned by members. Each person who deposits money is a member, not a customer. Surplus earnings go to the members in higher dividends, low-cost or free services, and lower loan rates. The National Credit Union Share Insurance Fund insures credit unions. All credit unions share ideas, information, and resources.

Federal Reserve System. The Federal Reserve System is the central banking system of the United States. It has a central board of governors in Washington, D.C. There are 12 Federal Reserve Bank districts in major cities throughout the nation. The district banks issue bank notes, lend money to member banks, maintain reserves, supervise member banks, and help set the national monetary policy.

Stock market. The stock market is an abstract concept. It is the mechanism that enables the trading of company stocks. It is different from the **stock exchange**, which is a corporation in the business of bringing together stock buyers and sellers.

The Role of Markets

A **market** is the interaction between potential buyers and sellers of goods and services. Money is the usual medium of exchange. **Market economies** have no central authority; custom plays a very small role. Every consumer makes buying decisions based on his or her own needs, desires, and income; individual self-interest rules. Every producer decides personally what goods or services to produce, what price to charge, what resources to employ, and what production methods to use. Profits motivate the producers. There is vigorous competition in a market economy. **Supply and demand** may affect the availability of resources needed for production, distribution, and consumption.

After production, the producer ideally distributes the product to the places where consumers need or want the product—and have the money to pay for the goods or services. In the United States, there is a large and active government (command) sector, but there is a greater emphasis on the market economy.

The following are the major types of economies in the world today:

Command economies. Command economies rely on a central authority to make decisions. The central authority may be a dictator or a democratically constituted government. Although a command economy relies mainly on the government to direct economic activity, there is a small market sector as well.

Traditional economies. Traditional economies largely rely on custom to determine production and distribution issues. While not static, traditional systems are slow to change and are not well-equipped to propel a society into sustained growth. Many of the poorer countries of the developing world have traditional systems.

Mixed economies. Mixed economies contain elements of each of the two previously defined systems. All real-world economies are mixed economies, but the proportions of the mixture can vary greatly.

Capitalist economies. Capitalist economies produce resources owned by individuals.

Socialist economies. Socialist economies produce resources owned collectively by society. In other words, resources are under the control of the government.

Efficiency occurs when a society produces the types and quantities of goods and services that most satisfy its people. Failure to do so wastes resources. **Technical efficiency** occurs when a society is able to use its resources to the best advantage and thus produce the most types and the largest quantity of goods and services. Again, failure to do so wastes resources. **Equity** occurs when the distribution of goods and services conforms to a society's notions of "fairness." These goals often determine the type of economic system that a country has.

Factors Affecting Consumer Decisions

Adam Smith (1723–1790) was a Scottish economist whose writings may have inaugurated the modern era of economic analysis. Published in 1776, *An Inquiry into the Nature and Causes of the Wealth of Nations* is an analysis of a market economy.

Smith believed that a market economy was a superior form of organization from the standpoint of both economic progress and human liberty. Smith acknowledged that **self-interest** was a dominant motivating force in a market economy; this self-interest, he said, was ultimately consistent with the **public interest**. An "invisible hand" guided market participants to act in ways that promoted the public interest. **Profits** may be the main concern of firms, but only firms that **satisfy** consumer demand and offer **suitable prices** earn profits. Goods and services refer to things that satisfy human **needs**, **wants**, or **desires**. **Goods** are tangible items, such as food, cars, and clothing; **services** are intangible items such as education and health care. A market is the interaction between potential buyers and sellers of goods and services. **Money** is usually the medium of exchange. The **supply** of a good is the quantity of that good that producers offer at a certain price. The collection of all such points for every price is the **supply curve**. **Demand** for a good is the quantity of a good that consumers are willing and able to purchase at a certain price. The **demand curve** is the combination of quantity and price, at all price levels.

Economic Interdependence Among Nations

Understanding global interdependence begins with recognizing that world regions include economic, political, historical, ecological, linguistic, and cultural regions. This understanding should include knowledge of military and economic alliances such as NATO, of cartels, and of the ways in which their existence affects political and economic policies within regions. Knowledge of world regions and alliances leads to identification of issues that affect people worldwide. Common issues that affect people everywhere include **finances**, **movement of labor**, **trade**, food production, human rights, use of natural resources, prejudice, and poverty.

A true sense of global interdependence results from an understanding of the relationship between local decisions and global issues; for example, how individual or community actions regarding waste disposal or recycling can affect the availability of resources worldwide. Fuel emission standards, for example, can affect air pollution, oil supplies, and gas prices. **Microeconomics** focuses on problems specific to a household, firm, or industry, rather than national or global issues. Microeconomics gives particular emphasis to how these units make decisions and the consequences of those decisions. **Macroeconomics** is the study of the economy as a whole. Some of the topics considered include inflation, unemployment, and economic growth. **Economic theory** is an explanation of why certain economic phenomena occur. For example, there are theories explaining the rate of inflation, how many hours people choose to work, and the amount of goods and

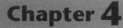

services a specific country will import. Economic theory is essentially a set of statements about cause-and-effect relationships in the economy.

Human, Natural, and Capital Resources and How These Resources Are Used in the Production of Goods and Services

Necessary for the production of goods and services are human resources, natural resources, and capital resources. **Human resources** are the people employed in a business or organization; in other words, a firm's human resources are its personnel. Originally, the term for human resources was *labor*. **Natural resources** are the material sources of wealth. Examples of natural or material resources are timber, fresh water, and mineral deposits that occur in a natural state and have economic value.

The word *capital* comes from the Latin word *caput*, which means "head." In economics, capital originally meant the profit that one made; the measure of profit was probably heads (*caput*) of cattle. In finance and economics today, **capital** means how much real, usable money a person or a company has.

How Transportation and Communication Networks Contribute to the Level of Economic Development in Different Regions

Economics is the study of society's choices among a limited amount of resources to attain the highest practical satisfaction. It is the allocation of scarce resources among competing ends.

Because people across the globe can now interact with each other instantaneously, the choices available to them throughout the world are more readily apparent today than they have been in the past. For example, advances in communication—especially through the development of satellites—made it possible for someone in Los Angeles to witness the devastation Hurricane Katrina wrought on the Gulf Coast in August 2005 and to become aware of the wants and needs there. Similarly, a person in Tokyo can see the goods and products readily available to American consumers in the newscasts and movies shown in Japan. People in New York can pick up the phone and call a person in London without delay to discuss the latest automobile designs. It is evident that people can see and hear about the goods and services available in other parts of the world; such knowledge affects the needs and wants of the world's people. Convenient transportation and even world travel is now possible for a large number of people throughout the world. Around the globe, people are becoming more aware of the world's products, services, and even clothing styles as they see people who live an ocean away using the products, services, and clothing. Even fast-food chains are familiar throughout the globe. As people become aware of lifestyles in other places, their wants and needs may change. People may aspire to what they perceive as a higher economic level. Transportation and communication networks, therefore, have helped initiate many changes in people's needs and wants and have ultimately contributed to the economic development of many regions.

REFERENCES

Alvarez, Lizette. "Census Director Marvels at the New Portrait of America." *New York Times*, January 1, 2001.

Cayne, Bernard S., ed. *Merit Students Encyclopedia*. Chicago: Crowell-Collier, 1969.

Chitwood, Oliver Perry, Frank Lawrence Owsley, and H. C. Nixon. *The United States: From Colony to World Power*. New York: D. Van Nostrand, 1949.

Congress for Kids. "Constitution: Amendments. *www.congressforkids.net/Constitution_ amendments.htm*.

Davis, Anita Price. *North Carolina during the Great Depression: A Documentary Portrait of a Decade*. Jefferson, NC: McFarland, 2003.

Florida Smart. "Florida Population and Demographics." *www.floridasmart.com/facts/ demographics.htm*.

Gordon, W. J. J. *Synectics*. New York: Harper and Row, 1961.

Halsey, William D., and Bernard Johnston, eds. *Merit Students Encyclopedia*. New York: Macmillan, 1991.

Harrington, Michael. *The Other America: Poverty in the United States*. New York: Macmillan, 1962.

Huitt, W. "Critical Thinking: An Overview." *Educational Psychology Interactive*. Valdosta, GA. 1998. *http://chiron.valdosta.edu/whuitt/col/cogsys/critthnk.html*. Last accessed July 11, 2008.

Martin, Philip L. "Immigration in the United States." Institute of European Studies, University of California, Berkeley. *http://ies.berkeley.edu/pubs/workingpapers/ay0102. html*.

Myrdal, Gunnar with the assistance of Richard Sterner and Arnold Rose. *An American Dilemma: The Negro Problem and Modern Democracy*. New York: Harper and Brothers Publishers, 1944.

NATO Official Homepage. *www.nato.int*

Schieffer, Bob. "Government Failed the People." *CBS News* (September 4, 2005).

Schug, Mark C., and R. Beery. *Teaching Social Studies in the Elementary.* Prospect Heights, IL: Waveland Press, 1987.

Schuncke, George M. *Elementary Social Studies: Knowing, Doing, Caring.* New York: Macmillan, 1988.

Smith, Adam. *An Inquiry into the Nature and Causes of the Wealth of Nations.* Dublin: Whitestone. 1776.

"United Nations Educational, Scientific, and Cultural Organization (UNESCO)," *http:// portal.unesco.org.* Last accessed July 16, 2008.

U.S. Census Bureau, *Current Population Survey*, March 2003. *www.census.gov/ population/socdemo/foreign/p20-534/tab0314.txt.* Last accessed July 16, 2008.

U.S. Census Bureau. "Countries of Birth of the Foreign-Born Population, 1850-2000." *Profile of the Foreign-Born Population in the United States: 2000. www.Infoplease. com/ipa/A0900547.html.* Last accessed July 11, 2008.

U.S. Census Bureau. "State and County QuickFacts: Florida." *http://quickfacts.census. gov/qfd/states/12000.html.*

Woolever, Roberta, and Kathryn P. Scott. *Active Learning in Social Studies: Promoting Cognitive and Social Growth.* Glenview, IL: Scott, Foresman, 1988.

Social Studies II
United States History, Government, Citizenship and Democracy

UNITED STATES HISTORY

European Exploration and Colonization

In 1497, King Henry VIII of England sponsored a voyage by **John Cabot** to try to discover a northwest passage through the New World to the Orient. However, the English made no real attempt to settle in the New World until nearly a century later. By the 1600s, the English became interested in colonizing the New World for several reasons.

Many people in England emigrated overseas because the country's population was increasing and because much of the land was being used for raising sheep for wool rather than for growing foodstuffs for survival. Scarce opportunities, like those for buying land, were primary motivators for emigration from England. Some people in England left their homeland because of the religious turmoil that engulfed England after the beginning of the Protestant Reformation. In addition to converts to Lutheranism and Calvinism, a major emigrating group was the Puritans, who called for reforms to "purify" the church.

Mercantilism also provided a motive for exploration and for the establishment of colonies. According to mercantile theories, an industrialized nation needed an inexpensive source of raw materials and markets for finished products. Colonies provided a way to obtain raw materials and to guarantee a market for industrial goods. Economic reasons, among others, motivated the French and the Dutch to explore and establish colonies in the New World.

In 1609, the year after the first English settlement, the French established a colony in Quebec. Overall, far fewer French settlers traveled to the New World than did English settlers, but the French were able to exercise a tremendous influence through the establishment of strong ties with the natives. The French created trading partnerships and a vast trading network; they often intermarried with the local native population. The Dutch financed an English explorer, **Henry Hudson**, who claimed for Holland the territory that is now New York. The Dutch settlements along the Hudson, Delaware, and Connecticut rivers developed into the colony of New Netherlands and established a vast trading network that effectively separated the English colonies of Jamestown and Plymouth.

One reason that English settlements became more prominent after 1600 was the defeat of the Spanish fleet, the supposedly invincible Armada, by the English in 1588. The changing power balance on the seas encouraged the English to increase their exploration and to attempt colonization of the Americas. The first few colonies founded by the English in America did not flourish. Sir Humphrey Gilbert, who had obtained a six-year grant giving him the exclusive rights to settle any unclaimed land in America, was planning to establish a colony in Newfoundland, but a storm sank his ship. Instead, **Sir Walter Raleigh** received the six-year grant. Raleigh explored the North American coast and named the territory through which he traveled Virginia, in honor of the "Virgin Queen" Elizabeth I of England. In addition, Raleigh convinced his cousin Sir Grenville to establish a colony on the island of Roanoke. **Roanoke** was off the coast of what later became North Carolina. The first settlers lived there for a year while Sir Grenville returned to England for supplies and additional settlers. However, when Sir Francis Drake arrived in Roanoke nearly a year later and found that Sir Grenville had not yet returned, the colonists left on his ship and abandoned the settlement. In 1587, Raleigh sent another group of colonists to Roanoke, but a war with Spain broke out in 1588 and kept him from returning until 1590. When Raleigh returned to Roanoke, the colonists had vanished and had left only one clue: a single word, *Croatan*, carved into a tree. This word could have referred to a nearby settlement of natives whom they might have joined or who might have attacked them. This suggested a number of possibilities in regard to the missing settlers; conclusive proof of their fate was never found.

Colonization: The Jamestown Settlement

In 1606, King James I of England granted to the Virginia Company a charter for exploration and colonization. This charter marked the beginning of ventures sponsored by merchants rather than directly by the Crown. The charter of the Virginia Company had two branches. James I gave one branch to the English city of Plymouth, which had the rights to the northern portion of territory on the eastern coast of North America, and he granted the London branch of the company the rights to the southern portion.

Considerable difficulties prevented the English from founding and maintaining a permanent settlement in North America. The Plymouth Company failed to establish a lasting settlement. The company itself ran out of money, and the settlers who had gone to the New World gave up and abandoned their established Sagadahoc Colony in Maine. Having decided to colonize the Chesapeake Bay area, the London Company sent three ships with about 104 sailors to that area in 1607. The company's ships sailed up a river, which they named the James in honor of the English king, and they established the fort and permanent settlement of Jamestown. The London Company and the men who settled Jamestown were hoping to find a northwest passage to Asia, gold, and silver or to be able to find lands capable of producing valuable goods, such as grapes, oranges, or silk. The colony at Jamestown did not allow the settlers to accomplish any of those things. Its location on the river, which became contaminated every spring, led to the outbreak of diseases such as typhoid, dysentery, and malaria. More than half the colonists died the first year, and by the spring of 1609, only one-third of the total number of colonists who had joined the colony were still alive.

The survival of the colony initially was largely accomplished through the efforts of **Captain John Smith**. Smith was a soldier who turned the colony's focus from exploration to obtaining food. Initially, Smith was able to obtain corn from the local Indians led by **Powhatan** and his 12-year-old daughter, **Pocahontas**. Smith also forced all able men in the colony to work four hours a day in the wheat fields. Attempts by the London Company to send additional settlers and supplies encountered troubles and delays. **Thomas Gates** and some 600 settlers, who left for Jamestown in 1609, ran aground on Bermuda and had to build a new ship. Although some new settlers did arrive in Jamestown, disease continued to shrink the population. When a seriously injured Smith had to return to England, his departure deprived the colony of its most effective and resourceful leader. It was not long after Smith left that the colonists provoked a war with Powhatan, who was beginning to tire of the colonists' demands for corn. Powhatan realized that the settlers intended to stay indefinitely and might challenge the Indians for control of the surrounding territory. Gates finally arrived in June 1610 with only 175 of the original 600 settlers. He found only 60 colonists who had survived the war with the Indians and the harsh winter of 1610, during which they had minimal food and other resources. Gates decided to abandon Jamestown and was sailing down the river with the surviving colonists on board when he encountered the new governor from England, **Thomas West**, Baron de la Warr. Gates and West returned to Jamestown, imposed martial law, responded to Indian attacks, and survived a five-year war with the Indians. Although the war did not end until 1614, when the colonists were able to negotiate a settlement by holding Pocahontas hostage, the situation in Jamestown began to improve in 1610. Some of the settlers went to healthier locations, and in 1613 one of them, **John Rolfe**, married Pocahontas. In 1614, the settlers planted a mild strain of tobacco, which gave them a crop they could sell for cash. The Crown issued two new charters that allowed Virginia to extend its borders all the way to the Pacific and made the London Company a joint-stock company. Changes in the company led to a new treasurer, **Sir Edwin Sandy**, who tried to reform Virginia.

Sandy encouraged settlers in Virginia to try to produce grapes and silkworms and to diversify the colony's economy in other ways. Sandy also replaced martial law with English common law. The colonists established a council to make laws, and settlers now had the right to own land. By 1623, about 4,000 additional settlers had arrived in Virginia. Attempts to produce and sell crops other than tobacco failed, however, and the arrival of large numbers of new colonists provoked renewed conflict with the Indians. A major Indian attack launched in March 1622 killed 347 colonists. Investors in the London Company withdrew their capital and appealed to the king, and a royal commission visited the colony. As a result of this investigation, the king declared the London Company bankrupt and assumed direct control of Virginia in 1624. Virginia became the first royal colony, and the Crown appointed a governor and a council to oversee its administration.

Three trends continued after the Crown assumed control. The first was unrelenting conflict with the Indians. By 1632, through war and raids, the colonists had killed or driven out most of the Indians in the area immediately around Jamestown. The other two trends were the yearly influx of thousands of new settlers and the high death rate in the colony. Despite the high mortality rate, the population of the colony began to increase gradually. The expansion of tobacco production led to a demand for labor, and thousands of the young men who came were indentured servants. In exchange for their passage to America and food and shelter during their terms of service, these men were bound to work for their masters for four or five years. After that time, they gained their freedom and often a small payment to help them become established. Most of these men were not able to participate in the running of the colony even after they became free, but some were able to acquire land.

In 1634, the Crown divided Virginia into counties, each with appointed justices and the right to fill all other positions. Under this type of system, individuals from a few wealthy families tended to dominate the government. Most of the counties became Anglican, and the colony continued to elect representatives to its House of Burgesses, an assembly that met with the governor to discuss issues of common law. The king, however, refused to recognize the colony's House of Burgesses. After 1660, the colony became even more dominated by the wealthiest 15 percent of the population, and these individuals and their sons continued to be the only colonists to serve as justices and burgesses. Settlement of the colonies continued, primarily for religious and economic reasons. Conflict between the colonists and the natives was constant.

Growth of the Slave Trade

The shortage of labor in the southern colonies and a drop in the number of people coming to the colonies as indentured servants forced the colonists to search for other sources of labor. Although the colonists began using African servants and slaves almost immediately after settling in the New World, the slave trade and the slave population in British North America remained small in the first half of the seventeenth century. Toward the end of the seventeenth century, increasing numbers of slaves from Africa became available, and the demand for them in North America further stimulated the growth of the transatlantic slave trade.

By the nineteenth century, millions of Africans had been forcibly taken from their native lands and sold into perpetual slavery. The Europeans bought slaves at forts that the slave traders had established on the African coast; the Europeans packed the slaves as closely as possible into the lower regions of ships for the long journey to the Americas. Chained slaves traveled in deplorable unsanitary conditions and received only enough food and water to keep them alive. Many slaves died during this Middle Passage voyage. Plantation owners in the Caribbean, Brazil, or North America bought the slaves to do the work. It was only after 1697 that English colonists began to buy large numbers of slaves. By 1760, the slave population had reached approximately a quarter of a million, with most of the slaves concentrated in the southern colonies. Slave labor replaced indentured servitude, and a race-based system of perpetual slavery developed. Colonial assemblies began to pass "slave codes" in the eighteenth century. These codes identified all non-whites or dark-skinned people as slaves, made their condition permanent, and legalized slavery in British North America.

Salem Witch Trials

During this period of increasing tensions brought about by fears of the occult, intolerance, and conflicts between the religious community and some less-understood individuals, several areas held witchcraft trials. In Salem, Massachusetts, a group of young girls accused servants from West India and older white members of the community, mostly women, of exercising powers that Satan had given to them. Other towns also experienced turmoil and charged residents with witchcraft. In Salem alone, the juries pronounced 19 people guilty; in 1692, after the execution of all 19 victims, the girls admitted their stories were not true.

The witchcraft trials illustrate the highly religious nature of New England society, but they also suggest that individuals who did not conform to societal expectations were at risk. Most of the accused were outspoken women who were often critical of their communities, were older, and were either widowed or unmarried. Some of these women had acquired property despite the accepted views and limitations regarding women's role in society.

Religion in the Colonies and the Great Awakening

The religious nature of colonial settlers did not lead to the kind of intolerance or persecution that had plagued Europe since the Reformation. Conflict among various religious groups did break out occasionally, but British North America enjoyed a far greater degree of religious toleration than anywhere else. Among the reasons this toleration existed were that several religious groups had immigrated to North America and that every colony, except Virginia and Maryland, ignored the laws establishing the Church of England as the official faith of the colony. Even among the Puritans, differences in religious opinion led to the establishment of different denominations.

Although there was some religious toleration, Protestants still tended to view Roman Catholics as threatening rivals. In Maryland, Catholics numbered about 3,000, the largest population of all the colonies, and were the victims of persecution. Jews were often victims of persecution; they could not vote or hold office in any of the colonies, and only in Rhode Island could they practice the Jewish religion openly. The other main trends in addition to toleration were the westward spread of communities, the rise of cities, and a decline in religious piousness. This sense of the weakening of religious authority and faithfulness led to the Great Awakening. The Great Awakening refers to a period beginning in the 1730s in which several well-known preachers traveled through British North America giving speeches and arguing for the need to revive religious piety and closer relationships with God. The main message of the preachers was that everyone has the potential, regardless of past behavior, to reestablish their relationship with God. This message appealed to many women and younger sons of landowners who stood to inherit very little. The best-known preacher during this period was **Jonathan Edwards**. Edwards denounced some current beliefs as doctrines of easy salvation. At his church in Northampton, Massachusetts, Edwards sermonized about the absolute sovereignty of God, predestination, and salvation by grace alone.

The Great Awakening further divided religion in America by creating distinctions among New Light groups (revivalists), Old Light groups (traditionalists), and new groups that incorporated elements of both. The various revivalists, or New Light groups, did not agree on every issue. Some revivalists denounced education and learning from books, while others founded schools in the belief that education was a means of furthering religion. While some individuals were stressing a need for renewed spiritual focus, others were beginning to embrace the ideas of the Enlightenment. As discussed earlier, the Scientific Revolution had demonstrated the existence of natural laws that operated in nature, and enlightened thinkers began to argue that humans had the ability to improve their own situation through the use of rational thought and acquired knowledge. Intellectuals of the **Enlightenment** shifted the focus from God to humans, introduced the idea of progress, and argued that people could improve their own situations and make decisions on how to live rather than just having faith in God and waiting for salvation and a better life after death.

Enlightenment thought had a tremendous impact on the North American colonists, who began to establish more schools, encourage the acquisition of knowledge, and become more interested in gaining scientific knowledge. The colleges founded in North America taught the scientific theories held by **Copernicus**, who argued that the planets rotated around the sun not the earth, and **Sir Isaac Newton**, who introduced the key principles of physics, including gravity. The colonists did not just learn European theories. **Benjamin Franklin** was among the colonists who began to carry out their own experiments and form their own theories. Franklin experimented with electricity and was able to demonstrate in 1752, by using a kite, that electricity and lightning were the same. Scientific theories also led to inoculations against smallpox. The Puritan theologian **Cotton Mather** convinced the population of Boston that injections with a small amount of the smallpox virus would build up their resistance to the disease and reduce the likelihood of reinfection. Leading theologians and scientists spread European scientific ideas and developed their own theories and applications using their acquired knowledge.

The American Revolution

The Coming of the American Revolution

In 1764, George Grenville pushed through Parliament the **Sugar Act** (the Revenue Act), which aimed to raise revenue by taxing goods imported by Americans. The **Stamp Act** (1765) imposed a direct tax on the colonists for the first time. By requiring Americans to purchase revenue stamps on everything from newspapers to legal documents, the Stamp Act would have created an impossible drain on hard currency in the colonies.

Americans reacted first with restrained and respectful petitions and pamphlets in which they pointed out that "taxation without representation is tyranny." The colonists began to limit their purchase of imported goods. From there, resistance progressed to stronger protests that eventually became violent. In October 1765, delegates from nine colonies met as the Stamp Act Congress, passed moderate resolutions against the act, and asserted that Americans could not be taxed without the consent of their representatives. The colonists now ceased all importation. In March 1766, Parliament repealed the Stamp Act. At the same time, however, it passed the **Declaratory Act**, which claimed for Parliament the power to tax or make laws for the Americans "in all cases whatsoever." In 1766, Parliament passed a program of taxes on items imported into the colonies. The taxes came to be known as the Townsend duties, a name that came from Britain's chancellor of the exchequer, Charles Townsend. American reaction was at first slow, but the sending of troops aroused them to resistance.

Again the colonies halted importation, and soon British merchants were calling on Parliament to repeal the Townsend duties. In March 1770, Parliament repealed all the taxes except that on tea; Parliament wanted to prove that it had the right to tax the colonies if it so desired. When Parliament ended the **Tea Act** in 1773, a relative peace ensued. In desperate financial condition—partially because the Americans were buying smuggled Dutch tea rather than the taxed British product—the British East India Company sought and obtained from Parliament concessions that allowed it to ship tea directly to the colonies rather than only by way of Britain. The result would be that the East India Company tea, even with the tax, would be cheaper than smuggled Dutch tea. The company hoped that the colonists would thus buy the tea—tax and all—save the East India Company, and tacitly accept Parliament's right to tax them. The Americans, however, proved resistant to this approach. Rather than acknowledge Parliament's right to tax, they refused to buy the cheaper tea and resorted to various methods, including tar and feathers, to prevent the collection of the tax on tea.

In most ports, Americans did not allow ships carrying the tea to land. In Boston, however, the pro-British governor **Thomas Hutchinson** forced a confrontation by ordering Royal Navy vessels to prevent the tea ships from leaving the harbor. After 20 days, this would, by law, result in selling the cargoes at auction and paying the tax. The night before the time was to expire, December 16, 1773, Bostonians thinly disguised as Native Americans boarded the ships and threw the tea into the harbor. This was the **Boston Tea Party**.

The British responded with four acts collectively titled the **Coercive Acts** (1774), in which they strengthened their control over the colonists. The **First Continental Congress** (1774) met in response to the acts. The First Continental Congress called for strict nonimportation and rigorous preparation of local militia companies.

The War for Independence

British troops went to Massachusetts, which the Crown had officially declared to be in a state of rebellion. General Thomas Gage received orders to arrest the leaders of the resistance or, failing that, to provoke any sort of confrontation that would allow him to turn British military might loose on the Americans. Americans detected the movement of Gage's troops toward Concord, however, and dispatch riders, like **Paul Revere** and **William Dawes**, spread the news throughout the countryside.

In Lexington, about 70 **minutemen** (trained militiamen who would respond at a moment's notice) awaited the British on the village green. A shot was fired; it is unknown which side fired first. This became **"the shot heard 'round the world."** The British opened fire and charged. Casualties occurred on both sides. The following month, the Americans tightened the noose around Boston by fortifying Breed's Hill (a spur of Bunker Hill). The British were determined to remove them by a frontal attack. Twice thrown back, the British finally succeeded when the Americans ran out of ammunition. There were more than 1,000 British casualties in what turned out to be the bloodiest battle of the war (June 17, 1775), yet the British had gained very little and remained "bottled up" in Boston.

Congress put **George Washington** (1732–1799) in charge of the army; called for more troops; and adopted the Olive Branch Petition, which pleaded with **King George III** to intercede with Parliament to restore peace. However, the king gave his approval to the Prohibitory Act, declaring the colonies in rebellion and no longer under his protection. Preparations began for full-scale war against America. In 1776, the colonists formed two committees to establish independence and a national government. One was to work out a framework for a national government. The other was to draft a statement of the reasons for declaring independence. The statement, called the **Declaration of Independence**, was primarily the work of Thomas Jefferson (1743–1826) of Virginia. It was a restatement of political ideas by then commonplace in America and showed why the former colonists felt justified in separating from Great Britain. Congress formally adopted the Declaration of Independence on **July 4, 1776**. The British landed that summer at New York City. Washington, who had anticipated the move, was waiting for them. However, the undertrained, underequipped, and badly outnumbered American army was no match for the British and had to retreat. By December, what was left of Washington's army had made its way into Pennsylvania.

With his small army melting away as demoralized soldiers deserted, Washington decided on a bold move. On Christmas night 1776, his army crossed the **Delaware River** and struck the Hessians (German mercenaries who often served with the British) at **Trenton, New Jersey**. Washington's troops easily defeated the Hessians, still groggy from their hard-drinking Christmas party. A few days later, Washington defeated a British force at **Princeton, New Jersey**. The Americans regained much of New Jersey from the British and saved the American army from disintegration. Hoping to weaken Britain, France began making covert shipments of arms to the Americans early in the war. These French shipments were vital for the Americans. The American victory at Saratoga, New York, convinced the French to join openly in the war against England. Eventually, the Spanish (1779) and the Dutch (1780) joined as well. The final peace agreement between the new United States and Great Britain became known as the Treaty of Paris of 1783. Its terms stipulated the following:

1. The recognition by the major European powers, including Britain, of the United States as an independent nation

2. The establishment of America's western boundary at the Mississippi River

3. The establishment of America's southern boundary at latitude 31° north (the northern boundary of Florida)

4. The surrender of Florida to Spain and the retainment of Canada by Britain

5. The enablement of private British creditors to collect any debts owed by United States citizens

6. The recommendation of Congress that the states restore confiscated loyalist property

New Politicians, New Governments, and Social Change

After the adoption and failure of the Articles of Confederation, Congress adopted a new constitution and the Americans elected George Washington as president under its guidelines.

The Federalist Era. George Washington received almost all the votes of the presidential electors. **John Adams** (1735–1826) received the next highest number and became the vice president. After a triumphant journey from his home at Mount Vernon in Virginia, Washington attended his inauguration in New York City, the temporary seat of government.

To oppose the antifederalists, the states ratified 10 amendments—the Bill of Rights—by the end of 1791. The first nine spelled out specific guarantees of personal freedoms, and the Tenth Amendment reserved to the states all powers not specifically withheld or granted to the federal government. **Alexander Hamilton** (1757–1804) interpreted the Constitution as having vested extensive powers in the federal government. This "implied powers" stance claimed that the federal government had all powers that the Constitution had not expressly denied it. Hamilton's was the "broad" interpretation of the Constitution. By contrast, Thomas Jefferson and **James Madison** (1751–1836) held the view that the Constitution prohibited any action not specifically permitted in the Constitution. Based on this view of government, adherents of this "strict" interpretation opposed the establishment of Hamilton's national bank. The Jeffersonian supporters, primarily under the guidance of Madison, began to organize political groups in opposition to Hamilton's program. The groups opposing Hamilton's view called themselves Democratic-Republicans or Jeffersonians.

The Federalists, Hamilton's supporters, received their strongest confirmation from the business and financial groups in the commercial centers of the Northeast and from the port cities of the South. The strength of the Democratic-Republicans lay primarily in the rural and frontier areas of the South and West. Federalist candidate John Adams won the election of 1796. The elections in 1798 increased the Federalists' majorities in both houses of Congress that used their "mandate" to enact legislation to stifle foreign influences.

The **Alien Act** raised new hurdles in the path of immigrants trying to obtain citizenship, and the **Sedition Act** widened the powers of the Adams administration to muzzle its newspaper critics. Democratic-Republicans were convinced that the Alien and Sedition

Acts were unconstitutional, but the process of deciding on the constitutionality of federal laws was as yet undefined.

The Jeffersonian Era. Thomas Jefferson and **Aaron Burr** ran for the presidency on the Democratic-Republican ticket, though not together, against John Adams and Charles Pinckney for the Federalists. Both Jefferson and Burr received the same number of votes in the electoral college, so the election went to the House of Representatives. After a lengthy deadlock, Alexander Hamilton threw his support to Jefferson. Burr had to accept the vice presidency, the result obviously intended by the electorate.

The adoption and ratification of the Twelfth Amendment in 1804 ensured that a tie vote between candidates of the same party could not again cause the confusion of the Jefferson-Burr affair. Following the constitutional mandate, an 1808 law prevented the importation of slaves. An American delegation purchased the trans-Mississippi territory from Napoleon for $15 million in April 1803 (the Louisiana Purchase), even though they had no authority to buy more than the city of New Orleans.

The War of 1812. Democratic-Republican **James Madison** won the election of 1808 over Federalist Charles Pinckney, but the Federalists gained seats in both houses of Congress.

The Native American tribes of the Northwest and the **Mississippi Valley** were resentful of the government's policy of pressured removal to the West, and the British authorities in Canada exploited their discontent by encouraging border raids against the American settlements. At the same time, the British interfered with American transatlantic shipping, including impressing sailors and capturing ships. On June 1, 1812, President Madison asked for a declaration of war, and Congress complied. After three years of inconclusive war, the British and Americans signed the Treaty of Ghent (1815). It provided for the acceptance of the status quo that had existed at the beginning of hostilities, and both sides restored their wartime conquests against the other.

The Monroe Doctrine. As Latin American nations began declaring independence, British and American leaders feared that European governments would try to restore the former New World colonies to their erstwhile royal owners. In December 1823, **President James Monroe** (1758–1831) included in his annual message to Congress a statement that the peoples of the American hemisphere were "henceforth not to be considered as subjects for future colonization by any European powers."

The Marshall Court. Chief Justice **John Marshall** (1755–1835) delivered the majority opinions in several critical decisions in the formative years of the U.S. Supreme Court. These decisions served to strengthen the power of the federal government (and of the Court itself) and restrict the powers of state governments. Here are two key examples:

- *Marbury v. Madison* (1803) established the Supreme Court's power of judicial review over federal legislation.

- In *Gibbons v. Ogden* (1824), a case involving competing steamboat companies, Marshall ruled that commerce includes navigation and that only Congress has the right to regulate commerce among states. Marshall's ruling voided the state-granted monopoly.

The Missouri Compromise. The Missouri Territory, the first territory organized from the Louisiana Purchase, applied for statehood in 1819. Because the Senate membership was evenly divided between slaveholding and free states at that time, the admission of a new state would give the voting advantage to either the North or the South. As the debate dragged on, the northern territory of Massachusetts applied for admission as the state of Maine. By combining the two admission bills, the Senate hoped to reach a compromise by admitting Maine as a free state and Missouri as a slave state. To make the Missouri Compromise palatable for the House of Representatives, the Senate added a provision prohibiting slavery in the remainder of the Louisiana Territory north of the southern boundary of Missouri (latitude 36°30′).

Jacksonian Democracy. Andrew Jackson (1767–1845), the candidate of a faction of the emerging Democratic Party, won the election of 1828. Jackson was popular with the common man. He seemed to be the prototype of the self-made Westerner: rough-hewn, violent, vindictive, with few ideas but strong convictions. He ignored his appointed cabinet officers and relied instead on the counsel of his "Kitchen Cabinet," a group of partisan supporters. He exercised his veto power more than any other president before him.

Jackson supported the removal of all Native American tribes to an area west of the Mississippi River. The **Indian Removal Act** of 1830 provided for the federal enforcement of that process. One of the results of this policy was the **Trail of Tears**, the forced march under U.S. Army escort of thousands of Cherokee Indians to the West. One-quarter or more of them, mostly women and children, perished on the journey.

The National Bank. The Bank of the United States had operated under the direction of Nicholas Biddle since 1823. He was a cautious man, and his conservative economic policy enforced conservatism among state and private banks—which many bankers resented. In

1832, Jackson vetoed the national bank's renewal, and it ceased being a federal institution in 1836.

The Antislavery Movement. In 1831, **William Lloyd Garrison** started his newspaper, *The Liberator*, and began to advocate total and immediate emancipation. He founded the New England Antislavery Society in 1832 and the American Antislavery Society in 1833. Theodore Weld pursued the same goals but advocated more gradual means.

The movement split into two wings: Garrison's radical followers and the moderates who favored "moral suasion" and petitions to Congress. In 1840, the Liberty Party, the first national antislavery party, fielded a presidential candidate on the platform of "free soil" (preventing the expansion of slavery into the new western territories).

The Role of Minorities. The women's rights movement focused on social and legal discrimination, and women like Lucretia Mott and Sojourner Truth became well-known figures on the speakers' circuit. By 1850, roughly 200,000 free blacks lived in the North and West. Prejudice restricted their lives, and "Jim Crow" laws separated the races.

Manifest Destiny and Westward Expansion. The coining of the term *Manifest Destiny* did not occur until 1844, but the belief that the destiny of the American nation was expansion all the way to the Pacific Ocean—and possibly even to Canada and Mexico—was older than that. A common conviction was that Americans should share American liberty and ideals with everyone possible, by force if necessary. In the 1830s, American missionaries followed the traders and trappers to the Oregon country and began to publicize the richness and beauty of the land. The result was the Oregon Fever of the 1840s, as thousands of settlers trekked across the Great Plains and the Rocky Mountains to settle the new Shangri-la.

Texas had been a state in the Republic of Mexico since 1822, following the Mexican revolution against Spanish control. The new Mexican government invited immigration from the North by offering land grants to Stephen Austin and other Americans. By 1835, approximately 35,000 "gringos" were homesteading on Texas land. Mexican officials saw their power base eroding as the foreigners flooded in, so they moved to tighten control through restrictions on immigration and through tax increases. The Texans responded in 1836 by proclaiming independence and establishing a new republic. Texas requested that the United States annex it. Many American citizens protested this annexation; they feared retaliation from Mexico and expressed concern about the annexation of such a large area with slavery. Congress learned that Great Britain might serve as protector for Texas, and this was a major reason for changing its vote. In 1845, after a series of failed attempts at annexation, the U.S. Congress admitted Texas to the Union.

The Mexican War

Though Mexico broke diplomatic relations with the United States immediately after Texas's admission to the Union, there was still hope of a peaceful settlement. In the fall of 1845, President **James K. Polk** (1795–1849) sent **John Slidell** to Mexico City with a proposal for a peaceful settlement, but like other attempts at negotiation, nothing came of it. Racked by coups and countercoups, the Mexican government refused even to receive Slidell. Polk responded by sending U.S. troops into the disputed territory. On April 5, 1846, Mexican troops attacked an American patrol. When news of the clash reached Washington, Polk sought and received from Congress a declaration of war against Mexico.

Negotiated peace came with the signing of the Treaty of Guadalupe Hidalgo on February 2, 1848. Under the terms of the treaty, Mexico ceded to the United States the southwestern territory from Texas to the California coast.

Sectional Conflict and the Causes of the Civil War

The Crisis of 1850. The Mexican War had barely started when, on August 8, 1846, a freshman Democratic congressman, **David Wilmot** of Pennsylvania, introduced his **Wilmot Proviso** as a proposed amendment to a war appropriations bill. It stipulated that "neither slavery nor involuntary servitude shall ever exist" in any territory to be acquired from Mexico. The House passed the proviso, but the Senate did not; Wilmot introduced his provision again amidst increasingly acrimonious debate.

One compromise proposal called for the extension of the 36°30′ line of the Missouri Compromise westward through the Mexican cession to the Pacific, with territory north of the line closed to slavery. Another compromise solution was *popular sovereignty*, which held that the residents of each territory should decide for themselves whether to allow slavery. Having more than the requisite population and being in need of better government, California petitioned in September 1849 for admission to the Union as a free state. Southerners were furious. Long outnumbered in the House of Representatives, the South would find itself, should Congress admit California as a free state, similarly outnumbered in the Senate. At this point, the aged **Henry Clay** proposed a compromise. For the North, Congress would admit California as a free state; the land in dispute between Texas and New Mexico would go to New Mexico; popular sovereignty would decide the issue of slavery in the New Mexico and Utah territories (all of the Mexican cession outside

California); and there would be no slave trade in the District of Columbia. For the South, Congress would enact a tougher fugitive slave law, promise not to abolish slavery in the District of Columbia, and declare that it did not have jurisdiction over the interstate slave trade; the federal government would pay Texas's $10 million preannexation debt.

The Kansas-Nebraska Act. All illusion of sectional peace ended abruptly in 1854 when Senator **Stephen A. Douglas** of Illinois introduced a bill in Congress to organize the area west of Missouri and Iowa as the territories of Kansas and Nebraska on the basis of popular sovereignty. The **Kansas-Nebraska Act** aroused a storm of outrage in the North, which viewed the repeal of the Missouri Compromise as the breaking of a solemn agreement; hastened the disintegration of the Whig Party; and divided the Democratic Party along North-South lines.

Springing to life almost overnight as a result of northern fury at the Kansas-Nebraska Act was the Republican Party. This party included diverse elements whose sole unifying principle was banning slavery from all the nation's territories, confining slavery to the states where it already existed, and preventing the further spread of slavery.

The Dred Scott Decision. In *Dred Scott v. Sanford* (1857), the Supreme Court attempted to settle the slavery question. The case involved a Missouri slave, **Dred Scott**, whom the abolitionists had encouraged to sue for his freedom on the basis that his owner had taken him to a free state, Illinois, for several years and then to a free territory, Wisconsin.

The Court attempted to read the extreme southern position on slavery into the Constitution, ruling not only that Scott had no standing to sue in federal court but also that temporary residence in a free state, even for several years, did not make a slave free. In addition, the Court ruling signified that the Missouri Compromise (already a dead letter by that time) had been unconstitutional all along because Congress did not have the authority to exclude slavery from a territory, nor did territorial governments have the right to prohibit slavery.

The Election of 1860. As the 1860 presidential election approached, the Republicans met in Chicago, confident of victory and determined to do nothing to jeopardize their favorable position. Accordingly, they rejected as too radical the front-running candidate, New York Senator **William H. Seward**, in favor of Illinois's favorite son **Abraham Lincoln** (1809–1865). The platform called for federal support of a transcontinental railroad and for the containment of slavery. On Election Day, the voting went along strictly sectional lines. Lincoln led in popular votes; though he was short of a majority of popular votes, he did have the needed majority in electoral college votes and won the election.

The Secession Crisis. On December 20, 1860, South Carolina, by vote of a special convention, seceded from the Union. By February 1, 1861, six more states (Alabama, Georgia, Florida, Mississippi, Louisiana, and Texas) had followed suit.

Representatives of the seceded states met in Montgomery, Alabama, in February 1861 and declared themselves to be the Confederate States of America. They elected former secretary of war and United States senator **Jefferson Davis** (1808–1889) of Mississippi as president and Alexander Stephens (1812–1883) of Georgia as vice president.

Civil War and Reconstruction

Hostilities Begin. In his inaugural address, Lincoln urged Southerners to reconsider their actions but warned that the Union was perpetual; that states could not secede; and that he would, therefore, hold the federal forts and installations in the South. Only two remained in federal hands: Fort Pickens, off Pensacola, Florida; and Fort Sumter, in the harbor of Charleston, South Carolina.

From **Major Robert Anderson**, commander of the small garrison at Sumter, Lincoln soon received word that supplies were running low. Desiring to send in the needed supplies, Lincoln informed the governor of South Carolina of his intention but promised that no attempt would be made to send arms, ammunition, or reinforcements unless Southerners initiated hostilities. Confederate **General P. G. T. Beauregard**, acting on orders from President Davis, demanded Anderson's surrender. Anderson said he would surrender if the fort were not resupplied. Knowing supplies were on the way, the Confederates opened fire at 4:30 AM on April 12, 1861. The next day, the fort surrendered. The day following Sumter's surrender, Lincoln declared an insurrection and called for the states to provide 75,000 volunteers to put it down. In response, Virginia, Tennessee, North Carolina, and

Arkansas declared their secession. The remaining slave states—Delaware, Kentucky, Maryland, and Missouri—wavered but stayed with the Union.

The North enjoyed many advantages over the South. It had the majority of wealth and was vastly superior in industry. The North also had an advantage of almost three to one in labor; over one-third of the South's residents were slaves, whom Southerners would not use as soldiers. Unlike the South, the North received large numbers of **immigrants** during the war. The North retained control of the U.S. Navy; it could command the sea and blockade the South. Finally, the North enjoyed a much superior system of railroads.

The South did, however, have some advantages. It was vast in size and difficult to conquer. In addition, its troops would be fighting on their own ground, a fact that would give them the advantage of familiarity with the terrain and the added motivation of defending their homes and families.

The Homestead Act and the Morrill Land Grant Act. In 1862, Congress passed two highly important acts dealing with domestic affairs in the North. The Homestead Act granted 160 acres of government land free of charge to any person who would farm it for at least five years. Many of the settlers of the West used the provisions of this act. The Morrill Land Grant Act offered large amounts of the federal government's land to states that would establish "agricultural and mechanical" colleges. The founding of many of the nation's large state universities occurred under the provisions of this act.

The Emancipation Proclamation. By mid-1862, Lincoln, acting under pressure from radical elements of his own party and hoping to make a favorable impression on foreign public opinion, determined to issue the **Emancipation Proclamation**, which declared free all slaves in areas still in rebellion as of January 1, 1863. At the recommendation of William Seward, former New York senator and now his secretary of state, Lincoln waited to announce the proclamation until the North won some sort of victory. The Battle of Antietam (September 17, 1862) provided this victory.

Northern Victory

Lincoln ran on the ticket of the National Union Party—essentially, the Republican Party with the addition of loyal or "war" Democrats. His vice presidential candidate was **Andrew Johnson** (1808–1875), a loyal Democrat from Tennessee.

In September 1864, word came that **General William Sherman** (1820–1891) had taken Atlanta. The capture of this vital southern rail and manufacturing center brought an enormous boost to northern morale. Along with other northern victories that summer and fall, it ensured a resounding election victory for Lincoln and the continuation of the war to complete victory for the North. **General Robert E. Lee** (1807–1870) abandoned Richmond, Virginia, on April 3, 1865, and attempted to escape with what was left of his army. Under the command of **Ulysses S. Grant** (1822–1885), Northern forces cornered Lee's troops and forced his surrender at Appomattox, Virginia, on April 9, 1865. Other Confederate troops still holding out in various parts of the South surrendered over the next few weeks. Lincoln did not live to receive news of the final surrenders. On April 14, 1865, **John Wilkes Booth** shot Lincoln in the back of the head while the president was watching a play in Ford's Theater in Washington, D.C.

Reconstruction. In 1865, Congress created the **Freedman's Bureau** to provide food, clothing, and education and generally to look after the interests of former slaves. To restore legal governments in the seceded states, Lincoln had developed a policy that made it relatively easy for Southern states to enter the collateral process.

Congress passed a **Civil Rights Act** in 1866, declaring that all citizens born in the United States are, regardless of race, equal citizens under the law. This act became the model of the Fourteenth Amendment to the Constitution. **President Andrew Johnson** obeyed the letter but not the spirit of the Reconstruction acts. Congress, angry at his refusal to cooperate, sought in vain for grounds to impeach him. In August 1867, Johnson violated the Tenure of Office Act, which forbade the president from removing from office those officials who had been approved by the Senate. This test of the act's constitutionality took place not in the courts but in Congress. The House of Representatives impeached Johnson, who came within one vote of being removed from office by the Senate.

The Fifteenth Amendment. In 1868, the Republicans nominated Ulysses S. Grant for president. His narrow victory prompted Republican leaders to decide that it would be politically expedient to give the vote to all blacks, Northern as well as Southern. For this purpose, leaders of the North drew up and submitted to the states the Fifteenth Amendment. Ironically, the idea was so unpopular in the North that it won the necessary three-fourths approval only because Congress required the Southern states to ratify it.

Industrialism, War, and the Progressive Era

The Economy. Captains of industry—such as **John D. Rockefeller** in oil, **J. P. Morgan** in banking, **Gustavus Swift** in meat processing, **Andrew Carnegie** in steel, and **E. H. Harriman** in railroads—created major industrial empires. In 1886, **Samuel Gompers** and **Adolph Strasser** put together a combination of national craft unions, the **American**

Federation of Labor (AFL), to represent labor's concerns about wages, hours, and safety conditions. Although aggressive in its use of the strike and in its demand for collective bargaining in labor contracts with large corporations, the AFL did not promote violence or radicalism.

The Spanish-American War. The Cuban revolt against Spain in 1895 threatened American business interests in Cuba. Sensational "yellow" journalism and nationalistic statements from officials such as Assistant Secretary of the Navy **Theodore Roosevelt** (1858–1919) encouraged popular support for direct American military intervention on behalf of Cuban independence.

On March 27, 1897, President **William McKinley** (1843–1901) asked Spain to call an armistice, accept American mediation to end the war, and stop using concentration camps in Cuba. Spain refused to comply. On April 21, Congress declared war on Spain, with the objective of establishing Cuban independence (the Teller Amendment). The first U.S. forces landed in Cuba on June 22, 1898, and by July 17, they had defeated the Spanish forces. Spain ceded the Philippines, Puerto Rico, and Guam to the United States in return for a payment of $20 million to Spain for the Philippines.

Theodore Roosevelt and Progressive Reforms. On September 6, 1901, while attending the Pan American Exposition in Buffalo, New York, President McKinley was shot by Leon Czolgosz, an anarchist. The president died on September 14. Theodore Roosevelt, at age 42, became the nation's twenty-fifth president and its youngest president to date.

In accordance with the Antitrust Policy (1902), Roosevelt ordered the Justice Department to prosecute corporations pursuing monopolistic practices. Attorney General P. C. Knox first brought suit against the Northern Securities Company, a railroad holding corporation put together by J. P. Morgan, and then moved against John D. Rockefeller's Standard Oil Company. By the time he left office in 1909, Roosevelt had indictments against 25 monopolies. Roosevelt engineered the separation of Panama from Colombia and the recognition of Panama as an independent country.

The **Hay-Bunau-Varilla Treaty** of 1903 granted the United States control of the Canal Zone in Panama for $10 million and an annual fee of $250,000; the control would begin nine years after ratification of the treaty by both parties. Construction of the **Panama Canal** began in 1904 and was completed in 1914.

In 1905, the African American intellectual and militant **W. E. B. DuBois** founded the **Niagara Movement**, which called for federal legislation to protect racial equality and to grant full citizenship rights. Formed in 1909, the **National Association for the Advancement of Colored People** pressed actively for the rights of African Americans. A third organization of the time, the radical labor organization called the **Industrial Workers of the World** (IWW, or Wobblies; 1905–1924) promoted violence and revolution. The IWW organized effective strikes in the textile industry (1912) and among a few western miners' groups, but it had little appeal to the average American worker. After the Red Scare of 1919, the government worked to smash the IWW and deported many of its immigrant leaders and members.

The Wilson Presidency. The nation elected Democratic candidate **Woodrow Wilson** (1856–1924) as president in 1912. Before the outbreak of World War I in 1914, Wilson, working with cooperative majorities in both houses of Congress, achieved much of the remaining progressive agenda, including tariff reform (Underwood-Simmons Act, 1913); the Sixteenth Amendment (graduated income tax, 1913); the Seventeenth Amendment (direct election of senators, 1913); the Federal Reserve banking system (regulation of and flexibility to monetary policy, 1913); the Federal Trade Commission (to investigate unfair business practices, 1914); and the Clayton Antitrust Act (improving the old Sherman Act and protecting labor unions and farm cooperatives from prosecution, 1914).

Wilson's Fourteen Points. When America entered World War I in 1917, President Wilson maintained that the war would make the world safe for democracy. In an address to Congress on January 8, 1918, he presented his specific peace plan in the form of the Fourteen Points. The first five points called for open rather than secret peace treaties, freedom of the seas, free trade, arms reduction, and a fair adjustment of colonial claims. The next eight points addressed national aspirations of various European peoples and the adjustment of boundaries. The fourteenth point, which he considered the most important and which he had espoused as early as 1916, called for a "general association of nations" to preserve the peace.

Social Conflicts. Although many Americans had called for immigration restriction since the late nineteenth century, the only major restriction imposed on immigration by 1920 had been the Chinese Exclusion Act of 1882. Labor leaders believed that immigrants depressed wages and impeded unionization. Some progressives believed that they created social problems. In June 1917, Congress, over Wilson's veto, imposed a **literacy test for immigrants** and **excluded many Asian nationalities**.

In 1921, Congress passed the **Emergency Quota Act.** The law became effective in 1922 and reduced the number of immigrants annually to about 40 percent of the 1921 total. Congress then passed the National Origins Act of 1924, which further reduced the number of southern and eastern European immigrants. In 1927, the nation set the annual maximum number of immigrants allowed into the United States to 150,000.

On Thanksgiving Day in 1915, **William J. Simmons** founded the second **Knights of the Ku Klux Klan**. Simmons intended to rebuild the Klan as depicted in the "Birth of a Nation." Its purpose was to intimidate African Americans, who were experiencing an apparent rise in status during World War I. The Klan's methods of repression included cross burnings, tar and featherings, kidnappings, lynchings, and burnings. The Klan was not a political party, but it endorsed and opposed candidates and exerted considerable control over elections and politicians in at least nine states.

Fundamentalist Protestants, under the leadership of **William Jennings Bryan**, began a campaign in 1921 to prohibit the teaching of evolution in the schools and protect the belief in the literal biblical account of creation. The South especially received the idea enthusiastically.

The Great Depression and the New Deal

The Crash. Signs of recession were apparent before the stock market crash in 1929. The farm economy, which involved almost 25 percent of the population; coal; railroads; and New England textiles had not been prosperous during the 1920s.

After 1927, new construction declined and auto sales began to sag. Many workers lost their jobs before the crash of 1929. Stock prices increased throughout the decade. The boom in prices and volume of sales was especially active after 1925 and was intensive from 1928 to 1929. Careful investors recognized the overpricing of stocks and began to sell to take their profits. During October 1929, prices declined as more people began to sell their stock. **Black Thursday**, October 24, 1929, saw the trading of almost 13 million shares; this was a large number for that time, and prices fell precipitously. Investment banks tried to boost the market by buying, but on October 29, **Black Tuesday**, the market fell about 40 points, with 16.5 million shares traded.

Hoover's Depression Policies. The nation had elected **Herbert Hoover** (1874–1964) to the presidency in 1928. In June 1929, Congress passed the Agricultural Marketing Act, which created the Federal Farm Board. The board had a revolving fund of $500 million to lend agricultural cooperatives to buy commodities, such as wheat and cotton, and hold them for higher prices.

The Hawley-Smoot Tariff of June 1930 raised duties on both agricultural and manufactured imports. Chartered by Congress in 1932, the Reconstruction Finance Corporation loaned money to railroads, banks, and other financial institutions. It prevented the failure of basic firms, on which many other elements of the economy depended, but many people criticized it as relief for the rich.

The Federal Home Loan Bank Act, passed in July 1932, created home loan banks, which made loans to building and loan associations, savings banks, and insurance companies. Its purpose was to help avoid foreclosures on homes.

The First New Deal. Franklin D. Roosevelt (1882–1945), governor of New York, easily defeated Hoover in the election of 1932. By the time of Roosevelt's inauguration on March 4, 1933, the American economic system seemed to be on the verge of collapse. In his inaugural address, Roosevelt assured the nation that "the only thing we have to fear is fear itself," called for a special session of Congress to convene on March 9, and asked for "broad executive powers to wage war against the emergency." Two days later, he closed all banks for a brief time and forbade the export of gold or the redemption of currency in gold. A special session of Congress from March 9 to June 16, 1933 ("The Hundred Days") passed a great body of legislation that has left a lasting mark on the nation. Historians have called Roosevelt's 1933–1935 legislation the First New Deal and a new wave of programs beginning in 1935 the Second New Deal.

Passed on March 9, the first day of the special session, the Emergency Banking Relief Act provided additional funds for banks from the Reconstruction Finance Corporation and the Federal Reserve, allowed the Treasury to open sound banks after 10 days and to merge or liquidate unsound ones, and forbade the hoarding or exporting of gold. On March 12, Roosevelt assured the public of the soundness of the banks in the first of many "fireside chats," or radio addresses. People believed him. Most banks were soon open, and their deposits were outnumbering withdrawals.

The **Banking Act of 1933**, or the Glass-Steagall Act, established the Federal Deposit Insurance Corporation to insure individual deposits in commercial banks and to separate commercial banking from the more speculative activity of investment banking. The Federal Emergency Relief Act appropriated $500 million for state and local governments to distribute to the poor. The act also established the Federal Emergency Relief Administration under **Harry Hopkins** (1890–1946). The **Civilian Conservation Corps** enrolled

250,000 young men aged 18 to 24 from families on relief to go to camps where they worked on flood control, soil conservation, and forest projects under the direction of the War Department. The **Public Works Administration** had $3.3 billion to distribute to state and local governments for building projects such as schools, highways, and hospitals. The Agricultural Adjustment Act of 1933 created the **Agricultural Adjustment Administration**. Farmers agreed to reduce production of principal farm commodities and received subsidies in return. Farm prices increased; when owners took land out of cultivation, however, tenants and sharecroppers suffered. The repeal of the law came in January 1936 on the grounds that the processing tax was not constitutional.

PRAXIS Pointer

Double-check the numbers on the question and on the answer sheet each time you mark your sheet. Marking one wrong answer can throw off your entire answer sheet and sink your score.

The **National Industrial Recovery Act** was the cornerstone of the recovery program; Congress passed it in June 1933. In executing the provisions of the code, President Roosevelt established the National Recovery Administration (NRA); the goal was the self-regulation of business and the development of fair prices, wages, hours, and working conditions. Section 7-a of the NRA permitted collective bargaining for workers; laborers would test the federal support for their bargaining in the days to come. The slogan of the NRA was, "We do our part." The economy improved but did not recover.

The Second New Deal. The **Works Progress Administration (WPA)** began in May 1935, following the passage of the Emergency Relief Appropriations Act of April 1935. The WPA employed people from the relief rolls for 30 hours of work a week at pay double that of the relief payment but less than private employment.

Created in May 1935, the **Rural Electrification Administration** provided loans and WPA labor to electric cooperatives so they could build lines into rural areas that the private companies did not serve. Passed in August 1935, the **Social Security Act** established for persons over age 65 a retirement plan to be funded by a tax on wages paid equally by employees and employers. The government paid the first benefits, ranging from $10 to $85 per month in 1942. Another provision of the act forced states to initiate unemployment insurance programs.

Labor Unions. The 1935 passage of the National Labor Relations Act, or the **Wagner Act**, resulted in massive growth in union membership—but at the expense of bitter conflict within the labor movement. Primarily craft unions made up the **American Federation of Labor (AFL)**, formed in 1886. Some leaders wanted to unionize mass-production industries, such as automobile and rubber manufacturing, with industrial unions.

In November 1935, **John L. Lewis** formed the **Committee for Industrial Organization (CIO)** to unionize basic industries, presumably within the AFL. **President William Green** of the AFL ordered the CIO to disband in January 1936. When the rebels refused, the AFL expelled them. The insurgents then reorganized the CIO as the independent Congress of Industrial Organizations. Labor strikes, particularly in the textile mills, marked the end of the 1930s. Soon the nation would receive another test.

World War II

The American Response to the War in Europe. In August 1939, Roosevelt created the War Resources Board to develop a plan for industrial mobilization in the event of war. The next month, he established the Office of Emergency Management in the White House to centralize mobilization activities.

Roosevelt officially proclaimed the neutrality of the United States on September 5, 1939. The Democratic Congress, in a vote that followed party lines, passed a new Neutrality Act in November. It allowed the cash-and-carry sale of arms and short-term loans to belligerents but forbade American ships from trading with belligerents or Americans from traveling on belligerent ships.

Roosevelt determined that to aid Britain in every way possible was the best way to avoid war with Germany. In September 1940, he signed an agreement to give Britain 50 American destroyers in return for a 99-year lease on air and naval bases in British territories in Newfoundland, Bermuda, and the Caribbean.

The Road to Pearl Harbor. In late July 1941, the United States placed an embargo on the export of aviation gasoline, lubricants, and scrap iron and steel to Japan and granted an additional loan to China. In December, additional articles—iron ore and pig iron, some chemicals, machine tools, and other products—fell under the embargo.

In October 1941, a new military cabinet headed by **General Hideki Tojo** took control of Japan. The Japanese secretly decided to make a final effort to negotiate with the United States and to go to war if there was no solution by November 25. A new round of talks followed in Washington, but neither side would make a substantive change in its position. The

Japanese secretly gave final approval on December 1 for a surprise attack on the United States.

The Japanese planned a major offensive to take the Dutch East Indies, Malaya, and the Philippines and to obtain the oil, metals, and other raw materials they needed. At the same time, they would attack Pearl Harbor in Hawaii to destroy the American Pacific fleet and keep it from interfering with their plans. At 7:55 AM on Sunday, December 7, 1941, the first wave of Japanese carrier-based planes unexpectedly attacked the American fleet in **Pearl Harbor**. A second wave followed at 8:50 AM. The United States suffered the loss of two battleships sunk, six damaged and out of action, three cruisers and three destroyers sunk or damaged, several lesser vessels destroyed or damaged, and the destruction of all 150 aircraft on the ground at Pearl Harbor. Worst of all, 2,323 American servicemen were killed and about 1,100 were wounded. The Japanese lost 29 planes, five midget submarines, and one fleet submarine.

Declared War Begins. On December 8, 1941, Congress declared war on Japan, with one dissenting vote—Representative Jeanette Rankin of Montana. On December 11, Germany and Italy declared war on the United States. Great Britain and the United States established the Combined Chiefs of Staff, headquartered in Washington, to direct Anglo-American military operations. On January 1, 1942, representatives of 26 nations met in Washington, DC, and signed the Declaration of the United Nations, pledged themselves to the principles of the Atlantic Charter, and promised not to make a separate peace with their common enemies.

The Home Front. In *Korematsu v. United States* (1944), the Supreme Court upheld sending the Issei (Japanese Americans from Japan) and Nisei (native-born Japanese Americans) to concentration camps. The camps did not close until March 1946—after the end of World War II.

President Roosevelt died on April 12, 1945, at Warm Springs, Georgia. **Harry S. Truman** (1884–1972), formerly a senator from Missouri and vice president of the United States, became president on April 12, 1945. (Harry Truman did not have a middle name; he used only the letter *S*, which he did not follow with a period.)

The Atomic Bomb. The Army Corps of Engineers established the Manhattan Engineering District in August 1942 for the purpose of developing an atomic bomb; the program eventually took the name the **Manhattan Project**. **J. Robert Oppenheimer** directed the design and construction of a transportable atomic bomb at Los Alamos, New Mexico. On

July 16, 1945, the Manhattan Project exploded the first atomic bomb at Alamogordo, New Mexico.

The *Enola Gay* dropped an atomic bomb on Hiroshima, Japan, on August 6, 1945, killing about 78,000 people and injuring 100,000 more. On August 9, the United States dropped a second bomb on Nagasaki, Japan. Japan surrendered on August 14, 1945, and signed the formal surrender on September 2.

The Postwar Era

The Cold War and Containment. In February 1947, Great Britain notified the United States that it could no longer aid the Greek government in its war against Communist insurgents. The next month, President Truman asked Congress for $400 million in military and economic aid for Greece and Turkey. In his **Truman Doctrine**, Truman argued that the United States must support free peoples who were resisting Communist domination.

> **PRAXIS Pointer**
>
> Remember this is a review. You have a foundation of knowledge of world and United States history from your secondary education—bring ALL your knowledge to the exam.

Secretary of State George C. Marshall proposed in June 1947 that the United States provide economic aid to help rebuild Europe. The following March, Congress passed the European Recovery Program; popularly known as the **Marshall Plan**, the program provided more than $12 billion in aid.

Anticommunism. On February 9, 1950, Senator **Joseph R. McCarthy** of Wisconsin stated that he had a list of known Communists who were working in the State Department. He later expanded his attacks. After McCarthy made charges against the army, the Senate censured and discredited him in 1954.

Korean War. On June 25, 1950, North Korea invaded South Korea. President Truman committed U.S. forces to the United Nations (UN) military effort; **General Douglas MacArthur** would command the troops. By October, UN forces (mostly American) had driven north of the thirty-eighth parallel, which divided North and South Korea.

Chinese troops attacked MacArthur's forces on November 26, pushing them south of the thirty-eighth parallel, but by spring 1951, UN forces had recovered their offensive.

The armistice of June 1953 left Korea divided along nearly the same boundary that had existed before the war.

Eisenhower-Dulles Foreign Policy. Dwight D. Eisenhower (1890–1969), elected president in 1952, chose **John Foster Dulles** as secretary of state. Dulles talked of a more aggressive foreign policy, calling for "massive retaliation" and "liberation" rather than containment. He wished to emphasize nuclear deterrents rather than conventional armed forces.

In July 1954, after several years of nationalist (Vietnamese) war against French occupation in Vietnam, France, Great Britain, the Soviet Union, and China signed the Geneva Accords, which divided Vietnam along the seventeenth parallel. The North would be under the leadership of **Ho Chi Minh** and the South under **Emperor Bao Dai**. The purpose of the scheduled elections was to unify the country, but **Ngo Dinh Diem** overthrew Bao Dai and prevented the elections from taking place. The United States supplied economic aid to **South Vietnam**.

In January 1959, **Fidel Castro** overthrew the dictator of Cuba. Castro criticized the United States, aligned Cuba more closely with the Soviet Union, and signed a trade agreement with the Soviets in February 1960. The United States prohibited the importation of Cuban sugar in October 1960 and broke off diplomatic relations in January 1961.

The New Frontier, Vietnam, and Social Upheaval

Kennedy's New Frontier. Democratic Senator **John F. Kennedy** (1917–1963) won the presidential election of 1960. The Justice Department, under Attorney General **Robert F. Kennedy**, began to push for civil rights, including desegregation of interstate transportation in the South, integration of schools, and supervision of elections. President Kennedy presented a comprehensive civil rights bill to Congress in 1963. With the bill held up in Congress, 200,000 people marched and demonstrated on its behalf, and Martin Luther King Jr. gave his "I Have a Dream" speech.

Cuban Missile Crisis. Under Eisenhower, the **Central Intelligence Agency** had begun training some 2,000 men to invade Cuba and to overthrow Fidel Castro. On April 19, 1961, this force invaded at the **Bay of Pigs**; opposing forces pinned them down, demanded their surrender, and captured some 1,200 men.

On October 14, 1962, a U-2 reconnaissance plane brought photographic evidence of the construction of missile sites in Cuba. On October 22, Kennedy announced a blockade of Cuba and called on the Soviet premier, **Nikita Khrushchev** (1894–1971), to dismantle the missile bases and remove all weapons capable of attacking the United States from Cuba. Six days later, Khrushchev backed down and withdrew the missiles. Kennedy lifted the blockade.

Johnson and the Great Society. On November 22, 1963, **Lee Harvey Oswald** assassinated President Kennedy in Dallas, Texas; **Jack Ruby** killed Oswald two days later. Debate still continues as to whether the assassination was a conspiracy. **Lyndon B. Johnson** (1908–1973) succeeded John Kennedy as president of the United States.

The **1964 Civil Rights Act** outlawed racial discrimination by employers and unions, created the Equal Employment Opportunity Commission to enforce the law, and eliminated the remaining restrictions on black voting. Michael Harrington's *The Other America: Poverty in the United States* (1962) showed that 20 to 25 percent of American families were living below the governmentally defined poverty line. The Economic Opportunity Act of 1964 sought to address the problem by establishing a job corps, community action programs, education programs, work-study programs, job training, loans for small businesses and farmers, and a "domestic peace corps" called Volunteers in Service to America. The Office of Economic Opportunity administered many of these programs.

Emergence of Black Power. In 1965, Dr. Martin Luther King Jr. announced a voter registration drive. With help from the federal courts, he dramatized his effort by leading a march from Selma, Alabama, to Montgomery, Alabama, between March 21 and 25. The Voting Rights Act of 1965 authorized the attorney general to appoint officials to register voters.

Seventy percent of African Americans lived in city ghettos. In 1966, New York and Chicago experienced riots, and the following year there were riots in Newark and Detroit. The Kerner Commission, appointed to investigate the riots, concluded that the focus of the riots was a social system that prevented African Americans from getting good jobs and crowded them into ghettos. On April 4, 1968, **James Earl Ray** assassinated Martin Luther King Jr. in Memphis, Tennessee. Ray was an escaped convict; he pled guilty to the murder and received a sentence of 99 years in prison. Riots in more than 100 cities followed.

Vietnam. After the defeat of the French in Vietnam in 1954, the United States sent military advisors to South Vietnam to aid the government of **Ngo Dinh Diem**. The pro-Communist Vietcong forces gradually grew in strength because Diem failed to follow through on promised reforms and because of the support from North Vietnam, the Soviet Union, and China.

"Hawks" in Congress defended President Johnson's policy and, drawing on the containment theory, said that the nation had the responsibility to resist aggression. The claim was that, if Vietnam should fall, all Southeast Asia would eventually go. Antiwar demonstrations were attracting large crowds by 1967. "Doves" argued that the war was a civil war in which the United States should not meddle. On January 31, 1968, the first day of the Vietnamese New Year (Tet), the Vietcong attacked numerous cities and towns, American bases, and even Saigon. Although they suffered large losses, the Vietcong won a psychological victory as American opinion began turning against the war.

The Nixon Conservative Reaction. Republican **Richard M. Nixon** (1913–1994), emphasizing stability and order, defeated Democratic nominee Hubert Humphrey by a margin of one percentage point. The Nixon administration sought to block renewal of the Voting Rights Act and delay implementation of court-ordered school desegregation in Mississippi. In 1969, Nixon appointed **Warren E. Burger**, a conservative, as chief justice. Although more conservative than the Warren court, the Burger court did declare in 1972 that the death penalty in use at the time was unconstitutional; it struck down state anti-abortion legislation in 1973.

The president turned to Vietnamization, the effort to build up South Vietnamese forces while withdrawing American troops. In 1969, Nixon reduced American troop strength by 60,000 but at the same time ordered the bombing of Cambodia, a neutral country. In the summer of 1972, negotiations between the United States and North Vietnam began in Paris. A few days before the 1972 presidential election, **Henry Kissinger**, the president's national security advisor, announced that "peace was at hand." Nixon resumed the bombing of North Vietnam in December 1972; he claimed that the North Vietnamese were not bargaining in good faith. In January 1973, the two sides reached a settlement in which the North Vietnamese retained control over large areas of the South and agreed to release American prisoners of war within 60 days. Nearly 60,000 Americans had been killed and 300,000 more wounded, and the war had cost American taxpayers $109 billion. On March 29, 1973, the last American combat troops left South Vietnam. The North Vietnamese forces continued to push back the South Vietnamese, and in April 1975, Saigon fell to the North.

Watergate, Carter, and the New Conservatism

Watergate. The Republicans renominated Nixon, who won a landslide victory over the Democratic nominee, Senator **George McGovern**. What became known as the Watergate crisis began during the 1972 presidential campaign. Early on the morning of June 17, a security officer for the Committee for the Reelection of the President, along with four other men, broke into Democratic headquarters at the Watergate apartment complex in Washington, DC. The authorities caught the men going through files and installing electronic eavesdropping devices.

In March 1974, a grand jury indicted some of Nixon's top aides and named Nixon an unindicted co-conspirator. Meanwhile, the House Judiciary Committee televised its debate over impeachment. The committee charged the president with obstructing justice, misusing presidential power, and failing to obey the committee's subpoenas. Before the House began to debate impeachment, Nixon announced his resignation on August 8, 1974, to take effect at noon the following day.

Gerald Ford (1913–2006) then became president. Ford was in many respects the opposite of Nixon. Although a partisan Republican, he was well liked and free of any hint of scandal. Ford almost immediately encountered controversy when, in September 1974, he offered to pardon Nixon. Nixon accepted the offer, although he admitted no wrongdoing and had not yet received any criminal charges.

Carter's Moderate Liberalism. In 1976, the Democrats nominated **James Earl Carter** (1924–), formerly governor of Georgia, who ran on the basis of his integrity and lack of Washington connections. Carter narrowly defeated Ford in the election.

Carter offered amnesty to Americans who had fled the draft and gone to other countries during the Vietnam War. He established the departments of energy and education and placed the civil service on a merit basis. He created a superfund for cleanup of chemical waste dumps, established controls over strip mining, and protected 100 million acres of Alaskan wilderness from development.

Carter's Foreign Policy. Carter negotiated a controversial treaty with Panama, affirmed by the Senate in 1978, that provided for the transfer of ownership of the canal to Panama in 1999 and guaranteed its neutrality. In 1978, Carter negotiated the Camp David Accords between Israel and Egypt. Israel promised to return occupied land in the Sinai to Egypt in exchange for Egyptian recognition, a process completed in 1982. An agreement to negotiate the Palestinian refugee problem proved ineffective.

The Iranian Crisis. In 1978, a revolution forced the **shah of Iran** to flee the country and replaced him with a religious leader, **Ayatollah Ruhollah Khomeini** (ca. 1900–1989). Because the United States had supported the shah with arms and money, the revolutionaries were strongly anti-American, calling the United States the "Great Satan."

After Carter allowed the exiled shah to come to the United States for medical treatment in October 1979, some 400 Iranians broke into the American embassy in Teheran on November 4 and took the occupants captive. They demanded the return of the shah to Iran for trial, the confiscation of his wealth, and the presentation of his wealth to Iran. Carter rejected these demands; instead, he froze Iranian assets in the United States and established a trade embargo against Iran. After extensive negotiations with Iran, in which Algeria acted as an intermediary, the Iranians freed the American hostages on January 20, 1981.

Attacking Big Government. Republican **Ronald Reagan** (1911–2004) defeated Carter by a large electoral majority in 1980. Reagan placed priority on cutting taxes. He based his approach on supply-side economics, the idea that if government left more money in the hands of the people, they would invest rather then spend the excess on consumer goods. The results would be greater production, more jobs, and greater prosperity, resulting in more income for the government despite lower tax rates. However, the federal budget deficit ballooned from $59 billion in 1980 to $195 billion by 1983. Reagan ended ongoing antitrust suits against IBM and AT&T and fulfilled his promise to reduce government interference with business.

A Woman on the Ticket. If not for anything else, the election of 1984 was a historic election because the Democratic party chose Representative Geraldine Ferraro D-NY to be former Vice-President Walter Mondale's running mate.

Iran-Contra. In 1985 and 1986, several Reagan officials sold arms to the Iranians in hopes of encouraging them to use their influence in obtaining the release of American hostages being held in Lebanon. Profits from these sales went to the Nicaraguan *contras*—a militant group opposed to the left-leaning elected government—thus circumventing congressional restrictions on funding the *contras*. The attorney general appointed a special prosecutor, and Congress held hearings on the affair in May 1987.

The Election of 1988. Vice President George H. W. Bush (1924–) won the Republican nomination. Bush defeated Democrat **Michael Dukakis**, but the Republicans were unable to make any inroads in Congress.

Operation Just Cause. Since coming to office, the Bush administration had been concerned that Panamanian dictator **Manuel Noriega** was providing an important link in the drug traffic between South America and the United States. After economic sanctions, diplomatic efforts, and an October 1989 coup failed to oust Noriega, Bush ordered 12,000 troops into Panama on December 20 for what became known as Operation Just Cause.

On January 3, 1990, Noriega surrendered to the Americans and faced drug-trafficking charges in the United States. Found guilty in 1992, his sentence was 40 years.

Persian Gulf Crisis. On August 2, 1990, Iraq invaded Kuwait, an act that Bush denounced as "naked aggression." The United States quickly banned most trade with Iraq, froze Iraq's and Kuwait's assets in the United States, and sent aircraft carriers to the Persian Gulf. On August 6, after the UN Security Council condemned the invasion, Bush ordered the deployment of air, sea, and land forces to Saudi Arabia and dubbed the operation Desert Shield.

On February 23, the allied air assault began. Four days later, Bush announced the liberation of Kuwait and ordered offensive operations to cease. The UN established the terms for the ceasefire, which Iraq accepted on April 6.

The Road to the Twenty-First Century

The Election of 1992. William Jefferson Clinton (1946–) won 43 percent of the popular vote and 370 electoral votes, while President Bush won 37 percent of the popular vote and 168 electoral votes. Although he won no electoral votes, the Independent Party candidate Ross Perot (1930–) gained 19 percent of the popular vote.

Domestic Affairs. The **North American Free Trade Agreement (NAFTA)**, negotiated by the Bush administration, eliminated most tariffs and other trade barriers among the United States, Canada, and Mexico. Passed by Congress and signed by Clinton in 1993, NAFTA became law in January 1994.

In October 1993, the Clinton administration proposed legislation to reform the health care system, which included universal coverage with a guaranteed benefits package, managed competition through health care alliances that would bargain with insurance companies, and employer mandates to provide health insurance for employees. With most Republicans and small business, insurance, and medical business interests opposed to the legislation, the Democrats dropped their attempt at a compromised package in September 1994.

Impeachment and Acquittal. Clinton received criticism for alleged wrongdoing in connection with a real estate development called Whitewater. While governor of Arkansas, Clinton had invested in Whitewater, along with **James B. and Susan McDougal**, owners of a failed savings and loan institution. After Congress renewed the independent counsel law, a three-judge panel appointed **Kenneth W. Starr** to the new role of independent prosecutor.

The Starr investigation yielded massive findings in late 1998, roughly midway into Clinton's second term, including information on an adulterous affair that Clinton had had with Monica Lewinsky while she was an intern at the White House. It was on charges stemming from this report that the House of Representatives impeached Clinton in December 1998 for perjury and obstruction of justice. The Senate acquitted him of all charges in February 1999.

Continuing Crisis in the Balkans. During Clinton's second term, continued political unrest abroad and civil war in the Balkans remained major foreign policy challenges. In 1999, the Serbian government attacked ethnic Albanians in Kosovo, a province of Serbia. In response, North Atlantic Treaty Organization (NATO) forces, led by the United States, bombed Serbia. Several weeks of bombing forced Serbian forces to withdraw from Kosovo.

The Election of 2000. Preelection polls indicated that the election would be close, and few ventured to predict the outcome. Indeed, the election outcome was much in doubt for several weeks after the election. Though Clinton's vice president, **Al Gore** (1948–), won the popular vote, the electoral college was very close, and Florida (the state governed by George W. Bush's brother) was pivotal in deciding the election.

George W. Bush (1946–), son of the former president **George H. W. Bush**, appeared to win Florida, but by a very small margin; a recount began. Then controversy over how to conduct the recount led to a series of court challenges, with the matter ultimately decided by the U.S. Supreme Court, which ruled in favor of Bush. George W. Bush thus became the forty-third president of the United States.

Terrorism Hits Home. The new president would soon face the grim task of dealing with a massive terrorist attack on major symbols of U.S. economic and military might. On the morning of September 11, 2001, hijackers deliberately crashed two U.S. commercial jetliners into the World Trade Center in New York City—toppling its 110-story twin towers. They crashed another plane into the Pentagon, just outside Washington, D.C. Passengers on yet another hijacked airplane took over the plane; by crashing it in Pennsylvania, they likely saved the lives of many others. Some 2,750 people died in the destruction of the World Trade Center, the deadliest act of terrorism in American history. One hundred eighty-four people died at the Pentagon and 40 in Pennsylvania.

Though the person behind the attacks was not immediately known, Bush cast prime suspicion on the Saudi exile Osama bin Laden, the alleged mastermind of the bombings of two U.S. embassies in 1998 and of a U.S. naval destroyer in 2000. The United States had earlier seen terrorism on its home soil carried out by Islamic militants in the 1993 bombing of the World Trade Center and by a member of the American militia movement in the bombing of the Oklahoma City federal building in 1995.

In retaliation for the terrorism brought against the United States, U.S. forces attacked Afghanistan. Many of these forces remain in Afghanistan to this day. The final outcome of the troop invasion is still uncertain. Disputes with Iraq continued when the United States reported that the country held weapons of mass destruction. Bush declared war (a disputed option) with Iraq. The outcome of sending troops to Iraq is undetermined.

The Election of 2008. A historic moment in United States elections, it was the first time a woman, **Hillary R. Clinton,** and a black man, **Barack H. Obama**, competed in a major party's primary for America's highest office. Obama won the Democratic party's nomination and ran against another historic ticket. The Republican party had nominated **Senator John McCain** for President and he chose Alaska Governor **Sarah Palin** to join him as running mate. On November 2008, Obama won the general election, and was sworn in on January 20, 2009.

Financial Crisis and Recession. Considered by many economists to be the worst financial crisis since the Great Depression of the 1930s, this crisis was triggered by a shortfall of liquidity in the United States banking system, and resulted in the collapse of large financial institutions, a bailout of banks by national governments, and downturns in stock markets around the world. In many areas, the housing market also suffered, resulting in numerous evictions, foreclosures and prolonged vacancies. It contributed to the failure of key businesses, declines in consumer wealth estimated in the trillions of United State dollars, and a significant decline in economic activity, leading to a severe global economic recession in 2008.

This global recession began in December 2007 in the United States and soon spread to the rest of the world. Although some economists declared an end to the recession in July 2009, many countries were still plagued with high unemployment. In the United States, it took until the end of 2009 before the GDP grew the requisite two consecutive quarters.

Immigration and Settlement Patterns

"The United States is a nation of immigrants" is a frequently quoted remark. The quotation, however, may cause some to forget that the Europeans came to a country already occupied by Native Americans.

The New World that Columbus and other explorers discovered in the late fifteenth and early sixteenth centuries was neither recently formed nor recently settled. It had actually been settled between 15,000 and 35,000 years before. As in other areas of the world, the native peoples of the so-called New World formed communities but did not immediately develop written languages. The lack of any kind of written record makes interpreting the prehistorical past more difficult. Archeologists and anthropologists working in North and South America have unearthed the remains of these early communities, and based on this evidence, anthropologists have formed the earliest theories about the origins, movements, and lifestyles of native peoples.

It is important to remember that there is not one universally accepted theory regarding the earliest history of the people who settled North and South America. By the time Europeans came into contact with the indigenous peoples of the Americas, more than 2,000 distinct cultures and hundreds of distinct languages existed. It is therefore necessary to trace not just the origins but also the developments, affected by various factors, e.g., the environment, that took place before the Europeans arrived. This provides an understanding of the various Indian cultures and societies and the resulting impact of contact with Europeans.

Previous sections and topics relate to the topic, "Identifying Immigration and Settlement Patterns That Have Shaped the History of the United States." The reader may wish to review the earlier sections/topics, such as "Prehistory and Early Civilization," "Causes and Consequences of Exploration, Settlement, and Growth," and "The Continued Exploration, Settlement, and Revolution in the 'New World'" to review some of the groups that came to America, their reasons for being here, and where they settled. The previous passages also give some attention to the legislation surrounding these immigrants, the Native Americans, human rights, and calls for immigration restriction.

Calls for immigration restriction had begun in the late nineteenth century, but the only major restriction imposed on immigration at the time had been the Chinese Exclusion Act of 1882. Labor leaders believed that immigrants depressed wages and impeded unionization. Some progressives believed that they created social problems. In June 1917, Congress, over President Wilson's veto, had imposed a literacy test for immigrants and excluded many Asian nationalities. In 1921, Congress passed the Emergency Quota Act. In practice, the law admitted almost as many immigrants as wanted to come from nations such as Britain, Ireland, and Germany but severely restricted Italians, Greeks, Poles, and eastern European Jews wanting to enter the country. The law became effective in 1922 and reduced the number of immigrants annually to about 40 percent of the 1921 total. Congress then passed the National Origins Act of 1924, which further reduced the number of southern and eastern European immigrants and cut the annual immigration total to 20 percent of the 1921 figure. In 1927, the annual maximum number of immigrants allowed into the United States was reduced to 150,000.

In *Korematsu v. United States* (1944), the Supreme Court upheld sending the Issei (Japanese Americans from Japan) and Nisei (native-born Japanese Americans) to concentration camps. The camps closed in March 1946. Some of the concentration camp victims remained on the West Coast, although some did return to their previous area of residence in the United States; some elected to relocate in Japan.

Since the United States first began tracking the arrival of immigrants within its boundaries in 1820, the United States has accepted 66 million legal immigrants, with 11 percent arriving from Germany and 10 percent from Mexico. However, two centuries of immigration and integration have not yielded consensus on the three major immigration questions: How many? From where? and what status should newcomers have when they arrive?

The U.S. immigration system in the early twenty-first century recognizes 800,000 to 900,000 foreigners a year as legal immigrants, admits 35 million nonimmigrant tourists and business visitors a year, and knows of another 300,000 to 400,000 unauthorized foreigners who settle in the country annually. Recent decades have witnessed contentious debates over the place of immigrants and their children in the educational, welfare, and political systems of the United States, or more broadly, whether the immigration system serves U.S. national interests (Martin, 2002). Restrictions have been more frequently proposed after the 9/11 attack, the war in Iraq, health care concerns for the population, and increased controversy surrounding illegal immigrants.

Table 5-1 on the next page ranks the ten leading countries of birth of the foreign-born resident population from 1850 to 2007. In 2003, the U.S. Census Bureau, in its Current Population Survey, indicated the regions of residence of foreign-born residents. Of the 33,500,000 foreign-born residents in the United States in 2000, 37 percent (12,395,000) resided in the West. The South had the second highest percentage, with 29 percent (9,715,000). The region with the third highest number of foreign-born residents (7,370,000) was the Northeast, which had almost 22 percent. Eleven percent (3,685,000) of the foreign-born residents lived in the Midwest (U.S. Census Bureau, *Current Population Survey*, March 2008, *www.census.gov/prod/2004pubs/p20-551.pdf*). Martin (2002) predicted that immigration was likely to continue at the current levels of 900,000 legal and 300,000 unauthorized a year. In the words of Kenneth Prewitt, a former director of the U.S. Census Bureau, America is "the first country in world history which is literally made up of every part of the world" (Alvarez 2001). Setting limits on the numbers of immigrants, providing services for those who are illegal immigrants in the United States, locating the immigrants who come to the United States, and finding work for those who are newly arrived without taking jobs from those who are already settled are some of the debates that concern legislators and citizens of the country.

Table 4-1. Countries of Birth of the Foreign-Born Population, 1850–2000 (Resident Population)

Ten leading countries	1850	1900	1930	1960	1970	1980	1990	2000	2007
1	Ireland 962,000	Germany 2,663,000	Italy 1,790,000	Italy 1,257,000	Italy 1,009,000	Mexico 2,199,000	Mexico 4,298,000	Mexico 7,841,000	Mexico 11,700,00
2	Germany 584,000	Ireland 1,615,000	Germany 1,609,000	Germany 990,000	Germany 833,000	Germany 849,000	China 921,000	China 1,391,000	China 1,900,000
3	Great Britain 379,000	Canada 1,180,000	United Kingdom 1,403,000	Canada 953,000	Canada 812,000	Canada 843,000	Philippines 913,000	Philippines 1,222,000	Phippines 1,700,000
4	Canada 148,000	Great Britain 1,168,000	Canada 1,310,000	United Kingdom 833,000	Mexico 760,000	Italy 832,000	Canada 745,000	India 1,007,000	India 1,500,000
5	France 54,000	Sweden 582,000	Poland 1,269,000	Poland 748,000	United Kingdom 686,000	United Kingdom 669,000	Cuba 737,000	Cuba 952,000	El Salvador 1,100,000
6	Switzerland 13,000	Italy 484,000	Soviet Union 1,154,000	Soviet Union 691,000	Poland 548,000	Cuba 608,000	Germany 712,000	Vietnam 863,000	Vietnam 1,100,000
7	Mexico 13,000	Russia 424,000	Ireland 745,000	Mexico 576,000	Soviet Union 463,000	Philippines 501,000	United Kingdom 640,000	El Salvador 765,000	Korea 1,000,000
8	Norway 13,000	Poland 383,000	Mexico 641,000	Ireland 339,000	Cuba 439,000	Poland 418,000	Italy 581,000	Korea 701,000	Cuba 983,000
9	Holland 10,000	Norway 336,000	Sweden 595,000	Austria 305,000	Ireland 251,000	Soviet Union 406,000	Korea 568,000	Dominican Republic 692,000	Canada 800,000
10	Italy 4,000	Austria 276,000	Czechoslovakia 492,000	Hungary 245,000	Austria 214,000	Korea 290,000	Vietnam 543,000	Canada 678,000	Dominican Republic 687,000

Source: U.S. Census Bureau. "Countries of Birth of the Foreign-Born Population, 1850–2000." *Profile of the Foreign-Born Population in the United States: 2001*

GOVERNMENT, CITIZENSHIP, AND DEMOCRACY

Ten-percent of your score will be obtained from this category. You will be expected to

- Understand the nature, purpose and forms (e.g., federal, state, local) of government

- Know key documents and speeches in the history of the United States (e.g., United States Constitution, Declaration of Independence, Gettysburg Address)

- Know the rights and responsibilities of citizenship in a democracy

Forms of Government

The U.S. Department of State identifies 26 forms of governments in the world (CIA, n.d.). Some of best-known forms of government listed are communism, socialism, democracy, monarchy, and oligarchy. A description of these types of government follows:

- **Communism** is a system in which the state controls economic activity in the nation. The state rejects free enterprise and capitalism; consequently, private ownership is discouraged and often prohibited. Usually the nation is ruled through a one-party system. In theory communism believes that the country should not have social classes, as a way to avoid the oppressor—oppressed dichotomy that exists in the world.

- **Socialism** is a system of government in which the central government controls the production and distribution of goods, services, and labor in the nation. The goal is to promote an equitable distribution of resources among the people. In theory, the working class should take over and administer collectively the resources for their benefit and the benefit of the national as a whole.

- **Democracy** is a form of government in which the majority rules. In practice it becomes a representative democracy, in which the people elect candidates to represent them in the government.

- **Monarchy** is a system in which a king or queen leads the nation. The monarch can have supreme powers and become dictator, or he/she can have limited or ceremonial powers limited by a parliament or a constitution.

There are three main broad classifications for these forms of government based on the number of people in power—government by one person, a group, or by many people:

Rule by One

In this form of government, one person becomes the supreme leader of the nation. Some of the terminology and concepts linked to this type of government are:

- **Autocracy**: Ruler has unlimited power, uses power in an arbitrary manner.

- **Monarchy**: Ruled by a king or queen who holds complete control over the subjects. Ruler sometimes claims birth and divine rights.

- **Dictatorship**: The ruler holds absolute power to make laws and to command the army.

Ruled by a Few

In this system, a group of influential people takes control of the government. Traditionally, these people appoint one of their own to function as the supreme leader of the government. Some examples of this type of government are:

- **Theocracy**: Ruled by a group of religious leaders, e.g., the Taliban in Afghanistan.

- **Aristocracy**: A group of nobles controls the economy and the government.

- **Oligarchy**: A small group of powerful and wealthy people rule the nation with the support of the military.

- **Military**: A committee of military officers or a junta rule the nation.

Rule by Many

In this type of government, the citizens of the nation, technically, become the government. In practice, the citizens elect members to represent them and become the government. Some examples of this type of government are:

- **Democracy**: The citizens of the nation directly or through elected members make important decisions, and become part of the government.

- **Constitutional Democracy**: It is a democratic form of government regulated by a constitution.

- **Parliamentarian Monarchy**: The monarch shares the power with the parliament. Often, the powers of the monarch are ceremonial in nature, as in Great Britain.

- **Federal Republic**: A constitutional government in which the powers of the central government are restricted to create semi-autonomous bodies (states or provinces) with certain degrees of self-governing powers, e.g., the United States.

The American Government

The governmental system of the United States has been identified as a federal republic and constitutional representative democracy. It is a federal republic because the U.S. government is limited by law; in this case, the government is limited by the Constitution. It is a constitutional representative democracy because the citizens elect senators and representatives to represent them in Congress.

The Constitution is the supreme law of the nation. It contains a description of the government and the rights and responsibilities of its citizens. The document can be amended with the approval of two-thirds of the House and the Senate and the ratification of individual state legislatures. Amendments to the U.S. Constitution have made it more democratic than the original document. The first ten amendments to the Constitution are known as the Bill of Rights.

Executive Branch

The executive branch of the U.S. government is composed of a president and a vice president elected every four years by electoral votes. The president is the commander-in-chief of the armed forces. He or she appoints cabinet members, nominates judges to the federal court system, grants pardons, recommends legislation, and has the power to veto legislation.

Judicial Branch

The judicial branch is composed of a federal court system that includes the Supreme Court and a system of lower courts—district courts, appeals courts, bankruptcy courts, and special federal courts. Federal judges are nominated by the president of the United States and confirmed by the Senate. All federal judges are appointed for life. The Supreme Court is composed of nine judges, and their ruling is considered final. Some of the major responsibilities of this body are to interpret the Constitution, resolve conflicts among states, and interpret laws and treaties.

Legislative Branch

The legislative branch is composed of the Congress, which is divided in two parts— the Senate and the House of Representatives. The Senate comprises two senators from each state, while the composition of the House is based on the population of each state. The Congress makes the laws of the nation, collects taxes, coins money and regulates its value, can declare war, controls appropriations, can impeach public officials, regulates the jurisdictions of federal courts, and can override presidential vetoes.

System of Checks and Balances

The U.S. Constitution provides for a system of checks and balances among the three branches of the government. In this type of system, individual branches check the others to be sure that no one assumes full control of the central government. The legislative branch can check the executive branch by passing laws over presidential veto (by a two-thirds majority in both houses). This branch exerts control over the judicial branch by refusing to confirm the president's judges. The executive can check the legislative branch by the use of the veto and the judicial branch by appointing federal judges. The judicial branch can check the other two branches through the process of judicial review, which can declare legislation unconstitutional or illegal.

Judicial Review Process—Marbury v. Madison

A dispute that occurred as the Thomas Jefferson administration came into power fundamentally altered the system of checks and balances of the American government. In this case, the judicial branch confirmed its power to review and assess the constitutionality of the legislation passed by Congress and signed by the president. This process is now called the judicial review.

Bill of Rights

After the U.S. Constitution was enacted in 1783, the founders felt that additional measures were necessary to preserve basic human rights. The first ten amendments to the U.S. Constitution came to be the Bill of Rights. A summary of the first ten amendments follows:

First Amendment—separation of church and state; freedom of religion, speech and press; and the right to peaceful assembly

Second Amendment—rights to keep and bear arms

Third Amendment—made it illegal to force people to offer quarters to soldiers in time of peace

Fourth Amendment—rights to privacy and unreasonable searches or seizures

Fifth Amendment—rights of due process, protection against self-incrimination, and protection from being indicted for the same crime twice (double jeopardy)

Sixth Amendment—rights to speedy public trial by an impartial jury and to counsel for one's defense

Seventh Amendment—right to sue people

Eighth Amendment—protection against cruel and unusual punishment

Ninth Amendment—enumeration of specific rights in the Constitution cannot be taken as a way to deny other rights retained by the people

Tenth Amendment—rights not delegated to the federal government by the Constitution are reserved to the states or to the people

Power Sharing Between State and Federal Governments

One of the most significant principles of the U.S. Constitution is the concept of power sharing between the federal and state governments. Some of the powers reserved to the federal and state governments follow.

Powers Reserved for the Federal Government

- Regulate interstate and foreign commerce

- Print money and regulate its value

- Establish the laws for regulation of immigration and naturalization

- Regulate admission of new states

- Declare war and ratify peace treaties

- Establish a system of weights and measures

- Raise and maintain armed forces

- Conduct relations with foreign nations

Powers Reserved for State Governments

- Conduct and monitor local, state, and federal elections

- Provide for local government

- Ratify proposed amendments to the Constitution

- Regulate intrastate commerce

- Provide education for its citizens

- Establish direct taxes like sales and state taxes

- Regulate and maintain police power over public health and safety

- Maintain control of state borders

In addition to the powers reserved to the states, the **Tenth Amendment** of the U.S. Constitution provides additional powers to the state. In this amendment, the powers not specifically delegated to the federal government are reserved for the states.

Local and State Governments

Most states in the United States follow the type of government established in the U.S. Constitution. State governments generally have three branches—executive, legislative, and judicial. The main difference is that the executive branch is led by a governor and the judicial branch is composed of a state court system subordinate to the federal court system. The city government is generally headed by a mayor or city manager with the support of a city council.

Citizenship

The development of civic ideas and practices is a lifelong process that begins in school by observing patriotic holidays, learning about the contribution of historical characters, and pledging allegiance to the American flag each day. In first grade, encouraging good citizenship continues with the introduction of the American anthem. Civic education and the principles of democracy are infused through active participation in community activities. To promote civic responsibility, students can get involved in discussions about issues that affect the community. Teachers guide students to suggest possible solutions to community problems, while students are guided to listen and analyze contributions. Through this exchange, students are guided to practice principles of democracy and to value individual contributions to solve community problems.

In grades K–6 students will become familiar with the meaning and importance of national holidays observed during the year. Holidays with historic significance observed during the year are Memorial Day, Labor Day, Columbus Day, Independence Day, Veteran's Day, and Martin Luther King Jr. Day. **Memorial Day** honors members of the military who died in war. **Labor Day** recognizes the importance of workers and labor unions. **Columbus Day** commemorates the arrival of Christopher Columbus to the Americas. **Independence Day** commemorates the adoption of the **Declaration of Independence**. **Martin Luther King Jr. Day** honors the leader of the civil rights movement. **Veteran's Day** celebrates all those who have served in our country's armed forces.

Children as early as prekindergarten can be guided to develop civic responsibility. Teachers can promote this sense of responsibility by involving students in real-life situations in which they take civic responsibility. For example, teachers can make children aware of how producing trash can affect the environment. As part of this process, students can be guided to examine the amount of trash that they produce daily and explore ways to reduce it. Promoting a sense of responsibility to the well-being of everyone constitutes the main principle for developing responsible citizenship.

American Symbols

Patriotic symbols are visible signs of national pride. The U.S. National Flag, the Pledge of Allegiance, the Statue of Liberty, the Liberty Bell, and the White House are important examples of patriotic symbols.

The United States of America **National Flag** has 50 stars represent the 50 states of the Union. The color red represents hardiness and valor, the white symbolizes purity and innocence and the blue symbolizes vigilance, perseverance, and justice. The Congress approved a new flag with 13 red and white alternating horizontal stripes and 13 stars representing the original colonies in 1777. A star and stripe were added to the flag each time a state entered the union. The Congress set the number of stripes at thirteen in 1818 and approved to continue to add a star for each new state.

The **Pledge of Allegiance** is a declaration of patriotism. It was first published in 1892 in The Youth's Companion and was believed to be written by the magazine's editor, Francis Bellamy. The original purpose was for the pledge was to be used by school children in activities to celebrate the 400th anniversary of the discovery of America. The Pledge was widely used in morning school routines for many years and received official recognition by Congress on 1942. The phrase "under God" was added in 1954 and a law indicating the proper behavior to adopt when reciting the pledge, which includes standing straight, removing hats or any other headgear, and placing the right hand over the heart.

The **Star-Spangled Banner** is the national anthem of the United States. It was originally a poem written by Francis Scott Key during the Battle of Baltimore in the War of 1812 against the British. In 1931, it was made the official national anthem of the United States.

The **Statue of Liberty** was a gift of friendship from the people of France to the people of the United States commemorating the United States' 100th anniversary. It is a universal symbol of freedom, democracy, and international friendship.

The **Liberty Bell** is a symbol of freedom and liberty. The Pennsylvania Assembly commissioned the Liberty Bell to commemorate the 50th anniversary of Pennsylvania's original constitution, the William Penn's Charter of Privileges. It is traditionally believed that it was rung to summon the people of Philadelphia to hear the Declaration of Independence. It became an icon when the abolitionists adopted it as a symbol of freedom. The abolitionists changed its name from The State House Bell to the Liberty Bell.

The **White House** was originally planned by President George Washington in 1791 and was completed in 1800 when its first resident, President John Adams, moved in with his wife, Abigail. It was originally called the President's House. President Theodore Roosevelt christened it with the name The White House in 1901, and for over 200 years it has been the home of the U.S. Presidents and their families. It is recognized as a symbol of the Presidency of the United States throughout the world.

The **Great Seal of the United States** consists of a bald eagle holding an olive branch and a bundle of arrows. The olive branch represents peace and the arrows represent military strength. The eagle holds a scroll in its beak with the nation's motto: "E Pluribus Unum" which means "Out of many, one."

For additional information about symbols of the United States go to http://govdocs. evergreen.edu/symbols.html, a website created and maintained by Evergreen State College in Olympia, Washington, or www.ushistory.org, a website created and hosted by the Independence Hall Association in Philadelphia.

Key Documents of the United States

The Magna Carta (1215 c.e.) Although it is an English charter requiring King John to extend certain liberties and accept that his will was not arbitrary, it inspired American colonists in their drafting of the United States Constitution. It is the first of a series of instruments that now are recognised as having a special constitutional status, the others being the Habeas Corpus Act, the Petition of Right, the Bill of Rights, and the Act of Settlement.

The Declaration of Independence (July 4, 1776) The Declaration of Independence pronounced the colonies free and independent states. It consists of a preamble, or introduction, followed by three main parts. The first part stresses natural unalienable rights and liberties that belong to all people from birth. The second part consists of a list of specific grievances and injustices committed by Britain. The third part announces the colonies as the United States of America. This document provided the foundation to establish equal rights for all people.

Articles of Confederation (November 15, 1777) During the Revolutionary War, the Second Continental Congress ran the government. After independence, the Articles of Confederation defined a new form of government. The new government was composed of representatives from thirteen independent states with limited power. The Congress could not declare war or raise an army. They could ask the states for money or for soldiers, but it was up to the states to agree to provide them. Under this type of government, each state printed its own money and imposed taxes on imports from the other states.

On the positive side, the new government provided for a common citizenship—citizens of the United States. It organized a uniform system of weights and measurements and the postal service. It also became responsible for issues related to Native Americans living within the borders of the new nation. The confederation served as the official government of the young republic until 1789, when the states ratified the Constitution.

United States Constitution (1787) After six years under the Articles of Confederation, the leaders of the nation realized that the American government needed revision to bolster its strength. To accomplish this goal, a constitutional convention was held in Philadelphia in 1787. The leaders of this initiative were George Washington, James Madison, Benjamin Franklin, and Alexander Hamilton. From this convention, a new form of government emerged. The Constitution was officially ratified in 1788, and in 1789 George Washington was selected to be the first president of the United States. The republic defined by the Constitution was composed of three branches, the executive, judicial, and legislative, and a system of checks and balances to regulate each branch.

The Declaration of Causes of Seceding States (Winter 1861) Several Southern wrote declarations dissolving their political connection with the Federal Government of the United States. They ceded to join the Confederation of States.

The Constitution of the Confederate States of America (March 11, 1861) was the supreme law of the Confederate States of America and in effect through the conclusion of the Civil War. The Confederacy also operated under a Provisional Constitution from February 8, 1861 to March 11, 1861. The original Provisional Constitution is currently located at the Museum of the Confederacy in Richmond, Virginia, and differs slightly from the version later adopted. In most articles of the Constitution, the document is a word-for-word duplicate of the United States Constitution. However, there are crucial differences between the two documents, in tone and legal content, specifically in the areas of states' rights and slavery.

The Gettysburg Address (November 19, 1863) One of the most famous speeches in United States history, the Gettysburg Address was given by President Abraham Lincoln, as the second speaker, at the dedication of Soldiers' National Cemetery at Gettysburg.

The Emancipation Proclamation (1862-1863) On Sept. 22, 1862, President Abraham Lincoln issued a preliminary proclamation declaring free all slaves residing in territory in rebellion against the federal government which would take affect on January 1, 1863. This Emancipation Proclamation actually freed few people. It did not apply to slaves in border states fighting on the Union side; nor did it affect slaves in southern areas already under Union control. Naturally, the states in rebellion did not act on Lincoln's order. But the proclamation did show Americans—and the world—that the civil war was now being fought to end slavery. Although the Emancipation Proclamation did not end slavery which, was achieved by the passage of the 13th Amendment, it did make that accomplishment a basic war goal and a virtual certainty.

The Declaration of War on Japan (Dec. 8, 1941) This speech, given to the United States Congress, is often referred to as Roosevelt's Infamy Speech because President Franklin D. Roosevelt declared war on Japan with these words:

> *Yesterday, December 7th, 1941—a date which will live in infamy—the United States of America was suddenly and deliberately attacked by naval and air forces of the Empire of Japan.*

Inaugural Address of President John F. Kennedy (1961) In his inaugural address, President Kennedy used the now famous phrase, "Ask not what your country can do for you; ask what you can do for your country." He asked the nations of the world to join together to fight the "common enemies of man: tyranny, poverty, disease, and war itself." He added: "All this will not be finished in the first one hundred days. Nor will it be finished in the first one thousand days, nor in the life of this Administration, nor even perhaps in our lifetime on this planet. But let us begin." In closing, he called for greater internationalism: "Finally, whether you are citizens of America or citizens of the world, ask of us here the same high standards of strength and sacrifice which we ask of you."

Reverend Martin Luther King Jr.'s "I Have A Dream Speech" (Aug. 28, 1963) Delivered on the steps at the Lincoln Memorial in Washington D.C., during the March on Washington for Jobs and Freedom, this speech has become a powerful symbol of the fight for civil rights in the United States. Reverend King called for racial equality and an end to discrimination with such eloquence that the speech has been ranked the top American speech of the 20th century by a 1999 poll of scholars of public address.

To learn more about historical American documents, go to "A Chronology of U.S. Historical Documents," a website created and maintained by the University of Oklahoma Law Center, at *www.law.ou.edu/hist*.

REFERENCES

Arends, R. 1998. *Learning to Teach*. 4th ed. Boston: McGraw-Hill.

CIA World Fact Book. Central Asia: Russia. *https://www.cia.gov/library/publications/the-world-factbook/geos/rs.html* (accessed October 1, 2009).

CIA World Fact Book. Nations: Forms of Government. *HistoryGuy.com*. *http://www.historyguy.com/nations/government_types.html* (accessed August 27, 2009).

Echevarria, J., M. Vogt, and D. Short. 2000. *Making content comprehensible for English language learners*: *The SIOP model*. Needham Heights, MA: Allyn and Bacon.

Ganeri, A., H. M. Martell, and B. Williams. 1999. *The World History Encyclopedia*. Bath, UK: Parragon.

Kagan, S. 1985. *Cooperative learning resources for teachers*. Riverside, CA: Spencer Kagan.

Kerr, A. 2006. Temperance and prohibition. History Department, Ohio State University. *http://prohibition.osu.edu/* (accessed October 1, 2009).

Lyman, F. T. 1981. The responsive classroom discussion: The inclusion of all students. In *Mainstreaming Digest,* ed. A. S. Anderson, 109–113. College Park: University of Maryland Press.

Marzano, R., and D. Pickering. 2005. *Building academic vocabulary*: *Teacher's manual*. Alexandria, VA: ASCD.

Mayell, H. 2004. Three high-altitude peoples, three adaptations to thin air. *National Geographic*. *http://news.nationalgeographic.com/news/2004/02/0224_040225_evolution.html* (accessed October 1, 2009).

Mendoza, V. 2001. Video review of *Chicano! History of the Mexican American Civil Rights Movement. The Journal for MultiMedia History*, Volume 3. *www.albany.edu/jmmh/vol3/chicano/chicano.html* (accessed August 28, 2009).

National Council for the Teaching of Social Studies (NCTSS) 2006. Expectations of Excellence: Curriculum Standards for Social Studies—Executive Summary. *www.socialstudies.org/standards/execsummary* (accessed October 1, 2009).

Parker, W. C. 2001. *Social Studies in Elementary Education*. 11th ed. Columbus, OH: Merrill Prentice-Hall.

Potts, J. 1994. *Adventure Tales of America*. Dallas, TX: Signal Media.

Rosado, L., and D. Salazar. 2002–2003. La Conexión: The English/Spanish connection. *National Forum of Applied Educational Research Journal* 15(4): 51–66.

Rosales Castañeda, O. 2006. *The Chicano Movement in Washington State* HistoryLink.org (accessed October 21, 2009) *1967-2006*.

Rowe, M. B. 1986. *Wait Times: Slowing Down May Be a Way of Speeding Up. Journal of Teacher Education*, 37, 43–50.

Schifini, A. 1985. *Sheltered English: Content area instruction for limited English proficiency students*. Los Angeles County Office of Education.

Schifini, A., H. García, D. J. Short, E. E. García, J. Villamil Tinajero, E. Hamayan, and L. Kratky. 2004. *Avenues: Success in language, literacy and content*. Carmel, CA: Hampton-Brown.

Slavin, R. 1986. *Student Learning: An Overview and Practical Guide*. Washington, DC: Professional Library National Education Association.

Science

The category of science will account for one-quarter of your score on the Elementary Education Content Knowledge 0014/5014 exam. You will be tested on your knowledge of earth science, life science, physical science, as well as your understanding of the personal and social aspects of study of science.

The National Science Teachers Association (NSTA) is in the process of reviewing its standards for teaching science in the United States and was scheduled to release a new framework in late Spring 2011. The NSTA promotes the idea that scientific inquiry should be a basic component of the curriculum in every grade in American schools (NSTA 2002). A position paper of the organization published in 2002 emphasizes the importance of offering students early experience in problem solving and scientific thinking. The report suggests that children learn science best under the following conditions:

- Students are actively involved in firsthand exploration of scientific concepts.

- Instruction is related and built on the abilities and experiences of the learners.

- Instruction is organized thematically.

- Mathematics and communication skills are integrated.

The report also indicates that curriculum should emphasize the contributions of people from a variety of cultures. Finally, the NSTA (2002) states that science education can be successful if teachers receive adequate professional development and school administrators show a genuine interest in science education.

PHYSICAL SCIENCE

Physical science is the study of universal forces that include gravity, electricity, and magnetism. This competency represents 30% of the science score and will test your understanding of

- the physical and chemical properties and structure of matter (e.g., changes of states, mixtures and solutions, atoms and elements)

- forces and motions (e.g., types of motion, laws of motion, forces and equilibrium)

- energy (e.g., forms of energy, transfer and conservation of energy, simple machines)

- the interactions of energy and matter (e.g., electricity, magnetism, sound)

Magnetism and Gravity

Magnetism is the force of attraction or repulsion between objects that results from the positive and negative ionic charges of the objects. Usually, the objects are metals, such as iron, nickel, and cobalt. Magnets have two poles that have opposing charges or forces: north (+) and south (−). When the north pole of a magnet is placed close to the north pole of a second magnet, repulsion occurs. When poles of different kinds (north and south) are placed close, they attract one another. The strength of the forces depends on the size and the proximity of the magnets. The charged area around a magnet is called a magnetic field. The Earth is like a large magnet, with opposing forces—the north pole and south pole—and the magnetic field of attraction of Earth that we know as gravity is like that of a magnet. Without gravity, all objects on Earth, including the atmosphere, would not be held onto its surface. Planets and other celestial objects that are more massive than Earth, such as Jupiter, have stronger gravitational forces, and those that are less massive and/or dense, such as our moon, have weaker gravitational forces.

Force and Motion

Force is defined as the action of moving an object by pulling or pushing it. Force can cause an object to move at a constant speed or to accelerate. When force is applied over a distance, work is done. **Work** is the product of the force acting in the direction of movement and causing displacement. **Energy** is defined as the ability to do work; when a tow truck uses force to pull a car and move it to a different location, energy is used and work is accomplished. Newton's laws of motion are important to understand in fulfilling this competency. Newton's first law is that an object at rest will remain at rest unless acted upon by an (unbalanced) force, and an object in motion will continue to stay in motion with the same speed and in the same direction unless acted upon by an (unbalanced) outside force. This first law is also called *inertia*. Newton's second law is that acceleration is produced when a force acts on mass and the greater the mass of the object being accelerated, the greater the amount of force needed to accelerate that object. Newton's third law of motion is that for every action there is an equal and opposite reaction.

See *http://teachertech.rice.edu/Participants/louviere/Newton/*

Force and motion, as well as changes in motion, may be measured through hands-on activities in which variables such as time, speed, distance, and direction can be recorded and graphed, and teachers need to know how to do so. For example, teachers can have students experience and record what happens when an object with higher mass (such as a large marble or ball bearing), collides with an object with less mass (e.g., a small marble or ball bearing). Teachers should also know what happens when the rate of speed is high when the objects collide compared to when the rate of speed is low. The game of pool or billiards is a good example. When forces are unbalanced, it may cause the object to change its motion or position.

Relationships between Force and Motion: Machines, Space, and Geologic Processes

A machine is something that makes work easier. Machines can be as simple as a wedge or a screw or as sophisticated as a computer or gas engine. A **simple machine** has few or no moving parts and can change the size and direction of a force. A screw, hammer, wedge, and incline plane are examples of simple machines. Simple machines are part of our daily activities. For example, children playing on a seesaw are using a simple machine called a **lever**. Thus, teachers and their students should know the practical use of these simple machines in everyday life. A **complex machine** is two or more simple machines working together to facilitate work. Some of the complex machines used in daily activities are a wheelbarrow, a can opener, and a bicycle.

Force and motion is what keeps the sun, Earth, moon, and planets in their orbits and explains the structure and changes of the universe. On Earth, force and motion are found in all geologic processes, explaining phenomena such as tides and tsunamis.

Matter

Matter is anything that takes up space and has mass. The **mass** of a body is the amount of matter in an object or thing, and **volume** describes the amount of space that matter takes up. Mass is also the property of a body that causes it to have weight. **Weight** is the amount of gravitational force exerted over an object. It is important not to confuse mass and weight. What students are measuring on their balances in the laboratory is an object's *mass*. Weight changes as an object goes from one level of gravitational force to another, for example, from Earth to the Moon, because the amount of "pull" on that object is different; but the mass of the object—how much matter or material is in the object—does not change unless we do something to actually take away or add matter to that object.

There are 112 basic kinds of matter, called **elements**, which are organized into the **periodic table**. An element is composed of microscopic components called **atoms**. Atoms are made up of particles called **electrons**, **neutrons**, and **protons**. The mass of the atom is located mostly in the nucleus, which is made up of protons and neutrons. The electron contains little mass and follows an orbit around the nucleus. **Molecules** are two or more atoms bonded together in a chemical bond. The atoms of a molecule can be more than one of the same *kind* of atom, as in the naturally occurring oxygen molecule, O_2, or a molecule can be two or more different atoms as in carbon dioxide, CO_2, ammonia, NH_3, and glucose, $C_6H_{12}O_6$. **Compounds** are when you have two or more *different* kinds of atoms in the molecule and you have a given amount of that substance. In other words, compounds consist of matter composed of atoms that are chemically combined with one another in molecules in definite weight proportions. An example of a compound is water; water is oxygen and hydrogen combined in the ratio of two hydrogen molecules to one molecule of oxygen H_2O. So, you can also call it *one* H_2O a molecule.

Properties of Matter

Matter has physical, thermal, electrical, and chemical properties. These properties are dependent upon the molecular composition of the matter.

Physical Properties

The physical properties of matter are the way matter looks and feels. It includes qualities like color, density, hardness, and conductivity. **Color** represents how matter is reflected or perceived by the human eye. **Density** is the mass that is contained in a unit of volume of a given substance. **Hardness** represents the resistance to penetration offered by a given substance. **Conductivity** is the ability of substances to transmit thermal or electric current.

Thermal Properties

Matter is sensitive to temperature changes. Heat and cold produce changes in the physical properties of matter; however, the chemical properties remain unchanged. For example, when water is exposed to cold temperature (release of heat), it changes from liquid to solid; and when water is exposed to heat, it changes from solid to liquid. With continued heat, the water changes from liquid to gas (water vapor). Water vapor can be cooled again and turned back into liquid. However, through all these states, water retains its chemical properties—two molecules of hydrogen and one molecule of oxygen or H_2O.

Electrical Properties

Matter can be classified as a conductor or nonconductor of electricity. Conductive matter allows the transfer of electric current or heat from one point to another. Metals are usually good conductors, while wood and rocks are examples of nonconductive matter.

Chemical Properties

The chemical properties of one type of matter (element) can react with the chemical properties of other types of matter. In general, elements from the same groups will not react with each other, while elements from different groups may. The more separated the groups, the more likely they will cause a chemical reaction when brought together. A type of matter can be chemically altered to become a different type of matter; for example, a metal trash can will rust if it is left out in the rain.

States of Matter

Matter can exist in four distinct states: solid, liquid, gas, and plasma. Most people are familiar with the basic states of matter, but they might not be familiar with the fourth one, plasma. Plasmas are formed at extremely high temperatures when electrons are stripped from neutral atoms (University of California, 2006). Stars are predominantly composed of plasmas. Solids have mass, occupy a define amount of space or *volume* or have a definite shape, and are more dense than liquids. Liquids have mass, occupy a definite volume, do not have a definite shape, but instead take the shape of their container. Gases have mass, do not have a definite volume, have no definite shape but take the shape of their container, and are the least dense of the three states of matter. Plasma has no definite shape or volume, and is a substance that cannot be classified as a solid, liquid, or gas. When substances change from one state of matter to another, such as ice melting, it is a physical change, and not a chemical change.

Mixtures and Solutions

Mixtures are combinations of two or more substances, where each substance is distinct from the other, that is, made up of two or more types of molecules and not chemically combined. The two substances in the mixture may or may not be evenly distributed, so there are no definite amounts or weight proportions. Mixtures may be *heterogeneous*, which means an uneven distribution of the substances in the mixture throughout. A mixture may be *homogeneous,* which means the components are evenly distributed throughout. Examples of mixtures include milk, which is a heterogeneous mixture of water and butterfat particles. The components of a mixture can be separated physically. For example, milk producers and manufacturers remove the butterfat from whole milk to make skim milk.

Solutions are *mixtures* that are *homogeneous,* which means that the components are distributed evenly and there is an even concentration throughout. The solute is the substance in the smaller amount that dissolves and that you add into the substance that is in the larger amount—the solvent. Water is a common solvent. Solids, liquids, and gases can be solutes. Examples of solutions are seawater and ammonia. Seawater is made up of water and salt, and ammonia is made up of ammonia gas and water. In these examples, the salt and the ammonia (NH_3) are the solutes; water is the solvent.

Physical and Chemical Changes in Matter

A **physical change** is a change in a substance that does not change what that substance is made of. Examples of physical changes are melting ice (boiling water), tearing paper, chopping wood, writing with chalk and mixing sugar and water together. In the mixing of sugar with water, or salt with water, even though the sugar or salt may not be visible to the naked eye in the water, it is still there and still has the same composition—that is, the molecules that make up the sugar or salt and water are still the same as when you mixed them. You can evaporate the water and you will recover your sugar or salt crystals.

A **chemical change** is when the substances that were combined are no longer the same molecules—they have changed to new substances. For example, burning wood, mixing baking soda and vinegar, or a rusting nail, which is when the iron of the nail (Fe) combines with oxygen (in the presence of water) to form a new substance—that is, a new molecule is formed, iron oxide Fe_2O_3.

Physical changes can be reversed, whereas chemical changes generally cannot be reversed. Evidence of a chemical change include that the combination of the substances gives off a gas (bubbles are observed), it changes color (not always a chemical change, but may be if the other evidences are also present), gives off heat and becomes warmer, or absorbs heat and becomes colder (temperature change), and forms a precipitate (a solid substance). When heat is given off in a chemical change, it is an **exothermic** reaction; and when heat is absorbed in a chemical change (the combination becomes colder), it is an **endothermic** reaction. Everyday examples of exothermic reactions are firewood burning or the use of a hand warmer that many mountain climbers and snow skiers use, and examples of endothermic reactions are a cold pack used in sports injuries or the combination of baking soda and vinegar (try it with a thermometer in the vinegar during the reaction and see!).

Chemical Reactions in Everyday Life

Chemical reactions occur in everyday life and are an essential part of our physical and biological world. The burning of gasoline in automobiles is a chemical change—and burning of any kind, for that matter. Burning is the combination of oxygen from the atmosphere with substances containing the carbon atom. The proper temperature has to be reached in order to begin this exothermic reaction, but once started, the chemical reaction can continue until the oxygen is used up or is prevented from entering into the reaction. So since gasoline is a fossil fuel (a once living organism), it contains carbon. When we provide the energy it needs to begin the reaction, called activation energy, as long as oxygen is present, the carbon substance will burn. Burning is a chemical reaction because the carbon and oxygen combine to form new substances such as carbon monoxide (CO) and carbon dioxide (CO_2). The same reaction occurs in burning wood, candles, and even in cell respiration—the oxygen we breathe and carry through our bloodstream is combined in our cells with carbon-containing glucose molecules in a type of "controlled" burning. Our bodies give off heat from this reaction, which is why we are able to maintain a fairly high temperature of about 98.6 degrees Fahrenheit. Other examples of chemical reactions in everyday life include chemical batteries, the digestion of food, and cooking/baking. Moreover, the process of photosynthesis, where plants use sunlight to convert carbon dioxide gas and water into food for the plant known as glucose (a simple sugar), is also an important chemical reaction responsible for providing food for and sustaining all life on Earth.

Principles of Energy

Energy is available in many forms, including heat, light, solar radiation, chemical, electrical, magnetic, sound, and mechanical energy. It exists in three states: potential, kinetic, and activation energies. An object possessing energy because of its ability to move has **kinetic energy**. The energy that an object has as the result of its position or condition is called **potential energy**. The energy necessary to transfer or convert potential energy into kinetic energy is called **activation energy**. All three states of energy can be transformed from one to the other. A vehicle parked in a garage has potential energy. When the driver starts the engine using the chemical energy stored in the battery and the fuel, potential energy becomes activation energy. Once the vehicle is moving, the energy changes to kinetic energy.

Heat and Temperature

Heat is a form of energy. Temperature is the measure of heat. The most common device used to measure temperature is the thermometer. Thermometers are made of heat-sensitive substances—mercury and alcohol—that expand when heated.

Heat and Light

The most common form of energy comes from the sun. Solar energy provides heat and light for animals and plants. Through **photosynthesis**, plants capture radiant energy from the sun and transform it into **chemical energy** in the form of glucose. This chemical energy is stored in the leaves, stems, and fruits of plants. Humans and animals consume the plants or fruits and get the energy they need for survival. This energy source is transformed again to create kinetic energy and body heat. **Kinetic energy** is used for movement and to do work, while **heat** is a required element for all warm-blooded animals, like humans. Cold-blooded animals also require heat, but rather than making it themselves through the transformation of plant sugar, they use solar energy to heat their body. Energy transformation constitutes the foundation and the driving force of an ecosystem. In addition to heat and solar radiation, energy is available in the forms of electricity and magnetism.

Heat Transfer

The transfer of heat is accomplished in three ways: conduction, radiation, and convection. **Conduction** is the process of transferring heat or electricity through a substance. It occurs when two objects of differing temperatures are placed in contact with each other and heat flows from the hotter object to the cooler object. For example, in the cooling system of a car, heat from the engine is transferred to the liquid coolant. When the coolant passes through the radiator, the heat transfers from the coolant to the radiator, and eventually, out of the car. This heat transfer system preserves the engine and allows it to continue working.

Radiation describes the energy that travels at high speed in space in the form of light or through the decay of radioactive elements. Radiation is part of our modern life. It exists in simple states as the energy emitted by microwaves, cellular phones, and sunshine or as potentially dangerous energy as X-ray machines and nuclear weapons. The radiation used in medicine, nuclear power, and nuclear weapons has enough energy to cause permanent damage and death.

Convection describes the flow of heat through the movement of matter from a hot region to a cool region. In its most basic form, the concept of convection is that warmer air rises and colder air sinks. The colder air contracts and so is denser, thus it sinks; the warmer air is expanded, or more spread out, and so is less dense and rises. Thus, convection occurs when the heating and circulation of a substance changes the density of the substance. A good example is the heating of air over land near coastal areas coupled with the influx of cooler sea breezes offshore. The heated air inland expands and thus decreases in density, causing the cooler, more dense air to rush in to achieve equilibrium. A more common example of convection is the process of heating water on a stove. In this case, heat is transferred from the stove element to the bottom of the pot to the water. Heat is transferred from the hot water at the bottom to the cooler water at the top by convection. At the same time, the cooler, denser water at the top sinks to the bottom, where it is subsequently heated. This circulation creates the movement typical of boiling water. Convection currents created by the combining or colliding of cold and warm air masses is one factor responsible for storms and circular rotation of the air in tornados and hurricanes. Ocean currents are also caused by the collision of cold water and warm water masses in the oceans (Cavallo, 2001).

Electricity and Magnetism

When you arrange an energy source, such as a battery, a wire, and a light bulb (or motor, or bell, or any electrical device) such that all *metal* parts are touching (metal is a good "conductor" of energy) in a circle—the bulb will light (the motor will run, the bell will ring, and so on). What has been created by arranging the items in this circle is known as an "electric circuit." The energy from the battery or other energy source is able to "flow" or be transferred through the metal wires and parts of the circuit. A **closed circuit** is when all metal parts are touching and the electrical charge is able to continue to be transferred through the circuit. A light switch or other "on button" closes the circuit and allows the electricity to flow. An **open circuit** is when there is a break someplace in the flow of electricity through the circuit. A switch or "off button" opens the circuit and stops the electricity flow. When you ring a door bell, you are closing the circuit or allowing all metal parts to touch and send electricity through it to make the bell ring; when you let go of the doorbell button, the circuit is open, and so the flow of electricity stops and so does the bell's ringing.

Lightning is a form of *static* electricity which means it is not "flowing" or being transferred in the way it is through a metal wire, but is caused by friction, much the same as walking across a carpet in socks and getting a shock when a metal doorknob is touched. In both kinds of electricity, the electrons in the atoms of the substance, which are negatively charged, are pulled away from their atom's nucleus, giving the object, or cloud, a negative charge. The negative charge is quickly attracted to a positive charge—in the case of lightning, that positive charge could be something (or someone!) on the ground. The positive charge quickly jumps toward the negative charge and the negative charge quickly jumps toward the positive charge, and a flash of lightning and clap of thunder is heard; or in the case of the doorknob, a spark and a snap sound. Electric circuits are just a way to channel the electricity and the opposing charges through a conductor such as metal wires to allow us to use the energy to do work and to transform the energy into different forms such as sound (a radio), light (light bulbs), mechanical (machinery), and/or heat energy.

Light Energy

Light energy, and all energy for that matter, travels in waves and in a straight-line path. The electromagnetic spectrum shows the different wavelengths and frequencies of energy, including the small portion that is visible light. The electromagnetic spectrum includes, for example, micro-waves, x-rays, radio waves, infrared radiation, visible light waves, and ultraviolet radiation, all of which have different wavelengths and frequencies that distinguish one type of wave from another.

For more information see *http://imagine.gsfc.nasa.gov/docs/science/know_l1/emspectrum.html*

Visible light is the wavelength of light we can see, which our eyes see as white light. However, this white light is composed of a host of other wavelengths of light that our eyes cannot always distinguish, which we know as the visible light spectrum, or a rainbow. The colors of white light include red, orange, yellow, green, blue, indigo, and violet (although some sources now eliminate indigo as separate from violet), or ROYGBIV. When light, again, traveling in a straight line, hits an object or substance and is *bent*, it is called **refraction**. The bending of light waves may result in the colors of light in the spectrum becoming visible, as when we see a rainbow in the sky (the water molecules in the air bend the light) or when light travels through cut glass such as with a prism. **Reflection** is when light waves bounce back, as when looking in a mirror. The principles of reflection and refraction are used in periscopes and telescopes in order to be able to see objects we may otherwise not be able to see. They are often popular in magic shows when objects are said to "disappear." In actuality, the light of the object has been refracted or reflected to a place away from our eyes so that we can no longer see it.

Refraction is also used to our advantage through concave and convex lenses. Concave or convex lenses work such that when light passes through it changes the focal point. The eye contains a lens, but when light passing through the eye cannot properly focus on the "screen" known as the retina, the object being viewed may be blurred. Concave or convex lenses are used in eyeglasses to adjust and correct the focal point. These lenses are also used in cameras, microscopes, and telescopes. A spoon is an example of both a concave and a convex lens—if you look into the concave side, you will see yourself upside down. If you look into the convex side of the spoon, you will see yourself right side up. This is due to refraction (and reflection) of light.

For more on this topic, see *http://camillasenior.homestead.com/optics4.html*.

Sound Energy

Sound also travels in waves. Sounds are caused by vibrations, such as a guitar string (or a rubber band), or banging on a drum or cymbal. Sound has a certain wavelength, frequency, pitch, and amplitude (loudness). Sound waves must travel through a medium, which may be solid, liquid, or gas. Sound travels best through solids because there are more molecules (particles) to vibrate, and least well through gases.

The types of sound waves are longitudinal and transverse. **Logitudinal** waves move parallel to the direction the wave moves, and transverse waves move perpendicular to the direction of the wave.

Electricity

Electricity is the flow of electrons or electric power or charge. The basic unit of charge is based on the positive charge of the proton and the negative charge of the electron. Energy occurs naturally in the atmosphere through light. However, it is not feasible to capture that type of energy. The electricity that we use comes from secondary sources because it is produced from the conversion of primary (natural) sources of energy like fossil fuels that are **nonrenewable** (natural gas, coal, and oil) and nuclear, and **renewable** resources such as wind and solar energy. All sources of energy are used to produce a common result—to turn a turbine that generates electricity (see *www.sce. com/kids/science/producing.html*). Electricity that is generated can then be sent through wires for human use, and can be transformed into other forms of energy, including sound, light, heat, and force.

Conservation of Energy

The main principle of energy conservation states that energy can change form but cannot totally disappear. For example, the chemical energy stored in a car battery is used to start the engine, which in turn is used to recharge the battery. Another example of energy conservation is placing merchandise on shelves. Energy was used to do the work (placing merchandise on a shelf) and it was stored as potential energy. Potential energy in turn can be converted to kinetic energy when the merchandise is pushed back to the floor. In this case, work was recovered completely, but often the recovered energy is less than the energy used to do the work. This loss of energy can be caused by friction or any kind of resistance encountered in the process of doing the work. For example, as a vehicle's tires roll across the pavement, doing the work of moving forward, they encounter friction. This friction causes heat energy to be released, as well as kinetic energy.

In essence, energy cannot be created or destroyed, only changed in form. Likewise, matter cannot be created or destroyed, only changed in form. Thus, energy from the sun is changed, for example, to chemical energy when plants use the energy to make glucose in photosynthesis. The energy from the sun is stored in the chemical bonds of the glucose molecule and will be released for use by the organism—the plant itself, or any organism that eats the plant and its glucose—when the molecule's chemical bonds are "broken" by oxygen in cell respiration and/or stored in another chemical form known as ATP. Likewise, electrical energy comes from burning, or breaking the bond of carbon-based molecules as in fossil fuels. This electricity generated is then transformed to another form by first capturing and sending that electrical energy through metal wires originating at the power generating plant, and sending it in a complete, closed circuit to homes, businesses, and industries. There the electrical energy may be transformed into sound, heat, light, and/or mechanical energy. In all cases, the energy is not lost, it is changed in form.

It is important to conserve matter and energy generated from fossil fuels as these are non-renewable sources and will one day be expended. It is also important to continue exploring alternative, renewable forms of energy and electricity generation to meet our society's energy demands and maintain our Earth's clean air and water supplies.

Key Principles of Physical Science

- To help students develop higher-order thinking skills, teachers need to guide students to analyze research data and make extrapolations or inferences based on data analysis.

- Matter is anything that has mass and takes up space.

- Mass is the amount of matter something contains.

- Volume refers to the amount of space taken up by an object.

- The states of matter are solid, gas, liquid, and plasma.

- There are 112 basic kinds of matter which are called elements.

- Elements are made up of atoms. An atom is the smallest part of matter.

- A compound is a kind of matter made up of two or more elements.

- A chemical formula describes the kinds of elements present in a compound. The chemical formula of water is H_2O because it has two molecules of hydrogen and one molecule of oxygen.

- Physical properties of matter are the characteristics that can be seen or measured without changing the material.

- Chemical properties of matter are the characteristics that can only be seen when the material changes and new materials are formed; for example, wood burns and turns into ashes. A chemical property of wood is its ability to burn.

- Water boils at 212 degrees Fahrenheit or 100 degrees Celsius, and it freezes at 32 degrees Fahrenheit or 0 degrees Celsius.

- Mass is the amount of matter or material of an object.

- Weight is the amount of gravitational force exerted over an object.

- When measuring dry chemicals on a balance scale, teachers should follow these steps: (1) Place and weigh a watch glass or dish, (2) place the dry chemical inside the watch glass or dish, and (3) subtract the weight of the glass or dish from the total to obtain the real weight of the chemical.

- Energy and matter may be changed from one form to another but are not lost.

- Heat is transferred by conduction, convection, and radiation.

- Electric circuits may be open or closed.

- Potential energy is stored energy; kinetic energy is energy in motion or actively being used. Activation energy is the energy it takes to change potential energy into kinetic energy.

- Light travels in waves and in a straight line; light may be refracted or bent and/or reflected.

- Sound is caused by vibrations.

LIFE SCIENCE

Also referred to as bioscience, life science includes any of several branches of science, such as biology, medicine, or ecology, that deal with living organisms and their organization, life processes, and relationships to each other and their environment. This competency will be 30% of your science score and tests your understanding of

- the structure and function of living systems (e.g., living characteristics and cells, tissues and organs, life processes)

- the reproduction and heredity (e.g., growth and development, patterns of inheritance of traits, molecular basis of heredity)

- change over time in living things (e.g., life cycles, mutations, adaptations and natural selection)

- regulation and behavior (e.g., life cycles, responses to external stimuli, controlling the internal environment)

- the unity and diversity of life, adaptation, and classification

- the interdependence of organisms (e.g., ecosystems, populations, communities)

Structure and Function

All living things carry on life functions such as respiration, nutrition, response, circulation, growth, excretion, regulation, and reproduction, all of which characterize them as *living* as opposed to nonliving. In addition, all living things are composed of the basic unit of life known as *cells*. Organisms, as well as individual cells of an organism and single-celled organisms, carry on these life functions using specialized structures. For example, earthworms carry on respiration through their moist skin; plants excrete gases from tiny pores on the underside of leaves called stomata; a single-celled amoeba ingests food by use of a "false foot" or pseudopodia; and insects respond to chemical attractants called pheromones of the opposite-sex insect for mating.

Animal and Plant Cells

Animal and plant cells are similar in appearance. Animal cells contain mitochondria, small round or rod-shaped bodies found in the cytoplasm of most cells. The main function of mitochondria is to produce the enzymes for the metabolic conversion of food to energy. This process consumes oxygen and is termed **aerobic respiration**.

Plants cells also contain mitochondria, which allow plants to carry on respiration where they use oxygen and excrete carbon dioxide and water just like animals. However, plants also have specialized organelles called chloroplasts that are used for taking in sunlight and using this energy to convert another gas, carbon dioxide, and water taken in from the roots to make glucose—a simple sugar that is the food for the plant. Chloroplasts contain chlorophyll, which is used in this process of converting light into chemical energy. This process is called **photosynthesis**. Photosynthesis is the process by which chlorophyll-containing organisms convert light energy to chemical energy.

Cell System

The cell is the basic unit of living organisms and the simplest living unit of life. Living organisms are composed of cells that have the following common characteristics:

- Have a membrane that regulates the flow of nutrients and water that enter and exit the cell

- Contain the genetic material (DNA) that allows for reproduction

- Require a supply of energy

- Contain basic chemicals to make metabolic decisions for survival

- Reproduce and are the result of reproduction

Eukaryotic and Prokaryotic Cells

There are two kinds of cells—prokaryotic and eukaryotic. **Prokaryotic cells** are the simplest and most primitive type of cells. They do not contain the structures typical of eukaryotic cells. Prokaryotic cells lack a nucleus and instead have one strand of deoxyribonucleic acid (DNA). Some prokaryotic cells have external whip like flagella for locomotion or a hairlike system for adhesion. Prokaryotic cells come in three shapes: cocci (round), bacilli (rods), and spirilla or spirochetes (helical cells). Bacteria (also called Monera) are prokaryotic cells. For more information and animated illustrations of pro- karyotic cells see *www.cellsalive.com/cells/bactcell.htm*.

Eukaryotic cells evolved from prokaryotic cells and in the process became structur- ally and biochemically more complex. The key distinction between the two cell types is that only eukaryotic cells contain many structures, or organelles, separated from other cytoplasm components by a membrane. The organelles within eukaryotic cells are the nucleus, mitochondria, chloroplasts, and Golgi apparatus. The nucleus contains the deoxyribonucleic acid (DNA) information. The mitochondria have their own membrane and contain some DNA information and proteins. They generate the energy for the cell. The chloroplast is a component that exists in plants only, allowing them to trap sunlight as energy for the process of photosynthesis. The Golgi apparatus secretes substances needed for the cell's survival.

Classifications of Living Things

Living things are divided into five groups, or **kingdoms**: Monera (bacteria), Protista (protozoans), Fungi, Plantae (plants), and Animalia (animals).

Monera consists of unicellular organisms. It is the only group of living organisms made of prokaryotic cells—the cells with a primitive organization system. Some exam- ples of this organism are bacteria, blue-green algae, and spirochetes.

Protista contains a type of eukaryotic cell with a more complex organization system. This kingdom includes diverse, mostly unicellular organisms that live in aquatic habitats, in both freshwater and saltwater. They are not animals or plants but unique organisms. Some examples of Protista are protozoans and algae of various types. The Amoeba, Para- mecium, and Euglena are in the Protista Kingdom.

Fungi are multicellular organisms with a sophisticated organization system—that is, containing eukaryotic cells. Fungi exist in a variety of forms and shapes. Because they do not have chlorophyll, they cannot produce food through photosynthesis. Fungi obtain energy, carbon, and water from digesting dead materials. Some examples of these types of organisms are mushrooms, mold, mildews, and yeast.

Plants are multicellular organisms with a sophisticated organization system. In addition to more familiar plants, moss and ferns also fall under this category. Plant cells have chloro- plasts, a component that allows them to trap sunlight as energy for the process of photosynthesis. In photosynthesis plants use carbon dioxide from the atmospheric environment and as the by-product of this process, supply the oxygen needed for the survival of animals.

Animals are also multicellular with multiple forms and shapes, and with specialized senses and organs. The Animalia kingdom is composed of organisms like sponges, worms, insects, fish, amphibians, reptiles, birds, and mammals. Animals are the most sophisticated type of living organisms and represent the highest levels of evolution. Animals live in all kinds of habitats, and they are as simple as flies or as sophisticated as humans.

Life Cycles

Life traditionally begins with a seed or a fertilized egg, which goes through metamorphosis until the organism is fully formed. The development and growth of organisms can take days, months, or years, but eventually they all go through similar stages: creation, maturation, reproduction, and death. Some organisms, like insects, go through a short cycle, reproducing once and then dying. Others, like vertebrates, spend more time in the reproductive stage. Some examples of living organisms and the changes that they go through are presented in Table 6.4.

Table 6-4. Life Cycles of Common Organisms

Organism	Stage 1	Stage 2	Stage 3	Stage 4	Stage 5
Darkling Beetle	Egg (fertilized by male sperm)	Larva—called "mealworm" though not a true worm	Pupa—mealworm curls up into a pupated or sleeplike state	Darkling Beetle	Reproduction—organisms lay eggs Death of the adult
Butterfly	Egg (fertilized by male sperm)	Larva—called caterpillar	Pupa—caterpillar forms a cocoon or chrysalis	Butterfly	Reproduction—organisms lay eggs Death of the adult
Frog	Egg (fertilized by male sperm)	Embryo	Tadpole	Frog	Reproduction—organism lays eggs Death of the adult
Human	Egg (fertilized by male sperm)	Embryo/Fetus	Child through adolescent	Human adult	Reproduction—organisms have live birth of offspring Death of the adult
					(continued)

Organism	Stage 1	Stage 2	Stage 3	Stage 4	Stage 5
Trees	Seed with embryo or "baby plant" inside (egg or ovule inside of flower, ovary fertilized by male sperm, nuclei inside of pollen grains)	Sprout	Growing plant	Mature tree	Reproduction—Tree produces flowers with new seeds that are dispersed Death of the adult

Some of the most spectacular metamorphoses (changes from one stage of life to another) are experienced by insects, amphibians, and humans. Insects, like the Darkling Beetle and the butterfly, go through drastic changes in a period of weeks. Frogs go through similar transmutations that allow them to move from an aquatic environment to land. Humans, on the other hand, begin life as microscopic beings and after nine months develop into a six- to nine-pound physically functional individual. The National Science Education Standards (NSES) emphasize that during the elementary school grades, students should be exposed to the concept of life cycles for plants and animals, including humans.

For additional information about living things, go to the website of the Behavioral Sciences Department of Palomar College, San Marcos, California, at *http://anthro.palomar.edu/animal/default.htm*.

Life Cycle of Plants

The life cycle of plants generally begins with seeds. Mature plants produce the seeds, which are transported through various means: wind, water, hitchhiking on animals, or ingested as food and released as droppings or waste. For the seeds to germinate, they need air, the right amount of heat or proper temperature specific for that seed, and water. They do not need light to *germinate* or initially sprout, but do need light to grow since they need to carry on photosynthesis for their source of food, and to mature into an adult plant that can reproduce new seeds. Growing plants also need the right kind of soil, sufficient water, and heat/light from the sun. As part of the growth process, plants develop a root system for support and to extract the water and minerals they need from the soil. It is important to understand that fertilizers are *not* food for the plant—they only provide vitamins and minerals for the plant to help it remain healthy. The only food the plant has is what it makes for itself through photosynthesis.

Through the process of **photosynthesis**, a plant containing chlorophyll captures energy from the sun and converts it into chemical energy. Part of the chemical energy is used for the plant's own survival, and the rest is stored in the stem and leaves. As part of the growth process, some plants produce flowers, which are pollinated by insects or through the wind. That is, the pollen, which contains sperm nuclei, is transferred from the male part of the flower, the stamen, to the female part of the flower, the pistil. Once pollination occurs, the sperm leaves the pollen and travels to the ovules or eggs inside the ovary of the pistil and fertilizes the ovules. The fertilized ovules become the seeds. The ovary swells to become the fruit, and the flower itself dies because it has now served its purpose. The fruits contain, carry, and protect the seeds until they are dispersed to a place where they can sprout, and the cycle of the plant continues.

For information on how this process can be presented to children in the elementary school grades, visit the following site: "The Life Cycle of Plants," at www.cast.org/teachingeverystudent. For additional information about photosynthesis, visit the following site: "Exploring Photosynthesis," at www.botany.uwc.ac.za/ecotree/photosynthesis/photosynthesis1.htm. An inquiry-based curriculum on the life cycle of plants can also be found in the NSTA publication, Science and Children by Cavallo (2005) titled, Cycling Through Plants.

Life Cycle of Animals

Many animals come from eggs. For some animals, the egg grows inside the female animal and is fertilized by the male, for others such as most fish species, the eggs are fertilized by the male after they have been expelled from the female's body. When fertilized internally, the fertilized egg may be laid externally from the female as in many insects, reptiles, and birds, or it may remain in the body of the female until birth. The egg has an outer lining to protect the animal growing inside. Bird eggs have hard shells, while the eggs of amphibians, like the turtle, have hard but flexible coverings. With the appropriate care and heat, an egg will hatch. After hatching, in some species, the parents protect and feed the newborn until it can survive on its own; in other species, the eggs are left on their own to survive. On reaching adulthood, females begin laying eggs, and the cycle of life continues. Mammals are also conceived through egg fertilization, but the resulting embryo is kept inside the mother until it is mature enough for life outside the womb.

Needs of Living Organisms

Living organisms like plants and animals need to have ideal conditions for their survival. They need nutrients, the appropriate temperature, and a balanced ecosystem to survive and reproduce. A healthy ecosystem must contain an appropriate system for energy exchange or a food chain. The right combination of herbivorous and carnivorous animals is necessary for a healthy ecosystem. The food chain generally begins with the primary source of energy, the sun. The sun provides the energy for plants; plants in turn are consumed by animals; and animals are consumed by other animals. These animals die and serve as food sources for fungi and plants. When this balance is disrupted either by the removal of organisms or the introduction of nonnative species, the ecosystem is affected, forcing animals and plants to adapt or else die. Thus, the common basic needs of all living organisms for survival are: *air, water, food,* and *shelter.*

Body Structure and Function

Cells are the basic unit of all living organisms. Within cells there are specialized organelles that carry on all of the life functions at a microscopic/chemical level. For example, the mitochondria carries on cell respiration, and ribosomes assemble proteins for use both inside the cell and out. Teachers should know the parts of the cell, called organelles, and their functions, particularly, the nucleus, mitochondria, chloroplasts (plants only), ribosomes, Golgi, endoplasmic reticulum, vacuoles, and cell membranes.

Moving outward from the *cell*, it is important to know that cells communicate with one another on a chemical level and work together to perform specific functions. The shape of these groups of cells and activity levels differ according to their particular function in the body; for example, muscle cells are long and narrow so they may better respond to stimuli and contract. Groups of cells with similar functions are called *tissues*. Tissues are organized together to perform a specific life function. A complex system of tissues working together to carry on one of the body's life functions is an *organ*. A group of different organs working together to support and help carry out a life function and keep the organism alive is called an *organ system*. Examples of systems include the digestive system, the respiratory system, the immune system, the muscular system, the skeletal system, the nervous system, and the circulatory system. Organ systems are organized into an *organism*. The order of organization is as follows:

Cells → Tissues → Organs → Systems → Organ Systems → Organism

For more information on the structure and function of organisms, see *www.palmbeach.k12.fl.us/MULTI-CULTURAL/ESOLCurriculumDocs/Secondary/SciOrganism.pdf*

Systems of the Human Body

Musculoskeletal System

The human skeleton consists of more than 200 bones held together by connective tissues called ligaments. Movements are effected by contractions of the *skeletal muscles*, and skeletal muscles are arranged in pairs, such as the biceps and triceps of the upper arm. When one of the pair contracts, it causes a certain movement of the bones; in the meantime the opposing muscle relaxes. When the opposing pair of muscle contracts, a different movement of the bones occurs, and the original muscle of the pair relaxes. For example, when the biceps (the muscle on top of the upper arm) contracts, the arm bends upwards; when the opposing muscle of the pairthe triceps, contract, the arm extends. Skeletal muscles are attached to bones with specialized connective tissue called tendons. The specialized connective tissue that attaches bones to other bones is called ligaments. The soft spongy tissue on the ends of bones is called cartilage. Muscular contractions are controlled by the nervous system.

In addition to skeletal muscle, the body also has muscles that are not part of the musculoskeletal system, thus not attached to bones. One such muscle type is called *smooth muscle*. Smooth muscle forms the inner linings of our digestive system and is controlled involuntarily by our autonomic (automatic) nervous system. A third type of muscle is *cardiac muscle*, which is the muscle of the heart, and is also controlled by our autonomic nervous system.

For a detailed analysis of each component of the body system go to the *Human Anatomy Online* website at *www.innerbody.com/htm/body.html*.

Nervous System

The nervous system has two main divisions: the somatic and autonomic. The somatic allows the voluntary control of skeletal muscles, and the automatic, or involuntary, controls cardiac and glandular functions. **Voluntary movement** is caused by nerve impulses sent from the brain through the spinal cord to nerves to connecting skeletal muscles. **Involuntary movement** occurs in direct response to outside stimulus. Involuntary responses are called reflexes. For example, when an object presents danger to the eye, the body responds automatically by blinking or retracting away from the object.

Circulatory System

The circulatory system follows a cyclical process in which the heart pumps blood through the right chambers of the heart and through the lungs, where it acquires oxygen. From there it is pumped back into the left chambers of the heart, where it is pumped into the main artery (aorta), which then sends the oxygenated blood to the rest of the body using a system of veins and capillaries. Through the capillaries, the blood distributes the oxygen and nutrients to tissues, absorbing from them carbon dioxide, a metabolic waste product. Finally, the blood completes the circuit by passing through small veins, which join to form increasingly larger vessels. Eventually, the blood reaches the largest veins, which return it to the right side of the heart to complete and restart the process.

Immune System

The main function of the body's immune system is to defend itself against foreign proteins and infectious organisms. The system recognizes organisms that are not normally in the body and develops the antibodies needed to control and destroy the invaders. When the body is attacked by infectious organisms, it develops what we know as a fever. Fever is the body's way of fighting invading molecules. The raised temperature of a fever will kill some bacteria. The major components of the immune system are the thymus, lymph system, bone marrow, white blood cells, antibodies, and hormones.

Respiratory System

Respiration is carried out by the expansion and contraction of the lungs. In the lungs, oxygen enters tiny capillaries, where it combines with **hemoglobin** in the red blood cells and is carried to the tissues through the circulatory system. At the same time, carbon dioxide passes through capillaries into the air contained within the lungs.

Animals inhale oxygen from the environment and exhale carbon dioxide. Carbon dioxide is used by plants in the process of photosynthesis, which produces the oxygen that animals use again for survival.

Digestive and Excretory Systems

The energy required for sustenance of the human body is supplied through the chemical energy stored in food. To obtain the energy from food, it has to be fragmented and digested. Digestion begins at the moment that food is placed in the mouth and makes contact with saliva. Fragmented and partially digested food passes down the esophagus to the stomach, where the process is continued by the gastric and intestinal juices. Thereafter, the mixture of food and secretions makes its way down the small intestine, where the nutrients are extracted and absorbed into the bloodstream. The unused portion of the food goes to the large intestine and eventually is excreted from the body through defecation.

Reproductive System

Students in the upper elementary grades (5 and 6) should know some basic biological facts about human reproduction. They should know that the body matures and develops in order for child-bearing to occur. The menstrual cycle should be understood by students, including what occurs in ovulation to prepare the egg cell, namely, the process of meiosis. In males, the process of meiosis occurs to produce the sperm cell. Students should know that these specialized cells, called gametes (egg and sperm), unite to form a fertilized egg, which grows and develops in distinct stages to produce new offspring.

Reproduction

An organism may consist of only one cell, or it may comprise many billions of cells of various dimensions. For example, cells are complete organisms, such as the unicellular bacteria; others, such as muscle cells, are parts of multicellular organisms. All cells have an internal substance called cytoplasm—a clear gelatinous fluid—enclosed within a membrane. Each cell contains the genetic material containing the information for the formation of organisms. Cells are composed primarily of water and the elements oxygen, hydrogen, carbon, and nitrogen.

Growth in most organisms is caused by nuclear cell division (**mitosis**.) In mitosis the chromosomes (containing DNA which is the genetic material of the cell or blueprint) first replicate—in humans the 46 chromosomes in the cell double. The cell then divides through a series of steps resulting in 2 new cells that each has the original 46 chromosomes, or the exact copy of the original. Through mitosis, new cells are made, for example, to form a scar after an injury, new bone cells, muscle cells, blood cells, and any cell that is needed by the body throughout life and growth.

However, in single-celled organisms, mitosis is the cell's form of reproduction—making exact copies of the DNA in each of the two "daughter" cells, and is often called binary fission. This type of reproduction is also called **asexual reproduction** because only one organism (the single cell) is involved and there is no exchange of genetic material or DNA. Thus, the two offspring cells, or daughter cells, are identical to the original or parent cell.

In humans and many other organisms, particularly mammals, another form of cell division occurs only in the reproductive organs (in most called the female ovaries and male testicles) where the DNA is replicated/copied; however, the cell divides *twice* in a process called **meiosis**. Meiosis is how sperm and egg cells are formed through a series of steps. The original cell in the female ovary or male testicle first duplicates (replicates) its 46 chromosomes (containing the genetic blueprint material, DNA) and then divides *twice,* the result is four cells with half the number of chromosomes, or 23 chromosomes each. In forming the egg cell, only one is a viable egg that can be fertilized and the remaining three are polar bodies that eventually dissolve. In the male, all four sperm cells that were formed by meiosis of the original cell are viable and capable of fertilizing the egg. The process is similar in other organisms; however, the number of chromosomes may be different, depending on the particular species—a similar process even occurs in plants, where the flower is the reproductive organ—the ovules are the egg cells, and the pollen contains the sperm. This form of reproduction is known as **sexual reproduction**, because it requires the combination of DNA between two organisms of the same species (male, female). The fertilization of the egg by sperm cells occurs through copulation in vertebrates, and for fish and some amphibians it occurs through cross-fertilization. Cross-fertilization occurs outside the body; the female lays the eggs (ovum), and the males spray them with sperm to fertilize them.

Plant Reproduction

The reproduction of plants can also be divided into asexual and sexual mechanisms. Asexual reproduction of plants takes place by cutting portions of the plant and replanting them. Sexual reproduction involves seeds produced by female and male plants, which are then cross-pollinated with help from insects or other animals. As mentioned, the flower is the reproductive organ of the plant. The flower consists of several parts that are the male and female reproductive organs. Some flowers may have only the male part, and likewise, some flowers contain only the female part of the same species of plant/tree. So there actually can be a "male" tree and a "female" tree for example. In the flower, the male reproductive organ is the stamen, which is divided into filament and anther. The filament simply holds up the anther, and the anther contains the pollen and in the pollen are the sperm nuclei. Flowers may also contain the female reproductive organ, or pistil, which consists of the ovary, style, and stigma. The ovary contains the egg cells, which in the flower are called ovules. The style is the tube above the ovary, and the stigma is the top of the style which has a sticky substance. The pollen needs to either be manually placed on the stigma, or blown there by the wind, or what usually happens, it needs to stick to the body of a bee or butterfly (who are actually in search of sugary nectar in the flower and not the pollen). When the pollen sticks to the body of the insect, it may then be transferred from the anther (male part) to the stigma (female part). In essence, the sperm nuclei then travel down the style until it reaches the ovules, where fertilization occurs. The fertilized egg then becomes the seed. The ovary of the flower may swell and become the fruit (as in a peach or apple). This process helps protect the seeds and also helps with seed dispersal (animals eat the fruit, the seed has a seed coat that protects it and is indigestible, the animals excretes the seed, unharmed, in its fecal matter). Seed germination—where the seed sprouts into a plant—requires the appropriate quantity of air, water, and heat.

Hereditary Material

Deoxyribonucleic acid or *DNA* is the hereditary material of living organisms. DNA has as its smallest complete component what is called a nucleotide. A single nucleotide consists of the sugar deoxyribose, a phosphate molecule, and a nitrogen base molecule. There are four nitrogen bases that are paired in the double-helix structure of DNA. These nitrogen bases are adenine, thymine, guanine, and cytosine. In DNA, adenine always pairs with a nucleotide having thymine as its nitrogen base (A-T); and guanine always pairs with a nucleotide having cytosine as its nitrogen base (G-C), and vice versa (T-A; C-G).

In bacteria, also called monera or prokaryotic cells, DNA is in a single strand. In more complex organisms including protista, fungi, animals and plants, all eukaryotic cells, the DNA is arranged in *chromosomes*, and these chromosomes with its DNA are located in the nucleus (though there is new evidence of DNA in other cell organelles, particularly the mitochondria). The number of chromosomes in the cells of organisms varies from one species to another—but it is the same for all members of that species. Along the strands of DNA that exist inside of chromosomes, there are certain locations that direct specific functions of cells, including hereditary traits, called *genes*. Certain genes give the cell directions, in the developing embryo for example, for the expression of traits such as eye color, hair color, and leg shape and size. In already developed organisms, as the human adult, other genes (sections of DNA) direct the production of substances and control specific activities and functions. The production of insulin in pancreatic cells, for example, is controlled by certain genes in the chromosomes in the cells of the organ known as the pancreas. In inheritance and cell functions, traits can be controlled or determined by more than one gene, located on the same, or even on different chromosomes. Likewise, there may be several traits influenced by one single gene.

As discussed earlier, the fertilized egg that eventually grows into the organism that then goes through its respective life cycle to adult contains half the number of chromosomes from the female egg (mother) and half the number of chromosomes from the male sperm (father). In the human, there are 23 chromosomes in the egg and 23 in the sperm, so the fertilized egg and, therefore, the offspring (baby) has 46 chromosomes—which is the normal number for all cells in all organisms of the human species. The 23 chromosomes of the egg have an exact pair or match in the sperm. That matching chromosome contains genes with DNA that direct the same traits. So along the length of chromosome number 20, for example, in the egg cell, you will find it controls the same traits that are along the length of chromosome number 20 in the male sperm. However, the 23 chromosomes in the egg contain the specific qualities or characteristics of the mother; whereas, the 23 chromosomes in the sperm contain the specific qualities or characteristics of the father.

Though more than one chromosome controls eye color—we will use one chromosome as an example. In one of the egg cell's chromosomes, there is a gene that controls eye color, and in the egg this eye color could be "blue." In the same number chromosome in the same location in the sperm cell, there will also be a gene for eye color, but the characteristic of that eye color may instead be "brown." So traits are located on the same number chromosome whether that chromosome originated from the egg or the sperm; however, the quality or characteristic may differ (that is, the pigment color that section of DNA or gene directs the cell to make). The gene for eye color and other traits that are the paired chromosomes in the same location are called *alleles*. When the egg is fertilized, the directions coded in the DNA alleles are set. In many alleles, one of the traits directed by the gene on one chromosome is **dominant**, and the other is **recessive**. The dominant trait is the one that typically "shows" or is *expressed* in the offspring. In the case of eye color, brown is usually dominant over blue eye color, so if one of the alleles is for "blue" eyes and the other allele from the other parent is for "brown" eyes, the offspring will show the dominant trait and have brown eyes. Again, it must be cautioned that many genes may direct eye color especially in an organism as complex as humans, but it is simply used as an example here. In addition, it is important to note that **environmental factors** play an important role in the expression (showing up) of traits in the offspring as they grow and develop. Sometimes environmental stressors, for example, can cause a genetic change in an organism that otherwise may not have been expressed, such as certain food allergies or intolerances.

Adaptations and Change over Time

Genetics plays an important role in the ability of organisms to be able to survive and thrive in their environment and, ultimately, produce new offspring where they can pass on similar genetic material, like that which allowed *them* to survive and thrive, and maybe survive and thrive even better. Some inherited traits, called *adaptations,* allow the organisms to best survive in their environment and others do not, and may even lead to their demise (and those prevent the prospect of future offspring). Adaptations do not suddenly arise or develop in the lifetime of organisms. They occur gradually in the species over time. For example, if a certain deer-like animal thousands of years ago was particularly fast—that is, it was born with stronger muscle tissue than most, and a better bone and muscle physical structure—perhaps it was better able to run away from predators and survive. Therefore, this deer-like animal was able to survive long enough for it to have offspring with similar genetic material. At the same time, those deer-like animals that were not born with the same muscular and structural soundness as this one were killed as prey before they could reproduce. The animal that was best adapted to its environment (needing to run from predators) was the first deer-like animal. In time, those animals that are best suited in this, as well as in other ways, are the organisms who survive, as do their offspring. Those not well adapted perish. It is also the case that the organism that survives will breed with another that also has better adapted characteristics, and was also able to survive in the natural environment.

A change or **mutation** in the genetic material, that is, the genes that direct the development of a trait, may give rise to a new characteristic that either is or is not better suited for the environment. In the case that it is better suited, the organism will survive and produce offspring with this same mutation. Over the years, mutations that are better suited to the environment may make the organism appear quite different than it did hundreds, thousands, and millions of years earlier. If the environment itself changes, however, organisms that were able to survive under the previous conditions (climate, water supply, vegetation, landscape) may be unable to survive in the new environmental conditions. Thus, a catastrophic event, such as perhaps a large asteroid striking the earth, could change the environmental conditions and either lead to the extinction of organisms, or the survival of organisms that would not have survived under the conditions before the strike. Likewise, selective breeding, which is human selection of which organisms breed with another, and thus, control of the genetic material that is passed onto offspring, also effects the change over time of organisms. The combination of genetics, adaptations, changes over time, mutations, selective breeding, and environmental conditions/changes contribute to the concept known as evolution.

Ecology

Ecology studies the relationship of organisms with their physical environment. The physical environment includes light, heat, solar radiation, moisture, wind, oxygen, carbon dioxide, nutrients, water, and the atmosphere. The biological environment describes living and nonliving organisms in the ecosystem. There are three main components of an ecosystem:

- **Producers** are green plants that produce oxygen and store chemical energy for consumers.

- **Consumers** are animals, both herbivores and carnivores. The herbivores take the chemical energy from plants, and carnivores take the energy from other animals or directly from plants.

- **Decomposers**, like fungi and bacteria, are in charge of cleaning up the environment by decomposing and freeing dead matter for recycling back into the ecosystem.

Maintaining a Healthy Balance

A successful ecosystem requires a healthy balance among producers, consumers, and decomposers. This balance relies on natural ways to control populations of living organisms and is maintained mostly through competition and predation.

Competition

When a shared resource is scarce, organisms must compete to survive. The competition, which occurs between animals as well as between plants, ensures the survival of the fittest and the preservation of the system.

Predation

Predation is the consumption of one living organism, plant or animal, by another. It is a direct way to control population and promote natural selection by eliminating weak organisms from the population. As a consequence of predation, predators and prey evolve to survive. If an organism cannot evolve to meet challenges from the environment, it perishes.

Adaptation for Survival

Changes in the environment force living organisms to modify their ways and even develop new physical features for survival. For example, over thousands of years, the anteater species and its offspring were able to survive better if they had a long snout to be able to reach for ants, and frogs developed a long, sticky tongue to catch flies. Adaptation for animals, plants, and even humans is a matter of life and death. Changes in the food chain of animals often force them to change their behaviors and adapt to new conditions.

For example, because their habitats are destroyed when land is developed by humans, raccoons and opossums have learned to coexist with humans and to get new sources of food. Bears have managed to successfully adapt to colder climates by hibernating during the winter and living on the fat they accumulate during the rest of the year. Other animals, like the chameleon or the fox, have developed camouflage to hide from predators. Humans are not exempt from the need to adapt to new situations. For example, humans have had to adapt and use tools to produce, preserve, and trade the food supplies they needed to sustain them. All these examples represent ways in which organisms adapt to deal with challenges in their ecosystem.

Key Principles of the Life Science

- When working with animals, teachers are ethically responsible for their well-being. Teachers need to provide an adequate environment for the survival and development of animals under their care.

- By observing the development of frogs and butterflies, students directly acquire information on the life cycles. Students can also observe how organisms adapt to their environment.

- Fungi obtain energy, carbon, and water from dead material. Fungi do not have chlorophyll, so they cannot produce food through photosynthesis.

- Chromosomes contain the genetic code, or DNA.

- Mitosis describes the process of a cell splitting to create two identical cells.

- Meiosis is the process of cells dividing to produce the egg and sperm cells, each with half the number of chromosomes as the parent cell so they are ready to restore the normal number of the species upon fertilization.

- Photosynthesis is the process of capturing, storing, and converting solar energy. It is also the source of oxygen in the atmosphere.

- Insects have three main parts: head, thorax, and abdomen.

- Humans have several body systems, including the musculoskeletal, nervous, circulatory, immune, respiratory, and digestive/excretory systems.

- Adaptations are features or characteristics of an organism that best help it survive in its environment.

- Organisms in the environment depend upon one another for survival and are inextricably linked in the ecosystem.

EARTH SCIENCE

Any of several sciences, such as geology, oceanography, and meteorology, that study the origin, composition, and physical features of the Earth are considered part of this topic. This category, like the other main categories, will account for 30% of your science score which will test your ability to

- Understand the structure of the Earth system (e.g., structure and properties of the solid Earth, the hydrosphere, the atmosphere)

- Understand processes of the Earth system (e.g., earth processes of the solid Earth, the hydrosphere, the atmosphere)

- Understand Earth history (e.g., origin of Earth, paleontology, the rock record)

- Understand Earth and the universe (e.g., stars and galaxies; the solar system and planets; Earth, Sun, and Moon relationships)

- Understand Earth patterns, cycles, and change

Structure and Composition of the Earth (Geology)

Landform Characteristics

The formation of deserts, mountains, rivers, oceans, and other landforms can be described in terms of geological processes. Mountains are formed by colliding plates. For example, the Appalachian Mountains in the United States were formed 250 million years ago when the tectonic plate carrying the continent of Africa collided with the plate carrying the North American continent (Badder et. al., 2000). Rivers and natural lakes form at low elevations where rainfall collects and eventually runs down to the sea. The sediment gathered by the rivers in turn accumulates at river mouths to create deltas. These are both constructive and destructive processes that form the Earth. Constructive processes include those that build mountains, such as the gradual (over millions of years) collision and crushing together of the Earth's tectonic plates. Destructive processes include weathering and erosion—the wearing down of mountains and rock by forces such as water, wind, and ice.

Layers of the Earth

The average circumference of the Earth at the equator is 25,902 miles, and its radius is about 3,959 miles. The Earth is divided into three main parts:

- The **crust** is the outer portion of the Earth where we live. The thickness of the crust varies from about 3 miles to 40 miles, depending on the location. It contains various types of soil, metals, and rocks. The crust is broken down into several floating tectonic plates. Movements of these plates cause earthquakes and changes in landforms.

- The **mantle** is the thickest layer of the Earth located right below the crust. It is composed mostly of rocks and metals. The heat in the mantle is so intense that rocks and metals melt, creating magma and the resulting lava that reaches the surface.

- The **core** is the inner part of the Earth. It is composed of a solid **inner core** and an **outer core** that is mostly liquid. The inner core is made of solid iron and nickel. Despite temperatures in the inner core that resemble the heat on the surface of the sun, this portion of the Earth remains solid because of the intense pressure there.

For more information about the layers of the Earth, go to the following website: *http://scign.jpl.nasa.gov/learn/plate1.htm*.

Continental Drift

In 1915, the German scientist Alfred Weneger proposed that all the continents were previously one large continent but then broke apart and drifted through the ocean floor to their present locations. This theory involved the concept of continental drift, which is the foundation of today's science of plate tectonics.

Tectonic Plates

Based on the theory of plate tectonics, the surface of the Earth is fragmented into large plates. These plates are in continuous motion, floating on the liquid mantel and always changing in size and position. The edges of these plates, where they move against each other, are sites of intense geologic activity, which results in earthquakes, volcanoes, and the creation of mountains. The generator for the movement of the continents/ Earth's plates is the mid-Atlantic ridge—a huge volcanic mountain range on the floor of the Atlantic Ocean that is continuously erupting and pushing the plates apart in opposite directions from each other.

For more information on plate motion go to *pubs.usgs.gov/gip/dynamic/understanding. html#anchor5567033*.

Forces That Change the Surface of the Earth

Three main forces and processes change the surface of the Earth: weathering, geological movements, and the creation of glaciers.

Weathering

Weathering is the process of breaking down rock, soils, and minerals through natural, chemical, and biological processes. Two of the most common examples of physical weathering are exfoliation and freeze thaw.

- **Exfoliation** occurs in places like the desert when the soil is exposed first to high temperatures, which cause it to expand, and then to cold temperatures, which make the soil contract. The stress of these changes causes the outer layers of rock to peel off.

- **Freeze-thaw** breaks down rock when water gets into rock joints or cracks and then freezes and expands, breaking the rock. A similar process occurs when water containing salt crystals gets into the rock.

Once the water evaporates, the crystals expand and break the rock. This process is called salt-crystal growth.

Weathering can be caused by chemical reactions. Two of the most common examples of chemical weathering are acid formation and hydration. Acid is formed under various conditions. For example, sulfur and rain are combined to create acid rain, which can weather and change the chemical composition of rock. Hydration occurs when the minerals in rock absorb water and expand sometimes changing the chemical composition of the rock. For example, through the process of hydration, a mineral like anhydrite can be changed into a different mineral, namely gypsum.

Erosion

After weathering, a second process called erosion can take place. **Erosion** is the movement of sediment from one location to the other through the use of water, wind, ice, or gravity. The Grand Canyon was created by the processes of weathering and erosion. The water movement (erosion) is responsible for the canyon being so deep, and the weathering process is responsible for its width (Badder et al., 2000).

Earthquakes and Geologic Faults

The movement of the Earth's plates has forced rock layers to fold, creating mountains, hills, and valleys. This movement causes **faults** in the Earth's crust, breaking rocks and reshaping the environment. When forces within the Earth cause rocks to break and move around geologic faults, earthquakes occur. A fault is a deep crack that marks the boundary between two plates. The San Andreas fault in central California is a well-known origin of earthquakes in the area. The epicenter of an earthquake is the point on the surface where the quake is the strongest. The **Richter scale** is used to measure the amount of energy released by the earthquake. The severity of an earthquake runs from 0 to 9 on the Richter scale. Small tremors occur constantly, but every few months, a major earthquake occurs somewhere in the world. Scientists are researching ways to predict earthquakes, but their predictions are not always accurate.

Volcanoes

Volcanoes are formed by the constant motion of tectonic plates. This movement creates pressure that forces magma from the mantle to escape to the surface, creating an explosion of lava, fire, and ash. The pressure of the magma and gases creates a monticule, or a small cone, that eventually grows to form a mountain-like volcano. Volcanic activity can create earthquakes, and the fiery lava can cause destruction.

Gravity

Gravity is the force of attraction that exists between objects. Gravity keeps the Earth in its orbit by establishing a balance between the attraction of the sun and the speed at which the Earth travels around it. However, gravity is also responsible for many of the Earth's forces that change the land. For example, when ice melts on the tops of mountains, it is because of gravity that the water will form streams and rivers that flow down the mountain, eventually making its way to the lowest point. Some of the main functions of gravity are listed here:

- Keeping the Earth's atmosphere, oceans, and inhabitants from drifting into space

- Pulling the rain to the rivers and eventually to the sea

- Guiding the development and growth of plants

- Affecting the way that our bones and muscles function

For information about the Earth and space, go to the official website of the National Aeronautics and Space Administration (NASA) at *www.nasa.gov/home/index.html?skipIntro=1*. This site includes special sections for children, students from kindergarten through grade 12, and teachers.

Surface Water and Groundwater

Surface water is the water in streams, lakes, and rivers, and all water that is on the surface of the land. Ground water is water that seeps beneath the surface of the land and forms an underground "river" of water. The groundwater seeps into the soil until it reaches an impermeable layer of rock. The water stays on top of this layer and is a source of drinking water. This water may be tapped into via aquifers and wells.

For more information, see *http://ga.water.usgs.gov/edu/earthgw.html*.

The Earth's Atmosphere

The Earth is surrounded by a large mass of gas called the atmosphere. Roughly 348 miles thick, this gas mass supports life on the Earth and separates it from space. Among the many functions of the atmosphere are these:

- Absorbing energy from the sun to sustain life

- Recycling water and other chemicals needed for life

- Maintaining the climate, working with electric and magnetic forces

- Serving as a vacuum that protects life

The atmosphere is composed of 78 percent nitrogen, 21 percent oxygen, and 1 percent argon. In addition to these gases, the atmosphere contains water, greenhouse gases like ozone, and carbon dioxide. The Earth's atmosphere has five layers. The layer closest to the Earth is called the troposphere, and the weather we experience occurs in this layer.

For more information on the atmosphere, go to *www.windows.ucar.edu/tour/link=/earth/Atmosphere/ layers.html&fr=t%20t.*

Natural and Human Influences on Earth Systems

It is important to understand that many natural processes on Earth can change its systems. For example, earthquakes and volcanoes can be destructive and change the structure and composition of the landscape. A tsunami is an enormous wall of water that crashes into shorelines caused by earthquakes under bodies of water such as oceans. It crashes and can create a dramatic change in that shoreline. However, human influences may also change Earth systems. The destruction of the rainforests, called deforestation can change the structure and composition of the land, and on a larger scale, affect the balance of atmospheric gases including carbon dioxide and oxygen levels. Carbon dioxide emissions from factories, automobiles, and airplanes, as examples, may play a role in changing the atmospheric composition as well. Carbon dioxide, called a "greenhouse gas" tends to trap heat energy and result in an overall warming of the atmosphere, which has an impact on climate and plant growth that in turn affects all living organisms on Earth. There are many natural and human influences that contribute to the increase of greenhouse gases in the atmosphere producing what is known as "global warming." Other greenhouse gases include methane (CH_4) and ozone, which is the molecule O_3, that when at the surface of the Earth, are components of smog.

It is important to distinguish global warming and the ozone that is in smog from the destruction of the ozone layer (hole in the ozone layer) which is a different phenomenon. Ozone forms a layer at the top of the atmosphere that blocks harmful ultraviolet rays from the sun from reaching the Earth's surface ("good ozone"). The "hole" in the ozone layer means there is a destruction of this ozone layer, and now harmful ultraviolet radiation is reaching Earth's surface where this hole is present. Chlorofluorocarbons, which are found in aerosols, contribute to the destruction of the ozone layer.

For more information on greenhouse gases and ozone, go to *http://hvo.wr.usgs.gov/volca-nowatch/2005/05_07_28.html*.

Rock Types

The hard, solid part of the Earth's surface is called rock. Rocks are made of one or more minerals. Rocks like granite, marble, and limestone are extensively used in the construction industry. They can be used in floors, buildings, dams, highways, or the making of cement. Rocks are classified by the way they are formed. Here are descriptions of the three types of rock:

- **Igneous** rocks are crystalline solids that form directly from the cooling of magma or lava. The composition of the magma determines the composition of the rock. **Granite** is one of the most common types of igneous rocks and is created from magma (inside the Earth). Once magma reaches the Earth's surface, it is called lava. Lava that has cooled forms a rock with a glassy look, called **obsidian**.

- **Sedimentary** rocks are called secondary rocks because they are often the result of the accumulation of small pieces broken off from preexisting rocks and then pressed into a new form. There are three types of sedimentary rocks:

  » **Clastic** sedimentary rocks are made when pieces of rock, mineral, and organic material fuse together. These are classified as conglomerates, sandstone, and shale.

  » **Chemical** sedimentary rocks are formed when water rich in minerals evaporates, leaving the minerals behind. Some common examples are gypsum, rock salt, and some limestone.

  » **Organic** sedimentary rocks are made from the remains of plants and animals. For example, coal is formed when dead plants are squeezed together. Another example is a form of limestone rock composed of the remains of organisms that lived in the ocean.

- **Metamorphic** rocks are also secondary rocks formed from igneous, sedimentary, or other types of metamorphic rock. When hot magma or lava comes in contact with rocks or when buried rocks are exposed to pressure and high temperatures, the result is metamorphic rocks. For example, exposing limestone to high temperatures creates marble. The most common metamorphic rocks are slate, gneiss, and marble.

For more information, go to *http://jersey.uoregon.edu/~mstrick/AskGeoMan/geoQuerry13.html*.

Rock Cycle

The formation of rock follows a cyclical process. For instance, rocks can be formed when magma or lava cools down, creating igneous rocks. Igneous rocks exposed to weathering can break into sediment, which can be compacted and cemented to form sedimentary rocks. Sedimentary rocks are exposed to heat and pressure to create metamorphic rocks. Finally, metamorphic rocks can melt and become magma and lava again (Badder et al., 2000).

An illustration of the rock cycle and forces causing the changes in rock can be found at *www.classzone. com/books/earth_science/terc/content/investigations/es0602/es0602page02.cfm*.

Minerals

Minerals are the most common form of solid material found in the Earth's crust. Even soil contains bits of minerals that have broken away from rock. To be considered a mineral, a substance must be found in nature and must never have been a part of any living organism. Minerals can be as soft as talc or as hard as emeralds and diamonds. Dug from the Earth, minerals are used to make various products:

- **Jewelry**—Gemstones such as amethysts, opals, diamonds, emeralds, topazes, and garnets are examples of minerals commonly used to create jewelry. Gold and silver are another type of mineral that can be used to create jewelry.

- **Construction**—Gypsum boards (drywall) are made of a mineral of the same name—gypsum. The windows in homes are made from another mineral, quartz.

- **Personal Use**—Talc is the softest mineral and it is commonly applied to the body in powder form.

Water Cycle

The hydrologic cycle describes a series of movements of water above, on, and below the surface of the Earth. This cycle consists of four distinct stages: storage, evaporation, precipitation, and runoff. It is the means by which the sun's energy is used to transport, through the atmosphere, stored water from the rivers and oceans to land masses. The heat of the sun evaporates the water and takes it to the atmosphere from which, through condensation, it falls as precipitation. As precipitation falls, water is filtrated back to underground water deposits called aquifers, or it runs off into storage in lakes, ponds, and oceans.

Tides

The word *tides* is used to describe the alternating rise and fall in sea level with respect to the land, produced by the gravitational attraction of the moon and the sun. Additional factors such as the configuration of the coastline, depth of the water, the topography of the ocean floor, and other hydrographic and meteorological influences may play an important role in altering the range, interval, and times of the arrival of the tides.

Nutrient Cycles

Nutrient cycles include the carbon and nitrogen cycle. The **carbon cycle** is the capture of carbon from carbon dioxide in the atmosphere by plants to make glucose. When this glucose is used as food for the plant or other organisms, it is digested, then by respiration, broken apart again into carbon dioxide and returned back to the atmosphere. The process continues in a life sustaining process.

More information on the carbon cycle can be found at *www.ucar.edu/learn/1_4_2_15t.htm*.

For the **nitrogen cycle** it is important to recognize that most of the air we breathe is nitrogen, but it is not useful to us in that form, so it is exhaled. Lightning causes nitrogen in the air to combine with oxygen. Certain bacteria that live on the roots of certain plants, called nitrogen-fixing bacteria, are able to take nitrogen in this combined form with oxygen and make it available for use by plants. The plants can incorporate the nitrogen into their plant structure, and when eaten by animals and other organisms, this nitrogen becomes available for use. The nitrogen returns to the soil when the plant or other living organism dies and decays, releasing nitrogen gas back into the atmosphere. Nitrogen is important to all living things because it is a major component of DNA, RNA, and amino acids, which are the building blocks of proteins.

A good animation of the nitrogen cycle is found at *www.classzone.com/books/ml_science_share/vis_sim/ em05_pg20_nitrogen/em05_pg20_nitrogen.html*, and further explanation is located at *http://eo.ucar.edu/ kids/green/cycles7.htm*.

Weather

The elements of weather include interactions between wind, water (precipitation), wind speed and direction, air pressure, humidity, and temperature. Wind is caused by air masses that have different amounts of heat (temperatures), where there may be a warm air mass that is moving toward a cold air mass for example. Air pressure is related to both the amount of water in the air mass and its temperature (heat content), in that warm air has higher pressure than cold air—warm, high pressure air masses move toward cold, low pressure air masses. One simple rule is that energy always moves from *warmer to colder*. So, if you open a window on a hot summer day when your air conditioning is on, the cold does *not go out*—the warm air comes in. The same is true on a larger scale with warm and cold air masses.

Humidity is a measure of the percentage of water that is in the air. Dew point is the temperature at which the air needs to be for the water to condense out of the air in liquid form as precipitation; or it may be observed as "dew." In other words, air has a certain amount of water vapor (water in the gas state) in it (the percent is measured as humidity). That water vapor will turn to liquid water as temperatures drop overnight, in which we observe dew, or when a cold front moves in that lowers the temperature, which can result in a rain or snow storm. Wind is measured by an instrument called an *anemometer*. Air pressure is measured by a *barometer*; *rain gauges* and other instruments measure precipitation. Temperature is measured by a *thermometer*. Relative humidity is measured by a *psychrometer*.

Climate

Weather is the result of the conditions of the atmosphere at a given, relatively short period of time. Climate, however, takes into account the longer-term weather conditions in an area on a continuous, seasonal basis. The climate is more complex and can be measured by the average variety of weather conditions, such as temperature and precipitation, that occur seasonally in that geographic region of the world over a long period of time.

More information, including the contrast between weather and climate, can be found at *www.nasa.gov/ mission_pages/noaa-n/climate/climate_weather.html*.

Predicting Weather

Weather can be predicted by tracking weather patterns using maps and charts. These maps have special symbols that indicate, for example, warm and cold air masses, air pressure, and relative humidity in a region. By knowing how air behaves, such as the fact that cold air goes down and warm air rises, warmer air always moves toward colder air, and high pressure always moves outward toward lower pressure, we can track the weather and make predictions. Clouds are also an indication of the type of weather occurring in an area. Interpreting weather maps is an important skill for weather prediction.

The Earth's Surface and Position as a Factor in Weather and Climate

The Earth's surface is primarily water, and bodies of water affect the weather and climate of an area. Water has a high specific heat, which means that it takes longer to take in heat and longer to release the heat it has absorbed than any other material on Earth. Therefore, coastal areas tend to be warmer than areas inland or away from water, because the water moderates the temperature, even if the locations are at the same latitude. In the U.S., for example, areas in the middle of the country will have greater extreme differences in the cold temperatures in the winter and warm temperatures in the summer compared to a location at the same latitude near the ocean.

Large lakes, such as the Great Lakes also create a situation called "lake effect" in the winter—the air over the lake is relatively warm, and so can carry water vapor (evaporation). As soon as that air carrying water moves over land, however, it rapidly cools and releases its water (precipitation) in the form of snow over the land. Mountains and other landforms also have an effect on the weather. When air holding water hits a mountain side, it is forced upward which makes the air cool and therefore rain (or snow) on that side of the mountain. This is typically the western side of the mountain in the U.S. as in the mountain ranges of the Rocky Mountains. Once the precipitation is gone from that air mass and the air mass crosses the mountain to the other side, it drops back down and warms, but now it is dry air and so may result in an arid region or desert. The Gobi Desert of the U.S. is a result of this phenomenon.

On a much larger scale, the tilt of the Earth itself—as a planet—is responsible for weather and climate. The Earth is on a 23° tilt on its axis in space. This tilt means the Earth's North Pole is pointed *away* from the sun when it is in one location in its orbit (path around the sun), and *toward* the sun when it is in the opposite orbital location. This tilt of the Earth results in the seasons, with extreme changes being in locations closer to the North and South poles.

See more information on this topic at *www.windows.ucar.edu/tour/link=/earth/climate/cli_seasons.html.*

Properties and Characteristics of Objects in the Sky

Galaxies

Galaxies are large collections of stars, hydrogen, dust particles, and other gases. The universe is made of countless galaxies. The solar system that includes Earth is part of a galaxy called the Milky Way.

Stars

Stars like the sun are composed of large masses of hydrogen pulled together by gravity. The hydrogen, with strong gravitational pressure, creates fusion inside the star, turning the hydrogen into helium. The liberation of energy created by this process causes solar radiation, which makes the sun glow with visible light, as well as forms of radiation not visible to the human eye.

The Earth-Sun-Moon System

Movements of Planet Earth

Earth performs two kinds of movement: rotation and revolution. **Rotation** describes the spinning of Earth on its axis. Earth takes approximately 24 hours to make a complete (360°) rotation, which creates day and night.

While Earth is rotating on its axis, it is also following an orbit around the sun. This movement is called **revolution**. It takes a year, or 365¼ days, for Earth to complete one revolution. The tilt of Earth as it moves around the sun and its curvature create **climate zones** and seasons. The zones immediately north and south of the equator are called the tropics—Cancer (north) and Capricorn (south). The Arctic Circle (North Pole) and Antarctic Circle (South Pole) are the area surrounding Earth's axis points. Latitude lines are imaginary horizontal lines around the Earth, and longitude lines are likewise vertical lines around the Earth from the North to the South Poles. These lines form a grid that helps us locate positions on Earth according to the location's specific latitude and longitude.

Phases of the Moon

During each lunar orbit around Earth (about 28 days), the moon appears to go through several stages based on the portion of the moon visible from Earth. The moon does not have its own source of light but reflects the light from the sun. The shape of the moon varies from a full moon, when Earth is between the sun and the moon, to a new moon, when the moon is located between the sun and Earth. A description of the major stages of the moon follows:

- **New Moon**—The moon is not visible to Earth because the side of the moon facing Earth is not being lit by the sun.

- **Crescent Moon**—At this stage between the half moon and the new moon, the shape of the moon is often compared to a banana.

- **Half Moon, or First Quarter**—During this stage, half of the moon is visible.

- **Gibbous Moon**—In this stage, about three quarters of the moon is visible.

- **Full Moon**—The whole moon is visible from Earth.

The term **blue moon** describes the appearance of two full moons in a single calendar month. The expression "once in a blue moon" represents an event that is not very frequent.

Components of Our Solar System

Solar System

The sun is the center of our solar system, which is composed of eight planets, many satellites that orbit the planets, and a large number of smaller bodies like comets and asteroids. Short definitions of these terms follow:

- Planets are large bodies orbiting the sun.

- Dwarf planets are small bodies orbiting the sun.

- Satellites are moons orbiting the planets. Our planet has one moon whereas other planets may have no moons (Mercury, Venus), or many moons (Jupiter, Saturn).

- Asteroids are small dense objects or rocks orbiting our star, the sun. The Asteroid Belt of our own solar system is located between Mars and Jupiter. Some theorize that the asteroids could be the remains of an exploded planet.

- Meteoroids are fragments of rock in space, most originating from the debris left behind by comets that burn up/vaporize upon entering Earth's atmosphere due to friction from the air molecules.

- Comets are small icy objects traveling through space in an elongated, elliptical orbit around the sun.

Planets

The objects in our solar system revolve around our star, which we call the sun. The **inner** solar system contains the planets Mercury, Venus, Earth, and Mars, in this order. The **outer** solar system comprises the planets Jupiter, Saturn, Uranus, and Neptune, and a number of dwarf planets, including Pluto, Ceres, Eris and others, with likely more yet to be found (see Table 6-5).

Table 6-5. Planets and Dwarf Planets of our Solar System

Inner Planets	Mercury Venus Earth Mars
Outer Planets	Jupiter Saturn Uranus Neptune
Dwarf Planets	Pluto Ceres Eris Haumea Makemake

Key Principles of the Earth Science Competencies

- Our solar system is part of the Milky Way, one of many galaxies in the universe.

- Minerals and rocks are commonly used in our daily life.

- The movement of tectonic plates creates intense geologic activity that results in earthquakes and volcanic activity.

- The Earth's atmosphere protects and preserves life.

- The water cycles are the movement and distribution of water within the Earth's atmosphere.

- The tilt of the Earth causes the seasons, and not the distance it is in its orbit away from the sun.

- Human activities as well as natural processes impact the landscape and processes on Earth.

- Weather is the interaction of many factors, including air temperature, air pressure, and humidity. Weather is the conditions in the atmosphere at a given location and time.

- The solar system consists of the sun, inner planets, outer planets, dwarf planets, satellites, asteroids, comets and meteoroids.

Planning and Implementing Scientific Inquiry

Scientific inquiry is promoted through students engaging in hands-on activities and experimentation. From their experiences conducting scientific experiments, students acquire information firsthand and develop problem-solving skills. Children in elementary grades are inquisitive and want to understand the environment around them. Teachers can use this interest to provide students with opportunities to use electronic and printed sources to find answers to their questions and to expand their knowledge about the topic. It is important for children to develop inquiry skills. This can only be accomplished by allowing them to experience science for themselves in hands-on investigations. By doing so, students develop important science inquiry and thinking skills (Table 6-6).

Table 6-6. Science Thinking Skills (FOSS, 2000)

Observing: Using the senses to get information
Communicating: Talking, drawing, and acting
Comparing: Pairing and one-to-one correspondence
Organizing: Grouping, seriating, and sequencing
Relating: Cause-and-effect and classification
Inferring: Super-ordinate/subordinate classification, if/then reasoning, and developing scientific laws
Applying: Developing strategic plans and inventing

The model of inquiry that best supports science learning is a model known as the *learning cycle*, consisting of three phases: *exploration*, *concept invention*, and *application* (Lawson, Abraham, and Renner 1989; Marek and Cavallo, 1997). Over time the learning cycle was extended with the addition of two new phases becoming what is known as the 5-E model (Bybee, 1989). What follows is some history on the development of inquiry-based teaching via the learning cycle and 5-E model.

The original three-phase learning cycle model developed by Robert Karplus in the early 1960s was based upon the following theoretical foundation:

1. Science must be taught in a way that is *consistent with the nature of science*. Science is discovery and investigation, and that means science must be taught as an active process—as something we *do*. The children need to have the opportunity to experience the true nature of science by doing science exploration for themselves through direct experiences and hands-on investigations.

2. Science teaching must be focused on promoting the main purpose of education, namely, to promote the development in our students of the *ability to think*—to be critical and independent thinkers. Science must be taught in a way that promotes the students' use of independent, critical, and higher-level thinking abilities (e.g., logic). Promoting this purpose of education is best accomplished by *not* giving or telling students the "answers" or information (e.g., as in giving a lecture); but instead by first giving students hands-on, direct experiences in which they use logic and reasoning to find "answers" or explanations for themselves; further discussion and teacher guidance can follow the students' direct experiences.

3. Science must be taught in a way that *matches how students learn,* described as the mental functioning model by Piaget (1964). How individuals learn is through mentally experiencing the following three-phase mental process. We first *assimilate* or "take in" information with our senses from our environment and what we are experiencing in our environment. During assimilation, we may have a sense of "disequilibrium," which is confusion or "cognitive conflict" as we try to make sense of our experiences. When in disequilibrium, we need to go back and *assimilate* more information—make more observations and gather more data, for example. When we have assimilated enough information and made sense of the information we have gathered, our minds experience *accommodation*. That is the "aha!" moment, the point when we ultimately feel "cognitive relief"—we figured it out, or what we have observed/experienced now makes sense! Third, our minds take that newly

accommodated information and we *organize* it into our mental structures. That is, we connect the new idea or what we have just figured out/made sense of to what we already know, what we experience in everyday life, and/or to new, related concepts.

The three phases of learning described by Piaget, assimilation-accommodation-organization, *match* the original learning cycle's three phases: Exploration-Concept Invention-Application. The logic in developing the learning cycle in these three phases was that, given what we know about how children (people) *learn*, we should be *teaching* in a sequence or way that matches this learning pattern. To do so, teachers should first provide children with an *Exploration* phase in which students can assimilate information using their senses. The students may or may not experience disequilibrium, but, as teachers, we should guide them (not tell them!) through the sense-making process. We should then carry out a discussion in the *Concept Invention* phase in which students share their observations and findings. With careful questioning, teachers guide students to review their data/observations toward helping them reach the "aha!" moment or accommodation. The summarizing statement the students are to write, post on the board, and/or state aloud to others in this phase represents their accommodation or understanding of the concept. The teacher then helps students organize the new concept by guiding them through *Application* of the concept in new contexts, in which students can connect the concept with what they observe in everyday life, or what they already know, for example.

Furthermore, by teaching via the learning cycle, we are teaching in a way that is consistent with the nature of science—as an active, hands-on process characterized by investigation and discovery—and we are teaching in a way that supports the purpose of education, that is, we are promoting children's development of higher level thinking abilities. The learning cycle and its origins and theory base is more fully described in a book by Marek and Cavallo (1997) titled *The Learning Cycle: Elementary School Science and Beyond.*

Over time, science educators added some additional phases to the learning cycle, namely, the *Engage* phase, with the idea that teachers need to do something that will gain the students' attention before beginning the exploration phase. *Engage* can be a demonstration (without explanation) or simply posing a question, challenge, or problem. So the original learning cycle model's first phase, *Exploration*, became two phases, *Engage* and *Explore*. Though identical, the *Concept Invention* phase's name was changed to *Explain* and *Application* phase had the name changed to *Elaborate,* to sustain the alliteration. Assessment or the measurement of learning in the original three-phase model was to take place throughout the learning cycle. However, science educators at the time preferred to have assessment articulated as an additional phase, which again to keep the "E" pattern, was termed *Evaluate*. So the three-phase **learning cycle** model was expanded into a **5-E Model**: *Engage, Explore, Explain, Elaborate, Evaluate*.

The two models are basically the same and grew out of the same underlying philosophy and theoretical foundation. However, the three phases more closely follow the model of learning—assimilation, accommodation and organization—as first described by Piaget; whereas the 5-E incorporates two additional essentials of classroom teaching, namely gaining students focus and attention, and measuring student learning.

Most importantly, in both models, the learning cycle and 5-E, students are *not told* the science concept or information before beginning the inquiry, but must discover the concept themselves through hands-on investigation, observation, and collection of data. In using the *Engage* phase (from 5-E) the students' learning experience begins with the teacher posing one or more questions, giving an interesting demonstration, or providing a laboratory guide; but in all of these, this phase captures their curiosity and motivates them to learn. Whether or not an *Engage* phase is used, students next (or first) experience an *Exploration* phase—and it must be a student-centered hands-on activity, investigation, or experiment. In the *Exploration* phase, students make observations and gather data on a science idea or topic area. In this phase, students can determine the experimental design or it can be pre-determined by the teacher. The main aspect, however, is that students are doing the lab activity themselves, and have not been told the expected outcome beforehand. For example, students may grow plants in the light and in the dark, and make observations, draw and/or take photos, and measure the plants grown under the two differing conditions over a period of time. All other variables are controlled (soil, water, air); only the light received by the plants is different, which is the variable.

After the observations have been made and data has been gathered by students, the teacher begins the next instructional phase called *Concept Invention*, or in the 5-E model, the *Explain* phase. In this phase the students present and share data with their classmates in a teacher-guided discussion of findings. The teacher uses questions to guide students' thinking and encourages the use of logic and reasoning as they interpret their data. For example, students may post the photos or drawings of plants grown in the dark and in the light, make line graphs of plant height over time, or share qualitative information about how the plant appeared after grown under the two conditions (e.g., plants in the light were green, whereas plants in the dark were yellow and pale). At the end of this phase, the students construct an overall statement that summarizes their data and observations, which is the central science *concept*. The science vocabulary is then linked to the concept students "invented."

Next the teacher helps students through the *Application* (from the learning cycle) or *Elaborate* (from the 5-E model) in which students use the new concept they learned as it is applied in new contexts. For example, students can create new questions to investigate or hypotheses to test based on what they just learned (the concept) and develop a way to answer their questions or test their hypotheses (e.g., what color of light is best for plants to grow?).They can also go to the Internet to learn more about the concept they just invented. In this phase the teacher can engage students in additional hands-on laboratories, readings, discussions, field trips, and/or writing activities that extend and expand upon the concept. These models of inquiry science teaching and learning are endorsed by NSTA (NSTA, 1998, 2003). The diagram in Figure 6-1 shows the inquiry-based learning cycle model as it corresponds to the 5-E model of science teaching.

Figure 6-1. The Learning Cycle and 5-E Model

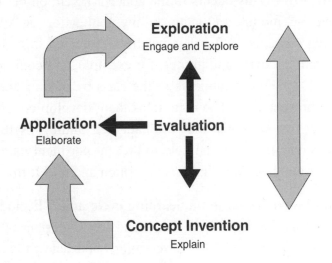

Interpreting Findings in Science Inquiry

In planning and conducting experiments, teachers should guide children to develop an appropriate procedure for testing hypotheses, including the use of instruments that can yield measurable data. Even at the early stages of scientific experimentation, the procedure must be clear and tangible enough to allow replication by other students or scientists. Help students understand the concept of controlling variables and testing only one variable at a time. Students need to learn to be precise in the collection of data and measurements. Ensure the use of the metric system in obtaining all measurement data.

Allowing students to gather their own data and observations for interpretation promotes their critical and logical thinking abilities. It also gives them experience with using appropriate tools, resources, and technology of science that will lead to accurate organization and analysis of data. The students will be able to experience and practice science skills by verifying their findings, basing findings on evidence, and analyzing sources of error. Having students collect and report their own data also brings the teacher opportunities to discuss scientific ethics with students.

In explaining data collection procedures and display of findings to English language learners, the teacher needs to demonstrate and provide a model of what the end results should look like. In using inquiry, students work in groups, which is particularly helpful for second language learners as they interpret and exchange ideas about data and scientific reasoning.

When students complete their experiments, teachers need to engage them in the process of analyzing their own, and other groups' data for similarities, differences, and variations including error. This occurs in the concept invention or "explain" phase of the learning cycle and 5-E model, and again in any application or "elaborate" activities in which data has been collected. After data has been collected from students' explorations, they display their data in charts and graphs, for example, and communicate their observations and, ultimately, concept statements to the class by posting them on the board and/ or through an oral presentation. The data helps them develop conclusions and form new research questions or hypotheses as they evaluate their findings, setting the foundation for new explorations. Students should be able to present pertinent data using graphic representations, and communicate their findings in written and oral forms to others.

In using scientific inquiry as in the learning cycle and 5-E model, scientific vocabulary is introduced *after* students have had hands-on experiences in the (engage and) exploration phase *and* have used their observations and data to construct meaning from their experiences in the *concept invention* or "explain" phase. Once students have had the hands-on direct experience with the concept, and have stated the meaning of their observations, the scientific vocabulary or terms that label the concept can be introduced by the teacher. In the application or elaborate phase, the teacher and students use the new vocabulary in extended experimentation, discussion, readings, writing, and other learning activities. Introducing terms after students have directly experienced the science inquiry and constructed meaning from their experiences by making a concept statement is especially important for second language learners in facilitating the development of understanding of science concepts. For all students, but especially for second language learners, this helps them understand concepts when terms are later *re-introduced*. By giving students the experience—something they *do*—and then allowing them to form meaning from their experience in ways that make sense to them, then when the term that labels what they learned is introduced, they are able to link it to prior knowledge and learning experiences in their minds. The terms are now able to build their background knowledge, which is critical for second language learners to understand the language of science. Making a connection between the hands-on activities and scientific vocabulary is beneficial to all students but especially to English language learners (ELLs), who can link the actions with the appropriate concept and vocabulary words without engaging in translations.

Promoting Logical Thinking and Scientific Reasoning

Interpreting results is one of the most challenging phases of scientific inquiry for children in the elementary grades. Students can easily discuss the observable results but might have difficulty interpreting their meaning. Teachers have to use developmentally appropriate practices to guide students to make extrapolations and infer information from the data, which involves the teachers' use of questioning, as addressed later in this chapter.

Scientific Tools and Equipment for Gathering and Storing Data

Various tools or instruments are used in scientific experimentation in kindergarten through grade 6. The classroom can be equipped with measuring devices like graduated cylinders, beakers, scales, dishes, thermometers, meter sticks, and micrometers. They might also have anatomical models showing the body systems. Teachers need to learn to use these tools and equipment properly in order to help their students know how to use them and to collect accurate data in their inquiry investigations.

History and Nature of Science, Diversity, and Equity in Science

The history and nature of science provides an important framework for student learning. By learning the history of science, students will come to understand that science is changing and dynamic rather than fixed and tentative. They will understand that their own conceptions and understandings of science can change in light of new experimental observations and evidence. Therefore, it is important to use the history and nature of science as a tool to promote students' learning. For example, the students can learn about the earth-centered model of the solar system that prevailed for hundreds of years before Copernicus, and then Galileo supported a new model, which is now the accepted view of a sun-centered model of the solar system. With better tools developed through time and the extension of findings through observations and experiments, our scientific knowledge constantly shifts and changes.

Science for all has long been the theme of science education's guiding documents such as Project 2061, a long-term initiative of the American Association for the Advancement of Science created in 1989, and the National Science Education Standards, published by the National Research Council in 1996. *Science for all* means that teachers need to help their students abandon stereotypes they may hold of science and scientists. For example, that science is a male-dominated profession. Teachers should help students to more appropriately view science as a field for males and females and for all cultures and ethnicities. To accomplish this goal, teachers need to be aware of their own potential, often not intentional, bias toward science and scientists that may be exclusionary. Posters of scientists displayed in the room should represent male and female scientists of diverse ethnicities and cultures, as well as of many different fields of science, such as environmental science, veterinary medicine, geology, engineering, and architecture, as well as the more traditionally represented physics and chemistry.

Likewise, discussions of science and scientific discovery should include contributions from a diverse range of scientists. In giving examples to students, it is important to alternate between the use of "he" and "she," and to use and or vary examples to be more gender neutral and meaningful to a variety of ethnicities. In laboratory activities it is important that all group members have the opportunity to handle the materials and perform the experiment, and that the same students are not delegated to note taking. Varying laboratory responsibilities can be accomplished by assigning each group member roles to perform when they are conducting a laboratory activity, such as materials collector, record keeper, reporter, and lab facilitator, and then rotating these roles from one laboratory activity to the next to ensure all have an opportunity to work in the various roles.

SCIENCE IN PERSONAL AND SOCIAL PERSPECTIVE

This category accounts for 5% of your science score.

- Knows about personal health (e.g., nutrition, communicable diseases, substance abuse

- Understands science as a human endeavor, process, and career

Science in Daily Life

Students need to be aware of how science is present and plays a role in their daily lives. The functioning of their bodies, the natural environment that is around them, and their everyday use of electrical appliances, bicycles, computers, and cell phones are examples of biological and physical science in their lives. However, students tend to keep the science they learn in school separate from the science they experience in everyday life! It is important that teachers help students connect the science they are learning in school to the world around them to broaden their understandings and promote the usefulness, value, and applicability of science. In the learning cycle and 5-E models, the best time to help students make these connections is in the application/elaboration phase. After students have experienced a hands-on lab activity and constructed an understanding of the concept, the teacher should help them relate that new concept to their everyday lives and see how the concept works in differing contexts. Connecting newly learned concepts to the students' life experiences makes the learning more meaningful for students and helps them retain understanding of the concept for later use. Relating science to what students already know and experience in life helps bridge the disconnections between "school science" and science they observe and experience in everyday life.

Science has brought society many advantages that have served to increase the health and longevity of humans, and to improve the quality of life for all. However, there may be consequences, often unforeseen, to scientific discovery and invention that impacts society and the natural environment, as well as the habitats and survival of the living organisms that share this planet. To better understand these issues, students need to gain scientific knowledge and evidence of what is known.

Armed with appropriate background knowledge, students will be in the position to weigh the pros and cons of various scientific discoveries and debate issues that prevail in our global community. Students should be apprised of issues such as global warming, for example, but before taking a position on the topic, they must be prepared with accurate scientific information on the topic. When students are given opportunities to use scientific concepts as support for sound logic and reasoning to debate or evaluate a scientific issue, they are operating at a high cognitive level important to their intellectual development.

Equally important is student awareness of the ethical, personal, societal, and economic implications of science, from both positive and negative perspectives. Students need to realize the trade-offs often present in scientific discovery and experimentation, for example, laboratory testing on animals. Many new and important discoveries have improved the quality of life at the cost of animals' lives. In order to best understand the complexity of how science interfaces with personal and societal issues, students need to be engaged in electronic and library research on impactful science topics and in discussion with peers and experts in the science fields. Topics such as cloning, global warming, alternative and fossil fuels, and acid rain are just a few additional topics tied to ethical, personal, societal, and economic concerns. It is important that students fully understand the scientific knowledge that underlies all such complex issues, and can formulate decisions based on this knowledge.

Energy as a source of fuel and electricity is a major issue threatening the economic, environmental, and personal status of living in the U.S. and global society. It is important to know about fossil fuels, their origin, how they are obtained, and how they are used for energy consumption. In addition, it is important to know that fossil fuels are nonrenewable and will one day be expended. Therefore, science must continue to develop and improve upon alternative sources of energy such as wind, hydroelectric, and geothermal. Teachers must be knowledgeable about these other sources of energy and be able to guide students toward understanding how these alternative, renewable energy sources are used and how they impact our society's energy needs.

A significant impact of science on daily life relates to student fitness and health. Childhood obesity is a serious problem in the United States, and teachers can play an important role in educating children on the negative health issues associated with poor nutrition and a lack of exercise. Students need to learn about factors that impact physical and psychological health and about how to make good choices on such factors, including nutrition, hygiene, physical exercise, smoking, drugs and alcohol. Understanding human biology, therefore, is important for students to realize how obesity and other factors such as substance use/abuse affect their physical and mental health. The topics of heart disease, diabetes, and cancer should be included in the curriculum as ways to help students understand the detrimental effects of unhealthy life choices.

SCIENCE AS INQUIRY AND SCIENCE PROCESSES

Five-percent of your science score will come from your

- Understanding of science as inquiry (e.g., questioning, gathering data, drawing reasonable conclusions)

- Understanding of how to use resource and research material in science

- Understanding the unifying processes of science (e.g., systems, order, and organization

Explanatory Framework across Science Disciplines

Science is a way of knowing, a process—it is a systematic way of looking at the world and how it works. This competency focuses on how science uses a regular, consistent method of collecting and reporting data about scientific phenomena. Science is a way of organizing observations and then seeking patterns and regularity in order to make sense of the world. In science we organize evidence, create models, and explain observations in a logical form. We make predictions and hypotheses and test our predictions and hypotheses through controlled experimentation, meaning all variables of the experiment remain constant except for the variable being tested. We repeat experiments multiple times and seek constancy in our findings in form and/or function. We seek patterns and consistency in our observations and data in order to construct explanations and make new predictions.

Science embraces a broad spectrum of subject matter, such as life science, physical science, and earth science, all of which is interrelated. For example, in studying the ecosystem, teachers must understand the biological aspects (e.g., the living organism) and how they interact, as in predator-prey relationships and symbiotic relationships (e.g., parasitism, commensalism), as well as the chemical aspects of the ecosystem (e.g., nitrogen cycle), the geologic or earth science aspects (e.g., the landscape, the water, and the climate) and the physics aspects (e.g., energy transfer, motion). Ecosystems, for example, regardless of location on earth, share unifying components and characteristics, and teachers must understand this unity. In life science, there is unity of what makes organisms "living"—they all must carry on life functions and are composed of one or more cells. These are the criteria that unify life forms and classify something like a virus, for example, as non-living (it does not carry on the life functions and is not composed of cells).

All scientific observations can be described by their characteristics or "properties." These properties organize the observations according to commonalities, or classification. Observed properties and patterns are centered on space, time, energy, and matter.

Scientific Models

Models are representations of the natural world and universe in order to help better understand how something appears, its form and/or its function. For example, we may make models of the solar system, cells, or an atom to help us better explain its form and function and interactivity with other structures. Such models can be helpful to us in understanding the actual concept the model represents, and scientists often make models for this purpose. However, it is important to understand that, though it represents the actual science phenomena or concept and provides explanatory power, it is not the same as the actual science concept and is limited. Models in science may be physical, as in a physical model of a cell; conceptual, as in a concept map or an analogy; and/or mathematical as in a formula showing relationships, such as $d = m/v$ (formula for density).

Developmentally Appropriate Practices

Children's processing of scientific inquiry can begin as early as age three or four. However, teachers must be aware of the stages of cognitive, social, and emotional development of children to appropriately introduce children to science concepts. For example, observing and experimenting with water and colors can easily be done by three- or four-year-olds, but using microscopes to observe and analyze animal or vegetable cells might be more appropriate for children in third and fourth grades. Students in the elementary grades need direct experiences in order to understand concepts. According to Piaget (1964), children are transitioning through stages of development that require direct involvement to make sense of their experience. The model of teaching described earlier, the learning cycle and 5-E model, are based upon promoting the intellectual development of children. Thus, these models of teaching were designed to be consistent with the nature of science—and importantly, to match how children naturally learn (Marek and Cavallo, 1997; Renner and Marek, 1990). It is important that teachers understand the theory and research that underlie such models, as well as know how to use these models in teaching.

Misconceptions or alternative conceptions are a pervasive problem in science teaching and learning. Children tend to view the world from their own perspectives and draw conclusions based on their limited experiences. Once misconceptions are established in learners' minds, they are difficult to change. Therefore, teaching needs to allow children the opportunity for direct experience and collecting evidence. The learning cycle has been established as a teaching model that promotes conceptual change, helps students resolve misconceptions, and leads to more scientifically accurate understandings (Sandoval, 1995).

Teachers need to begin lessons with direct, concrete activities giving students experience with objects. After concept understandings are established in learners, then teachers can move them from the concrete to more abstract reasoning. For example, in learning the concept of density, it is important that students have objects to touch, feel, weigh (take the mass of) and measure first, as in the exploration phase of the learning cycle. From direct experience with the objects, students should construct the concept that "a certain amount of matter (mass) is packed into a given amount of space (volume)." The term that labels this concept is "density." As application, teachers help students develop their abstract-thinking abilities by having them solve problems using the formula for density, $d=m/v$. Teachers need to select instruction appropriately such that concrete experiences are used first, leading the students to later use abstract reasoning. Teachers need to select learning experiences that will promote the students' scientific knowledge, skills, and use of inquiry. Further, the students are able to use the prior knowledge they have formed about density to learn more extended, related concepts such as buoyancy. This example demonstrates the instructional knowledge and skills teachers need to have to prepare the best possible science learning experiences for students. The learning cycle or 5-E model are consistent with the goals of this competency.

The use of good questions by the teacher is critical to promoting logical thinking and scientific reasoning among students. Good questioning causes students to reflect upon the logic of their data and observations with confidence and also identify possible misinformation or misunderstanding of important concepts. Students learn to effectively use scientific argumentation and respond to challenges to their findings in order to support their conclusions. Teachers use questioning to reveal student learning and assess their progress in forming sound scientific frameworks of understanding. Questioning is the hallmark of science inquiry and should be used throughout inquiry instruction. In the learning cycle/5-E model, questioning must be designed to lead students toward being able to state the concept, so it is especially critical in the concept invention or "explain" phase.

Teachers can guide students at various levels of development to observe events; and through questioning, teachers can help students develop high-order thinking skills. For example, a teacher can lead children to make predictions while conducting experiments with objects that float or sink in water. By asking students to predict and explain why an object might sink or float, the teacher is leading students to analyze the properties of the object and the water to make an evaluative decision; that is, the children are using analysis and evaluation to complete that simple task. The following guide, based on Bloom's Revised Taxonomy, will help teachers best promote and elevate logical thinking abilities among students. (Bloom & Krathwohl, 1956; Anderson & Krathwohl, 2001).

1. Use key questioning terms aimed at the full range of the cognitive domain

LEVEL 1: Knowledge

Recall of factual information

> *List* the five Kingdoms.
>
> *Label* the parts of the cell in the diagram provided.
>
> *Write* the formula for density.

LEVEL 2: Comprehension

Communicate an idea in a different form

> *Explain* heat transfer through conduction.
>
> *Restate* what a habitat is in your own words.
>
> *Submit* a definition of photosynthesis in your own words.

LEVEL 3: Application

Use what is known to find new solutions or apply in new situations

> *Relate* the concept of convection to lake turn over.
>
> *Utilize* your understanding of burning to explain why sand works to put out a fire.
>
> *Making use of* the clothes you are wearing, how can you stay afloat for several hours?

LEVEL 4: Analysis

Break things and ideas down into component parts and find their unique characteristics

> *Examine* blueprints of the electrical circuitry of your school building and explain how it works to bring electricity to your laboratory station.
>
> *Study* the diagram of human digestion and *reason* what the organ marked #7 might be and explain its function.

Using the given laboratory materials, *deduce* the identities of the substances labeled "A," "B," and "C."

LEVEL 5: Synthesis

Use what is known to think creatively and divergently; make something new or original; pattern ideas or things in a new way

Create a burglar alarm system for the classroom.

Build a telescope for classroom use.

Develop a plan for cleaning the pollutants in the Trinity River.

LEVEL 6: Evaluation

Use what is known to make judgments and ratings; accept or reject ideas; determine the worthiness of an idea or thing

Decide whether or not you agree with the production of more nuclear power plants and provide justification for your decision.

Make a ruling you would give to car manufacturers on global warming and provide support for your ruling.

Rank the top five greatest discoveries in scientific history and *explain* why you have chosen those discoveries and ranked them in that particular order.

2. Avoid yes/no questions (unless part of a game) and questions with obvious answers.

Showing a picture of a cell
Not so good

Is this a cell?
Better

What is this structure and how do you know?
(Students watching a chemical reaction in which the solution turns blue)
Not so good

Did it turn blue?
Better

What happened? What did you observe? Why did this happen?

3. **Use questions beginning with the words why, how, what, where, and when that probe students' thinking.**

How do you know?

Why do you think that?

Where did you see a change?

What is your explanation for this observation?

When did you notice the change occur?

What do you think?

Measuring Student Learning

Teaching cannot occur without student *learning*, and in order to determine that learning is occurring, student progress needs to be assessed on a regular basis. Assessment of learning should occur on some scale, large or small, every class day, and as students move through the learning of concepts, as in the learning cycle and 5-E models. Measuring learning as it is occurring is "authentic assessment" and allows teachers to adjust the instruction according to student learning and potential difficulties in learning. Alternative assessment methods, in addition to the more traditional testing formats (e.g., multiple-choice) should be used to obtain a full picture of what students know and do not know or can and cannot do. Alternative assessments include techniques such as verbal reports, laboratory practical exams, story writing, developing advertisements or brochures, constructing a concept map, writing essays, creating drawings or models, and developing a play or skit. In each assessment, the concepts to be learned are represented in alternative ways—yet clearly communicate what students have learned and understand.

It is essential that teachers monitor and assess students' understanding of concepts and skills on a regular, consistent basis and use this information to adjust instruction. The results of frequent informal and formal/traditional and alternative assessments should be used as a tool for planning subsequent instruction. Teachers must communicate progress to students so they can learn to self-monitor their own learning and understand what is needed to achieve learning goals.

REFERENCES

American Association for the Advancement of Science. 1989. *Science for All Americans: A Project 2061 Report on Literacy Goals in Science, Mathematics, and Technology.* Washington, DC.

Anderson, L. W., D. R. Krathwohl, et al., Eds. 2001. *A Taxonomy for Learning, Teaching, and Assessing: A Revision of Bloom's Taxonomy of Educational Objectives.* Boston, MA: Allyn & Bacon (Pearson Education Group)

Badder, W., D. Peck, L. J. Bethel, C. Sumner, V. Fu, and C. Valentino. 2000. *Discovery works.* (Texas ed.). Boston: Houghton Mifflin.

Bloom, B. S. and D. R. Krathwohl. 1956. *Taxonomy of Educational Objectives: The Classification of Educational Goals, by a committee of college and university examiners. Handbook I: Cognitive Domain.* NY, NY: Longmans, Green

Bybee, R., Buchwald, C.E., Crissman, S. Heil, D., Kuerbis, P., Matsumoto, C. & McInerney 1989. *Science and Technology Education for Elementary Years: Frameworks for Curriculum and Instruction.* Washington, DC: The National Center for Improving Science Education.

Cavallo, A.M.L. 2005. Cycling through plants. *Science and Children, 4,* 22–27.

Cavallo, A.M.L. 2001. Convection connections: Integrated learning cycle investigations that explore convection—the science behind wind and waves. *Science and Children, 38,* 20–25.

Full Option Science System (FOSS). 2000. Lawrence Hall of Science, University of California, Berkeley, CA.

Lawson, A.E., M.R. Abraham, and J. W. Renner. 1989. *A theory of instruction: Using the learning cycle to teach science concepts and thinking skills.* NARST Monograph No. 1.

Marek, E. A., & Cavallo, A. M. L. (1997). *The Learning Cycle: Elementary School Science and Beyond* (Rev. ed.). Portsmouth, NH: Heinemann.

National Science Teachers Association. 2003. *Standards for Science Teacher Preparation: Skills of Teaching* (Revised Version). Washington, DC: National Science Teachers Association.

National Science Teachers Association (NSTA). 2002. Elementary school science. Position paper. Retrieved September 22, 2009, from *www.nsta.org/positionstatement&psid=8/*.

National Science Teachers Association. 1998. *Standards for Science Teacher Preparation: Skills of Teaching*. Washington, DC: National Science Teachers Association.

National Research Council. 1996 *National Science Education Standards*. Washington, D.C.: National Academy Press.

Piaget, J. 1964. Cognitive development in children: Piaget, development and learning. *Journal of Research in Science Teaching,* 2, 176–80.

Renner, J. W., and Marek, E. A. 1990. An educational theory base for science teaching. *Journal of Research in Science Teaching.* 27(3): 241–46.

Sandoval, J. S. 1995. Teaching in subject matter areas: Science. *Annual Review of Psychology*, 46, 355–74.

University of California, Lawrence Livermore National Laboratory. 2006. Plasma: The fourth state of matter. Retrieved September 18, 2009, from *http://FusEdWeb.llnl.gov/CPEP/*.Ma nem experum quidus. Quid quatiat atesequam, nonse am fuga. Lestotam, od min pedio ellandae nestias ut veliquae posam, sitaqui diosam autemo to int officit veriost voluptam dolor sam volupta tatur?

Practice Test 1

Elementary Education: Content Knowledge (0014/5014)

This test is also on CD-ROM in our special interactive PRAXIS Elementary Education: Content Knowledge (0014/5014) TestWare®. It is highly recommended that you first take this exam on computer. You will then have the additional study features and benefits of enforced timed conditions and instantaneous, accurate scoring. See page 12 for instructions on how to get the most out of REA's TestWare®.

1. Ⓐ Ⓑ Ⓒ Ⓓ
2. Ⓐ Ⓑ Ⓒ Ⓓ
3. Ⓐ Ⓑ Ⓒ Ⓓ
4. Ⓐ Ⓑ Ⓒ Ⓓ
5. Ⓐ Ⓑ Ⓒ Ⓓ
6. Ⓐ Ⓑ Ⓒ Ⓓ
7. Ⓐ Ⓑ Ⓒ Ⓓ
8. Ⓐ Ⓑ Ⓒ Ⓓ
9. Ⓐ Ⓑ Ⓒ Ⓓ
10. Ⓐ Ⓑ Ⓒ Ⓓ
11. Ⓐ Ⓑ Ⓒ Ⓓ
12. Ⓐ Ⓑ Ⓒ Ⓓ
13. Ⓐ Ⓑ Ⓒ Ⓓ
14. Ⓐ Ⓑ Ⓒ Ⓓ
15. Ⓐ Ⓑ Ⓒ Ⓓ
16. Ⓐ Ⓑ Ⓒ Ⓓ
17. Ⓐ Ⓑ Ⓒ Ⓓ
18. Ⓐ Ⓑ Ⓒ Ⓓ
19. Ⓐ Ⓑ Ⓒ Ⓓ
20. Ⓐ Ⓑ Ⓒ Ⓓ
21. Ⓐ Ⓑ Ⓒ Ⓓ
22. Ⓐ Ⓑ Ⓒ Ⓓ
23. Ⓐ Ⓑ Ⓒ Ⓓ
24. Ⓐ Ⓑ Ⓒ Ⓓ
25. Ⓐ Ⓑ Ⓒ Ⓓ
26. Ⓐ Ⓑ Ⓒ Ⓓ
27. Ⓐ Ⓑ Ⓒ Ⓓ
28. Ⓐ Ⓑ Ⓒ Ⓓ
29. Ⓐ Ⓑ Ⓒ Ⓓ
30. Ⓐ Ⓑ Ⓒ Ⓓ

31. Ⓐ Ⓑ Ⓒ Ⓓ
32. Ⓐ Ⓑ Ⓒ Ⓓ
33. Ⓐ Ⓑ Ⓒ Ⓓ
34. Ⓐ Ⓑ Ⓒ Ⓓ
35. Ⓐ Ⓑ Ⓒ Ⓓ
36. Ⓐ Ⓑ Ⓒ Ⓓ
37. Ⓐ Ⓑ Ⓒ Ⓓ
38. Ⓐ Ⓑ Ⓒ Ⓓ
39. Ⓐ Ⓑ Ⓒ Ⓓ
40. Ⓐ Ⓑ Ⓒ Ⓓ
41. Ⓐ Ⓑ Ⓒ Ⓓ
42. Ⓐ Ⓑ Ⓒ Ⓓ
43. Ⓐ Ⓑ Ⓒ Ⓓ
44. Ⓐ Ⓑ Ⓒ Ⓓ
45. Ⓐ Ⓑ Ⓒ Ⓓ
46. Ⓐ Ⓑ Ⓒ Ⓓ
47. Ⓐ Ⓑ Ⓒ Ⓓ
48. Ⓐ Ⓑ Ⓒ Ⓓ
49. Ⓐ Ⓑ Ⓒ Ⓓ
50. Ⓐ Ⓑ Ⓒ Ⓓ
51. Ⓐ Ⓑ Ⓒ Ⓓ
52. Ⓐ Ⓑ Ⓒ Ⓓ
53. Ⓐ Ⓑ Ⓒ Ⓓ
54. Ⓐ Ⓑ Ⓒ Ⓓ
55. Ⓐ Ⓑ Ⓒ Ⓓ
56. Ⓐ Ⓑ Ⓒ Ⓓ
57. Ⓐ Ⓑ Ⓒ Ⓓ
58. Ⓐ Ⓑ Ⓒ Ⓓ
59. Ⓐ Ⓑ Ⓒ Ⓓ
60. Ⓐ Ⓑ Ⓒ Ⓓ

61. Ⓐ Ⓑ Ⓒ Ⓓ
62. Ⓐ Ⓑ Ⓒ Ⓓ
63. Ⓐ Ⓑ Ⓒ Ⓓ
64. Ⓐ Ⓑ Ⓒ Ⓓ
65. Ⓐ Ⓑ Ⓒ Ⓓ
66. Ⓐ Ⓑ Ⓒ Ⓓ
67. Ⓐ Ⓑ Ⓒ Ⓓ
68. Ⓐ Ⓑ Ⓒ Ⓓ
69. Ⓐ Ⓑ Ⓒ Ⓓ
70. Ⓐ Ⓑ Ⓒ Ⓓ
71. Ⓐ Ⓑ Ⓒ Ⓓ
72. Ⓐ Ⓑ Ⓒ Ⓓ
73. Ⓐ Ⓑ Ⓒ Ⓓ
74. Ⓐ Ⓑ Ⓒ Ⓓ
75. Ⓐ Ⓑ Ⓒ Ⓓ
76. Ⓐ Ⓑ Ⓒ Ⓓ
77. Ⓐ Ⓑ Ⓒ Ⓓ
78. Ⓐ Ⓑ Ⓒ Ⓓ
79. Ⓐ Ⓑ Ⓒ Ⓓ
80. Ⓐ Ⓑ Ⓒ Ⓓ
81. Ⓐ Ⓑ Ⓒ Ⓓ
82. Ⓐ Ⓑ Ⓒ Ⓓ
83. Ⓐ Ⓑ Ⓒ Ⓓ
84. Ⓐ Ⓑ Ⓒ Ⓓ
85. Ⓐ Ⓑ Ⓒ Ⓓ
86. Ⓐ Ⓑ Ⓒ Ⓓ
87. Ⓐ Ⓑ Ⓒ Ⓓ
88. Ⓐ Ⓑ Ⓒ Ⓓ
89. Ⓐ Ⓑ Ⓒ Ⓓ
90. Ⓐ Ⓑ Ⓒ Ⓓ

91. Ⓐ Ⓑ Ⓒ Ⓓ
92. Ⓐ Ⓑ Ⓒ Ⓓ
93. Ⓐ Ⓑ Ⓒ Ⓓ
94. Ⓐ Ⓑ Ⓒ Ⓓ
95. Ⓐ Ⓑ Ⓒ Ⓓ
96. Ⓐ Ⓑ Ⓒ Ⓓ
97. Ⓐ Ⓑ Ⓒ Ⓓ
98. Ⓐ Ⓑ Ⓒ Ⓓ
99. Ⓐ Ⓑ Ⓒ Ⓓ
100. Ⓐ Ⓑ Ⓒ Ⓓ
101. Ⓐ Ⓑ Ⓒ Ⓓ
102. Ⓐ Ⓑ Ⓒ Ⓓ
103. Ⓐ Ⓑ Ⓒ Ⓓ
104. Ⓐ Ⓑ Ⓒ Ⓓ
105. Ⓐ Ⓑ Ⓒ Ⓓ
106. Ⓐ Ⓑ Ⓒ Ⓓ
107. Ⓐ Ⓑ Ⓒ Ⓓ
108. Ⓐ Ⓑ Ⓒ Ⓓ
109. Ⓐ Ⓑ Ⓒ Ⓓ
110. Ⓐ Ⓑ Ⓒ Ⓓ
111. Ⓐ Ⓑ Ⓒ Ⓓ
112. Ⓐ Ⓑ Ⓒ Ⓓ
113. Ⓐ Ⓑ Ⓒ Ⓓ
114. Ⓐ Ⓑ Ⓒ Ⓓ
115. Ⓐ Ⓑ Ⓒ Ⓓ
116. Ⓐ Ⓑ Ⓒ Ⓓ
117. Ⓐ Ⓑ Ⓒ Ⓓ
118. Ⓐ Ⓑ Ⓒ Ⓓ
119. Ⓐ Ⓑ Ⓒ Ⓓ
120. Ⓐ Ⓑ Ⓒ Ⓓ

PRACTICE TEST 1

TIME: 120 minutes
120 questions

Four-Function or Scientific Calculator Permitted

I. READING/LANGUAGE ARTS

1. A phrase can NEVER be

   (A) a fragment of a sentence.
   (B) a modifier.
   (C) a complete thought.
   (D) prepositional.

2. The proverb "Death is a black camel, which kneels at the gates of all" is an example of

   (A) alliteration.
   (B) simile.
   (C) metaphor.
   (D) hyperbole.

3. Literacy is a person's ability to

   (A) hop and skip.
   (B) read and write.
   (C) encode and be pragmatic.
   (D) comprehend and engage.

4. In general, the entries in a table of contents are arranged according to which of the following relationships?

   (A) Alphabetical
   (B) Concrete and abstract
   (C) Linear and recursive
   (D) Order of occurrence in the book

Questions 5 and 6 refer to the following poem.

> Old Time is still a-flying;
> And this same flower that smiles today,
> Tomorrow will be dying.
> The glorious lamp of heaven, the sun,
> The higher he's a-getting,
> The sooner will his race be run,
> And nearer he's to setting.

5. Which of the following best describes the theme of the poem?

   (A) Races are to be won.
   (B) Father Time is destructive.
   (C) God is watching.
   (D) Time marches on.

6. The poet uses the examples of flowers and the sun to illustrate

   (A) love of humanity.
   (B) love of nature.
   (C) the fleeting nature of life.
   (D) the arbitrary death of natural things.

Question 7 refers to the following essay.

   Creating an English garden on a mountainside in the Ouachita Mountains in central Arkansas may sound like an impossible endeavor, but after two years, this dream is becoming my reality. By digging up the rocks and replacing them with bags of topsoil, humus, and peat, the persistent gardener now has sprouts that are not all weeds. Gravel paths meander through the beds of Shasta daisies, marigolds, lavender, valerian, iris, day lilies, Mexican heather, and other flowers. Ornamental grasses, dogwood trees, and shrubs back up the flowers. Along the periodic waterway created by an underground spring, swamp hibiscus, helenium, hosta, and umbrella plants display their colorful and seasonal blooms. Large rocks dug up by a pickax outline the flowerbeds. Blistered hands are worth the effort when people stop by to view the mountainside beauty.

7. This essay can be described as being

(A) speculative.
(B) argumentative.
(C) narrative.
(D) expository.

8. What is is incorrect about the following statement? "You will have 40 minutes to complete the assignment. When your finished, give it to Ms. Fletcher or myself."

I. "40" should be spelled out as forty.
II. The clauses should be joined by a semicolon, not a period.
III. "myself" should be "me."
IV. "your" should be "you're."

(A) Both I and II
(B) Only III
(C) Both III and IV
(D) Only IV

9. Which of the following is the term given for the written symbols for the speech sounds?

(A) Graphemes

(B) Semantics
(C) Phonemes
(D) Phonics

10. Ms. Thompson wants to teach her students about methods of collecting data in science. This is an important skill for first graders. Which of the following describes the most appropriate method of teaching students about collecting data in science?

(A) Ms. Thompson should arrange the students into groups of four. She should then have each group observe the class's pet mouse while she gently touches it with a feather. The students should record how many times out of 10 the pet mouse moves away from the feather. Then she should gently touch the class's philodendron 10 times with a feather. The students should record how many out of 10 times the philodendron moves away from the feather.
(B) Ms. Thompson should arrange the students into groups of four. She should give each group five solid balls made of materials that will float and five solid balls made of materials that will not float. She should have the students drop the balls into a bowl of water and record how many float and how many do not.
(C) Ms. Thompson should show the students a video about scientific methods of gathering data.
(D) Ms. Thompson should have a scientist come and talk to the class about methods of collecting data. If she cannot get a scientist, she should have a science teacher from the high school come and speak about scientific methods of data collection.

Questions 11–15 are based on the following passage.

Frederick Douglass was born Frederick Augustus Washington Bailey in 1817 to a white father and a slave mother. Frederick was raised by his grandmother on a Maryland plantation until he was eight. Then he was sent to Baltimore by his owner to be a servant to the Auld family. Mrs. Auld recognized Frederick's intellectual acumen and defied the law of the state by teaching him to read and write. When Mr. Auld warned that education would make the boy unfit for slavery, Frederick sought to continue his education in the streets. When his master died, Frederick, who was only 16 years of age, was returned to the plantation to work in the fields. Later, he was hired out to work in the shipyards in Baltimore as a ship caulker. He plotted an escape, but was discovered before he could get away. It took five years before he made his way to New York City and then to New Bedford, Massachusetts. He managed to elude slave hunters by changing his name to Douglass.

At an 1841 anti-slavery meeting in Massachusetts, Douglass was invited to give a talk about his experiences under slavery. His impromptu speech was so powerful and so eloquent that it thrust him into a career as an agent for the Massachusetts Anti-Slavery Society. To counter those who doubted his authenticity as a former slave, Douglass wrote his autobiography in 1845. This work became a classic in American literature and a primary source about slavery from the point of view of a slave. Douglass went on a two-year speaking tour abroad to avoid recapture by his former owner and to win new friends for the abolition movement. He returned with funds to purchase his freedom and to start his own anti-slavery newspaper. Douglass became a consultant to Abraham Lincoln, and throughout the Reconstruction period he fought doggedly for full civil rights for freedmen; he also supported the women's rights movement.

11. According to the passage, Douglass's writing of his autobiography was motivated by

    (A) the desire to make money for the anti-slavery movement.
    (B) his desire to become a publisher.
    (C) his interest in authenticating his life as a slave.
    (D) his desire to travel and speak to slaves.

12. The central idea of the passage is that Douglass

    (A) was instrumental in changing the laws regarding the education of slaves.
    (B) was one of the most eminent human rights leaders of the nineteenth century.
    (C) was a personal friend and confidant to a president.
    (D) wrote a classic in American literature.

13. According to the author of this passage, Mrs. Auld taught Douglass to read because

    (A) Douglass wanted to go to school like the other children.
    (B) she recognized his natural ability.
    (C) she wanted to comply with the laws of the state.
    (D) he needed to be able to read so that he might work in the home.

14. The title that best expresses the ideas of this passage is

    (A) The History of the Anti-Slavery Movement in America.

(B) The Outlaw Frederick Douglass.

(C) Reading: A Window to the World of Abolition.

(D) Frederick Douglass's Contributions to Freedom.

15. In the context of the passage, *impromptu* is the closest in meaning to

(A) unprepared.

(B) nervous.

(C) angry.

(D) loud.

Questions 16–18 refer to the following passage.

Gary Harris, a farmer from Conrad, Montana, has invented and patented a motorcycle helmet. It provides a brake light, which can signal traffic intentions to other drivers behind. In the United States, all cars sold are now required to have a third, high-mounted brake light. Harris's helmet will meet this requirement for motorcyclists.

16. The passage tells about

(A) a new invention for motorcyclists.

(B) a brake light for motorcyclists.

(C) Harris's helmet.

(D) Gary Harris, inventor.

17. An implication regarding the new invention is

(A) the new brake light requirement for cars should likewise apply to motorcycles.

(B) the new brake light requirement for cars cannot apply to motorcycles.

(C) If you buy a car from outside of the United States, you are exempt from the brake light requirement.

(D) As an inventor, Gary Harris can make more money if he leaves farming.

18. Because of the new brake light requirement for cars,

(A) drivers can readily see the traffic signals of car drivers ahead of them.

(B) fewer accidents can happen on the road.

(C) car prices will go up and will be less affordable to buy.

(D) the additional lights on the road will become hazardous.

Questions 19 and 20 are based on the following passage.

America's national bird, the mighty bald eagle, is being threatened by a new menace. Once decimated by hunters and loss of habitat, the bald eagle is facing a new danger, suspected to be intentional poisoning by livestock ranchers. Authorities have found animal carcasses injected with restricted pesticides. These carcasses allegedly are placed to attract and kill predators such as the bald eagle in an effort to preserve young grazing animals. It appears that the eagle is being threatened again by the consummate predator, humans.

19. One can conclude from this passage that

(A) the pesticides used are beneficial to the environment.

(B) ranchers believe that killing the eagles will protect their ranches.

(C) ranchers must obtain licenses to use illegal pesticides.

(D) poisoning eagles is good for livestock.

20. The author's attitude is one of

(A) uncaring observation.

(B) concerned interest.

(C) uniformed acceptance.

(D) suspicion.

21. Which of the following is NOT synonymous with the word *mediocre*?

    (A) Original
    (B) Commonplace
    (C) Passable
    (D) Ordinary

22. Which author wrote: "What's in a name? That which we call a rose/ By any other name would smell as sweet"?

    (A) Christopher Marlowe
    (B) Ben Johnson
    (C) William Shakespeare
    (D) Geoffrey Chaucer

23. The meaning of *protagonist* is

    (A) the landscape.
    (B) a villain.
    (C) the central character.
    (D) a quest.

24. The literary technique of foreshadowing is often used

    (A) in novels, short stories, and drama to manifest the characters' emotions by reflecting them in the natural world.
    (B) in novels, short stories, and drama to hint at future developments in the plot.
    (C) in lyric poetry to manifest the speaker's emotions by reflecting them in the natural world.
    (D) in myths and ballads to hint at future developments in the plot.

Question 25 is based on the following passage.

Water is a most unusual substance because it exists on the surface of Earth in its three physical states: ice, water, and water vapor. Other substances exist in a solid and liquid or gaseous state at temperatures normally found at Earth's surface, but water is the only pure substance to occur in all three states on Earth.

Water is odorless, tasteless, and colorless. It is a universal solvent. Water does not corrode, rust, burn, or separate into its components easily. It is chemically indestructible. It can, however, corrode almost any metal and erode the most solid rock. A unique property of water is that, when frozen in its solid state, it expands and floats on liquid water. Water has a freezing point of 0°C and a boiling point of 100°C. Water has the capacity to absorb great quantities of heat with relatively little increase in temperature. In addition, *distilled* water is a poor conductor of electricity, but when salt is added, it is a good conductor of electricity.

25. According to the passage, what is the most unusual property of water?

    (A) Water is odorless, tasteless, and colorless.
    (B) Water exists on the surface of the Earth in three physical states.
    (C) Water is chemically indestructible.
    (D) Water is a poor conductor of electricity.

Question 26 refers to the following statement.

The disparaging remarks about her performance on the job made Margaret uncomfortable.

26. The word *disparaging* is closest in meaning to

    (A) congratulatory.
    (B) immoral.
    (C) whimsical.
    (D) insulting.

27. The Japanese form of poetry called *haiku* is known for its

 (A) brevity and concision.
 (B) elaborate and flowery description.
 (C) logic and directness of statement.
 (D) humor and lifelike detail.

28. Hamlet's "To Be or Not to Be" speech, in the play by William Shakespeare, is an example of the dramatic technique known as

 (A) aside.
 (B) dialogue.
 (C) soliloquy.
 (D) comic relief.

29. Which of the following types of literature is characterized as realistic and contains a moral?

 (A) Fairy tale
 (B) Myth
 (C) Legend
 (D) Parable

II. MATHEMATICS

30. Inside a barn were lambs and people. If we counted 30 heads and 104 legs in the barn, how many lambs and how many people were in the barn?

 (A) 10 lambs and 20 people
 (B) 16 lambs and 14 people
 (C) 18 lambs and 16 people
 (D) 22 lambs and 8 people

Use the figure below and the following facts to answer Question 31.

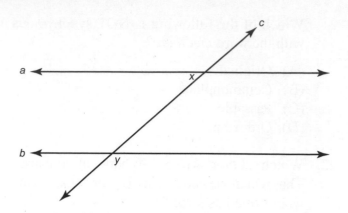

Lines *a* and *b* are parallel, *c* is a line, and the measure of angle *x* is 50°.

31. What is the measure of angle *y*?

 (A) 50°
 (B) 100°
 (C) 130°
 (D) 80°

32. In the given figure, assume that *AD* is a line. What is the measure of angle *AXB*?

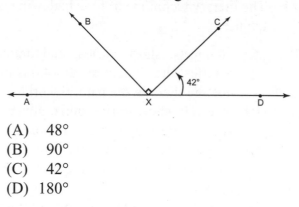

 (A) 48°
 (B) 90°
 (C) 42°
 (D) 180°

33. Which formula can be used to find the area of the triangle shown below?

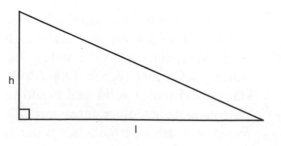

(A) $A = (l \times h)/2$
(B) $A = (l + h)/2$
(C) $A = 2(l + h)$
(D) $A = 2(l \times h)$

34. Which formula can be used to find the area of the figure below? (Assume the curve is a *half circle*.)

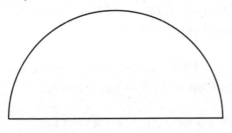

(A) $A = \pi r$
(B) $A = 2\pi r^2$
(C) $A = \pi r^2$
(D) $A = \pi r^2/2$

35. What is the greatest common divisor of 120 and 252?

(A) 2
(B) 3
(C) 6
(D) 12

36. How many odd prime numbers are there *between* 1 and 20?

(A) 7
(B) 8
(C) 9
(D) 10

37. Round the following number to the nearest hundredths place: 287.416.

(A) 300
(B) 290
(C) 287.42
(D) 287.4139

38. According to the following graph which one of the following statements is true?

Age of Household Head

Percentage Distribution of Households and Discretionary Income (Total U.S. = 100%)

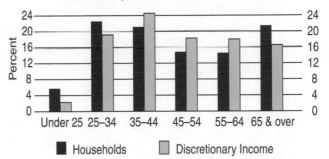

(A) Middle-aged households tend to have greater discretionary income.
(B) The youngest have the most discretionary income.
(C) The oldest have the most discretionary income.
(D) The older people get, the less discretionary income they have.

39. The floor of a 9 foot × 12 foot rectangular room depicted in the diagram is to be covered in two different types of material. The total cost of covering the entire room is $136. The cost of covering the inner rectangle is $80. The cost of covering the shaded area is $56. To compute the cost of material per square foot used to cover the shaded area, which of the following pieces of information is (are) NOT necessary?

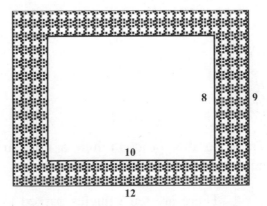

I. The total cost of covering the entire room.
II. The cost of covering the inner rectangle.
III. The cost of covering the shaded area.

(A) I only
(B) II only
(C) I and II only
(D) I and III only

40. How many cups of water does a 7-gallon container of water hold?

(A) 28
(B) 56
(C) 70
(D) 112

41. If the two triangles, *ABC* and *DEF*, shown below, are similar, what is the length of side *DF*?

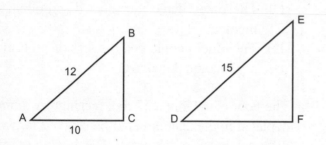

(A) 12.5 units
(B) 13 units
(C) 12 units
(D) 13.5 units

42. What is the solution to the equation
$\dfrac{x}{3} - 9 = 15$?

(A) 18
(B) 8
(C) 36
(D) 72

43. Translate this problem into a one-variable equation and then solve the equation.

There are ten vehicles parked in a parking lot. Each is either a car with four tires or a motorcycle with two tires. (Do not count any spare tires.)

There are 26 wheels in the lot. How many cars are parked in the lot?

(A) 8
(B) 6
(C) 5
(D) 3

44. Which equation could be used to solve the following problem?

Three consecutive odd numbers add up to 117. What are they?

(A) $x + (x + 2) + (x + 4) = 117$
(B) $1x + 3x + 5x = 117$
(C) $x + x + x = 117$
(D) $x + (x + 1) + (x + 3) = 117$

45. Use the pie chart below to answer the following question: If the total number of people voting was 600, which of the following statements are true?

Votes for City Council

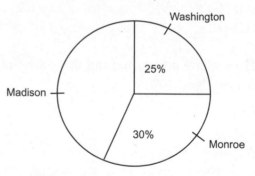

I. Madison received more votes than Monroe and Washington combined.
II. Madison received 45% of the votes.
III. Monroe received 180 votes.
IV. Madison received 180 votes.

(A) I and III only
(B) I and IV only
(C) II and III only
(D) II and IV only

46. Which of the following scenarios could be represented by the graph shown below?

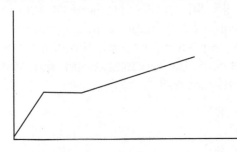

(A) Mr. Cain mowed grass at a steady rate for a while, took a short break, and then finished the job at a steady but slower rate.
(B) Mr. Cain mowed grass at a steady rate for a while, mowed at a steady but slower rate, and then took a break.
(C) Mr. Cain mowed grass at a variable rate for a while, took a short break, and then finished the job at a variable rate.
(D) Mr. Cain mowed grass at a steady rate for a while, took a short break, and then finished the job at a steady but faster pace.

47. Which one of the statements below is necessarily true according to the bar graph below?

Ms. Patton's Earnings, 1998–2002

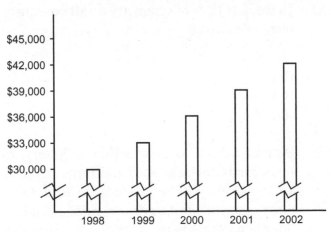

(A) The range of Ms. Patton's earnings for the years shown is $15,000.
(B) Ms. Patton's annual pay increases were consistent over the years shown.
(C) Ms. Patton earned $45,000 in 2003.

(D) Ms. Patton's average income for the years shown was $38,000.

48. Which equation could be used to solve the following problem?

Acme Taxicab Company computes fares for riders by the following formula: A passenger is charged three dollars for getting into the cab, then is charged two dollars more for every mile or fraction of a mile of the ride. What would be the fare for a ride of 10.2 miles?

(A) $3 \times (2 \times 10.2) = y$
(B) $3 + (2 + 11) = y$
(C) $3 \times (2 + 10.2) = y$
(D) $3 + (2 \times 11) = y$

49. What does it mean that multiplication and division are *inverse operations*?

(A) Multiplication is commutative, whereas division is not. For example: 4×2 gives the same product as 2×4, but $4 \div 2$ is not the same as $2 \div 4$.
(B) Whether multiplying or dividing a value by 1, the value remains the same. For example, 9×1 equals 9; $9 \div 1$ also equals 9.
(C) When performing complex calculations involving several operations, all multiplication must be completed before completing any division, such as in $8 \div 2 \times 4 + 7 - 1$.
(D) The operations "undo" each other. For example, multiplying 11 by 3 gives 33. Dividing 33 by 3 then takes you back to 11.

50. The daily high temperatures in Frostbite, Minnesota, for one week in January were as follows:

Sunday:	−2°F
Monday:	3°F
Tuesday:	0°F
Wednesday:	−4°F
Thursday:	−5°F
Friday:	−1°F
Saturday:	2°F

What was the mean daily high temperature for that week?

(A) 7
(B) −7
(C) −1
(D) 1

51. Which of the following illustrates the distributive property?

(A) Multiplying 23 by 16 gives the same product as multiplying 16 by 23.
(B) The numbers 65, 70, and 12 can be added together in any order; the sum will always be the same.
(C) The sum of 102 and 9 is the same as the sum of 9 and 102.
(D) The product of 3 and 42 is the same as the sum of the products 3×2 and 3×40.

52. Which equation could be used to answer the following question?

Together, a pen and a pencil cost $2.59 (ignoring tax). The pen cost $1.79 more than the pencil. What was the cost of the pencil?

(A) $x = (2.59 - 1.79) \times 2$
(B) $2.59 = x - 1.79$
(C) $2.59 = x + (x + 1.79)$
(D) $x = 2.59 - 1.79$

53. Matt has earned the following scores on his first six weekly mathematics tests: 91, 89, 82, 95, 86, and 79. He hopes for an average (mean) of 90 percent, which would just barely give him an A− in math class on his first report card. By how many points did Matt miss earning an A−?

(A) 87
(B) 3
(C) 90
(D) 18

54. Ms. Williams plans to buy carpeting for her living room floor. The room is a rectangle measuring 14 feet by 20 feet. She wants no carpet seams on her floor, even if that means that some carpeting will go to waste. The carpeting she wants comes in 16-foot-wide rolls. What is the minimum amount of carpeting that will have to be wasted if Ms. Williams insists upon her no-seams requirement?

(A) 40 square feet
(B) 60 square feet
(C) 80 square feet
(D) 100 square feet

55. How many lines of symmetry do all nonsquare rectangles have?

(A) 0
(B) 2
(C) 4
(D) 8

56. Bemus School is conducting a lottery to raise funds for new band uniforms. Exactly 1,000 tickets will be printed and sold. Only one ticket stub will be drawn from a drum to determine the single winner of a big-screen television. All tickets have equal chances of winning. The first 700 tickets are sold to 700 different individuals. The remaining 300 tickets are sold to Mr. Greenfield. Given this

information, which of the following statements are true?

I.   It is impossible to tell in advance who will win.
II. Mr. Greenfield will probably win.
III. Someone other than Mr. Greenfield will probably win.
IV. The likelihood that Mr. Greenfield will win is the same as the likelihood that someone else will win.

(A) I and II only
(B) I and III only
(C) II and IV only
(D) III and IV only

57. How many ten thousands are there in 1 million?

(A) 100
(B) 10
(C) 1,000
(D) 10,000

58. An owner of twin Siamese cats knows the following data:

I.   the cost of a can of cat food
II. the volume of a can of cat food
III. the number of cans of cat food eaten each day by one cat
IV. the weight of the cat food in one can

    Which of the data above can be used to determine the cost of cat food for seven days for the two cats?

(A) I and II only
(B) I and III only
(C) I and IV only
(D) III and IV only

59. The distance from Tami's house to Ken's house is three miles. The distance from Ken's house to The Soda Depot is two miles. Which of the following statements are true?

I.   The greatest possible distance between Tami's house and The Soda Depot is five miles.
II. The greatest possible distance between Tami's house and The Soda Depot is six miles.
III. The shortest possible distance between Tami's house and The Soda Depot is one mile.
IV. The shortest possible distance between Tami's house and The Soda Depot is two miles.

(A) I and III only
(B) I and IV only
(C) II and III only
(D) II and IV only

III. SOCIAL STUDIES

60. The characteristics of fascism include all of the following EXCEPT

(A) totalitarianism.
(B) democracy.
(C) romanticism.
(D) militarism.

61. The industrial economy of the nineteenth century was based on all of the following EXCEPT

(A) the availability of raw materials.
(B) an equitable distribution of profits among those involved in production.
(C) the availability of capital.
(D) a distribution system to market finished products.

62. "Jim Crow" laws were laws that

(A) effectively prohibited blacks from voting in state and local elections.

(B) restricted American Indians to United States government reservations.

(C) restricted open-range ranching in the Great Plains.

(D) established separate segregated facilities for blacks and whites.

63. Which of the following is used to effect the release of a person from improper imprisonment?

(A) A writ of mandamus

(B) A writ of habeas corpus

(C) The Fourth Amendment requirement that police have probable cause in order to obtain a search warrant

(D) The Supreme Court's decision in *Roe v. Wade*

64. The intellectual movement that encouraged the use of reason and science and anticipated human progress was called the

(A) American system.

(B) mercantilism.

(C) Enlightenment.

(D) Age of Belief.

65. Which of the following is the correct chronological order for the events in history listed below?

I.   Puritans arrive in New England.

II. Protestant Reformation begins.

III. Columbus sets sail across the Atlantic.

IV. Magna Carta is signed in England.

(A) IV, III, II, I

(B) IV, III, I, II

(C) III, IV, II, I

(D) III, II, I, IV

66. Thomas Paine's pamphlet *Common Sense* was significant because it

(A) alerted thousands of colonists to the abuses of British rule, the oppressiveness of the monarchy, and the advantages of colonial independence.

(B) rallied American spirit during the bleak winter of 1776, when it appeared that Washington's forces, freezing and starving at Valley Forge, had no hope of surviving the winter, much less defeating the British.

(C) called for a strong central government to rule the newly independent American states and foresaw the difficulties inherent within the Articles of Confederation.

(D) asserted to its British readers that they could not beat the American colonists militarily unless they could isolate New England from the rest of the American colonies.

67. In the United States government, the function of checks and balances is meant to

(A) regulate the amount of power each branch of government has.

(B) make each branch of government independent from the others.

(C) give more power to the president.

(D) give more power to the Supreme Court.

68. The Fifteenth Amendment of the United States Constitution was ratified in 1870 to grant

(A) black women and men the right to vote.

(B) citizenship for blacks.

(C) freedom of slaves.

(D) black men the right to vote.

69. Which of the following groups did NOT play a role in the settlement of the English colonies in America?

(A) Roman Catholics

(B) Puritans

(C) Mormons

(D) Quakers

70. On the following map, which letter represents the Philippines?

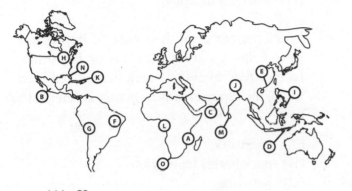

(A) K

(B) D

(C) I

(D) M

71. The Bill of Rights

(A) listed the grievances of the colonists against the British.

(B) forbade the federal government from encroaching on the rights of citizens.

(C) gave all white males the right to vote.

(D) specified the rights of slaves.

Use the bar graph to answer Questions 72 and 73.

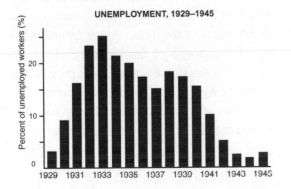

72. According to the bar graph, the unemployment rate was *highest* in

(A) 1929.

(B) 1933.

(C) 1938.

(D) 1944.

73. According to the graph, the unemployment rate was *lowest* in

(A) 1929.

(B) 1933.

(C) 1938.

(D) 1944.

74. According to the following graph, which one of the following statements is true?

Households by Income Class

Percentage Distribution of Households and Discretionary Income (Total U.S. = 100 percent)

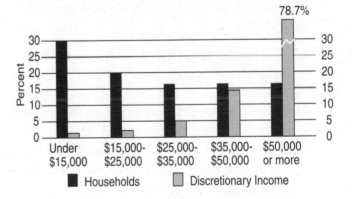

(A) About 50% of households had annual incomes of less than $15,000.

(B) Almost 75% of households had annual incomes of $50,000 or more.

(C) About 78% of households had annual incomes of $50,000 or more.

(D) About 20% of households had annual incomes between $15,000 and $25,000.

75. The launching of *Sputnik* by the Soviet Union in 1957 triggered increased emphasis on all of the following areas of study EXCEPT

    (A) world history.
    (B) math.
    (C) science.
    (D) foreign languages.

76. All of the following were true of education in the southern colonies EXCEPT

    (A) Private tutors were used to educate the sons of wealthy plantation owners.
    (B) The education of girls was limited to the knowledge of how to manage a household.
    (C) Slaves were taught to read so that they could study the Bible.
    (D) Teaching a slave to read or write was a criminal act.

77. The ruling of the Supreme Court in *Brown v. Board of Education of Topeka, Kansas* (1954) found that

    (A) separate educational facilities could offer equal educational opportunities to students.
    (B) students could be placed in segregated tracks within desegregated schools.
    (C) segregated schools resulted in unequal educational opportunity but caused no psychological effects.
    (D) separate educational facilities were inherently unequal and violated the Fourteenth Amendment.

78. President Lyndon B. Johnson's "War on Poverty" resulted in all of the following EXCEPT

    (A) the Peace Corps.
    (B) Head Start.
    (C) the Elementary and Secondary Education Act.
    (D) VISTA.

79. The Education for All Handicapped Children Act of 1975 mandates that schools provide free and appropriate education for all of the following EXCEPT the

    (A) mentally handicapped.
    (B) physically handicapped.
    (C) socially–emotionally handicapped.
    (D) learning disabled.

80. When a member of the House of Representatives helps a citizen from his or her district receive federal aid to which that citizen is entitled, the representative's action is referred to as

    (A) casework.
    (B) pork barrel legislation.
    (C) lobbying.
    (D) logrolling.

81. The term *Trail of Tears* refers to the

    (A) Mormon migration from Nauvoo, Illinois, to what is now Utah.
    (B) forced migration of the Cherokee tribe from the southern Appalachians to what is now Oklahoma.
    (C) westward migration along the Oregon Trail.
    (D) migration into Kentucky along the Wilderness Road.

82. The United States Constitution defines the powers of the United States Congress and the states. The United States Constitution reserves powers to the states in the Tenth Amendment, while Article I, Section 8 of the United States Constitution delegates powers to the federal government. Some powers are shared concurrently between the states and federal government. Which of the following powers are concurrent powers?

    I. Lay and collect taxes
    II. Regulate commerce
    III. Establish post offices
    IV. Borrow money

(A) I and II only
(B) II and III only
(C) III and IV only
(D) I and IV only

83. Which of the following statements best defines the role of the World Trade Organization (WTO)?

    (A) It resolves trade disputes and attempts to formulate policy to open world markets to free trade through monetary policy and regulation of corruption.
    (B) It is an advocate for human rights and democracy by regulating child labor and providing economic aid to poor countries.
    (C) It establishes alliances to regulate disputes and polices ethnic intimidation.
    (D) It regulates trade within the United States in order to eliminate monopolistic trade practices.

84. The drought of the 1930s that spanned from Texas to North Dakota was caused by

    I.   overgrazing and overuse of farmland.
    II. natural phenomena, such as below-average rainfall and wind erosion.
    III. environmental factors, such as changes in the jet stream.
    IV. the lack of government subsidies for new irrigation technology.

    (A) I and II only
    (B) II and III only
    (C) I and III only
    (D) II and IV only

85. Which of the following best describes a major difference between a state government and the federal government?

    (A) State governments have more responsibility for public education than the federal government.

(B) State governments are more dependent on the personal income tax for revenue than the federal government.
(C) State governments are more dependent on the system of checks and balances than the federal government.
(D) State governments are subject to term limits, whereas federal government representatives serve unlimited terms.

86. The Battle of Waterloo is historically significant because it marked which of the following?

    (A) The defeat of William the Conqueror
    (B) The end of the French Revolution
    (C) The defeat of Napoleon
    (D) The start of the Thirty Years' War

87. The most advanced pre-Columbian civilizations of Mesoamerica were the

    (A) Aztecs and Incas.
    (B) Maya and Aztecs.
    (C) Toltecs and Pueblos.
    (D) Olmecs and the Iroquois.

IV. SCIENCE

88. To apply the concept of time zones, students need to have a clear understanding of

    (A) the International Date Line.
    (B) the Earth's yearly revolution.
    (C) the concept of meridians of longitude.
    (D) the concept of the parallels of latitude.

89. Which of the following is considered to be evidence for plate tectonics?

    (A) Continental coastline "fit"
    (B) Identical fossil evidence at "fit" locations
    (C) Intense geological activity in mountainous regions
    (D) All of the above

90. The Pacific Northwest receives the greatest annual precipitation in the continental United States. Which of the following statements best identifies the reason that this occurs?

    (A) The jet stream moving south from Canada is responsible for pushing storms through the region.
    (B) The region's mountains along the coast cause air masses to rise and cool, thereby reducing their moisture-carrying capacity.
    (C) Numerous storms originating in Asia build in intensity as they move across the Pacific Ocean and then dump their precipitation upon reaching land.
    (D) The ocean breezes push moisture-laden clouds and fog into thc coastal region, producing humid, moist conditions that result in precipitation.

91. The probability of parents' offspring showing particular traits can be predicted by using

    (A) the Linnaean System.
    (B) DNA tests.
    (C) the Punnett Square.
    (D) Phenotypic traits

92. A material with definite volume but no definite shape is called

    (A) titanium.
    (B) a gas.
    (C) a liquid.
    (D) a solid

93. The intensity of an earthquake is measured by a(n)

    (A) thermograph.
    (B) seismograph.
    (C) telegraph.
    (D) odometer.

94. Which of the following types of pollution or atmospheric phenomena are correctly matched with their underlying causes?

    I.   Global warming—carbon dioxide and methane
    II. Acid rain—sulfur dioxide and nitrogen dioxide
    III. Ozone depletion—chlorofluorocarbons and sunlight
    IV. Aurora borealis—solar flares and magnetism

    (A) I and II only
    (B) II and III only
    (C) I and IV only
    (D) I, II, III, and IV

95. Which of the following observations best describes the "Ring of Fire"?

    (A) Similarities in rock formations and continental coastlines created the "Ring of Fire."
    (B) Earth's plates collide at convergent margins, separate at divergent margins, and move laterally at transform-fault boundaries.
    (C) Earthquakes produced waves that continue to travel through the Earth in all directions and created the "Ring of Fire."
    (D) Volcanoes form when lava accumulates and hardens.

96. _____ is defined as the ability to do work.

    (A) Force
    (B) Energy
    (C) Speed
    (D) Distance

97. The atomic number for neutral (unionized) atoms as listed in the periodic table refers to

    (A) the number of neutrons in an atom.
    (B) the number of protons in an atom.
    (C) the number of electrons in an atom.
    (D) both (B) and (C).

98. Which of the following is a phenomenon involving the physical properties of a substance?

    (A) Corrosion of iron
    (B) Burning of wood
    (C) Rocket engine ignition
    (D) Melting of ice

99. Isotopes of a given element contain

    (A) more electrons than protons with equal numbers of neutrons.
    (B) more protons than electrons with equal numbers of neutrons.
    (C) equal numbers of protons and electrons with differing numbers of neutrons.
    (D) unequal numbers of protons and electrons with differing numbers of neutrons.

100. Newton's second law of motion states that "the net force acting on a body is equal to the product of its mass and its acceleration." Which of the following is a good example of the law's application?

    (A) Decreased friction between surfaces by means of lubrication
    (B) Potential energy stored in a compressed spring
    (C) A rocket lifting off at Cape Canaveral with increasing speed
    (D) Using a claw hammer to pull a nail out with multiplied force

101. Which of the following is most likely to contain the greatest thermal energy?

    (A) The Pacific Ocean with an average temperature of $\approx 5°F$
    (B) A 1 g sample of molten metal at 2,000°F
    (C) A bucket of water at 75°F
    (D) Lake Michigan at an average temperature of $\approx 5°F$

102. Which cellular component is responsible for the regulation of exchanges of substances between a cell and its environment?

    (A) The endoplasmic reticulum
    (B) The cell nucleus
    (C) The cytoplasm
    (D) The cell membrane

103. Humans have 46 chromosomes in their body cells. How many chromosomes are found in the zygote?

    (A) 2
    (B) 10
    (C) 23
    (D) 46

104. All of the following are true EXCEPT:

    (A) Heredity is the study of how traits are passed from parent to offspring.
    (B) The chemical molecule that carries an organism's genetic makeup is called DNA.
    (C) Sections of the DNA molecule that determine specific traits are called chromosomes.
    (D) The genetic makeup of an organism is altered through bioengineering.

105. Which of the following sources of energy is nonrenewable?

    (A) Hydrogen cell
    (B) Geothermal
    (C) Nuclear
    (D) Hydroelectric

106. Darwin's original theory of natural selection asserts that

    (A) all organisms have descended with modification from a common ancestor.
    (B) random genetic drift plays a major role in speciation.
    (C) species characteristics are inherited by means of genes.

(D) speciation is usually due to the gradual accumulation of small genetic changes.

107. The lunar period is nearest in length to

(A) 24 hours.
(B) 30 days.
(C) 365 days.
(D) 1 week.

108. A supernova normally occurs when

(A) a star first initiates fusion.
(B) galaxies collide.
(C) the end of a star's lifetime nears, with its nuclear fuel exhausted.
(D) a wandering comet plunges into a star's interior.

109. The most important factor in Earth's seasonal patterns is the

(A) distance from the sun to Earth.
(B) Earth's rotation period of 24 hours.
(C) tilting of the Earth's axis.
(D) the moon and associated tides.

110. Metamorphic rocks are

(A) derived from igneous rocks.
(B) unrelated to igneous rocks.
(C) a type of sedimentary rock.
(D) a type of rock not found on this planet.

111. Seafloor spreading is characterized as

(A) plate spreading with upwelling magma forming ridges.
(B) plate collisions with associated ridge formation.
(C) plate spreading with no ridge formation.
(D) plate collisions with no ridge formation.

112. Igneous rocks are formed by

(A) magma cooling in underground cells and pockets.
(B) magma ejected above ground as lava, which cools.
(C) layers of sediment collecting and compacting at the bottom of lakes and seas.
(D) both (A) and (B).

113. Which of the following is the name of the cell formed by the union of a male sperm and a female ovum that develops into the embryo?

(A) Haploid
(B) Zygote
(C) Diploid
(D) Cytoplasm

114. The diagram below shows a path for electric flow. As the electrically charged particle flow moves through one complete circuit, it would NOT have to go through

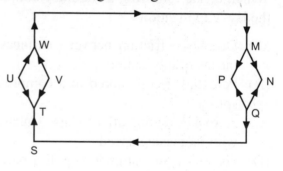

(A) V to get to W.
(B) W to get to M.
(C) Q to get to T.
(D) T to get to S.

115. A positive condition depending on the absence of cold is

(A) Fahrenheit.
(B) intense artificial cold.
(C) heat.
(D) Celsius.

116. A hot-air balloon rises when propane burners in the basket are used to heat the air inside the balloon. Which of the following statements correctly identifies the explanation for this phenomenon?

    (A) Heated gas molecules move faster inside the balloon; their force striking the inside causes the balloon to rise.
    (B) Hot gas molecules are themselves larger than cool gas molecules, resulting in the expansion of the gas.
    (C) The amount of empty space between gas molecules increases as the temperature of the gas increases, resulting in the expansion of the gas.
    (D) The combustion of propane releases product gases that are lighter than air and that are trapped in the balloon, causing it to rise.

117. A rock picked up at a bottom of a hill was found to contain tiny pieces of seashells. Which of the following is the best explanation of how this rock was formed?

    (A) It was formed on or near Earth's surface from magma or lava that flowed during a volcanic eruption.
    (B) It was formed when minerals deep inside Earth were subjected to great heat and pressure.
    (C) It was formed when sediments sank to the bottom of an ancient sea and were subjected to great pressure for long periods of time.
    (D) It was formed by seafloor spreading and erosion of the mid-ocean ridge deep in the ocean.

118. Earth's moon is

    (A) generally closer to the sun than it is to Earth.
    (B) generally closer to Earth than it is to the sun.
    (C) generally equidistant between Earth and the sun.
    (D) closer to Earth during part of the year and closer to the sun for the rest of the year.

119. Which of the following statements correctly describes each group of vertebrates?

    I.   Amphibians are cold-blooded and spend part of their life cycle in water and part on land.
    II. Reptiles are warm-blooded and have scales that cover their skin.
    III. Fish are cold-blooded, breathe with gills, and are covered by scales.
    IV. Mammals are warm-blooded and have milk glands and hair.

    (A) I and IV only
    (B) I, III, and IV only
    (C) IV only
    (D) I, II, III, and IV

120. Which of the following statements is NOT true?

    (A) Infectious diseases are caused by viruses, bacteria, or protists.
    (B) Cancers and hereditary diseases can be infectious.
    (C) Environmental hazards can cause disease.
    (D) The immune system protects the body from disease.

Practice Test 1
Answer Explanations

Elementary Education:
Content Knowledge (0014/5014)

ANSWER KEY FOR PRACTICE TEST 1

1. (C)	25. (B)	49. (D)	73. (D)	97. (D)
2. (C)	26. (D)	50. (C)	74. (D)	98. (D)
3. (B)	27. (A)	51. (D)	75. (A)	99. (C)
4. (D)	28. (C)	52. (C)	76. (C)	100. (C)
5. (D)	29. (D)	53. (D)	77. (D)	101. (A)
6. (C)	30. (D)	54. (A)	78. (A)	102. (D)
7. (C)	31. (C)	55. (B)	79. (C)	103. (D)
8. (C)	32. (A)	56. (B)	80. (A)	104. (C)
9. (A)	33. (A)	57. (A)	81. (B)	105. (C)
10. (B)	34. (D)	58. (B)	82. (D)	106. (A)
11. (C)	35. (D)	59. (A)	83. (A)	107. (B)
12. (B)	36. (A)	60. (B)	84. (A)	108. (C)
13. (B)	37. (C)	61. (B)	85. (A)	109. (C)
14. (D)	38. (A)	62. (D)	86. (C)	110. (A)
15. (A)	39. (C)	63. (B)	87. (B)	111. (A)
16. (A)	40. (D)	64. (C)	88. (C)	112. (D)
17. (A)	41. (A)	65. (A)	89. (D)	113. (B)
18. (A)	42. (D)	66. (A)	90. (B)	114. (A)
19. (B)	43. (D)	67. (A)	91. (C)	115. (C)
20. (B)	44. (A)	68. (D)	92. (C)	116. (C)
21. (A)	45. (C)	69. (C)	93. (B)	117. (C)
22. (C)	46. (A)	70. (C)	94. (D)	118. (B)
23. (C)	47. (B)	71. (B)	95. (B)	119. (B)
24. (B)	48. (D)	72. (B)	96. (B)	120. (B)

PRACTICE TEST 1 PROGRESS CHART

Language Arts Content   ____/29

1	2	3	4	5	6	7	8	9	10	11

12	13	14	15	16	17	18	19	20	21	22

23	24	25	26	27	28	29

Mathematics Content   ____/30

30	31	32	33	34	35	36	37	38	39	40

41	42	43	44	45	46	47	48	49	50	51

52	53	54	55	56	57	58	59

Social Studies Content   ____/28

60	61	62	63	64	65	66	67	68	69	70

71	72	73	74	75	76	77	78	79	80	81

82	83	84	85	86	87

Science Content   ____/33

88	89	90	91	92	93	94	95	96	97	98

99	100	101	102	103	104	105	106	107	108	109

110	111	112	113	114	115	116	117	118	119	120

PRACTICE TEST 1
ANSWER EXPLANATIONS

1. (C)

The correct answer is (C). A phrase cannot be a complete thought. A clause, on the other hand, can be a complete thought.

2. (C)

A metaphor is a comparison between two items without the use of *like* or *as*. In the proverb, "death" is called a "black camel." A simile is a comparison that uses *like* or *as*. Alliteration is the repetition of a consonant sound, and hyperbole is an exaggeration.

3. (B)

The most basic definition of literacy is the ability to read and write.

4. (D)

The index of the book (A) is arranged in alphabetical order according to topic; the page number is generally given directly after the topic. The entries are not according to concrete and abstract (B) or linear and recursive (C) relationships. Answer choice (D) is the best answer; it gives the order of occurrence.

5. (D)

Choice (D) "time marches on" is the best answer. The first line of the poem points to the theme of this poem. Answers (B) and (C) are only partially true: (B) does not reflect the gentleness of the poem, and (C) requires introducing the concept of reading into the poem, something that is not immediately present.

6. (C)

Choice (C) is the best answer. One can interpret the poem to be an expression of love of nature (B) and humanity (A), but there is no option to choose both. (D) is not a good answer because the poem illustrates the cycle of life as opposed to the "arbitrary nature of natural things."

7. (C)

Essays fall into four rough categories: speculative, argumentative, narrative, and expository. The purpose of this essay is narrative (C). The narrative essay may recount an incident or a series of incidents and is almost always autobiographical, in order to make a point. The informality of the storytelling makes the narrative essay less insistent than the argumentative essay but more directed than the speculative essay. But the thesis may not be as obvious or clear-cut as that in an expository or argumentative essay. This essay is not speculative (A). The speculative essay (A) is so named because, as its Latin root suggests, it looks at ideas and explores them rather than explaining them. The purposes of the argumentative essay (B) are always clear: to present a point and provide evidence, which may be factual or anecdotal, and to support it. The structure is usually very formal, as in a debate, with counterpositions and counterarguments. An expository essay (D) may have narrative elements, but that aspect is minor and subservient to that of explanation.

8. (C)

Both the use of "your" and "myself "is incorrect, so (C) is the correct answer. While the misuse of "myself" is rampant in spoken English, the correct usage is only reflexive—that is, when the subject and the object of the sentence (I gave myself a raise). In all other cases, "I" or "me" should be used. Both (A) and (B) are tempting choices but neither the use of numerals instead of words nor the use of a period instead of a semicolon is grammatically incorrect.

9. (A)

The correct answer is (A). *Graphemes* are "the written symbols for the speech sounds." The word *phonemes* refers to "the speech sounds." *Phonics* refers to "the method of teaching reading that emphasizes the association between the grapheme and the phoneme." *Semantics* refers to "the study of the meaning of language."

10. (B)

A hands-on activity will best help the students learn about data collection. (B) is the only choice that employs a hands-on activity, so this is the best answer. The students would learn about direct observation by watching Ms. Thompson tickle the mouse and the philodendron (A); however, this method would not be as effective as allowing the students to conduct their own data collection. Research suggests that viewing a video (C) is an inefficient method of learning. Having a guest speaker

tell the students about data collection (D) is not a good choice for first graders.

11. (C)

The passage suggests that Douglass was concerned with raising social consciousness about slavery. His interest in refuting those who doubted his claims was for the sake of authenticity.

12. (B)

Douglass was one of the eminent human rights leaders of the nineteenth century. All the other choices, while true, are irrelevant to the question and are not supported by the text.

13. (B)

The passage states, "Mrs. Auld recognized Frederick's intellectual acumen." A synonym for *acumen* is *intelligence*, *insight*, or *natural ability*. The other choices are incorrect.

14. (D)

Choices (A), (B), and (C) are too vague or ill-defined. Thus, choice (D) is correct.

15. (A)

An "impromptu" speech is one given extemporaneously, without prior preparation, or "off the cuff."

16. (A)

The best answer is (A)—it is the main idea of the passage. Choice (B) is partially correct—if it has to be specific, it should refer to the brake lights on the helmet. Choice (C) is incomplete as a key or main idea of the passage, and the same could be said of choice (D).

17. (A)

It would follow that the rationale behind the new brake-light requirement for cars in California is the same for all other vehicles on the road. Hence, choice (A) is the correct answer. (B) is illogical; in (C), any car driven in California, wherever it has been bought, cannot be exempt from the requirement; in (D), Harris can go on inventing while remaining a farmer—he'll make more money doing both.

18. (A)

Choice (A) is the most logical and appropriate answer. Hence, it is the correct answer. Choice (B) can be, but is not necessarily true; (C) is a logical possibility but will not drastically raise car prices beyond affordability; (D) may be true, but not as road hazards.

19. (B)

The ranchers believe that killing the eagles will protect their ranches. This is understood by the implication that "attract[ing] and kill[ing] predators . . . in an effort to preserve young grazing animals" will protect their ranches.

20. (B)

The author's use of words such as "mighty bald eagle" and "threatened by a new menace" supports concern for the topic. For the most part, the author appears objective; thus, choice (B), concerned interest, is the correct answer.

21. (A)

(A) is correct since something that is *original* is new, fresh, inventive, or novel: an original way of advertising. By definition, *mediocre* means that something is ordinary or of moderate quality; neither good nor bad; barely adequate. *Ordinary* (D) and *commonplace* (C) are probably closest to the meaning of *mediocre*. *Passable* (B), suggests bare adequacy.

22. (C)

Choice (C) is the correct answer. Juliet in *Romeo and Juliet*, by William Shakespeare, speaks those lines.

23. (C)

The protagonist is the central character (C).

24. (B)

Foreshadowing is used to hint at future plot developments, not to manifest characters' or speakers' emotions. It is not used prominently in lyric poetry or in ballads.

25. (B)

The first paragraph states that this is the reason that water is a most unusual substance. Choices (A) and (C) list unusual properties of water, but they are not developed in the same manner as the property stated in choice (B). Choice (D) is not correct under any circumstances.

26. (D)

Insulting (D) is the correct definition. The other terms are either antonyms or incorrect interpretations.

27. (A)

(A) is correct. By definition, haiku poetry is too short to contain much elaborate description. The haiku form does not emphasize logic or direct statements. And while some haiku poetry is humorous and/or contains lifelike details, these qualities do not characterize all haiku poems.

28. (C)

The "To Be or Not to Be" speech is a soliloquy in which Hamlet utters his thoughts aloud at length. It is not an aside because he is not speaking briefly to the audience in the midst of other action. Because Hamlet is the only one speaking, it is not a dialogue, nor is it an example of comic relief, due to the serious tone of the speech.

29. (D)

A parable is a story that is realistic and has a moral that teaches a lesson. (D) is the correct answer. Fairy tales have the element of magic, often have a certain pattern, and may present an ideal to the reader. Myths are stories written to explain things that the teller does not understand. Legends are usually exaggerated stories about real people, places, and things.

30. (D)

Let x be the number of lambs in the barn. Then, because each person and lamb has only one head, the number of people must be $30 - x$. Because lambs have four legs, the number of lamb legs equals $4x$. Similarly, the number of human legs equals $2(30 - x)$. Thus, the equation for the total number of legs (104) is

$$4x + 2(30 - x) = 104$$

Use the distributive property, $a(b - c) = ab - ac$, to get

$$4x + 60 - 2x = 104$$

which reduces to

$$2x + 60 = 104$$

Subtract 60 from each side to get

$$2x = 44, \text{ or } x = 22.$$

So the number of lambs is 22, and the number of people is $30 - 22 = 8$.

31. (C)

When two parallel lines are crossed by another line (called a transversal), eight angles are formed. However, there are only two angle measures among the eight angles, and the sum of the two measures is 180°. All the smaller angles will have the same measure, and all the larger angles will have the same measure. In this case, the smaller angles all measure 50°, so the larger angles (including angle y) all measure 130°. To solve this problem: the smaller angle + the larger angle = 180; substitute 50 for the smaller angle: $50 + y = 180$; subtract 50 from both sides: $y = 130$.

32. (A)

One must know two things to answer the question. One is the meaning of the small square at the vertex of angle *BXC*. That symbol means that angle *BXC* is a *right angle* (one with 90°). The second is that a straight line, such as *AXD*, can be thought of as a *straight angle*, which measures 180°. Therefore, because the sum of the angles *DXC* (42°) and *BXC* (90°) is 132°, the remaining angle on the line must measure 48° (180° − 132°).

33. (A)

The area of any rectangle is equal to the measure of its length times the measure of its width (or, to say it differently, the measure of its base times the measure of its height). A right triangle can be seen as half of a rectangle (sliced diagonally). Answer (A) represents, in effect, half of a rectangle's area (i.e., the area divided by 2).

34. (D)

The formula for finding the area of any circle is $A = \pi r^2$ (about 3.14 times the length of the radius times itself). In this case, take half of πr^2; hence, answer choice (D) is correct.

35. (D)

To find the greatest common divisor (GCD), factor both numbers and look for common factors. The product of these common factors is the GCD. The GCD here is the greatest integer that divides into both 120 and 252.

$$120 = 2^3 \times 3 \times 5 \text{ and}$$
$$252 = 2^2 \times 3^2 \times 7,$$

so the GCD = $2^2 \times 3 = 12$.

36. (A)

A prime number is an integer that is greater than 1 and that has no integer divisors other than 1 and itself. So the prime numbers between 1 and 20 (not including 1 and 20) are: 2, 3, 5, 7, 11, 13, 17, and 19. But 2 is not an odd number, so the odd primes between 1 and 20 are: 3, 5, 7, 11, 13, 17, and 19. Hence, there are seven odd primes between 1 and 20.

37. (C)

Place values are as follows: 1,000s, 100s, 10s, 1s, decimal point, 10ths, 100ths, 1,000ths. The 1 is in the hundredths place. If the number to the immediate right of the 1 (i.e., the number in the thousandths place) is greater than or equal to 5, we increase 1 to 2; otherwise, we do not change the 1. Then we leave off all the numbers to the right of the 1. In our problem, a 6 is in the thousandths place, so we change the 1 to a 2 to get 287.42 as our answer.

38. (A)

Graph reading and interpretation is the primary focus of this question. Choice (B) is obviously wrong because the youngest have the least discretionary income. The oldest group has less discretionary income than those between the ages of 25 and 65; therefore, item (C) is wrong. The discretionary income for all ages over 25 is more than for those under 25; (D) is incorrect.

39. (C)

To find the cost per square foot of material to cover the shaded area, divide the total cost of covering the shaded area (III) by the square footage of the shaded area. Only option III is necessary; I and II are *not* necessary. The answer is therefore (C). The problem would be solved as follows: The total area of the larger rectangle is the base times the height, 12 ft × 9 ft, which equals 108 sq. ft. Therefore, the area of the shaded portion surrounding the inner rectangle is

$$108 \text{ sq ft} - 80 \text{ sq ft} = 28 \text{ sq ft}$$

If the total cost of material is $56 to cover the shaded area of 28 square feet, the cost per square foot is $56/28 sq ft = $2/sq ft.

40. (D)

The best way to solve this problem is to see it as unit analysis. Keep in mind that you want your answer in cups, so write the measurements as fractions with denominators of 1. You will need the conversion factor and, therefore, you need to know how many quarts are in a gallon, etc.

$$\frac{7 \text{ gal}}{1} \times \frac{4 \text{ qt}}{1 \text{ gal}} \times \frac{2 \text{ pt}}{1 \text{ qt}} \times \frac{2 \text{ c}}{1 \text{ pt}}$$

Just like numbers in a fraction, the measurements (e.g., gal, qt) cancel each other out, leaving you with the numbers:

$$7 \times 4 \times 2 \times 2 = 112,$$

so the answer is (D) 112 cups.

41. (A)

If two triangles are similar, they have the exact same shape (although not necessarily the same size). This means that the corresponding angles of the two triangles have the same measure and the corresponding sides are proportional. To find the missing side (side DF), set up the proportion:

$$AB/AC = DE/DF$$

or, by substituting the given values,

$$12/10 = 15/x$$

where x is the length of side DF. This can be read as "12 is to 10 as 15 is to x." The problem can be solved by using cross multiplication. Thus, $12x = 150$, or $x = 12.5$.

42. (D)

Using the rules for solving one-variable equations, the original equation is transformed as follows:

$$x/3 - 9 = 15$$

Adding 9 to each side of the equation gives

$$x/3 = 24$$

Multiplying both sides by 3 gives

$$x = 72$$

43. (D)

One way to solve the problem is by writing a one-variable equation that matches the information given:

$$4x + 2(10 - x) = 26$$

The $4x$ represents four tires for each car. Use x for the number of cars because you do not know this number at first. Then $(10 - x)$ represents the number of motorcycles in the lot. (If there are 10 vehicles total, and x of them are cars, subtract x from 10 to get the number of "leftover" motorcycles.) Then $2(10 - x)$ stands for the number of motorcycle tires in the lot. The sum of the values $4x$ and $2(10 - x)$ is 26, which gives the equation above. Using the standard rules for solving a one-variable equation, x (the number of cars in the lot) equals 3. Another approach to answering a multiple-choice question is to try substituting each choice for the unknown variable in the problem to see which one makes sense.

44. (A)

The correct equation must show three consecutive odd numbers being added to give 117. Odd numbers (just like even numbers) are each two units apart. Only the three values $(x, x + 2, x + 4)$ given in choice (A) are each two units apart. Because the numbers being sought are odd, one might be tempted to choose (D). However, the second value in choice (D), $(x + 1)$, is not two units apart from the first value (x); it is different by only one.

45. (C)

Washington and Monroe together received 55 percent of the votes. Everyone else voted for Madison; Madison must have received 45 percent of the votes. (All of the candidates' percentages must add up to 100 percent.) Statement I cannot be true, and statement II must be true. Monroe received 30 percent of the 600 votes; 0.30 times 600 is 180, so statement III is true. Madison received 45 percent of the vote, and 45 percent of 600 is 270, so statement IV is false. Therefore, only II and III are true, and the correct answer is (C).

46. (A)

The somewhat steep straight line to the left tells you that Mr. Cain worked at a steady rate for a while. The completely flat line in the middle tells you he stopped for a while—the line does not go up because Mr. Cain did not cut grass then. Finally, the line continues upward (after his break) less steeply (therefore more flatly), indicating that he was working at a slower rate.

47. (B)

Because Ms. Patton's increases were constant ($3,000 annually), and because the directions tell you that only one statement is true, choice (B) must be the correct answer. To be more confident, however, you can examine the other statements. The range of Ms. Patton's earnings is $12,000 (the jump from $30,000 to $42,000), not $15,000, so choice (A) cannot be correct. Although Ms. Patton may have earned $45,000 in 2003, you do not know this because the graph goes only to 2002; choice (C) cannot be correct. Choice (D) gives the incorrect earnings average: it was $36,000, not $38,000.

48. (D)

All riders must pay at least $3, so 3 will be added to something else in the correct equation. Only choices (B) and (D) meet that requirement. The additional fare of $2 "for every mile or fraction of a mile" tells you that you will need to multiply the number of miles driven (use 11 because of the extra fraction of a mile) by 2, leading to the correct answer of (D).

49. (D)

It is true that multiplication is commutative and division is not (A), but that is not relevant to their being inverse operations. Choice (B) also contains a true statement, but again the statement is not about inverse operations. Choice (C) gives a false statement; in the example shown, the order of operations tells you to compute $8 \div 2$ before any multiplication. As noted in choice (D), two operations being inverse indeed depends on their ability to undo each other.

50. (C)

To find the average (mean) of a set of values, first add them together. In this case, the negative and the positive integers should be added together separately. Those two sums are -12 and 5. (The zero can be ignored; it does not affect either sum.) Then -12 and 5 should be added together for a sum of -7. To complete the work, the sum of -7 must be divided by the number of values (7), giving -1.

51. (D)

In simple notation form, the distributive property is as follows:

$$a(b + c) = (a \times b) + (a \times c)$$

This means that, when multiplying, you may have some computational options. Consider answer choice (D). The distributive property allows us to break 42 down into the convenient addends 2 and 40. You can then multiply each addend separately by 3. Thus, 3×2 equals 6, and 3×40 equals 120. Then, courtesy of the distributive property, we can add those products together to get 126. Only answer choice (D) is illustrative of the distributive property.

52. (C)

The total price of the two items in the original problem is given as $2.59, hinting that equation (B) or (C) may be correct. (In both cases, $2.59 is shown as the sum of two values.)

Examine the right side of equation (C): Note that one value is $1.79 higher than the other. That is, in equation (C), x could stand for the price of the pencil, and $(x + 1.79)$ could stand for the price of the more expensive pen. Hence, equation (C) is the right one. None of the others fits the information given.

53. (D)

It is helpful to compute Matt's current average. Adding his scores, you get 522. Dividing that by 6 (the number of scores), you find that his average is 87%. Similarly, you can multiply 90 by 6 to compute the number of total points it would take to have an average of 90 ($90 \times 6 = 540$). Matt earned only 522 points, so he was 18 shy of the A−.

54. (A)

The only way carpet from a 16-foot-wide roll will cover Ms. Williams' floor without seams is if she buys 20 feet of it. She can then trim the 16-foot width to 14 feet so that it fits her floor. Buying 20 feet of a 16-foot-wide roll means that she will have to buy 320 square feet. Her living room has an area of only 280 square feet (14 feet × 20 feet), so she'll be wasting 40 square feet (320 − 280), but no more.

55. (B)

If you can fold a two-dimensional figure so that one side exactly matches or folds onto the other side, the fold line is a line of symmetry. The figure below is a nonsquare rectangle with its two lines of symmetry shown.

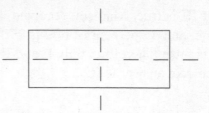

One might think that lines drawn from opposite corners are lines of symmetry, but they're not. The two halves would be the same size and shape, but wouldn't fold onto each other. Note that the question asked about nonsquare rectangles. Squares (which are rectangles) have four lines of symmetry.

56. (B)

Statement I is true because the winner could be Mr. Greenfield and it could be someone else. Statement II is not true, even though Mr. Greenfield bought many more tickets than any other individual. He still has a block of only 300; 700 ticket stubs in the drum aren't his. This tells us that statement III is true. Finally, statement IV is false. Don't confuse the true statement "all tickets have an equal chance of winning" with the false statement that "all persons have an equal chance of winning."

57. (A)

You know that 10,000 contains 4 zeros, or 10^4 in place value. The number 1,000,000 contains 10^6, or 6 zeros. Thus, 10^6 divided by 10^4 is 10^2, or 100. You may divide 10,000 into 1,000,000, but that is the laborious way to solve this. Choice (A) is correct.

58. (B)

You are challenged to analyze which data you would need to calculate the cost of feeding two cats for seven days. If you calculate the cost for one cat for seven days, then double the answer, you will have an approximate cost for two cats. The total cost for one cat is the cost of a can of food times the number of cans of food eaten each day by one cat, times seven days. Double this figure to find the answer for both cats.

59. (A)

Drawing a sketch with dots marking the possible locations of the two houses and The Soda Depot is a good idea. You can start with dots for the two houses, using inches for miles:

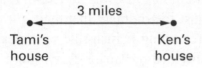

If you then draw a dot representing The Soda Depot two miles (inches) to the right of Ken's house, as in the figure that follows, you see that the greatest possible distance between Tami's house and The Soda Depot is five miles:

If you draw The Soda Depot dot to the left of Ken's house, as in the figure below, you see that The Soda Depot could be as close as one mile to Tami's house, but no closer. Only statements I and III, then, are true.

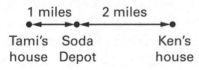

60. (B)

"Democracy" is the correct response because it is the antithesis of the authoritarianism of fascism. Indeed, facism romantizes a bygone time and relies on

the military to right the wrong. Nationalism is another tool used to rally the public in a fascist system.

61. (B)

The industrial economy of the nineteenth century was not based on an equitable distribution of profits among all those who were involved in production. Marxists and other critics of capitalism condemned the creed of capitalists and the abhorrent conditions of the industrial proletariat. Raw materials, a constant labor supply, capital, and an expanding marketplace were critical elements in the development of the industrial economy.

62. (D)

In the 1880s and 1890s, the United States Supreme Court upheld the doctrine of segregated "separate but equal" facilities for blacks and whites in *Plessy v. Ferguson*. Restrictive laws that kept blacks and whites separated became known as "Jim Crow" laws. Their impact was to allow racist governments in the South to set up "separate but unequal" facilities in which blacks were forced to sit in the rear of streetcars and buses and to eat in the back rooms of restaurants, were excluded completely from white businesses, and had to use separate and usually inferior public restroom facilities. These laws allowed white supremacists to "put blacks in their place" and effectively kept blacks from achieving anything near equal status. It wasn't until the 1950s and 1960s that new Supreme Court decisions finally forced the repeal of these laws.

63. (B)

A writ of habeas corpus (B) is a court order that directs an official who is detaining someone to produce the person before the court so that the legality of the detention may be determined. The primary function of the writ is to gain the release of someone who has been imprisoned without due process of law. For example, if the police detained a suspect for an unreasonable time without officially charging the person with a crime, the person can seek relief from a court in the form of a writ of habeas corpus. (A) is incorrect because a writ of mandamus is a court order commanding an official to perform a legal duty of his or her office. It is not used to prevent persons from being improperly imprisoned. The Fourth Amendment requirement that police have probable cause in order to obtain a search warrant regulates police procedure. It is not itself a mechanism for gaining the release of a person for improper imprisonment, so (C) is incorrect. Answer (D) is incorrect because the decision in *Roe v. Wade* dealt with a woman's right to have an abortion; it had nothing to do with improper imprisonment.

64. (C)

The American system (A), as conceived by Henry Clay, referred to the nationalist policy of uniting the three economic sections of the United States in the time following the War of 1812. Mercantilism (B) was an economic theory whose principal doctrine was the belief that the wealth of nations was based on the possession of gold. The Age of Belief (D) is tied to tradition and emotion. The Enlightenment (C) is the best possible answer.

65. (A)

The Magna Carta was signed in 1215. Columbus's voyages began in the fifteenth century. The Protestant Reformation occurred in the sixteenth century. The Puritans came to America in the seventeenth century. Therefore, the best choice is (A).

66. (A)

Thomas Paine wrote several pamphlets before and during the American Revolution. *Common Sense* was the most significant because it carefully documented abuses of the British parliamentary system of government, particularly in its treatment of the American colonies. Paine portrayed a brutish monarchy interested only in itself and pointedly argued how independence would improve the colonies' long-term situation. His argument was directed at the common man, and it struck a chord unlike anything previously written in the colonies. Its publication in 1774 was perfect in reaching the public at just the moment that their questions and concerns regarding British rule were peaking. The answers provided in Paine's essays were pivotal in the subsequent behavior of many colonists who, until that time, had been unsure of what they believed regarding independence and British rule. Answer (B) is incorrect. Paine wrote another essay called *American Crisis* during the winter of 1776. This essay, not *Common Sense*, helped rally American spirits during that long, demoralizing winter. Answers (C) and (D) are also incorrect. Paine wrote to an American, not a British, audience. He also wrote *Common Sense* well before American independence was achieved.

67. (A)

Choice (A) is correct; checks and balances provide each of the branches with the ability to limit the actions of the other branches. (B) is incorrect; branches of the federal government do not achieve independence from each other because of checks and balances. Choices (C) and (D) are also incorrect because they deal with only one branch, whereas the system of checks and balances involves the manner in which the three branches are interrelated.

68. (D)

The best choice is (D). The Fifteenth Amendment granted black males the right to vote. (A) is incorrect because the voting right was given to black males only, not women of any race. (B) is incorrect because the Fourteenth Amendment granted citizenship to former slaves. (C) is incorrect because the Thirteenth Amendment granted freedom to slaves.

69. (C)

Choices (A), (B), and (D) all played a role in the early settlements of the English colonies in America. The correct response is answer choice (C); Mormonism was founded at Fayette, New York, in 1830, by Joseph Smith. *The Book of Mormon* was published in 1830; it describes the establishment of an American colony from the Tower of Babel.

70. (C)

The letter *K* represents Cuba, the letter *D* represents Indonesia, and the letter *M* represents Sri Lanka. The correct answer is (C) because the letter *I* represents the Philippine Islands.

71. (B)

The Bill of Rights clearly states that Congress may not make laws abridging citizens' rights and liberties. Choices (C) and (D) are incorrect because the Bill of Rights does not talk about voting rights or slaves. A list of grievances (A) is contained in the Declaration of Independence.

72. (B)

The 1933 bar is highest, and the graph measures the percentage of unemployment by the height of the bars. The bars for 1929 (A), 1938 (C), and 1944 (D) are all lower than the bar for 1933, the year in which unemployment was the highest.

73. (D)

The bar for the year 1944 (the bar between 1943 and 1945) is the lowest bar on the graph. As previously mentioned, the graph measures the percentage of unemployment by the height of the bars. The bars for 1929 (A), 1933 (B), and 1938 (C) are all higher than the bar for 1944.

74. (D)

Choice (A) is wrong because about 30 percent, not 50 percent, of households had under $15,000. Choices (B) and (C) are also incorrect because slightly more than 15 percent fell into this category.

75. (A)

The United States was shocked when the Soviet Union launched *Sputnik* in 1957, ushering in the space age. Comparisons between Soviet education and the education available in United States public schools indicated a need to emphasize math (B), science (C), and foreign languages (D) for the United States to compete with other countries and to remain a world power.

76. (C)

The general public believed that the slaves would be more submissive if they remained illiterate; therefore, most slaves were never taught to read or write. Teaching a slave to read or write was, in fact, a criminal act.

77. (D)

In handing down its decision in *Brown v. Board of Education of Topeka, Kansas* in 1954, the Supreme Court stated that "Separate but equal has no place . . . Separate educational facilities are inherently unequal and violate the equal protection clause of the Fourteenth Amendment."

78. (A)

The Peace Corps (A) was established by President John F. Kennedy. Johnson's VISTA (D) was modeled after the Peace Corps. Head Start (B) and the Elementary and Secondary Education Act (C) were also put into effect as part of President Johnson's "War on Poverty."

79. (C)

The Education for All Handicapped Children Act of 1975 provides for mentally (A) and physically (B) handicapped as well as learning-disabled children (D). It does not include socially-emotionally handicapped youngsters.

80. (A)

The term *casework* (A) is used by political scientists to describe the activities of members of Congress on behalf of individual constituents. These activities might include helping an elderly person secure social security benefits or helping a veteran obtain medical services. Most casework is actually done by congressional staff and may take as much as a third of the staff's time. Representatives supply this type of assistance for the good public relations it provides. Pork barrel legislation (B) is rarely, if ever, intended to help individual citizens. Rather, such legislation authorizes federal spending for special projects, such as airports, roads, or dams, in the home state or district of the representative. It is meant to help the entire district or state. Also, there is no legal entitlement on the part of a citizen to a pork barrel project, such as exists with social security benefits. Choice (C) is not the answer because lobbying is an activity directed toward the representative, not one done by the member of Congress. A lobbyist attempts to get members of Congress to support legislation that will benefit the group that the lobbyist represents. Logrolling (D) is incorrect because it does not refer to a congressional service for constituents. It refers instead to the congressional practice of trading votes on different bills. Representative X will vote for Representative Z's pork barrel project, and in return representative Z will vote for representative X's pork barrel project.

81. (B)

The term *Trail of Tears* is used to describe the forced relocation of the Cherokee tribe from the southern Appalachians to what is now Oklahoma (B). The migration of Mormons from Nauvoo, Illinois, to the Great Salt Lake in Utah (A), and the westward movements along the Oregon Trail (C) and, much earlier, the Wilderness Road (D) all took place and could at times be as unpleasant as the Cherokees' trek. They were voluntary, however, compared to the Cherokee migration and therefore did not earn such sad titles as the "Trail of Tears."

82. (D)

Both state and federal governments have the power to lay and collect taxes and to borrow money.

Article I, Section 8 of the Constitution establishes the powers of Congress, whereas the Tenth Amendment to the Constitution (the last amendment within the Bill of Rights) sets forth the principle of reserved powers to state governments. State constitutions give states the power to lay and collect taxes.

83. (A)

The main purposes of the WTO are to open world markets to all countries and thus promote economic development, and to regulate the economic affairs between member states

84. (A)

Overgrazing, overuse of farmland, and a lack of rainfall caused the drought of the 1930s.

85. (A)

The responsibility for public education belongs to the state governments. The federal government has often passed legislation to regulate and provide funds for public education, but the main responsibility for establishing and regulating education resides with the states.

86. (C)

French-ruled peoples viewed Napoleon as a tyrant who repressed and exploited them for the glory and advantage of France. The Battle of Waterloo is historically significant because it marked the defeat of Napoleon in 1815.

87. (B)

The Maya and the Aztecs occupied the area of Central America and Southern Mexico called Me-soamerica. Both groups were accomplished builder, astronomers, and mathematicians. Choice (A) is incorrect because the Inca civilization was not a Mesoamerican group. They developed an advanced civilization in South America, in present-day Peru and Ecuador. Choice (C) is incorrect because only the Toltecs were from Mesoamerica; the Pueblo Indians were from present-day New Mexico in North America. Choice (D) is incorrect because only the Olmecs were Mesoamerican. The Iroquois civilizations developed in North America.

88. (C)

The best choice is (C); the Earth is divided into 24 zones based on the meridians of longitude, which are determined using the rotation of the Earth and its exposure to sunlight. This rotation creates day and night, and consequently the concept of time. Choice (A) is incorrect because the International Date Line is only one of 24 meridians of the Earth. Choice (B) is incorrect because the term revolution describes the movement of the Earth around the sun, which affects the seasons but not necessarily the time zones. Choice (D) is incorrect because the parallels of latitude do not affect the time zones.

89. (D)

The east coast of South America and the west coast of Africa fit together like pieces of a jigsaw puzzle. Fossil remains in locations where "fit" is observed are too well matched to be coincidental. Earthquakes and volcanism are more prevalent in mountainous regions, where plates collided, than in other regions. Thus, all these factors support the theory of plate tectonics.

90. (B)

The region's mountain ranges are the main reason for the high precipitation.

91. (C)

All known living things are grouped in categories according to shared physical traits. The process of grouping organisms is called classification. Carl Linné, also known as Linnaeus, devised the classification system used in biology today. In the Linnaean system (A), all organisms are given a two-word name (binomial). The name consists of a genus (e.g., *Canis*) and a species (e.g., *lupus*) designation. The DNA holds the genetic materials of a cell, so (B) could not be the correct answer. (D) is not a correct choice since both (A) and (B) are incorrect. When the genetic type of parents is known, the probability of the offspring showing particular traits can be predicted by using the Punnett Square (C). A Punnett Square is a large square divided into four small boxes. The genetic symbol of each parent for a particular trait is written alongside the square, for one parent along the top and for the other parent along the left side, as shown in the figure.

Each gene symbol is written in the boxes below or to the right of it. This results in each box having two gene symbols in it. The genetic symbols in the boxes are all the possible genetic combinations for a particular trait of the offspring of these parents. Each box has a 25 percent probability of being the actual genetic representation for a given child.

92. (C)

A liquid has a definite volume, but it molds to the shape of the container holding it. Titanium (A) is a solid (D), and solids have a definite shape and volume, so (A) and (D) are not the best answers. A gas will expand to fit the container in both volume and shape, so (B) is not the correct answer.

93. (B)

The instrument for measuring the intensity of an earthquake is a seismograph. A thermograph (A) measures temperature; a telegraph (C) is a communication device; and an odometer (D) measures distance traveled, so (A), (C), and (D) are not correct.

94. (D)

All are correctly matched.

95. (B)

Expansion occurring on the ocean floor creates pressure around the edges of the Pacific Plate and produces geologic instability where the Pacific Plate collides with the continental plates on all sides. Neither earthquakes (C), hardened lava (D), nor rock similarities (A) alone are sufficient to account for the "Ring of Fire."

96. (B)

Energy is defined as the ability to do work. Work occurs when a force (push or pull) is applied to an object, resulting in movement. Work = force × distance. The greater the force (A) applied, or the longer the distance traveled (D), or the greater the interval between two points, the greater the work done, but they are not the ability to do the work. Speed is rate of movement, so (C) is not the best answer.

97. (D)

Atoms are neutral, so the net charge must be zero, requiring that the number of negative particles (electrons) equals the number of positive particles (protons).

98. (D)

(A), (B), and (C) all involve chemical changes in which iron, wood, and rocket fuel, respectively, react with other substances to produce a reactant product with different chemical properties. Melted ice in the form of water still has the same chemical formula, so the correct answer is (D).

99. (C)

Isotopes are atoms with the same number of protons and electrons but different number of neutrons. Isotopes for a given element all have the same chemical properties, differing only in their atomic weight, or number of neutrons.

100. (C)

Newton's second law states that an unbalanced force acting on a mass causes the mass to accelerate. In equation form, $F = ma$, where F is force, m is mass, and a is acceleration. Only (C) involves a mass that is being accelerated by an unbalanced force.

101. (A)

Thermal energy is the total amount of internal energy of a given body, whereas temperature is a measure of the vibrational activity of atoms or molecules within the material. Therefore, thermal energy involves both the mass and temperature of a given body. Thus, (A) is the most likely answer

because its mass far exceeds 1 g, a bucket of water, and Lake Michigan. (B) is ruled out because, even though its temperature is very high, its mass is extremely small.

102. (D)

The cell membrane (D) is a selectively permeable barrier that permits some substances to pass through while forming a barrier for others. None of the other choices have this property.

103. (D)

A zygote is the cell formed by the union of a male sperm and a female ovum. The zygote develops into the embryo following the instruction of its DNA. (D) is correct because the zygote of a human is a cell derived from a sperm containing 23 chromosomes and an egg containing 23 chromosomes. A haploid has only one copy of each chromosome and therefore half the number of chromosomes found in other cells of the body. A diploid has two copies of each chromosome. (A) cannot be the correct answer because it represents too few chromosomes for either a haploid sex cell or a diploid body cell. (B) cannot be the correct answer because it also represents too few chromosomes for either a haploid sex cell or a diploid body cell. (C) cannot be the correct answer because it represents the number of chromosomes in a sperm or an egg.

104. (C)

Genes are the sections of the DNA molecule that determine specific traits.

105. (C)

Nuclear energy (C) is nonrenewable. Nuclear energy has potential advantages in providing large quantities of energy from a small amount of source material, but the process of radioactive decay is nonreversible.

106. (A)

Choices (B), (C), and (D) are ruled out because Darwin was unaware of the genetic work that was later done by Mendel. Darwin and most other nineteenth-century biologists never knew of Mendel and his research. It was not until the beginning of the twentieth century that Mendel's pioneering research on genetic inheritance was rediscovered.

107. (B)

The lunar period is about 30 days, or one month, which is the time it takes for the moon to orbit Earth one time.

108. (C)

A star "going nova" is presumed to be at the end of its life. As hydrogen (or sometimes helium) is depleted, the fusion reaction becomes incapable of sustaining the pressures required to push the star's mass outward against the pull of gravity. The star then collapses, resulting in a gigantic explosion known as a supernova. Choice (A) is neither observed nor possible; (B) is not observed; and (D), although occasionally observed, does not trigger nova-sized explosions.

109. (C)

The tilting of Earth's axis causes the Northern Hemisphere to point more sunward in the summer months and away from the sun in the winter months (with the reverse being true for the Southern Hemisphere), so (C) is the correct answer. (B) is ruled out because the rotation period is the same from season to season. (A) is ruled out because Earth is actually somewhat closer to the sun in December through January than it is in June through July, which is winter for the Southern Hemisphere. (D) is ruled out because this is a daily, not a seasonal, phenomenon.

110. (A)

Igneous rocks are transformed, or "metamorphosed," into metamorphic rocks. Thus, they are related to igneous, not sedimentary, rocks and are found on this planet.

111. (A)

According to the theory of plate tectonics, plate spreading is associated with magma upwelling to fill the vacated space, which forms ridges at these locations. This is true also under the oceans.

112. (D)

The raw material for igneous rock formation is magma, which—when cooled either above or below ground—becomes igneous rock.

113. (B)

The correct answer is (B). A zygote is the cell formed by the union of a male sperm and a female ovum. The zygote develops into the embryo following the instruction of its DNA. A haploid has only one copy of each chromosome and therefore half the number of chromosomes found in other cells of the body. A diploid has two copies of each chromosome. Cytoplasm is the contents of a cell, outside the nucleus.

114. (A)

Note that the particle flow divides at two points, T and M. At these points, the flow has two paths to reach either point W or point Q. Thus, the correct choice is (A). Particle flow can reach point W by going through point U, rather than V. It would have to flow through all other points listed in order to make a complete circuit or total clockwise path.

115. (C)

Because heat is a positive condition depending on the absence of cold, (C) is the correct answer. Fahrenheit and Celsius are measures of temperature, not conditions; therefore, (A) and (D) are incorrect choices. Heat is the opposite of intense artificial cold; (B) is not acceptable.

116. (C)

The gas molecules themselves do not expand in size when heated, but the spaces between them increases as the molecules move faster. The expanding hot air leaves the balloon body through the opening at the bottom. With less air in the balloon casing, the balloon is lighter. The combustion products of propane are carbon dioxide (molar mass 44 g/mol), which is heavier than air, and water (molar mass 18 g/mol), which is lighter.

117. (C)

The correct answer is (C). The question asks you to apply your knowledge of rock formation and the processes of Earth's history to a single sample, a rock containing tiny pieces of seashells. The presence of seashells in a rock on a hillside indicates that the hillside was under water many years ago. When the ancient sea existed, shells, which are "houses" of sea creatures, would have fallen to the seabed when the animals died. The pressure of the water over very long periods of time would have compacted and cemented the sediment and the

shells into rocks that were later exposed when the sea dried up. Hence, the answer (C).

118. (B)

The moon is much closer to Earth than it is to any other celestial body or to the sun.

119. (B)

Reptiles are never warm-blooded although they normally have scales all over their body; all the other statements are correct.

120. (B)

Cancers and hereditary diseases (B) are *not* infectious. Diseases caused by viruses, bacteria, or protists (A) that invade the body are called infectious diseases. These disease-causing organisms are collectively referred to as germs. Despite the fact that the immune system protects the body from disease (D), environmental hazards can still cause disease (C). (B) is the only answer that is false and therefore is the answer to this question.

Practice Test 2

Elementary Education: Content Knowledge (0014/5014)

This test is also on CD-ROM in our special interactive PRAXIS Elementary Education: Content Knowledge (0014/5014) TestWare®. It is highly recommended that you first take this exam on computer. You will then have the additional study features and benefits of enforced timed conditions and instantaneous, accurate scoring. See page 12 for instructions on how to get the most out of REA's TestWare®.

ANSWER SHEET FOR PRACTICE TEST 2

1. (A) (B) (C) (D)
2. (A) (B) (C) (D)
3. (A) (B) (C) (D)
4. (A) (B) (C) (D)
5. (A) (B) (C) (D)
6. (A) (B) (C) (D)
7. (A) (B) (C) (D)
8. (A) (B) (C) (D)
9. (A) (B) (C) (D)
10. (A) (B) (C) (D)
11. (A) (B) (C) (D)
12. (A) (B) (C) (D)
13. (A) (B) (C) (D)
14. (A) (B) (C) (D)
15. (A) (B) (C) (D)
16. (A) (B) (C) (D)
17. (A) (B) (C) (D)
18. (A) (B) (C) (D)
19. (A) (B) (C) (D)
20. (A) (B) (C) (D)
21. (A) (B) (C) (D)
22. (A) (B) (C) (D)
23. (A) (B) (C) (D)
24. (A) (B) (C) (D)
25. (A) (B) (C) (D)
26. (A) (B) (C) (D)
27. (A) (B) (C) (D)
28. (A) (B) (C) (D)
29. (A) (B) (C) (D)
30. (A) (B) (C) (D)

31. (A) (B) (C) (D)
32. (A) (B) (C) (D)
33. (A) (B) (C) (D)
34. (A) (B) (C) (D)
35. (A) (B) (C) (D)
36. (A) (B) (C) (D)
37. (A) (B) (C) (D)
38. (A) (B) (C) (D)
39. (A) (B) (C) (D)
40. (A) (B) (C) (D)
41. (A) (B) (C) (D)
42. (A) (B) (C) (D)
43. (A) (B) (C) (D)
44. (A) (B) (C) (D)
45. (A) (B) (C) (D)
46. (A) (B) (C) (D)
47. (A) (B) (C) (D)
48. (A) (B) (C) (D)
49. (A) (B) (C) (D)
50. (A) (D) (C) (D)
51. (A) (B) (C) (D)
52. (A) (B) (C) (D)
53. (A) (B) (C) (D)
54. (A) (B) (C) (D)
55. (A) (B) (C) (D)
56. (A) (B) (C) (D)
57. (A) (B) (C) (D)
58. (A) (B) (C) (D)
59. (A) (B) (C) (D)
60. (A) (B) (C) (D)

61. (A) (B) (C) (D)
62. (A) (B) (C) (D)
63. (A) (B) (C) (D)
64. (A) (B) (C) (D)
65. (A) (B) (C) (D)
66. (A) (B) (C) (D)
67. (A) (B) (C) (D)
68. (A) (B) (C) (D)
69. (A) (B) (C) (D)
70. (A) (B) (C) (D)
71. (A) (B) (C) (D)
72. (A) (B) (C) (D)
73. (A) (B) (C) (D)
74. (A) (B) (C) (D)
75. (A) (B) (C) (D)
76. (A) (B) (C) (D)
77. (A) (B) (C) (D)
78. (A) (B) (C) (D)
79. (A) (B) (C) (D)
80. (A) (B) (C) (D)
81. (A) (B) (C) (D)
82. (A) (B) (C) (D)
83. (A) (B) (C) (D)
84. (A) (B) (C) (D)
85. (A) (B) (C) (D)
86. (A) (B) (C) (D)
87. (A) (B) (C) (D)
88. (A) (B) (C) (D)
89. (A) (B) (C) (D)
90. (A) (B) (C) (D)

91. (A) (B) (C) (D)
92. (A) (B) (C) (D)
93. (A) (B) (C) (D)
94. (A) (B) (C) (D)
95. (A) (B) (C) (D)
96. (A) (B) (C) (D)
97. (A) (B) (C) (D)
98. (A) (B) (C) (D)
99. (A) (B) (C) (D)
100. (A) (B) (C) (D)
101. (A) (B) (C) (D)
102. (A) (B) (C) (D)
103. (A) (B) (C) (D)
104. (A) (B) (C) (D)
105. (A) (B) (C) (D)
106. (A) (B) (C) (D)
107. (A) (B) (C) (D)
108. (A) (B) (C) (D)
109. (A) (B) (C) (D)
110. (A) (B) (C) (D)
111. (A) (B) (C) (D)
112. (A) (B) (C) (D)
113. (A) (B) (C) (D)
114. (A) (B) (C) (D)
115. (A) (B) (C) (D)
116. (A) (B) (C) (D)
117. (A) (B) (C) (D)
118. (A) (B) (C) (D)
119. (A) (B) (C) (D)
120. (A) (B) (C) (D)

TIME: 120 minutes
120 questions

| Four-Function or Scientific Calculator Permitted |

I. LANGUAGE ARTS

Questions 1 and 2 refer to the following paragraph:

(1) One potential hideaway that until now has been completely ignored is De Witt Isle, off the coast of Australia. (2) Its assets are 4,000 acres of jagged rocks, tangled undergrowth, and trees twisted and bent by battering winds. (3) Settlers will have avoided it like the plague, but bandicoots (rat like marsupials native to Australia), wallabies, eagles, and penguins think De Witt is just fine. (4) Why De Witt? (5) So does Jane Cooper, 18, a pert Melbourne High School graduate, who emigrated there with three goats, several chickens, and a number of cats brought along to stand guard against the bandicoots. (6) "I was frightened at the way life is lived today in our cities," says Jane. (7) "I wanted to be alone, to have some time to think and find out about myself."

1. Which of these changes is grammatically correct?

   (A) Sentence 1—Change "has been" to "have been."
   (B) Sentence 7—Delete "to have."

   (C) Sentence 3—Change "will have" to "have."
   (D) Sentence 4—Change "emigrated" to "immigrated."

2. Which one of these changes would make the passage flow more logically?

   (A) Put Sentence 5 before Sentence 4.
   (B) Begin the passage with Sentence 4.
   (C) In Sentence 1, delete "off the coast of Australia."
   (D) Begin the passage with Sentence 2.

Questions 3 and 4 are based on the following:

In a unit on ecology for a fifth-grade class, the teacher presents the following poem:

The days be hot, the nights be cold,
But cross we must, we rush for gold.

The plants be short, the roots spread wide,
Me leg she hurts, thorn's in me side.

I fall, I crawl, I scream, I rave,
Tiz me life that I must save.

How can it be, I've come undone,
Here 'neath this blazin' eternal sun?

The days be hot, the nights be cold,
Me lonely bones alone grow old.

3. What physical setting is the poem describing?

   (A) A forest
   (B) A tundra
   (C) A swamp
   (D) A desert

4. The type of writing in the poem can best be described as

   (A) colloquial.
   (B) narrative.
   (C) metaphoric.
   (D) factual.

5. Mrs. Nemetski is preparing a unit on literary genres. She presents the class with the following story:

   > A fisherman was trying to lure fish to rise so that he could hook them. He took his bagpipes to the banks of the river and played them. No fish rose out of the water. Next he cast his net into the river and when he brought it back, the net was filled with fish. Then he took his bagpipes again and as he played, the fish leaped up in the net.
   >
   > "Ah, now you dance when I play," he said to an old fish.
   >
   > "Yes," said the old one, "when you are in a person's power you must do as he commands."

   To which genre does this story belong?

   (A) Narrative
   (B) Character analysis
   (C) Editorial
   (D) Fable

Questions 6–8 refer to the following:
A flea and a fly in a flue
Were caught, so what could they do?
Said the fly, "Let us flee."

"Let us fly," said the flea.
So they flew through a flaw in the flue.

—Anonymous

6. What form of poetry did the teacher present to her class?

   (A) An elegy
   (B) A ballad
   (C) A limerick
   (D) A haiku

7. The repetition of the *fl-* in *flea*, *fly*, and *flue* is called

   (A) alliteration.
   (B) onomatopoeia.
   (C) imagery.
   (D) symbolism.

8. A follow-up assignment to the above presentations might include:

   I.   having students illustrate the poem.
   II.   asking students to write their own poem in this form.
   III. having students clap their hands to practice the rhythm of the poem.

   (A) I only
   (B) I and II only
   (C) I and III only
   (D) I, II, and III

"If turnips are not blue, then the sky is falling."

9. Given that the previous sentence is true, which one of the following sentences MUST also be true?

   (A) If turnips are blue, then the sky is not falling.
   (B) If the sky is falling, then turnips are not blue.
   (C) If the sky is not falling, then turnips are blue.
   (D) If the sky is not falling, then turnips are not blue.

10. Sequential language acquisition occurs when students

    (A) learn a second language after mastery of the first.
    (B) learn a second language at the same time as the first.
    (C) learn two languages in part.
    (D) develop language skills.

11. Mr. Chan is teaching his class how to recognize propaganda. He presents his class with the slogan "Buy a brand-new Whizzer bike like the ones all your friends have." Which propaganda device is he illustrating?

    (A) Bandwagon
    (B) Testimonial
    (C) Card-stacking
    (D) Glittering generality

12. What do the following sentences illustrate?

    Laura tried to do her best.

    The judge tried the case harshly.

    (A) Grammatical errors
    (B) Synonyms and antonyms
    (C) Rules of spelling
    (D) Words with multiple meanings

Question 13 is based on the following poem:

Richard Cory
By Edwin Arlington Robinson

Whenever Richard Cory went down town,
We people on the pavement looked at him:
He was a gentleman from sole to crown,
Clean favored, and imperially slim.

And he was always quietly arrayed,
And he was always human when he talked;
But still he fluttered pulses when he said,
"Good-morning," and he glittered when he
   walked.

And he was rich—yes, richer than a king—
And admirably schooled in every grace;
In fine we thought that he was everything
To make us wish that we were in his place.

So on we worked, and waited for the light,
And went without the meat, and cursed the
   bread;
And Richard Cory, one calm summer night,
Went home and put a bullet through his head.

13. Richard Cory represents the

    (A) wisdom of age.
    (B) happiness of love.
    (C) deception of appearance.
    (D) contentment of youth.

14. A teacher presents the following sentences to her class. Which one is **CORRECT**?

    (A) I don't like hiking as much as I like cross-country skiing.
    (B) I don't like to hike as much as cross-country skiing.
    (C) I don't like hiking as much as I like to ski cross-country.
    (D) I don't like to hike as much as I like going cross-country skiing.

Read the passage below, and then answer Questions 15–18.

The issue of adult literacy has finally received recognition as a major social problem. Unfortunately, the issue is usually presented in the media as a "women's interest issue." Numerous governors' wives and even Laura Bush have publicly expressed concern about literacy. As well-meaning as the politicians' wives may be, it is more important that the politicians themselves recognize the seriousness of the problem and support increased funding for literacy programs.

Literacy education programs need to be directed at two different groups of people with very different needs. The first group is composed of people who have very limited reading and writing skills. These people are complete illiterates. A second group is composed of people who can read and write but whose skills are not sufficient to meet their needs. This second group is called functionally illiterate. Successful literacy programs must meet the needs of both groups.

Instructors in literacy programs have three main responsibilities. First, the educational needs of the illiterates and functional illiterates must be met. Second, the instructors must approach the participants in the program with empathy, not sympathy. Third, all participants must experience success in the program and must perceive their efforts as worthwhile.

15. What is the difference between illiteracy and functional illiteracy?

   (A) There is no difference.
   (B) A functional illiterate is enrolled in a literacy education program but an illiterate is not.
   (C) An illiterate cannot read or write; a functional illiterate can read and write but not at a very high skill level.
   (D) There are more illiterates than functional illiterates in the United States today.

16. What does "women's interest issue" mean in the passage?

   (A) The issue is interesting to women only.
   (B) Many politicians' wives have expressed concern over the issue.
   (C) Women illiterates outnumber male illiterates.

(D) Politicians interested in illiteracy often have their wives give speeches on the topic.

17. According to the passage, which of the following is NOT a characteristic of successful literacy programs?

   (A) Participants should receive free transportation.
   (B) Participants should experience success in the program.
   (C) Instructors must have empathy, not sympathy.
   (D) Programs must meet the educational needs of illiterates.

18. What is the author's opinion of the funding for literacy programs?

   (A) Too much
   (B) Too little
   (C) About right
   (D) Too much for illiterates and not enough for functional illiterates

Read the passage below, and then answer Questions 19–22.

Language not only expresses an individual's ideology, it also sets perimeters while it persuades and influences the discourse in the community that hears and interprets its meaning. Therefore, the language of failure should not be present in the learning environment (i.e., the classroom) because it will have a prohibitive impact on the students' desire to learn as well as a negative influence on the students' self-esteem. The *Oxford English Dictionary* defines *failure* as "a fault, a shortcoming, a lack of success, a person who turns out unsuccessfully, becoming insolvent, etc." We as educators might well ask ourselves if this is the sort of doctrine that we want to permeate our classrooms. Perhaps our own university maxim, *mens agitat molem* (literally " mind moves the mass," or "the mind can move mountains") will help us discover if, indeed, the concepts of failure are really the types of influences we wish to introduce to impressionable new students. Is the mind capable of moving a mountain when it is already convinced it cannot? One must remain aware that individuals acquire knowledge at independent rates of speed. Certainly no one would suggest that one infant "failed" the art of learning to walk because she acquired the skill two months after her infant counterpart. Would anyone suggest that infant number one failed walking? Of course not. What would a mentor project to either toddler were he to suggest that a slower acquisition of walking skills implied failure? Yet we as educators feel the need to suggest student A failed due to the slower procurement of abstract concepts than student B. It is absolutely essential to shift the learning focus from failure to success.

19. Which of the following statements best conveys the meaning of the passage?

   (A) Learning is something that happens at different speeds and is, therefore, natural.
   (B) Instructors need to be sensitive to students' individual needs.
   (C) Instructors need to shift the educational focus from failure to success in learning environments.
   (D) Failure is a potential hazard in the classroom and should be avoided at all costs.

20. As stated in the context of the passage, what does "university maxim" mean?

   (A) University Latin
   (B) University motto
   (C) University rhetoric
   (D) University sophomore

21. According to the passage, what will have a negative effect on students' self-esteem?

   (A) The rhetoric of diction
   (B) The slower procurement of abstract concepts
   (C) The learning focus from failure to success
   (D) The language of failure

22. According to the passage, what does language do besides aid individual expression?

   (A) It establishes individual thought and tells of individual philosophies.
   (B) It paints visual images and articulates individual declaration.
   (C) It suggests individual axioms and community philosophy.
   (D) It persuades and influences the discourse in the community that hears and interprets its meaning.

23. To explain and clarify ideas is the purpose of which of the following types of writing?

   (A) Expository
   (B) Persuasive
   (C) Descriptive
   (D) Narrative

24. *Hiss* is an example of

   (A) metaphor
   (B) personification
   (C) simile
   (D) onomatopoeia

Read the passage below, and then answer Questions 25–27.

   The early decades of the fifteenth century were a period in our history when English took a "great (linguistic) vowel shift" by redistributing the vowel pronunciation and configuration. Each vowel changed its sound quality, but the distinction between one vowel and the next was maintained. There was a restructuring of the sounds and patterns of communication. One has to conclude that a concurrent stress and exhilaration was also occurring within the perimeters of the literate society. Musicians, artists, poets, and authors all must have relished the new freedom and experimentation that was now possible with the newfound linguistic shifts.

25. The passage tells about

(A) a shift in vowel pronunciation and configuration.
(B) a fifteenth-century renaissance for musicians, artists, poets, and authors.
(C) a newfound linguistic freedom from conventional sound and linguistic structure.
(D) various vowel stresses and their effect on artistic expression.

26. What is the meaning of the word *linguistic* as used in the passage?

(A) Artistic freedom
(B) Verbal or rhetorical
(C) Social or expressive
(D) Vowel configuration

27. Because "each vowel changed its sound quality,"

(A) there was a restructuring of the sounds and patterns of communication.
(B) language could never be spoken in the same way again.
(C) artists had to develop new means of expression.

(D) communication went through a divergent change of status and culture.

Read the passage below, and then answer Questions 28–30.

The teaching apprentice initiated the discussion in a clear and well-prepared manner. To _____ the lecture topic, the teaching apprentice utilized overhead transparencies of both lexicon and abstract representation to better _____ the theories behind various pedagogical concepts. The class culminated whereby students established enthymemes extrapolated from the class discussion. The class maintained integrity and continuity.

28. Which of these grouped words, if inserted in order into the passage's blank lines, would address the logical sequencing of the narrative?

(A) refute; criticize
(B) conflate; discern
(C) undermine; explain
(D) support; illustrate

29. The definition of the term *pedagogical* as used in the passage means

(A) "academic."
(B) "abstract."
(C) "meaningless."
(D) "obtuse."

30. The passage suggests that the author's classroom experience was

(A) a needless waste of time and energy.
(B) intelligible and pragmatic.
(C) haphazard and disorderly.
(D) too advanced and complicated.

31. Which of the following is NOT a type or form of poetry?

    (A) Limerick
    (B) Couplet
    (C) Free verse
    (D) Metaphor

II. MATHEMATICS

32. The following data represent the ages of 17 people enrolled in an adult education class:

    32, 33, 34, 35, 36, 42, 42, 42, 43, 50, 51, 61, 61, 62, 63, 68, 79

    Adina organized the data as follows:
    3   2, 3, 4, 5, 6
    4   2, 2, 2, 3
    5   0, 1
    6   1, 1, 2, 3, 8
    7   9

    The display Adina used is called which one of the following?

    (A) Box-and-whisker plot
    (B) Stem-and-leaf plot
    (C) Cumulative histogram
    (D) Pictograph

33. The Ungerville cafeteria offers a choice for lunch on its Mexican Day special. You can choose either a taco or a burrito. You can choose a filling of chicken, beef, or beans, and you have a choice of six different beverages. To determine the total number of possible different lunches consisting of a taco or burrito, one filling, and one beverage, which mathematical process would be most useful?

    (A) Factor tree
    (B) Conditional probability

    (C) Factorials
    (D) Counting principle

34. The spinner shown below is divided into equal sections.

    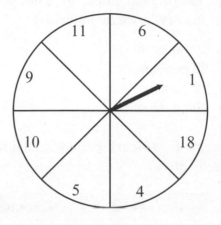

    What is the probability of landing on a section with a number that is a multiple of 3?

    (A) $\dfrac{5}{8}$

    (B) $\dfrac{5}{6}$

    (C) $\dfrac{3}{8}$

    (D) $\dfrac{3}{10}$

35. The average speed of a plane is 600 kilometers per hour. How long does it take the plane to travel 120 kilometers?

    (A) 0.2 hour
    (B) 0.5 hour
    (C) 0.7 hour
    (D) 5 hours

36. Nathan stayed up all night studying for his exams. He began his studies at 9:45 P.M. and ended at 6:22 A.M. How long did he study?

    (A) 7 hr 23 min
    (B) 7 hr 37 min

(C) 8 hr 37 min
(D) 8 hr 23 min

37. The price of a sweater was reduced by 50 percent during a clearance sale. To sell the sweater at the original price, by what percentage must the new price be increased?

(A) 200 percent
(B) 50 percent
(C) 75 percent
(D) 100 percent

38. A recipe for spinach pasta uses the following ingredients:

Ingredient	Amount
Oranges	2
Scallions	¾ bunch
Cream	1 cup
Angel-hair pasta	12 oz.
Baby spinach	3 bags

This recipe serves 4 people and takes 17 minutes to prepare. To serve 10 people, how many ounces of angel-hair pasta are required?

(A) 15
(B) 20
(C) 25
(D) 30

39. Given the following numerical computation, which operation should be performed first?

$$\frac{5 + 3(4 - 2)^2}{4}$$

(A) Addition
(B) Subtraction
(C) Division
(D) Powering

40. Jose conducted a survey of 20 classmates to determine their favorite breakfast drink. The results are shown in the following table:

Beverage	Number of Classmates
Orange juice	6
Milk	4
Tea	2
Soda	2
Other	6

To create a pie chart for this data, how many degrees should be used for the sector representing milk?

(A) 40°
(B) 72°
(C) 86°
(D) 90°

41. Joshua's tie has three colors. One-half of the tie is blue, one-fifth is brown, and the rest is burgundy. What fraction of the tie is burgundy?

(A) $\frac{5}{7}$
(B) $\frac{2}{10}$
(C) $\frac{3}{10}$
(D) $\frac{7}{10}$

42. Dawn draws a picture of a parallelogram on the board. All of the following are properties of a parallelogram EXCEPT:

(A) Opposite sides are equal.
(B) Opposite angles are equal.
(C) Diagonals are equal.
(D) Diagonals bisect each other.

43.

> A number diminished by 5 is
> 3 more than 7 times the number.

If we let *n* represent the number referred to above, which one of the following best represents the statement shown above?

(A) $n + 5 > 7n + 3$
(B) $n - 5 > 7n + 3$
(C) $n - 5 > 7(n + 3)$
(D) $n - 5 = 7n + 3$

44. Which of the following is the equivalent of 6^6?

(A) 36
(B) 66
(C) 46,656
(D) 7,776

45. Which types of graphs or charts would be appropriate for displaying the following information?

**Favorite lunch foods of
40 surveyed sixth graders:**

Pizza	18
Chicken Nuggets	12
Macaroni and Cheese	4
Tacos	4
Hamburgers	2

I.   Bar graph
II. Circle (pie) chart
III. Scatter plot
IV. Broken-line graph

(A) I and II only
(B) III and IV only
(C) I and III only
(D) II and IV only

46. Dividing 6.2 by 0.05 yields

(A) 124.
(B) 1.24.
(C) 12.4.
(D) 0.124.

47. Use the figure that follows to answer the question.

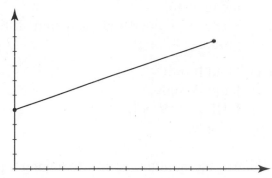

Which of the following situations might the graph illustrate?

I.   The varying speed of an experienced runner over the course of a 26-mile race.
II. The number of households a census taker still has to visit over the course of a week.
III. The value of a savings account over time, assuming steady growth.
IV. The changing height of a sunflower over several months.

(A) I and II only
(B) III and IV only
(C) II, III, and IV only
(D) I, III, and IV only

48. The following graph shows the distribution of test scores in Ms. Alvarez's class.

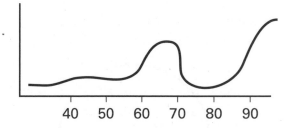

Which of the following statements do you know to be true?

I.   The majority of students scored higher than 60.

II. The test was a fair measure of ability.
III. The mean score is probably higher than the median.
IV. The test divided the class into distinct groups.

(A) I and II only
(B) I and IV only
(C) I, III, and IV only
(D) IV only

49. What is the solution to the following equation?

$$\frac{x}{4} + 6 = 10$$

(A) 1
(B) 4
(C) 8
(D) 16

50. What are the solutions to the following equation?

$$3x^2 - 11 = 1$$

(A) 2 and –2
(B) 3 and –3
(C) 4 and –4
(D) 1 and –1

51. Three small circles, all the same size, lie inside a large circle as shown below. The diameter AB of the large circle passes through the centers of the three small circles. If each of the smaller circles has area 9π, what is the circumference of the large circle?

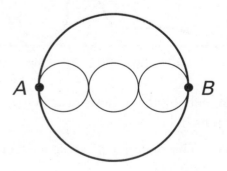

(A) 9
(B) 18
(C) 18π
(D) 27π

52. One day, 31 students were absent from Pierce Middle School. If that represents about 5.5 percent of the students, what is the population of the school?

(A) 177
(B) 517
(C) 564
(D) 171

53. Which of the following are equivalent to 0.5 percent?

I.   One-half of one percent
II. 5 percent
III. $\dfrac{1}{200}$
IV. 0.05

(A) I and III only
(B) I and IV only
(C) II and III only
(D) II and IV only

54. Which point represents the y-intercept of the equation $2x = 3y - 12$?

(A) (4, 0)
(B) (0, –6)
(C) (–6, 0)
(D) (0, 4)

55. The slope m passes through points (–6, 0) and (0, 4) on the coordinate plane. Using the formula $m = \dfrac{y_2 - y_1}{x_2 - x_1}$ $(x_1 \neq x_2)$, which of the following statements are true?

I.   The slope of the line is negative.
II. The slope of the line is positive.
III. The y-intercept of the line is –6.
IV. The y-intercept of the line is 4.

(A) I and III only
(B) I and IV only
(C) II and III only
(D) II and IV only

56. Use the graph below to answer the follow-ing question: Which inequality describes the graph?

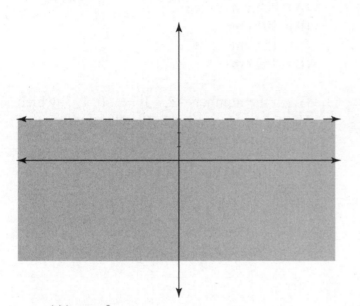

(A) $y < 3$
(B) $x < 3$
(C) $y > 3$
(D) $x > 3$

57. Which of the following comes closest to the actual length of side x in the triangle below?

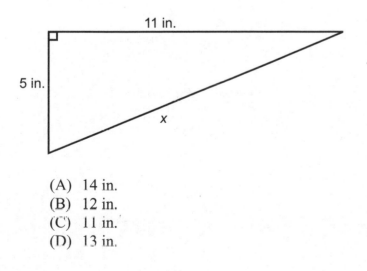

(A) 14 in.
(B) 12 in.
(C) 11 in.
(D) 13 in.

58. Use the figure below to answer the question that follows.

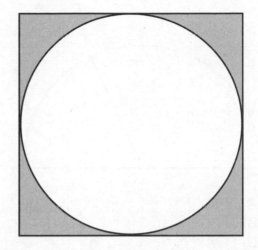

What is the approximate area of the shaded region, given that the radius of the circle is 6 units and the square inscribes the circle?

(A) 106 square units
(B) 31 square units
(C) 77 square units
(D) 125 square units

59. Use the figure below to answer the question that follows.

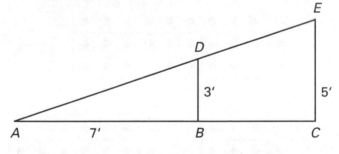

The figure is a sketch of a ramp. Given that the two ramp supports (*DB* and *EC*) are perpen-dicular to the ground, and the dimensions of the various parts are as noted, what is the approxi-mate distance from point *B* to point *C*?

(A) 4.7 feet
(B) 4.5 feet
(C) 4.3 feet
(D) 4.1 feet

60. The needle on the dial points most nearly to which reading?

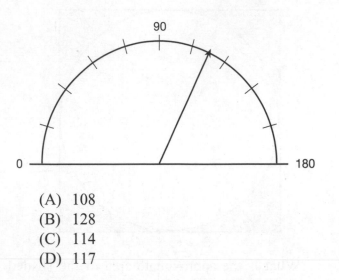

(A) 108
(B) 128
(C) 114
(D) 117

61. The diagram below could be used to model which one of the following?

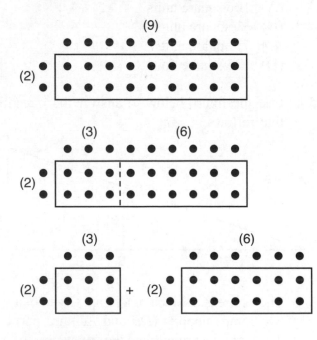

(A) Distributive property
(B) Associative property of addition
(C) Commutative property of multiplication
(D) Associative property of multiplication

62. What is the approximate volume of the following cylinder?

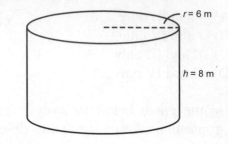

(A) 904 cm³
(B) 301 cm³
(C) 151 cm³
(D) 452 cm³

63. Given the numbers −2, −1, −½, 0, 1, 3, which Venn diagram expresses the characteristics of the numbers correctly by type?

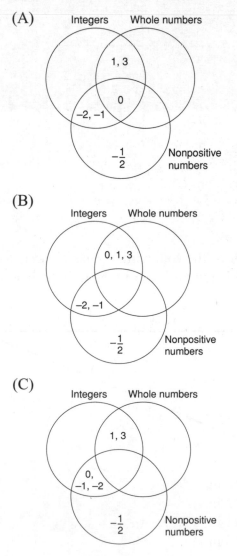

(D)

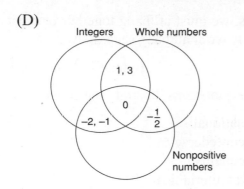

64. The diagram below displays a factor tree for the number *x*. What is the value of *x*?

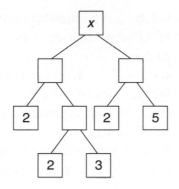

(A) 14
(B) 80
(C) 100
(D) 120

65. Assume that one pig eats 4 pounds of food each week. There are 52 weeks in a year. How much food do 10 pigs eat in a week?

(A) 40 lb.
(B) 520 lb.
(C) 208 lb.
(D) 20 lb.

III. SOCIAL STUDIES

66. A topographical map is one that shows the

(A) population distribution of a region.

(B) climate of a region.
(C) landscape and water of a region.
(D) political boundaries of a region.

67. The culture of a people consists of its

I. religion.
II. language.
III. social organization.

(A) I only
(B) I and II only
(C) II and III only
(D) I, II, and III

68. The monotheism of the ancient Hebrews spread throughout the ancient world and led to the formation of Christianity and Islam. This is an example of

(A) cultural diffusion.
(B) religious homogeneity.
(C) global interdependence.
(D) demographic data.

69. A nomadic lifestyle would most likely be found in the

(A) English countryside.
(B) Scandinavian fjords.
(C) Sahara Desert.
(D) Canadian Rockies.

70. Which of the following are research tools?

I. The library
II. The Internet
III. Interviews

(A) I only
(B) I and II only
(C) I and III only
(D) I, II, and III

71. The term *colonialism* can be used to describe

(A) Spanish conquests in the sixteenth century.
(B) the medieval system of guilds.

(C) Haitian independence from France in 1804.

(D) the sale of indulgences by the Catholic Church.

72. Mr. DeVito's class is studying immigration to the United States. Which concept would be appropriate to introduce?

(A) Divestment
(B) Assimilation
(C) Feudalism
(D) Nationalism

73. Ms. Rodriguez is teaching social studies and outlining skills. What would be the most appropriate heading for the following outline list?

    I. _____

    A. More government regulation
    B. Reform of corrupt political practices
    C. Concern for the problems of workers

(A) Reconstruction
(B) The Progressive Era
(C) The Cold War Era
(D) The New Frontier

74. The widespread use of computers has led to national concern over

(A) increased environmental pollution.
(B) guarding the right to privacy.
(C) protection of the right to petition.
(D) a decrease in television viewing.

75. Economic resources include all of the following EXCEPT

(A) land.
(B) labor.
(C) capital.
(D) values.

76. In teaching social studies, a teacher puts these two quotations on the board:

By uniting we stand, by dividing we fall.

—John Dickinson, 1768

Yes, we must all hang together or most assuredly we shall hang separately.

—Benjamin Franklin, 1776

These quotations illustrate the concept of

(A) nationalism.
(B) confederacy.
(C) equality.
(D) totalitarianism.

77. Mr. Galili is teaching about the Civil War and its aftermath in social studies. He explains that the Jim Crow laws were attempts by the

(A) federal government to improve the status of African Americans and Native Americans.
(B) state and local governments to restrict the freedom of African Americans.
(C) states to ban organizations such as the Ku Klux Klan.
(D) Radical Republicans in Congress to carry out reconstruction plans.

78. In announcing the Emancipation Proclamation, Lincoln's immediate purpose was to

(A) free black slaves in all of the slave states.
(B) free black slaves in only the border slave states that had remained loyal to the Union.
(C) let the Southern states know that whether or not they chose to secede from the Union, slavery would not be tolerated by his administration once he took office.
(D) rally Northern morale by giving the war a higher moral purpose than just preserving the Union.

79. Which of the following was NOT associated with the Civil War era?

(A) Morrill Land Grant
(B) Emancipation Proclamation
(C) Manifest Destiny
(D) The Homestead Act

80. Which of the following was NOT a main motivating factor for European explorers?

    (A) Protecting royalty
    (B) Fame and fortune
    (C) Control of trade routes
    (D) Spreading Christianity

81. The United States has a two-party system, while several European governments have a multiparty system. Which of the following statements is true about political parties in the United States but not true about political parties in multiparty European governments?

    (A) Political parties form coalitions in order to advance their policy initiatives through Congress.
    (B) Single-member district voting patterns clearly identify candidates for seats in political offices.
    (C) Parties provide candidates for office and organize campaigns to get the candidate elected.
    (D) Political parties are linked to religious, regional, or social class groupings.

82. In what year did the Salem Witch Trials take place?

    (A) 1492
    (B) 1692
    (C) 1792
    (D) 1592

83. Which of the following best describes the western, or Pacific region of Canada, comprising British Columbia and the Yukon?

    (A) The area contains many uninhabitable areas, including a mix of arid terrain and rugged mountain ranges that hinder rail and car transportation, resulting in minimal population settlement.
    (B) The area contains arid deserts and vast grasslands that are ideal for cattle farming and oil production.
    (C) The area contains the vast majority of Canada's natural resources and the greatest diversity of native peoples in Canada.
    (D) The area contains 50 percent of Canada's population, resulting in 70 percent of Canada's manufacturing.

84. The concept of the division of power between the state governments and the federal government is known as

    (A) separation of church and state.
    (B) socialism.
    (C) federalism.
    (D) feudalism.

85. The New Deal legislation developed to alleviate the strain of the Great Depression on the nation's economy was under which president?

    (A) Franklin D. Roosevelt
    (B) Herbert Hoover
    (C) Theodore Roosevelt
    (D) Harry S. Truman

86. Which of the following would be considered a primary source in researching the factors that influenced U.S. involvement in the Korean War?

    I.   The personal correspondence of a military man stationed with the 5th Regimental Combat Team (RCT) in Korea.
    II. A biography of Harry S. Truman by David McCullough, published in 1993.
    III. A journal article about the beginning of the Korean War by a noted scholar.
    IV. An interview with U.S. Secretary of Defense George Marshall.

    (A) I and II only
    (B) II and IV only
    (C) II and III only
    (D) I and IV only

87. Which of the following were major causes of the Great Depression?

    I.   Hoarding money greatly reduced the money supply, resulting in higher prices for consumer goods.
    II. The gold standard limited the amount of the money supply, reducing money circulation and causing a drop in prices and wages.
    III. The Smoot-Hawley Tariff Act increased tariffs, which resulted in increased prices for consumer goods.
    IV. The stock market crash reduced the value of companies, causing them to raise prices of consumer goods.

    (A) I and II only
    (B) II and III only
    (C) III and IV only
    (D) I, II, and III

88. Which Revolutionary War battle is considered the turning point in the war because it led to direct French assistance for the Americans?

    (A) Trenton
    (B) Bunker Hill
    (C) Yorktown
    (D) Saratoga

89. Which of the following is NOT one of the five themes of geography?

    (A) Location
    (B) Economic growth
    (C) Human-environmental interaction
    (D) Regions, patterns, and processes

90. According to the feudal system, serfs were

    (A) peasants.
    (B) lords.
    (C) property owners.
    (D) clergy.

91. Martin Luther is associated with which of the following?

    (A) *The Last Supper*
    (B) *Institutes of the Christian Religion*
    (C) *The Prince*
    (D) *95 Theses*

92. Which of the following is the study of the social behavior of humans within a group?

    (A) Sociology
    (B) Anthropology
    (C) Physiology
    (D) Psychology

93. Supply and demand refers to

    (A) resources owned by individuals.
    (B) resources owned collectively by society.
    (C) when society produces the types and quantities of goods that most satisfy its people.
    (D) the availability of resources based on consumer consumption.

94. "The shot heard 'round the world" is associated with which of the following events?

    (A) The settlement of Jamestown
    (B) The Civil War
    (C) The Boston Tea Party
    (D) The Revolutionary War

95. December 7, 1941, is the date of what major event in history?

    (A) The United States drops the atomic bomb on Hiroshima.
    (B) Castro overthrows the Cuban government.
    (C) The Japanese attack Pearl Harbor.
    (D) Rosa Parks refuses to give up her seat on a public bus to a white man.

96. The war powers of Congress include which of the following?

    I.   Declare war
    II. Raise and support armies
    III. Provide and maintain a navy
    IV. Provide for organizing, arming, and calling forth the militia

    (A) I and II only
    (B) III only
    (C) I, II, III, and IV
    (D) II and III only

97. The main purpose of the Monroe Doctrine was to

    (A) end European colonial interference in Latin America.
    (B) increase U.S. colonial efforts in Asia.
    (C) assist Spain in maintaining its Latin American empire.
    (D) monitor the 13 colonies.

98. The central banking system of the United States that issues bank notes and lends money to member banks is known as which of the following?

    (A) The stock market
    (B) The stock exchange
    (C) The Federal Reserve
    (D) The Bank of the United States

IV. SCIENCE

99. The atmospheres of the moon and other celestial bodies were studied by using telescopes and spectrophotometers long before the deployment of interplanetary space probes. In these studies, scientists used the spectral patterns of sunlight that passed through the atmosphere of distant objects to learn what elements make up those atmospheres. Which of the following explains the source of the black-line spectral patterns?

    (A) When an element is excited, it gives off light in a characteristic spectral pattern.
    (B) When light strikes an object, some wavelengths of light are absorbed by the surface and others are reflected to give the object its color.
    (C) When light passes through a gas, light is absorbed at wavelengths characteristic of the elements in the gas.
    (D) The black lines are the spectra of ultraviolet light, which is called black light because it cannot be seen with the human eye.

100. Ms. Rosenberg writes these words on the chalkboard:

    Igneous
    Sedimentary
    Metamorphic

    She is going to teach a lesson on
    (A) geography.
    (B) biology.
    (C) chemistry.
    (D) geology.

101. A teacher takes a beaker of colored water and pours it from a long, slim vessel into a short, wide vessel. The teacher is illustrating the principle of

    (A) natural selection.
    (B) deduction.
    (C) conservation.
    (D) accommodation.

102. The creation of wildlife refuges and the enforcement of game hunting laws are measures of

    (A) conservation.

(B) exploitation.

(C) conservatism.

(D) population control.

103. Diagrams, tables, and graphs are used by scientists mainly to

(A) design a research plan for an experiment.

(B) test a hypothesis.

(C) organize data.

(D) predict an independent variable.

104. Mrs. Korenge is teaching a unit on ecology. She tells her class, "A new type of fuel gives off excessive amounts of smoke. Before this type of fuel is used, an ecologist would most likely want to know

(A) what effect the smoke will have on the environment."

(B) how much it will cost to produce the fuel."

(C) how long it will take to produce the fuel."

(D) if the fuel will be widely accepted by the consumer."

105. The data table below shows average daily air temperature, wind speed, and relative humidity for four days at a single location.

Day	Air Temperature (°c)	Wind Speed (Mph)	Humidity (%)
Monday	40	15	60
Tuesday	65	10	75
Wednesday	80	20	30
Thursday	85	0	95

On which day was the air closest to being saturated with water vapor?

(A) Monday

(B) Tuesday

(C) Wednesday

(D) Thursday

106. Ms. Posner is doing a unit on plants with her class. She took three seeds and put them in three different locations. Each seedling was grown in the same soil and each received the same amount of water. At the end of six days, the results were put in this table:

Location	Height (cm)	Leaf Color
Sunny windowsill	7	Green
Indirect sunlight	9	Green
Closed closet	11	Whitish yellow

What hypothesis was most likely being tested here?

(A) A plant grown in the dark will not be green.

(B) The type of soil a plant is grown in influences how tall it will be.

(C) Plants need water to grow.

(D) Plants grown in red light are taller than plants grown in green light.

107. Which of the following is a cone-shaped formation one might find on the floor of a cave?

(A) Stalactite

(B) Stalagmite

(C) Graphite

(D) Magmite

108. We may be told to "gargle with saltwater" when we suffer from a sore throat. Which of the following phenomena would be used to explain this advice?

(A) Lowering of vapor pressure
(B) Increasing osmotic pressure
(C) Increasing boiling point
(D) Decreasing freezing point

109. Which of the following is not the direct result of volcanic activity?

(A) Sedimentary rock
(B) Igneous rock
(C) Magma
(D) Lava

110. Each population lives in a particular area and serves a special role in the community, which is known as its *niche*. For example, the niche of a hawk is to eat mice in fields. Sometimes one population replaces another in a *niche*. This occurrence is known as which of the following?

(A) Natural selection
(B) Adaptation
(C) Conservation
(D) Succession

111. Which of the following characteristics of a sound wave represents the number of waves that pass through a given point each second?

(A) Amplitude
(B) Frequency
(C) Wavelength
(D) Intensity

112. The flowchart below shows part of the water cycle. The question marks indicate the part of the flowchart that has been deliberately left blank.

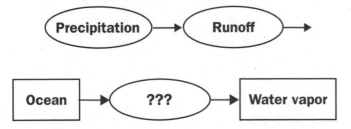

Which process should be shown in place of the question marks to best complete the flowchart?

(A) Condensation
(B) Deposition
(C) Evaporation
(D) Infiltration

113. Producing and distributing chemicals that aid digestion, growth, and metabolism is known as

(A) excretion.
(B) secretion.
(C) reproduction.
(D) respiration.

114. The smallest possible uncharged unit of ordinary matter identifiable as an element is

(A) compound.
(B) molecule.
(C) cytoplasm.
(D) atom.

115. Which of the following directs cell activities and holds DNA?

(A) Ribosome
(B) Cell membrane
(C) Nucleus
(D) Cell wall

116. A cycling of materials is represented in the diagram below.

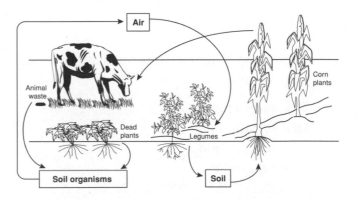

Which of the following statements is supported by the events shown in the diagram?

(A) Materials are cycled among living organisms only.

(B) Materials are cycled among heterotrophic organisms only.

(C) Materials are cycled between the living and nonliving components of the environment.

(D) Materials are cycled among the physical factors of the environment by the processes of condensation and evaporation.

117. Over time, mutations within individuals give them differing abilities to adapt and survive to changing environments and habitats. The survival of some individuals who are better able to adapt to change is known as which of the following?

(A) Natural selection
(B) Evolution
(C) Overpopulation
(D) Adaptation

118. To move a heavy book across a tabletop at a constant speed, a person must continually exert a force on the book. This force is primarily used to overcome which of the following forces?

(A) The force of gravity
(B) The force of air resistance
(C) The force of friction
(D) The weight of the book

119. Human body temperature regulation via the skin involves

(A) respiration.
(B) transpiration.
(C) perspiration.
(D) sensation.

120. Photosynthesis ($CO_2 + H_2O \Rightarrow$ glucose + oxygen) is a

(A) reduction process in which oxygen is reduced by a coenzyme.

(B) reduction process in which hydrogen is oxidized by a coenzyme.

(C) reduction process in which hydrogen is reduced by a coenzyme.

(D) reduction process in which oxygen is oxidized by a coenzyme.

Practice Test 2
Answer Explanations

Elementary Education:
Content Knowledge (0014/5014)

1. (C)	25. (A)	49. (D)	73. (B)	97. (A)
2. (A)	26. (B)	50. (A)	74. (B)	98. (C)
3. (D)	27. (A)	51. (C)	75. (D)	99. (C)
4. (A)	28. (D)	52. (C)	76. (A)	100. (D)
5. (D)	29. (A)	53. (A)	77. (B)	101. (C)
6. (C)	30. (B)	54. (D)	78. (D)	102. (A)
7. (A)	31. (D)	55. (D)	79. (C)	103. (C)
8. (D)	32. (B)	56. (A)	80. (A)	104. (A)
9. (C)	33. (D)	57. (B)	81. (B)	105. (D)
10. (A)	34. (C)	58. (B)	82. (B)	106. (A)
11. (A)	35. (A)	59. (A)	83. (C)	107. (B)
12. (D)	36. (C)	60. (D)	84. (C)	108. (B)
13. (C)	37. (D)	61. (A)	85. (A)	109. (A)
14. (A)	38. (D)	62. (A)	86. (D)	110. (D)
15. (C)	39. (B)	63. (A)	87. (A)	111. (B)
16. (B)	40. (B)	64. (D)	88. (D)	112. (C)
17. (A)	41. (C)	65. (A)	89. (B)	113. (B)
18. (B)	42. (C)	66. (C)	90. (A)	114. (D)
19. (C)	43. (D)	67. (D)	91. (D)	115. (C)
20. (B)	44. (C)	68. (A)	92. (A)	116. (C)
21. (D)	45. (A)	69. (C)	93. (D)	117. (A)
22. (D)	46. (A)	70. (D)	94. (D)	118. (C)
23. (A)	47. (B)	71. (A)	95. (C)	119. (C)
24. (D)	48. (B)	72. (B)	96. (C)	120. (C)

PRACTICE TEST 2 PROGRESS CHART

Language Arts Content

/31

1	2	3	4	5	6	7	8	9	10	11

12	13	14	15	16	17	18	19	20	21	22

23	24	25	26	27	28	29	30	31

Mathematics Content

/34

32	33	34	35	36	37	38	39	40	41	42	43

44	45	46	47	48	49	50	51	52	53	54	55

56	57	58	59	60	61	62	63	64	65

Social Studies Content

/33

66	67	68	69	70	71	72	73	74	75	76	77

78	79	80	81	82	83	84	85	86	87	88	89

90	91	92	93	94	95	96	97	98

Science Content

/22

99	100	101	102	103	104	105	106	107	108	109

110	111	112	113	114	115	116	117	118	119	120

1. (C)

The verb phrase "will have avoided" implies that an action will occur in the future. However, it is clear that the author is describing what has already happened; therefore, "have avoided" is the correct verb usage.

2. (A)

Sentence 3 ends by describing all of the animals who have made De Witt Isle their home. The best transition to sentence 4 introduces Jane Cooper and then explains why she chose this particular place.

3. (D)

The poem describes a blazing hot environment with cold nights. Plants are small with wide roots, and no mention is made of rain; therefore, it would be a desert. The plants are not the type to be found in a forest, where there would be natural covering from the sun. A swamp would be rainy, and a tundra is a cold, icy environment.

4. (A)

Colloquial language is informal or conversational. The author's use of "The days be hot, the nights be cold" and "Tiz me life that I must save" is nonstandard English; thus, it is considered colloquial. A narrative is a long story, while factual writing, as the name implies, gives readers facts. Metaphors are comparisons without the use of the words *like* or *as*.

5. (D)

A fable is a story that teaches a lesson; therefore, the passage can be classified as a fable. A narrative is generally a long, fictional piece. A character analysis scrutinizes one or more characters that are presented. An editorial gives an opinion on a specific subject.

6. (C)

A limerick is a humorous poem in the rhythm a-a-b-b-a. The first two lines rhyme; the second two lines rhyme; and the last line rhymes with the first two lines. An elegy is a mournful poem. A ballad is a long poem that tells a story. Haiku is a form of poetry with a 17-syllable verse, divided into three units of 5, 7, and 5 syllables.

7. (A)

Alliteration is the repetition of consonant sounds. Onomatopoeia occurs when a word actually sounds like the sound it makes. Imagery is a way to portray something by comparison. Symbolism occurs when a word or phrase represents something else.

8. (D)

Illustrating the poem would allow younger children to visualize its humor, while clapping their hands as the poem is read reinforces its rhythm.

Older children could write their own poems in this style.

9. (C)

In an if/then statement, the phrase following the *if* is called the hypothesis and the phrase following the *then* is called the conclusion. Given an original statement, only the contrapositive is guaranteed to have the same truth-value. The contrapositive is obtained by swapping the hypothesis and conclusion phrases and also negating them. *Note:* The negative of "turnips are not blue" is "turnips are blue."

10. (A)

Students speaking two languages learn one of two ways: sequentially, in which one language is mastered before the study of the second language has begun, or simultaneously, in which both languages are learned concurrently (B). Sequential language acquisition does not mean a student learns two languages in parts (C) or develops language skills (D).

11. (A)

The statement tries to influence readers by telling them that all of their friends own this particular item. This device is known as bandwagon. A testimonial is a quote by someone, whether by name or anonymously, that vouches for a product. Card-stacking is the intentional organization and arrangement of material to make one position look good and another position look bad. A glittering generality is the use of an emotionally appealing word or concept to gain approval without thinking.

12. (D)

The two sentences show two meanings for the verb *try*. In the first sentence, the word means "attempted"; in the second sentence, it means "judged."

13. (C)

Robinson shows the reader that, although Richard Cory seems to have everything—riches, grace, and the respect of others—he isinwardly very unhappy and commits suicide.

14. (A)

These sentences illustrate the grammatical rule of parallelism. The phrase before the "like" or "as" have to match, or be parallel to the phrase after the "like" or "as." Choice (B) states: "to hike" and "skiing." Choice (C) states: "hiking" and "to ski." Choice (D) gives us "to hike" and "going cross-country skiing." Only choice (A) shows parallelism in its use of "hiking" and "skiing." Therefore, choice (A) is correct.

15. (C)

Choice (C) is correct because these are the definitions of *illiterate* and *functional illiterate* stated in paragraph 2.

16. (B)

Choice (B) is correct because the passage begins by stating that many politicians' wives have expressed interest in literacy.

17. (A)

This question must be answered using the process of elimination. You are asked to select a statement that names a possible program component that is not characteristic of successful literacy programs. Choice (A) is correct because the other choices are specifically mentioned in the passage.

18. (B)

Choice (B) is correct because the author specifically states that politicians should support increased funding for literacy programs.

19. (C)

The passage suggests that education is at present based primarily on failure and negative reinforcement and that, in order to create a more productive and positive learning environment, the emphasis must shift to success.

20. (B)

Maxim in this case is another word for "motto." *Mens agitat molen* is actually the motto of the University of Oregon. Answers (A), (C), and (D) are erroneous definitions; therefore, (B), university motto, is the correct answer.

21. (D)

The passage states that "the language of failure . . . will have a prohibitive impact on the students' . . . self-esteem," so (D) is the correct answer.

22. (D)

The first paragraph of the passage tells the reader that, in addition to personal expression, language also has the power to persuade and influence.

23. (A)

The purpose of expository writing is to explain and clarify ideas. The purpose of persuasive writing is to convince the reader of something. The purpose of descriptive writing is to provide information about a person, place, or thing. A narrative is a story or an account of an incident or a series of incidents.

24. (D)

A metaphor is a comparison between two items without the use of *like* or *as*. Personification is attributing human characteristics to an inanimate object. A simile is a comparison that uses *like* or *as*. Onomatopoeia is the use of a word that connotes or produces the sound it is meant to convey. The correct answer, onomatopoeia, is (D).

25. (A)

The passage tells of the "great (linguistic) vowel shift" of the early fifteenth century. While the passage speaks of (B), an artistic renaissance; (C), new linguistic freedoms; and (D), effects on artistic expression, these are all *results* of the shift and not the shift itself. The shift is what the passage is about.

26. (B)

In this case, *linguistic* refers to speaking, talking, verbiage, and/or the act of oration. Choice (B), verbal or rhetorical, is the correct answer.

27. (A)

Answers (B), (C), and (D) are generalized answers resulting from the vowel shift. Choice (A) is a direct result of the shift and is quoted directly from the passage.

28. (D)

A teaching apprentice would be expected to lay the foundation for her lecture and then support her points by presenting greater detail by way of example, or as the passage puts it, "illustration." Someone in this position, having set this task for herself, would not be prone to refuting (A) or criticizing her own lecture notes. Nor would she want to conflate topics which would cause confusion (B); or, perhaps least of all, working to undermine (C) the lecture topic she had elected to teach.

29. (A)

The definition of the term *pedagogical* is "academic." Answers (B), "abstract"; (C), "meaningless"; and (D), "obtuse," are incorrect.

30. (B)

The author's classroom experience was answer (B), intelligible (understandable) and pragmatic (practical or utilitarian). The passage gives credence to this by the author's discription of the discussion as "clear and well-prepared."

31. (D)

A metaphor is not a type or form of poetry, so (D) is the correct answer. Metaphors are figures of speech that help create imagery in poems or other forms of writing. Limericks, couplets, and free verse are all types or forms of poetry.

32. (B)

A stem-and-leaf plot shows the data in numerically increasing order. The leaf is the last digit to the right, and the stem is the remaining digit or digits disregarding the leaf. For example, given the number 27, 7 is the leaf, 2 is the stem.

Stem	Leaf
2	7

33. (D)

The counting principle states the following:

If there are m different ways to choose a first event and n different ways to choose a second event, then there are $m \times n$ different ways of choosing the first event followed by the second event.

There are three stages in this example:

Stage 1	taco or burrito	2 choices
Stage 2	filling	3 choices
Stage 3	beverage	6 choices

Total possible different outcomes: $2 \times 3 \times 6 = 36$.

34. (C)

Successful events are multiples of 3. This includes 6, 9, and 18. There are three successful events. The total number of possible outcomes is 8.

The probability of landing on a multiple of $3 = \frac{3}{8}$.

35. (A)

The plane travels 600 kilometers in 1 hour. To travel 120 kilometers, you need $\frac{1}{5}$ of an hour, or 0.2 hour. 120 is what part of 600? Write it as a fraction:

120/600, which reduces to $\frac{1}{5}$. Change to a decimal by dividing 1.00 by 5 = 0.2.

36. (C)

Nathan studied for 8 hours and 37 minutes. Answer (C) is correct. One way to calculate elapsed time is to start with the hours: 8 hours elapse from 9:45 P.M. to 5:45 A.M.; 15 minutes elapse from 5:45 to 6:00 A.M.; 22 minutes elapse from 6:00 to 6:22 A.M. Add the 15 minutes to the 22 minutes for a total of 37 minutes. Add this to the 8 hours for the total time spent studying.

37. (D)

The sweater's price was cut by half. Therefore, it needs to be doubled to sell at the original price. For example,

Original price:	$20.00
50 percent sale:	$10.00

To go back to the original price, you must double the sale price, which is the same as increasing it by 100 percent.

38. (D)

We establish a proportion relating the number of people to the ounces of angel-hair pasta. The proportion would be $\frac{4}{10} = \frac{12}{x}$. Then cross-multiply and divide by 4.

39. (B)

The order of operations requires us to do all operations within grouping symbols first. A parenthesis is a grouping symbol. The first operation to be performed is 4 − 2.

40. (B)

Four of the twenty people chose milk. That is, $\frac{4}{20}$, or $\frac{1}{5}$, of the people chose milk. Consequently, $\frac{1}{5}$ of the 360° pie chart should be associated with milk.

41. (C)

The blue and the brown comprise $\frac{1}{2} + \frac{1}{5}$ of the tie. Use 10 as the lowest common denominator. Thus, the blue and brown make up $\frac{7}{10}$ of the tie. The balance $\left(1 - \frac{7}{10}\right) = \frac{3}{10}$ belongs to the burgundy.

42. (C)

Properties of a parallelogram include:

- The sum of its angles equals 360°.
- Opposite sides are equal.
- Opposite sides are parallel.
- Opposite angles are equal.
- Adjacent angles are supplementary (add to 180°).
- Diagonals bisect each other.

Diagonals are equal only if the parallelogram is a rectangle.

43. (D)

Diminished means "made smaller." This implies subtraction; therefore, a number n diminished by 5 means $n - 5$. Three more than 7 times the number n is $7n + 3$, and finally, *is* means "equals." Putting it all together, $n - 5 = 7n + 3$.

44. (C)

6 to the 6th power is $6 \times 6 \times 6 \times 6 \times 6 \times 6$, or 46,656. It is not 36, which would be only 6×6, or 6^2. Choice (B), or 66, represents placing the 6 beside another 6; that is not the correct answer. The answer 7,776 represents 6 only to the 5th power.

45. (A)

A bar graph works well here. The height of each of the five bars is determined by the number of votes for each lunch food. A circle or pie chart could also be used. The 18 votes for pizza give the fraction $\frac{18}{40}$, so pizza would be assigned 45% of the area of a circle chart, or 162°. The same approach would tell us the appropriate size of each lunch food's slice of the pie chart. A scatter plot illustrates the relationship between sets of data. A broken-line graph generally illustrates change over time. Neither is appropriate for illustrating the given data.

46. (A)

In order to solve this problem, you need to move the decimal point to the right two places., until you are working with whole numbers. Then divide the whole numbers:

$$\frac{6.2}{0.05} = \frac{62.0}{.5} = \frac{620}{5} = 124$$

The correct answer is 124.

47. (B)

One way to approach the problem is to examine each scenario for reasonableness. Even though a runner's mile-by-mile pace in a marathon varies up and down, the runner continually increases the distance covered, and the graph will always move upward, so situation I doesn't go with the graph.

The number of households a census taker has left to visit decreases with each visit, so situation II doesn't fit either. Both situations III and IV are examples of steady growth, so both match the graph.

48. (B)

Just from looking at the graph, it's clear that most of the space under the curve is past the "60" mark on the x-axis, so answer (D) is eliminated because it doesn't include statement I. Statement II can't be answered by what the graph shows. It appears possible that certain questions were too hard for many in the class and that there weren't enough questions to differentiate B students from C students, but perhaps the class performed exactly as it should have, given the students' ability and Ms. Alvarez's teaching. The distribution can give a teacher many clues about the test and the students, and even herself, but by itself, it tells us nothing about the fairness of the test. Thus, answer (A) can be eliminated. Statement III is also false; in left-skewed distributions such as this one, the median is higher than the mean. This is true because the mean is lowered by the lowest scores, while the median is relatively unaffected by them. Statement IV is true: one fairly large group has scored in the high 80s and 90s and another discernible group in the low to mid-60s, whereas few students fall outside these two groups. Thus, the answer has to be (B).

49. (D)

Using the rules for solving one-variable equations, the original equation,

$$\frac{x}{4} + 6 = 10$$

is transformed by subtracting 6 from each side,

49. (D)

Using the rules for solving one-variable equations, the original equation,

$$\frac{x}{4} + 6 = 10$$

is transformed by subtracting 6 from each side, $6 - \frac{x}{4} + 6 = 10 - 6$ which obtains $\frac{x}{4} = 4$. Then, multiply both sides by 4 which solves for $x = 16$

50. (A)

Again, using the rules for solving one-variable equations produces these transformations:

$$3x^2 - 11 = 1$$

Adding 11 to each side of the equation gives

$$3x^2 = 12$$

Dividing both sides by 3 gives

$$x^2 = 4$$

Next, find the square roots of 4: 2 and –2.

The solutions can be checked by substituting them (one at a time) into the original equation to see if they work. In this case, both 2 and –2 work.

51. (C)

Let r be the length of the radius of each of the small circles and let R be the length of the radius of the large circle. Then, $R = 3r$. The area of each of the small circles is $\pi r^2 = 9\pi$. Now divide both sides of the equation by π:

$$r^2 = 9, r = 3.$$

Then,

$$R = 3r = 3 \times 3 = 9.$$

Therefore, the circumference of the large circle is

$$C = 2\pi R = 2\pi \times 9 = 18\pi.$$

52. (C)

One way to arrive at the answer is to set up a proportion, with one corner labeled x:

$$\frac{31}{x} = \frac{5.5}{100}$$

To complete the proportion (and to find the answer), cross-multiply 31 and 100, giving 3,100, then divide by 5.5, giving approximately 564.

53. (A)

The value 0.5 is equivalent to $\frac{5}{10}$ or $\frac{1}{2}$. That means that 0.5 percent (which is one way to read the original numeral) is the same as one-half of 1 percent, so answer I is correct.

One-half of 1 percent is not the same as 5 percent, so answer II cannot be correct.

$\frac{1}{200}$ is equivalent to 0.5 percent. Here's why: 1 percent is equivalent to $\frac{1}{100}$. Half of 1 percent (0.5 percent, as noted above) is $\frac{.5}{100}$; therefore, answer III is correct. Choice IV is not correct because 0.05 is equivalent to 5 percent, which is not the same as .5 percent. Therefore, only I and III are correct, which yields choice (A) as the correct answer.

determine slope is to use the slope formula, which would give you $\dfrac{4-0}{0-(-6)} = \dfrac{4}{6} = \dfrac{2}{3}$ which is positive.

54. (D)

The y-intercept of a linear equation is the point at which its graph passes through, or intercepts, the vertical y-axis. One way to determine the y-intercept is by rewriting the equation in y-intercept form:

$$y = mx + b$$

If a linear equation is in that form, b tells you where the graph of the line intercepts the y-axis. In this case, you rewrite (or transform) the equation following these steps:

$$2x = 3y - 12$$

Switch around to: $\qquad 3y - 12 = 2x$

Add 12 to both sides $\qquad 3y - 12 + 12 = 2x + 12$

Simplify $\qquad 3y = 2x + 12$

Divide by 3 $\qquad y = \dfrac{2}{3}x + 4$

That final version of the equation is indeed in y-intercept form. The 4 tells you that the graph of the equation intercepts the y-axis at point (0, 4).

55. (D)

It is helpful to make a sketch of the line on the coordinate plane. (To do this you need to know how to plot individual points.) The line "travels" from the lower left to the upper right, meaning that it has a positive slope. Statement II is therefore true. The y-intercept of a line is the spot at which the line crosses, or intercepts, the vertical axis. In this case, that's at point (0, 4). (You can simply say that the y-intercept is 4, without mentioning the 0.) Statement IV is therefore true as well. A second way to

56. (A)

Consider various random points in the shaded area: (5, –2), (–1, 2), (12, 2.5), and (–9, 1). Notice that all points in the shaded area have a y-coordinate value less than 3. The inequality that states this fact is the one in (A) ("y is less than 3").

57. (B)

Use the Pythagorean theorem to compute the length of any side of any right triangle, as long as you know the lengths of the other two sides. Here is the theorem: For any right triangle with side lengths of a, b, and c, and where c is the length of the hypotenuse (the longest side, and the one opposite the right angle), $c^2 = a^2 + b^2$.

$$c^2 = 11^2 + 5^2$$

$$\text{or}$$

$$c^2 = 146$$

$$c = \sqrt{146} \approx 12$$

58. (B)

First, it is helpful to view the shaded area as the area of the square minus the area of the circle. With that in mind, you simply need to find the area of each simple figure, and then subtract one from the other.

You know that the radius of the circle is 6 units in length. That tells you that the diameter of the circle is 12 units. Because the circle is inscribed in the square (meaning that the circle fits inside the square touching it as many places as possible), you see that the sides of the square are each 12 units in length. Knowing that, you compute the area of the square as 144 square units (12×12).

Using the formula for finding the area of a circle (πr^2), and using 3.14 for π, you get approximately 113 square units (3.14 × 6 × 6). Then, you subtract 113 (the area of the circle) from 144 (the area of the square) for the answer of 31.

59. (A)

To answer the question, you must recognize that triangles *ADB* and *AEC* are similar triangles, meaning that they have the same shape. That also means that the corresponding angles of the two triangles are the same, or congruent, and that corresponding sides of the two triangles are proportional. Given that, you can set up the following proportion, where *x* is the distance from point A to point C:

$$\frac{3}{7} = \frac{5}{x}$$

Solving the proportion by cross multiplication, you see that the length of segment *AC* is about 11.7. Knowing that the length of segment *AB* is 7 feet, you subtract to find the length of *BC* (11.7 − 7 = 4.7).

60. (D)

You should first count the number of spaces on the dial: There are 10. Five spaces equals 90 units, and 90 divided by 5 is 18 units. Each space is worth 18 units. The needle points to about halfway between marks 6 and 7. Thus, one-half of 18, plus 6 times 18, is 117. Choice (D) is the correct reading.

61. (A)

The distributive property (of multiplication over addition) can be demonstrated algebraically as

$$a(b + c) = ab + bc$$

The diagrams in the example display as follows:

$$2(9) = 18$$

$$2(3 + 6) = 18$$

$$2(3) + 2(6) = 18$$

62. (A)

The formula for finding the volume of a cylinder is:

$$V = \pi r^2 h$$

This means that the volume is equal to π (about 3.14) times the measure of the radius squared, times the height of the cylinder. In this case, that's

$$3.14 \times 6^2 \times 8$$

or

$$3.14 \times 36 \times 8$$

or about 904 cm. (Note that the final answer is given in cubic centimeters.)

63. (A)

Venn diagrams are overlapping circles that display elements of different sets. They show elements common to more than one set as well as elements unique to only one set.

−2, −1, 0, 1, 3 are integers

−2, −1, −½, 0 are nonpositive numbers (Note: Zero is neither positive nor negative.)

0, 1, 3 are whole numbers

64. (D)

A factor tree decomposes an integer into its prime factors by continuously factoring a given number into two factors until there are no further factors other than 1 and the number. For example, the factor tree for 12 appears as follows:

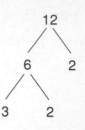

To work a factor tree backward (from the bottom up), multiply the factors to obtain the composite number they come from.

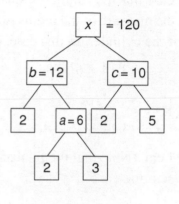

$$a = 2 \times 3 = 6$$
$$b = 6 \times 2 = 12$$
$$c = 2 \times 5 = 10$$
$$x = 12 \times 10 = 120$$

65. (A)

Here one must use only needed information. Do not be distracted by superfluous data. Simple multiplication will do. If one pig eats four pounds of food per week, how much will 10 pigs eat in one week? $10 \times 4 = 40$ pounds. The problem intentionally contains superfluous data (52 weeks), which should not distract the reader from its easy solution. Ratio and proportion will also work here:

$$\frac{1}{10} = \frac{4}{x}$$

$x = 40$ pounds per week

66. (C)

The topography of a region is specifically the nature of its landscape—mountains, deserts, plateaus, oceans, and lakes. Population distribution would be shown on a demographic map. Climate and political boundaries are separate entities.

67. (D)

The culture of a people is the way in which the people live. It encompasses their religion, language, social organization, customs, traditions, and economic organization.

68. (A)

Cultural diffusion refers to the extending of an aspect of culture from one area to another and its inclusion in the culture(s) of other people. Religious homogeneity is the similitude of religion, not its spread. Global interdependence refers to the importance of one country to another, usually in terms of economics. Demographics is the study of population trends.

69. (C)

A nomadic lifestyle is one in which people do not settle in one area; instead, they roam from place to place and set up temporary living arrangements in each place. The desert is an area of nomadic lifestyle because it generally does not support agriculture and does not have sufficient water for people to settle in one place permanently.

70. (D)

The library offers the student books, articles, journals, and so on, with which to do research. The Internet is a very useful tool because of its convenience and the access it affords to thousands of sites. Interviews with relevant people can offer an important glimpse into the personal stories or issues of a topic.

71. (A)

Colonialism is the extension of a nation's rule beyond its borders by the establishment of settlements in which indigenous populations are directly ruled or displaced. Colonizers generally dominate the resources, labor, and markets of the colonial territory. In the sixteenth century, Spain extended its rule to parts of North America, South America, and the Caribbean. Guilds were the forerunners of modern trade unions, a system in which people who practiced similar crafts joined together. Haiti's independence from France removed the colonialism that France had imposed upon this island. Indulgences were practices of the Catholic Church in medieval times in which Catholics bought pardons from the church.

72. (B)

Assimilation is the process in which a minority racial, cultural, religious, or national group becomes part of the dominant cultural group. Divestment occurs when a country removes itself, whether economically, militarily, or socially, from something in which it had previously invested. Feudalism was a system in which people were protected by lords in exchange for their labor. Nationalism, or patriotism, is the feeling of pride and belonging that people have for their country.

73. (B)

The Progressive Era in the early twentieth century can be described as one in which government concerned itself with reform. The Progressives, as they called themselves, worked to make American society a better and safer place in which to live. They tried to make big business more responsible through regulations of various kinds. They worked to clean up corrupt city governments, to improve working conditions in factories, and to improve living conditions for those who lived in slum areas, a large number of who were recent immigrants.

74. (B)

A great concern of educators, parents, and the general public is privacy in using computers. The Internet is a vast worldwide network, and users worry that what is sent over the Internet may not always be secure.

75. (D)

Economic resources are those that provide goods and services to people. Economic resources are considered to be scarce, while wants are unlimited. Therefore, land, labor, and capital are considered resources, while values are not goods or services that are limited.

76. (A)

Both speakers are referring to the colonies that were later to become the United States of America. This feeling of togetherness and pride for one's country is called nationalism. Confederacy occurs when one group joins in opposition to another. Totalitarianism is the rule by a dictator—the antithesis of these quotes; while equality denotes equal rights.

77. (B)

The Jim Crow laws were in existence from the 1880s (post–Civil War) to the 1960s. A majority of American states enforced segregation using these laws. States and cities could impose legal punishment on people for a variety of "infractions" dealing with African Americans. Intermarriage between the races was forbidden, and in both the public and private sectors, blacks and whites were separated.

78. (D)

Lincoln's immediate purpose in announcing the Emancipation Proclamation was to rally flagging Northern morale. Lincoln waited until after a major Union victory, at Antietam in 1862, so he couldn't be charged with making the announcement as an act of desperation. He recognized that the costs of the war had reached a point where preserving the Union would not be a powerful enough reason to motivate many Northerners to continue the war. Framing the war as a war against slavery would mobilize powerful abolitionist forces in the North and perhaps create an atmosphere of a holy crusade rather than one of using war to resolve a political conflict. While the Emancipation Proclamation had the announced purpose of freeing the slaves, Lincoln himself indirectly stated that freeing the slaves was a means to a greater end, preserving the Union.

79. (C)

The Morrill Land Grant, Emancipation Proclamation, and The Homestead Act were all parts of the post–Civil War Reconstruction efforts. Manifest Destiny refers to the belief in the expansion of the American nation to the Pacific Ocean and beyond.

80. (A)

Exploration was based on many motivating factors. Some sought fame and fortune, others wanted control of the trade routes, and others sought adventure. Many explorers had religion as their main incentive, either the desire to spread the word or to find freedom from persecution. While royal figures sponsored and encouraged voyages, protecting royalty was not a central motivating factor for exploration. (A) is the correct answer.

81. (B)

Multiparty systems use an electoral system based on proportional representation. Therefore, each party gets legislative seats in proportion to the votes it receives. In the United States, the candidate who receives a plurality of the votes is declared the winner.

82. (B)

In Salem, Massachusetts, a group of young girls accused servants from West India and older white members of the community, mostly women, of exercising powers that Satan had given them. Other towns also experienced turmoil and charged residents with witchcraft. In Salem alone, the juries pronounced 19 people guilty; in 1692, after the execution of all 19 victims, the girls admitted their stories were not true.

83. (C)

The western, or Pacific coast, of Canada receives an exceptional amount of rain and includes some of the tallest and oldest trees in Canada, similar to northern California. The region has the greatest diversity of native peoples in Canada.

They belong to seven distinct groups and speak 19 different languages.

84. (C)

Separation of church and state refers to the idea that church administration and public administration should be under different authorities. Socialism is an economic system in which the basic means of production are primarily owned and controlled collectively. Feudalism is a concept of land management in which lords pledge service to the king in order to maintain title to their lands. Division of power between the state governments and the federal government is known as federalism. This is the constitutional framework in which all power not given to the federal government is reserved for the states.

85. (A)

In his inaugural address, Roosevelt assured the nation that "the only thing we have to fear is fear itself." He called a special session of Congress from March 9 to June 16, 1933, which led to the passage of a great body of legislation that has left a lasting mark on the nation. Historians have divided Roosevelt's legislation into the First New Deal (1933–1935) and a new wave of programs beginning in 1935 called the Second New Deal.

86. (D)

Both the personal correspondence of a military man stationed with the 5th RCT in Korea and an interview with Secretary of Defense George Marshall are primary sources because they involve correspondence or testimony from individuals who were actually involved in the Korean War.

87. (A)

A limited money supply and rising prices were major causes of the Great Depression. The money supply was most affected by the gold standard, and the Smoot-Hawley Tariff Act further affected consumer prices.

88. (D)

The battle at Saratoga marked the end to a British three-pronged campaign to split New England from the other colonies. With the surrender of Burgoyne's army, the Americans had won a major victory and captured an entire British army. This victory gave the French the evidence they needed that the Americans could actually win the war, and gave them a chance to avenge their loss to the British in the Seven Years' War. The French now recognized the American government and declared war on England.

89. (B)

The five themes of geography are (1) place; (2) location; (3) human-environmental interaction; (4) movement and connections; and (5) regions, patterns and processes.

90. (A)

According to the feudal system, serfs or peasants served the landlords who owned the land they worked.

91. (D)

Martin Luther authored the *95 Theses*. Leonardo da Vinci painted *The Last Supper*. John Calvin wrote *Institutes of the Christian Religion. The Prince* was written by Machiavelli.

92. (A)

Sociology is the study of the social behaviors of human beings in group settings.

93. (D)

The economic principle of supply and demand refers to the availability of resources based on consumer consumption.

94. (D)

In Lexington, Mass., 77 local minutemen (trained militiamen who would respond at a moment's notice) and others, having been alerted by Paul Revere's ride and other communications, awaited the British on the village green. A shot was fired; it is unknown which side fired first, but this became "the shot heard 'round the world."

95. (C)

December 7, 1941, marks the attack on Pearl Harbor. The United States dropped the atomic bomb on Hiroshima, Japan, on August 6, 1945. Fidel Castro overthrew the dictator-led government in Cuba in January 1959. On December 11, 1955, Rosa Parks refused to give up her seat on a public bus to protest discriminatory laws.

96. (C)

The war powers of Congress include the right to declare war; raise and support armies; provide and maintain a navy; and provide for organizing, arming, and calling forth the militia.

97. (A)

The main purpose of the Monroe Doctrine was to stop European colonial interference in Latin America. In December 1823, President Monroe included in his annual message to Congress a statement that the peoples of the American hemisphere were "henceforth not to be considered as subjects for future colonization by any European powers."

98. (C)

The Federal Reserve issues bank notes, lends money to member banks, maintains reserves, supervises member banks, and helps set the national monetary policy. The stock market is the mechanism that enables the trading of company stocks. It is different from the stock exchange, which is a corporation in the business of bringing together stock buyers and sellers. The Bank of the United States was proposed by Alexander Hamilton to standardize currency and manage the debt created by the Revolutionary War.

99. (C)

All of the choices are true, but only choice (C) addresses the exercise. Black line spectra are formed when the continuous spectra of the sun pass through the atmosphere. The elements in the atmosphere absorb wavelengths of light characteristic of their spectra (these are the same wavelengths given off when the element is excited—for example, the red color of a neon light). By examining the line spectral gaps, scientists can deduce the elements that make up the distant atmosphere. Choice (A) is true, but it explains the source of a line spectrum. Choice (B) is true, and it explains why a blue shirt is blue when placed under a white or blue light source. Recall that a blue shirt under a red light source will appear black because there are no blue wavelengths to be reflected. Choice (D) is partially true because black lights do give off ultraviolet light that the human eye cannot see.

100. (D)

Igneous, *sedimentary*, and *metamorphic* are terms that describe varieties of rocks; therefore, they would be taught in a lesson on geology, which is the study of the earth's history.

101. (C)

The law of conservation states that a material will have the same volume regardless of the shape of the container in which it is placed. Accommodation and its sister concept, assimilation, is the way in which one incorporates new information into one's way of thinking. Piaget is the Swiss psychologist who did experimental work on these concepts. Natural selection is a Darwinian concept stating that a species will naturally evolve to retain useful adaptive characteristics. Deduction is a method of reasoning.

102. (A)

Wildlife refuges are places specifically created so that animals can have a safe haven. Similarly, game hunting laws prevent hunters from killing animals indiscriminately. Exploitation is the opposite: It means using a resource for our own ends, regardless of the effects on the resource. Conservatism is a political point of view that espouses keeping the status quo in society.

103. (C)

Diagrams, tables, and graphs are different ways to display information. These would be most useful in organizing that information. They would not assist in making predictions, testing a hypothesis, or designing a research plan, but they could be helpful in any of these endeavors.

104. (A)

An ecologist is concerned about environmental issues; therefore, he or she would be most interested in the effect of the fuel's smoke emissions. Cost and time factors do not concern the environmentalist. Similarly, consumer acceptance is not the domain of the environmentalist.

105. (D)

Relative humidity measures the percentage of water vapor in the air. The higher the humidity, the more water vapor exists in the air. Thursday had the highest relative humidity (95%), so (D) is the correct answer.

106. (A)

The variable in this experiment is light. The three plants were given different amounts of light, so choice (A) is the correct answer. The plants were grown in the same soil and given the same amount of water. The experiment does not deal with red light.

107. (B)

A stalagmite is a cone-shaped deposit form on the floor of the cave; (B) is the correct answer. A stalactite is an icicle-shaped lime deposit hanging from the roof or sides of a cave. Graphite is the material found in a pencil.

108. (B)

Salt is a strong electrolyte that completely dissociates in solution. When this solution is in contact with a semipermeable membrane, like the inflamed cells in the throat, water moves across the membrane from the side with the lowest solute concentration to the side of higher solute concentration. In the case of the sore throat, water from inside the inflamed cells moves out toward the higher concentration salt water, and the throat cells shrink due to the loss of water. All the items listed are colligative properties that, like osmotic pressure, are a function of the number, but not the nature, of particles in solution.

109. (A)

Sedimentary rock may be formed by pressure over a period of time; it is not always the direct result of volcanic activity. (A) is the correct answer. Igneous rock is formed from heat and can be the result of volcanic activity. Magma is molten rock within the earth; it may pour forth during a volcanic eruption. Lava is a product of a volcanic eruption.

110. (D)

Natural selection occurs when the stronger or more advantageous traits of a species are continued through reproduction. An adaptation is a structure or behavior that increases a living thing's ability to survive and reproduce. Conservation is the practice of using natural areas without disrupting their ecosystems. The correct answer is (D). Succession is the orderly and predictable change of communities as a result of population replacement in niches.

111. (B)

The frequency represents the number of sound waves that pass through a given point each second. Amplitude and intensity refer to the amount of energy in a sound wave. Wavelength refers to the distance from the crest of one wave to the crest of the next wave.

112. (C)

To turn water (a liquid) into water vapor (a gas) the process of evaporation must occur. Condensation is the reverse—turning a gas into a liquid. Deposition occurs when something is deposited in an area, and infiltration is the process by which one item permeates another item.

113. (B)

Secretion is the process of producing and distributing chemicals that aid digestion, growth, and metabolism. Excretion is the elimination of wastes. Reproduction is the process of making new living things. Respiration is the process of exchanging gases.

114. (D)

The atom is the smallest possible uncharged unit of ordinary matter, so (D) is the answer. While a molecule (B) is also fundamental to matter, it is larger than an atom. A compound (A) is a combination of two or more elements, which cannot be smaller than an atom. A cytoplasm (C) is the jelly-like substance inside a cell.

115. (C)

The nucleus directs cell activities and holds the DNA. A ribosome makes protein from amino acids. The cell membrane controls movement of materials in and out of the cell. The cell wall gives rigid structure to plant cells.

116. (C)

The diagram shows cycling among air, legumes, soil organisms, dead plants, live plants, and animals. This means that the cycling occurs between the living and nonliving parts of the environment.

117. (A)

The survival of some individuals who are better able to adapt to change is known as natural selection. This concept is also explained as "survival of the fittest."

118. (C)

The force of friction between the book and the table is the primary force that must be overcome to move the book. An experiment to study these frictional forces could keep all other variables (size and weight of the book, speed of travel) constant while measuring the force needed to move the book using a spring scale. Different experiments could change the surface of the book by covering the book with wax paper, construction paper, or sandpaper.

119. (C)

The body regulated water and heat through perspiration. Transpiration describes a process not involving humans. Thus, (B) is not correct. Respiration (A) is breathing in humans and will cause some water loss. However, the question asks how the body regulated substances through the skin. (D), sensation, is the ability to process or perceive. The skin does have nerve endings

that can sense, but this does not involve temperature or water regulation.

120. (C)

The answer is (C) because by definition photosynthesis is the chemical reaction that results in a reduction.

Index

PRAXIS 0014/5014

Index

INSTALLING REA'S TESTWARE®

SYSTEM REQUIREMENTS

Pentium 75 MHz (300 MHz recommended) or a higher or compatible processor; Microsoft Windows 98 or later; 64 MB available RAM; Internet Explorer 5.5 or higher.

INSTALLATION

1. Insert the PRAXIS Elementary Education 0014/5014 CD-ROM into the CD-ROM drive.

2. If the installation doesn't begin automatically, from the Start Menu choose the RUN command. When the RUN dialog box appears, type d:\setup (where d is the letter of your CD-ROM drive) at the prompt and click OK.

3. The installation process will begin. A dialog box proposing the directory "C:\Program Files\REA\Praxis_ElEd014\" will appear. If the name and location are suitable, click OK. If you wish to specify a different name or location, type it in and click OK.

4. Start the PRAXIS Elementary Education TestWare® application by double-clicking on the icon.

REA's PRAXIS Elementary Education TestWare® is **EASY** to **LEARN AND USE**. To achieve maximum benefits, we recommend that you take a few minutes to go through the on-screen tutorial on your computer. The "screen buttons" are also explained here to familiarize you with the program.

SSD ACCOMMODATIONS FOR STUDENTS WITH DISABILITIES

Many students qualify for extra time to take the PRAXIS Elementary Education Content Knowledge exam, and our TestWare® can be adapted to accommodate your time extension. This allows you to practice under the same extended-time accommodations that you will receive on the actual test day. To customize your TestWare® to suit the most common extensions, visit our website at www.rea.com/ssd.

TECHNICAL SUPPORT

REA's TestWare® is backed by customer and technical support. For questions about **installation or operation of your software**, contact us at:

> **Research & Education Association**
> Phone: (732) 819-8880 (9 a.m. to 5 p.m. ET, Monday–Friday)
> Fax: (732) 819-8808
> Website: *www.rea.com*
> E-mail: info@rea.com

Note to Windows XP Users: In order for the TestWare® to function properly, please install and run the application under the same computer administrator-level user account. Installing the TestWare® as one user and running it as another could cause file-access path conflicts.